S0-AFK-792

PSYCHIATRY AND CATHOLICISM

PSYCHIATRY AND CATHOLICISM

James H. VanderVeldt, O.F.M., Ph.D.

Associate Professor of Psychology, The Catholic University of America; Professor of Psychology, Trinity College

Robert P. Odenwald, M.D., F.A.P.A.

Director of the Child Center and Assistant Professor of Psychiatry, The Catholic University of America

FIRST EDITION

McGRAW-HILL BOOK COMPANY, INC.

New York Toronto London

1952

PSYCHIATRY AND CATHOLICISM

Library of Congress Catalog Card Number: 51-12652

IMPRIMI PERMITTITUR

Father Thomas Plassmann, O.F.M., Provincial, January 16, 1952

NIHIL OBSTAT

Francis J. Connell, C.SS.R., S.T.D., Censor Deputatus

IMPRIMATUR

✠ Patrick A. O'Boyle, Archbishop of Washington, D.C., January 16, 1952

FOREWORD

From the time of the beginning of modern psychiatry to the present there have been problems concerning its relationship to Christianity. Many of the opinions voiced have been extreme. For some psychiatry has supplanted Christianity. Others find no room in the Christian fold for psychiatry, which they consider necessarily heathen. Neither of these extreme positions is true and both are harmful. Hence there has been a long-felt need of a book that would present a scientifically sane integration of psychiatry and Christianity. Therefore it was with great pleasure that I received the present manuscript for it admirably satisfies an urgent need.

The moral and ethical implications of some of the principles and practices of psychiatry involve thorny problems which are baffling not only for the educated layman but also for the doctor and the priest. The authors of this study make no pretense of offering the last word on these important, evolving, and controversial topics. In my opinion, however, they do present a safe and scientific synthesis of modern psychiatry and Christian ethics. This is a book that can be read with the assurance that the reliable findings of modern psychiatry are here fully and accurately presented with no prejudice to the teachings of Christianity. Since truth is one, the valid teachings of psychiatry cannot fail to harmonize with Christian ethics. By brilliantly using this norm as their flail in the rich harvest of psychiatric research, the authors have competently winnowed the wheat from the chaff.

In the first part of this work one finds the general principles of psychiatry with a careful evaluation based on Christian morality as proposed by the Catholic Church. The latter section treats clearly and in readily understandable language the complete range of psychiatric disorders. To all these topics the authors bring extraordinarily well balanced judgments acquired during years of experience in their respective fields.

Both authors are professors in the Department of Psychiatry and Psychology at the Catholic University of America. Father James Vander-Veldt, O.F.M., is a doctor and agrégé in philosophy from the University of Louvain. In his many years of teaching and writing he has abundantly merited the high degree of esteem that is accorded him by scholars both in this country and abroad. Robert Odenwald, M.D., Director of the Child Guidance Center at Catholic University, is a man who has dedicated his life to the study of psychiatry and has practiced in this field for many years with notable success. As a Fellow of the American Psychiatric Association and a diplomate in neuropsychiatry, Dr. Odenwald is well qualified to speak with authority in this field. With Father VanderVeldt contributing to the religio-philosophic aspect of the problem and Dr. Odenwald to the practical medical aspect, the relationship of psychiatry and Christian ethics receives ample and competent treatment.

As Chancellor of the Catholic University, I am proud that two of its professors have brought forth this worthwhile work. I am gratefully conscious of the fine contribution that these two men have made; and I trust that the success which this book will undoubtedly attain will induce them to continue to collaborate on problems in this field, and will inspire others to imitate their scholarly activities. They have done a great service for all those who are seeking to know psychiatry and its relationship to natural law morality and Christian ethics which are the bases of the American tradition.

✠ PATRICK A. O'BOYLE
Archbishop of Washington

ACKNOWLEDGMENT

The authors feel profoundly grateful to His Excellency, the Most Reverend Patrick A. O'Boyle, Archbishop of Washington, D.C., for introducing this work to the public and for the kindly interest he has taken in it.

They are greatly indebted to Rev. Albert F. Grau, S.J., for writing the chapter on counseling and for other valuable assistance; to Rev. Robert A. Ford and Rev. Louis B. Snider, S.J., for their participation in composing the chapters on social work and clinical psychology. They wish to express their appreciation to Misses Elizabeth Barham and Margaret M. Scanlon for reading the manuscript; to Mrs. Margery Hohman and Misses Elizabeth Clift and Lois Gannon who assisted in the typing.

CONTENTS

Chapter 1

PERSON AND PERSONALITY

A human being, in contrast with animals and plants, is called a person, and philosophers have presented a variety of definitions of this term. Catholic philosophy for the most part has adopted the definition that was formulated by Boethius (*c.* A.D. 470–525) and states that a person is an individual substance endowed with reason. This definition involves the concept of substances—a concept that has become alien to nonscholastic thinking. A brief explanation, therefore, seems to be in order. Here, as elsewhere throughout this book, when the authors explain certain concepts of Catholic philosophy and theology, they intend to do so by simply stating the Catholic position, avoiding, as far as it seems feasible, controversial issues and technical terminology. But one cannot clarify his philosophical position without speaking about philosophy.

Lecturing before an audience largely composed of physicians, one of the present authors stated that the human soul is a substance. A physician objected that this could not be so because, he said, the soul was a spiritual entity. This episode is worthy of mention because it shows that, although this physician had a correct notion of the soul, he was thrown off the track by the term "substance." He conceived of the term as it is used in science, particularly in chemistry, where it means an elementary body or a compound of such chemical units. In other words, he believed that "substance" always referred to something material. However, this notion was incorrect, for substance in the philosophical sense may be spiritual or may involve matter. Substance means any entity which by its very nature exists in itself and for itself, *i.e.*, which needs no other entity in which to inhere. One may best understand substance by comparing it with accidents. The latter are such things as color, thought, and movement, which cannot exist without something that is colored, that thinks, or that moves. Accidents cannot naturally exist by themselves but need something in which to inhere. In contrast, a substance subsists in itself.

God is a purely spiritual substance, whereas men and animals are substances that include matter. A human person consists of two coprinciples, matter and soul. A discussion of how scholastic philosophy conceives of matter would take this discussion too far afield, but it may be helpful to concentrate upon the concept of the soul.[1] The soul of man is an incomplete spiritual substance. A spiritual or immaterial substance is a thing that is neither composed of or dependent on matter for its existence or activities. Now, the human soul is such a spiritual entity, but in an incomplete manner. The latter concept requires some clarification. To say that the soul is an incomplete substance means that, although it can exist separated from the body—and, as a matter of fact, does exist in that way after death until the resurrection of the flesh—yet it is unable while so separated to exercise all its functions. The soul, apart from the body, can display its spiritual powers, intellect and will, but it cannot see, hear, have sensory feelings, emotions, etc., because for the exercise of sensory reactions it is dependent on the body and its organs. Hence, the human soul needs to be united with its coprinciple, the body, for the complete exercise of all its powers. In that sense, the soul is said to be an incomplete substance: it belongs to the very nature of the human soul to be conjoined with the body. When body and soul are united, they form a complete substance, and for that reason this union is called a substantial union. When such a union takes place, a human person is present, possessing a complete human nature.

Since the soul needs the body for the full display of all its functions, an important corollary of the substantial union is that the human person is the ultimate agent to whom all reactions and everything that occurs within man should be attributed. This statement must be enlarged a little, because it has a direct bearing on the very topic of this book.

The body-machine alone, *i.e.*, not animated by the soul, does not live, nor can it perceive, think, feel, or suffer emotions. No materialist has ever proved that it can. It is only through the soul that a man lives and performs these various activities. However, as has been said, the soul alone cannot perform all these activities. It cannot at all exercise the vegetative and sensory functions without the body, and although it can think and will when separated, as long as it is united with the body it depends for these rational activities on sensory and organic functions; *e.g.*, a man needs perceptions and images for his thinking. Furthermore, a man does not say that his body walks or that his soul smells fish. Therefore, all these activities are, in the final analysis, to be ascribed to the substantial unit that is called a human person.[2] The person is the ultimate agent of all his reactions and of whatever happens to him. No human activity derives exclusively from the body, nor from the soul; such activity derives from the substantial unit.

An important application of this principle deals with sickness. According to the principles just set forth, it does not make sense to say that the soul is sick or that the body is sick. The body without the soul is not sick, but dead; the soul, with or without the body, is a spirit, and spirits do not get sick. The man, the person, is sick. Using a terminology that is Cartesian rather than scholastic in origin, one may distinguish between what is called physical disease and what is called mental disease, but these terms should be interpreted in the correct sense. Physical or organic disease, like cancer or pneumonia, means that the vegetative system of a living person is affected; and a man is mentally sick when his sensory functions are disturbed, regardless of the cause and of whether or not this sensory disturbance influences the exercise of his rational powers. But in either case it is the person who is sick. It will be shown later that this corollary is strongly confirmed by the findings of psychosomatic medicine.

At the beginning of this chapter the human person was defined as an individual rational substance. It is now in order to concentrate upon the term "individual." The first question that arises is how to recognize the individuality that distinguishes one man from another. The obvious answer is that the only way to know individual differences is by observing a person's behavior—this term being taken in the sense of both "external" and "internal" behavior.[3]

Now, the study of individual differences forms the subject matter of what is usually called the psychology of personality. Thus far, the use of the word "personality" has been purposely avoided. It should be made clear that the term "personality" for what has been described as a "person" should be interpreted as personality in the metaphysical sense. The study of metaphysical personality tells what a man is, philosophically speaking. And the study of behavioral, observational characteristics by which a man reveals or expresses himself is the study of empirical personality, or personality *tout court.* A man is a person, and he reveals a personality. And indeed every human being shows a set of reactions, a typically characteristic way of acting that is individual to him.[4]

Psychologists and psychiatrists approach the study of personality in various ways. One approach, which is called the typological study of personality, classifies all people into a number of broad categories believed to be the fundamental or basic types of man. Among the best known are the typologies of Spranger and Jung. C. Jung distinguishes the extrovert type characterized by objective thinking, *i.e.*, thinking in which the object or outer world plays the determining role, and the introvert type characterized by subjective thinking, *i.e.*, thinking in which the subject or world of inner experience predominates. Each type is subdivided into two rational types, one in which thought prevails and one in which emotion prevails, and two irrational types, one determined by sensation and one determined by intuition.[5]

E. Spranger divides people according to the value that predominates in their lives, and thus he arrives at six personality types: the theoretical man, who is predominantly interested in explaining things and systematizing knowledge; the economic man, who is out primarily for practical, profitable things; the aesthetic man, whose interest is in beauty and art; the social man, whose prominent feature is love of people and the desire to make them happy and promote their welfare; the political man, whose greatest ambition is to wield power over other people; and the religious man, who is defined according to whatever definition of religion one follows.[6]

The trend among present-day psychologists is away from typologies, in spite of the remarkable fact that some of the critics make use of them. The main objection is that types are too theoretical, abstract, and artificial to be of much practical use. Taking Spranger's typology as an example, it will in practice be easily found that an individual may fit two or more of the categories; if he fits them all, one might, with equal right, say that he fits none of them. Besides, the present authors believe that at least two more categories should be added: the hedonistic and the ethical types.

For these reasons, the majority of psychologists, particularly those in the United States, feel that the psychology of personality is best served by the study of the traits that we actually observe in an individual. The important advantage of this method is that it allows for a fairly accurate measurement of personality traits.

Personality traits are the characteristic modes of acting by which a person reveals himself more or less consistently. Looking at them from the standpoint of adjustment, one may say that an individual's traits determine his adjustment, both mental and physical, to reality. A trait, *e.g.*, aggressiveness, is found in a great number of people; in fact, the assumption is that basic personality traits are present in all people, and, for that reason, they are called common traits. However, traits are found in different degrees in different people and are normally distributed through the population ranging from minimal to maximal intensity. Just as the height or weight of a large number of people is represented in the normal curve of distribution, so people can be arranged on a scale of aggressiveness, or any other basic trait, with the majority being at, or near, an average of that trait and a few at each end being either very aggressive or very nonaggressive. The range of a person's aggressiveness can be determined by observing how he reacts in various situations; *e.g.*, one person may show his aggressive personality only when dealing with inferiors, while another may show it also when he is dealing with equals or even superiors.

Now, it is this difference of degree that enables the psychologist to measure the basic variables. Hence, the degree to which a person possesses the trait gives a clue as to the individuality of that trait.

What are these common measurable traits? The answers to this question are far from unanimous, but it seems that the number of basic traits is not so large as it would appear at first view. At least, factorial analysis seems to point in that direction. Among the common traits that have been fairly well isolated is ascendance-submission. It is assumed to be one single trait, of which each individual is supposed to have a certain amount, but the amount varies in such a way that in some people the ascending, dominating tendency prevails while in other people the submissive, yielding tendency is foremost. Introversion-extroversion is another such continuum; in extreme cases, a person is sometimes said to be an almost perfect introvert, or an almost perfect extrovert, but in most cases people show a mixture of both tendencies. Many authors include general intelligence among personality traits. Those traits which express a person's attitude toward values are of particular importance for the subject matter of this book. One may measure a man's interest in theoretical values, or aesthetic, economic, political, religious, and perhaps still other values on which Spranger based his typology. However, in the present procedure these interests and attitudes are not used to put an individual into a certain category or type, but serve as one of the many measurable traits by which a person can be revealed.

The main methods that are used to identify or measure personality traits are questionnaires, standardized rating scales, and projective techniques. A description of these personality tests will be given in Chapter 13.

How do personality traits come to be what they are in an individual, *e.g.*, an adult? In other words, how does a man's personality originate? Personality comes into existence as the result of a number of factors, which may be considered as belonging to four groups.

Whatever happens during a lifetime that helps shape a personality presupposes the existence of a basic something that can be influenced or molded. This basic something is properly found in the constitutional, congenital, native endowment of an individual. How far this native endowment is hereditary is a question of minor importance here, but it comprises, in the first place, the individual's organic, somatic, or biological constitution; in scholastic terminology, one would say that it includes anything that pertains to vegetative life. The glandular, particularly the endocrine, system and the neuromuscular system are of more direct importance for the personality make-up. The constitutional endowment determines, among other things, a person's sex, physique, certain innate dispositions such as motility (the muscular tonus and speed of movement), vitality or energy output (some people can work all day without tiring, while others tire easily), and emotionality (the bodily resonance of emotions).

These latter three dispositions—emotionality, vitality, and motility—constitute what is called by the group name of "temperament." Although some writers identify temperament with the whole of personality, the present authors designate as temperament the native dispositions that derive from a man's somatic constitution. The nearest approach to the primitive form of temperament is to be found in a child; in an adult, temperament never appears in its native form because it is overlaid with influences due to learning, training, and the individual's own will. But, although temperament in adults is inextricably interwoven with the other determinants of personality, which will be mentioned presently, enough of it is assumed to be present in a person's behavior to permit investigations of temperament. This has been done ever since the time of Hippocrates, who presented the world with his renowned humoral division of temperaments, comprising the choleric or irascible, the sanguine or impulsively hopeful, the melancholy or sad, and the phlegmatic or apathetic types.

Since inborn temperament is largely determined by the same factors as physique, physical appearance, or body build, by the biochemical factors especially, it could be expected that attempts would be made to establish the correlation between temperament and physique. Among the more recent attempts, the study by Kretschmer and that by Sheldon should be mentioned.

Kretschmer's investigation on physique and character, according to the title of his book, presumably is an attempt to correlate body build with character, the latter term meaning the whole of personality. But the title is misleading. Kretschmer himself makes it clear in the text that he intends to compare physique with what he calls the foundational core or elementary, native basis of personality. And this foundational core coincides to a large extent with the authors' definition of temperament.[7]

Kretschmer distinguished, in brief, the following body types: the asthenic or leptosome physique, characterized by underdeveloped, sharp, lean features, and the pyknic type, characterized by a rounded, thickset build. Inasmuch as the leptosomatic constitution is sometimes associated with a more or less strongly developed skeleton and musculature, he singled out a third body build which he called the athletic form. And he grouped all abnormal physiques under the term "dysplastic type." Basing his opinion on the statistical analysis of mental patients, Kretschmer held the view that the asthenic physique was strongly represented among schizophrenic patients and that the pyknic body build was particularly characteristic of manic-depressive patients. The two mixed types of physique were also found among schizophrenics, but they occurred more frequently among epileptics. Kretschmer then made the assumption that the abnormal is merely an exaggeration of the normal, and he attempted to prove this assumption to be true by showing that the asthenic physique correlated not only with the pathological schizophrenics but also with the borderline cases of the schizoids as well as with the type of normal temperament that he called schizothymic. Likewise, he held that the pyknic physique was correlated not only with the manic-depressive but also with the borderline cases of the cycloids and with the cyclothymic temperament of normal, well-adjusted personalities.

Kretschmer's theory has been examined from different angles and has met not only with enthusiastic approval but also with severe criticism.[8] For instance, Garvey examined 260 patients equally divided between manic depressives and schizophrenics and found little to support Kretschmer's theory.

Sheldon and his coworkers,[9] on the basis of the measurement of photographs, distinguish three body types: endomorphy, characterized by "soft roundness"; mesomorphy, in which muscle and bone predominate; and ectomorphy, which discloses "linearity and fragility." The somatotype of every single individual is expressed by a seven-point scale by which the degree of that individual's endomorphy, mesomorphy, and ectomorphy is indexed. Likewise, Sheldon, on the basis of factorial analysis of some sixty traits, finds three components of temperament, which he calls (*a*) viscerotonia, expressed in such traits as relaxation, love of comfort, sociability, and the like; (*b*) somatotonia, disclosed by such traits as directness of manner, assertive posture, and unrestrained voice; and (*c*) cerebrotonia, in which a certain tenseness, restraint, and social inhibition predominate. Again, a seven-point scale is used to determine to what degree any single individual possesses the three dimensions of temperament. Thereupon, comparing the varieties of physique with those of temperament, the authors find a high correlation between endomorphy and viscerotonia, between mesomorphy and somatotonia, and between ectomorphy and cerebrotonia.

Although this work is welcomed as the most careful investigation on the subject to date, some criticism has already been leveled against it. One of the more serious objections is that Sheldon's choice of what he calls temperament traits is, if not arbitrary, at least unilateral.

Up to this point, only the physiological, somatic factors of a person's native endowment have been mentioned. But a human being is not only a biological somatic entity, but a psychobiological or psychosomatic unit; *i.e.,* his constitutional make-up comprises also some basic psychic potentialities or dispositions. Every individual possesses from childhood on a set of drives and impulses, native abilities to perceive, to learn, to remember, and a certain amount of potential, native intelligence. These inborn capabilities will develop with time, but one has to admit a certain fund of native equipment in order to make development possible. And this inborn equipment varies from person to person. Despite the claims of some die-hard behaviorists to the contrary, no amount of training will make a Beethoven out of an individual who has only a fair amount of inborn musical ability.

The individual's constitutional endowment, both somatic and psychic, which is given at birth, forms what is variously called the raw material, the rudimentary basis, the matrix, the foundational core of his personality. In this respect, a newborn child may be said to possess personality only in a rudimentary form. This rudimentary endowment gradually develops during a lifetime into a more or less organized and integrated personality. It is capable of natural growth and maturation, and it is molded by the other three kinds of factors. A person's basic equipment is, in the first place, influenced by his environment. Some of the environmental factors are of a physical or biological nature, such as the climate, the food, the air, and whatever diseases, injuries, and accidents may befall him. The social surroundings in which a man lives and the cultural group of which he is a member are of greater importance for personality development. Everyone is strongly influenced by his family background, his nationality, the race to which he belongs, the gang into which he drifted in his youth, the circle of his cronies and other group memberships, the school he attends, the teachings of his church, and the experiences of his profession. Each one of these, and many other environmental factors, have been made the subject matter of special studies, which undoubtedly contribute to a better understanding of the manner in which certain personality traits come into existence. The danger of some of these studies is that the investigators, apparently overwhelmed by their own findings, raise the factor that they singled out for their study to the status of being the one all-embracing factor accounting for personality.

Obviously, personality is not the sum of a man's native endowment plus environmental influences; it is, rather, the result or product of the interplay between the two. The demands of environment interact with native equipment and modify it within limits.

Moreover, a point not to be overlooked is that some of the environmental factors are themselves the result of personality structure. One of the factors mentioned was a man's profession. Some of the personality traits of an individual who has chosen to be a politician or a priest or a psychiatrist or a member of any group are certainly determined by the exigencies of his profession, but the very choice of that profession was influenced by the preexisting features of his personality, such as capacity, interest, and ideals. This observation leads to the third major factor that is responsible for the development of personality.

This extremely important factor is a man's will. Personality traits are not simply the result of environmental influences passively received into the psychophysical organism; a man can actively shape his life, destiny, and personality by means of his own will power. True, he cannot change his organic constitution or his physical environment, nor can he escape the influence of his sociocultural milieu; but he can use his will to exploit his mental abilities to the utmost, and he can cause his life experiences to serve the purpose that he outlines for himself. Although he necessarily undergoes the influence of the sociocultural standards of his environment, he need not be a slave of those standards. There are many examples of people who, although living in the midst of a certain culture, say the so-called culture of the Nazis, refused to submit to its impact.

Man may formulate for himself ideals and principles of conduct and, by abiding by them, gradually develop personal attitudes. Now, the whole of these attitudes acquired under the influence of the will is called character. Character, therefore, is the disposition that prompts the will to react in a habitual manner to the motives that stimulate a man. Since many of the personality traits due to the activity of the will have a moral connotation, *i.e.*, since they constitute moral habits, virtues or vices, some authors limit the term "character" precisely to designating the whole of these moral habits; but this definition seems to be inspired by an ethical theory denying the existence of morally indifferent acts. On the other hand, there are some who extend the word "character" to a meaning covering the whole of personality, an extension that would seem to make the word quite superfluous. Others, and it would seem the majority of present-day writers, simply ignore the term, because, as they say, they do not believe in the will. Determinism will be taken up in the next chapter; here it may simply be observed that the problem of the existence of the will is not only a question of belief, but one that should be settled in the first place by an analysis of psychological data.

Finally, Catholics, as well as many Protestants, Jews, and Mohammedans, admit the existence of a fourth factor that helps to shape one's personality—divine grace. If one wishes to call the will a constitutional factor, one might put grace in the group of "environmental" factors, with the understanding that it belongs to the supernatural "environment." History pictures numerous individuals whose personality seems to have changed, sometimes radically and suddenly, as in the cases of such saints as St. Paul, St. Augustine, St. Francis of Assisi, and St. Ignatius of Loyola. Similar changes of attitude can be observed in the lives of a great many other individuals whose names will never figure in history books, such as reformed alcoholics and convicts. Such cases demand explanation, and many of these persons themselves attribute the change in their personality to God's grace. Then there are the millions of people who are forced to drag on a life of perpetual sacrifice, day after day, in monotonous drudgery; they, too, are convinced that they could never stand the strain and stress of life unless God helped them.

If psychology of personality aims at understanding individuals, it should not exclude those whose conduct may be difficult to explain. One may try to extricate himself from such a difficulty by saying that people who believe that God helps them with His grace suffer an illusion, but that is only a gratuitous, aprioristic statement. The other way out is the perennially repeated objection that scientific psychology can do nothing with factors like grace and will, because these factors make human behavior unpredictable. However, the answer is just as perennial—*viz.*, that science should not sacrifice factual reality to a preconceived ideal. When real tests are ahead, no man's reactions are fully predictable.

In the preceding pages, an attempt has been made to review briefly the sources from which personality springs. Since the factors mentioned vary from individual to individual, it is clear that each particular individual can be expected to develop his own personality traits.

Now suppose that a number of traits of a particular individual have been measured; his standing in each trait can then be represented graphically in the form of a psychograph or personality profile. Such a graph shows the degree to which he possesses each of the various traits, and the connecting lines between the scores represent a kind of profile.

Does the psychograph give a picture of the homogeneity of a total personality? No, because it gives only a quantitative view of the sum of his traits. But personality is not synonymous with the sum of an individual's traits, because traits are never completely independent of one another; there is a certain interfusion, overlapping, and blending, inasmuch as every trait is colored by all the others. The psychograph represents only the quantitative scores of a man's traits, but—as Allport rightly observes—"it fails to express the qualitative balance between two or more traits," [10] in spite of its connecting lines.

Psychology has still a long way to go toward the solution of the problem concerning the integration and organization of personality traits. Some psychologists see the solution of it in what is variously called the cardinal trait, the dominant trait, or the master-sentiment, and they point out that such dominant traits largely depend on the values that an individual primarily seeks to achieve in life, on his principles and ideals. For instance, the motivational attitudes and interests of the aesthetic, religious, selfish, or altruistic man may color all his personality traits and make for a certain harmony of striving toward a goal. The result will be a more or less organized, integrated personality. There are obviously many individuals who have little or no fixed purpose in life; in that case, the personality is only loosely organized and the summative picture that the psychograph presents would approach somewhat an adequate representation of it.

It would seem that the existence of a central trait which gives aim to an individual life and around which all personality traits are organized makes for an integrated personality.[11] At this point an interesting question may be raised. Is integration of personality synonymous with normality, and is a loosely integrated personality synonymous with a personality that is abnormal in the medical or psychiatric sense of the word? The answer seems to be negative. On the one hand, it can hardly be maintained that all people with loosely organized personality structure should be classified as abnormal; on the other, not only normal but also some abnormal people may disclose a dominant trait in which their entire personality is centered. To be sure, many abnormal personalities present a picture of disintegration; unity and consistency of action is impaired for one or another reason, *e.g.*, because of a clash between the aims of life. But there are others who must be considered abnormal and who, nevertheless, disclose an astonishing harmony of striving, which gives their personality an integrated character. The megalomaniac who considers himself the President of the United States or Napoleon may display a surprisingly consistent way of acting according to his assumed role. The criminal who lives only for one purpose, crime, may perhaps possess a better self, but if he does, it seems to be altogether subordinated to his pretty well organized "bad self." Adolf Hitler organized his personality around his one dominating master sentiment—the glory of the German "race," of which he believed himself to be the personification—and colored his entire behavior by this dominant trait. Of course, the picture that such abnormal individuals present is distorted, sometimes into the grotesque, but it is a kind of homogeneous distortion, inasmuch as the distortions follow a sort of consistent pattern. Hence, it would seem that some abnormal people, too, may exhibit a kind of integrated personality.

What, then, puts the label of abnormality on such individuals? The main criterion that serves to distinguish abnormal from normal people seems to lie in the adjustment to reality. A normal person's reactions are usually proportionate to the situation in which they occur. True, he may occasionally give in to an emotional outburst or display of childish behavior, much the same as an abnormal person, but such maladjustive behavior is only passing and the normal person soon recovers his old self. Things are different with abnormal personalities; *e.g.*, the lack of maturity of a hysteric who tries to dominate her surroundings as a child does is, in an adult person, obviously not in keeping with reality; neither is the asocial, undisciplined behavior of the psychopath.

It is clearly impossible to draw a sharp dividing line between normal and abnormal personalities. As a matter of fact, adjustment or lack of it may run the entire gamut from perfect or nearly perfect adaptation to well-nigh complete maladjustment. It is also clear that the sources from which personality springs are the same for both normal and abnormal individuals; but, in the latter, any of these factors, either the constitutional, or the environmental, or both, are impaired.

NOTES AND REFERENCES

1. For an excellent discussion of the nature of matter, see MOORE, THOMAS V., "Cognitive Psychology" (Philadelphia: J. B. Lippincott Company, 1939), pp. 560–578.
2. See ST. THOMAS AQUINAS, S. *Theol.* I, Q. 76, a. 3.
3. In the text, the study of personality was approached from the logical standpoint, *i.e.*, how one comes to know a person's individuality. From the ontological angle, it should be noted that the soul is the formal principle of individual characteristics. True, all these characteristics are to be attributed to the composite of soul and body, *i.e.*, the person, as the ultimate agent, but they are his through the soul. The ontological principle of a man's individuality is, therefore, to be found in his soul. In other words, the souls of different men should be conceived of as—numerically—different one from another: Mr. Jones' soul is individually different from Mr. Smith's. This is precisely the opinion of St. Thomas Aquinas, who further points out that the reason for each soul's individuality is to be found in the particular disposition of the body with which that soul is united. See ST. THOMAS, *Contra Gent.*, 2, c. 75, c. 83; *Q. Disp. de An.*, a. 3; *Q. Disp. de Pot.*, a. 10; S. *Theol.* I, Q. 85, a. 7.
4. The following form a selected bibliography of studies on personality:

ALLERS, RUDOLPH, "Character Education in Adolescence" (New York: Joseph F. Wagner, Inc., 1940); *id.*, "The Psychology of Character" (New York: Sheed & Ward, Inc., 1943); *id.*, "Self Improvement" (New York: Benziger Bros., 1939).

ALLPORT, GORDON W., "Studies in Expressive Movement" (New York: The Macmillan Company, 1933); *id.*, "Trait-names, a Psycho-lexical Study" (Princeton, N.J.: Psychological Review Company, 1936); *id.*, "Personality, a Psychological Interpretation" (New York: Henry Holt and Company, Inc., 1937); *id.*, "The Nature of Personality: Selected Papers" (Cambridge, Mass.: Addison-Wesley Press, 1950).

ANGYAL, ANDRAS, "Foundations for a Science of Personality" (New York: Commonwealth Fund, Division of Publication, 1941).

BEERS, CLIFFORD, "A Mind That Found Itself" (New York: Doubleday, & Company, Inc., 1935).

CATTELL, C. A., "Personality: A Systematic, Theoretical and Factual Study" (New York: McGraw-Hill Book Company, Inc., 1950).

CATTELL, RAYMOND B., "Description and Measurement of Personality" (Milwaukee: The Bruce Publishing Co., 1948).

HARSH, CHARLES M., and H. G. SCHRICKEL, "Personality: Development and Assessment" (New York: The Ronald Press Company, 1950).

KLUCKHOHN, CLYDE, "Personality in Nature, Society, and Culture" (New York: Alfred A. Knopf, Inc., 1948).

LEWIN, KURT, "A Dynamic Theory of Personality" (New York: McGraw-Hill Book Company, Inc., 1935).

MAGNER, JAMES A., "Personality and Successful Living" (Milwaukee: The Bruce Publishing Company, 1944).

MURPHY, G., "Personality: a Biosocial Approach to Origins and Structure" (New York: Harper & Brothers, 1947).

MURRAY, H. A., *et al.*, "Explorations in Personality" (New York: Oxford University Press, 1938).

STAGNER, ROSS, "Psychology of Personality" (2d ed.; New York: McGraw-Hill Book Company, Inc., 1948).

THORNE, FREDERICK C., "Principles of Personality Counseling" (University of Vermont, 1950).

WHITE, ROBERT W., "The Abnormal Personality" (New York: The Ronald Press Company, 1948).

WOLFF, W., "Values and Personality" (New York: Grune and Stratton, 1950).

5. JUNG, C. J., Metamorphoses and Symbols of Libido, *Annual of Psychoanalytic and Psychopathological Research,* 1913; *id.,* "Psychological Types," translated by Godwin Baynes (New York: Harcourt, Brace and Company Inc., 1923).
6. SPRANGER, E., "Lebensformen" (6th ed.; Halle: M. Niemeyer, 1927), English translation by Paul J. W. Pigors, "Types of Man" (Halle: M. Niemeyer, 1928).
7. KRETSCHMER, E., "Körperbau und Charakter" (Berlin: Springer-Verlag, 1921), English translation by W. J. Sprott, "Physique and Character" (New York: Harcourt, Brace and Company, 1925).
8. Among the critics may be mentioned CONNOLLY, C. J., "Physique in Relation to Psychosis" in "Studies in Psychology and Psychiatry," (Washington, D.C.: The Catholic University of America Press, 1939), Vol. IV, No. 5; GARVEY, R., Comparative Body Build of Manic-Depressives and Schizophrenic Patients, *Psychological Bulletin,* Vol. 30 (1933), pp. 567–739; ALLPORT, "Personality," pp. 72–78.
9. SHELDON, W. H., S. S. STEVENS, and W. B. TURNER, "The Varieties of Human Physique" (New York: Harper & Brothers, 1940); SHELDON, W. H., and S. S. STEVENS, "The Varieties of Temperament" (New York: Harper & Brothers, 1942).
10. ALLPORT, "Personality," p. 404.
11. A special problem concerning the integration of personality seems to be created by cases of double or multiple personality. One and the same man may present the picture of the more or less integrated personality of Mr. Burke in one phase and that of the more or less integrated personality of Mr. Jackson in another phase. Although the two personalities are completely disconnected, the unity of the person in the metaphysical sense of the word remains unimpaired, because both empirical personalities are phases of one person, composed of one and the same body and soul. If one wishes to speak in terms of unity, one should say that the functional unity is impaired because the memory functions are split into two disconnected chains.

Chapter 2

THE MORAL LAW, CONSCIENCE, AND RESPONSIBILITY

THE MORAL ORDER

Most systems of psychology and psychiatry long ago severed all relationship with morality, professing that they are not, and should not be, concerned with the problem of whether an individual's behavior is desirable or undesirable from the moral standpoint. Theoretical psychology largely pursues this course still, but some branches of practical psychology seem to have arrived at a turning point in the road of development. This turning of the tide is gradually becoming more and more noticeable in the case of that extremely practical branch of psychology which deals with mental health.

The present world condition probably has something to do with the turning of the tide. Serious people have begun to think about the reasons for an ever-lengthening chain of global wars and about the unbalanced state of our tottering society; they have asked themselves if the mental confusion in the world is not, in the final analysis, a moral problem. More and more people seem willing to agree that the problem of rebuilding our present world on a sounder basis involves the reestablishment of moral principles and ideals. Obviously, the rebuilding of our disorganized world can be achieved only through the restoration of the mental health of the individuals who make up that world. Hence, a growing number of those who are interested in restoring mental health feel that they must concern themselves also with the problems of moral values.

However, it would be a serious mistake to believe that psychology, psychiatry, sociology, anthropology, or any other such science is by itself in a position to establish the ultimate and stable principles of morality. Such a task does not belong to their jurisdiction, for no psychological or sociological theory is a substitute for ethics. Ethics, and especially moral theology, have the task and the exclusive right to lay down the norms and rules of the moral order, *i.e.*, to teach what is morally good and what is morally evil, and also to show why certain actions are either good or bad.

In presenting an exposition of the Catholic system of morality, the authors do not intend to enter into the countless discussions that surround this topic, but according to the rule already expressed, they intend to set forth as briefly and succinctly as possible the main tenets of the Catholic doctrine.

The Catholic moral system presupposes as a basic condition the existence of a personal God Who created the world and rules it with infinite intelligence. This ruling is called the eternal law—the plan, exemplar, and source of all law. God is the supreme lawgiver with regard to not only physical but also moral events; in other words, God has established not only a physical but also a moral order. This means that God has laid down a set of rules that form the standard by which a person's actions must be judged either morally right or morally wrong. God did not formulate these norms arbitrarily, as a human tyrant might do who today might issue a decree or edict and tomorrow might revoke or change it; they are the expression of God's eternal, infinite reason and therefore irrevocable and eternal. This ruling, as it exists in God's mind, is the objective norm of morality.

Anyone who denies the existence of an ultimate objective norm of morality to be found in the mind of the Creator is bound to look somewhere else in order to find the source of morality; he may try to locate that source in society, tradition, customs, the state, or dictators, but then he has to bear the consequences of his system. All such theories proclaim that the moral order is man-made. If there is no absolute norm of morality, man has to decide for himself or, more often, other men decide for him what is morally good and bad. Such a refusal to acknowledge an objective, absolute norm undermines all moral stability. Although this is not the place to present a refutation of relativistic theories of morality, it is important to point out that refusal to admit absolute ethical standards results in the construction of the most ingenious theories which, when put to the test, fall to pieces.

A simple example may clarify this statement. When Hitler and his abettors exterminated thousands of Jews by locking them up in gas chambers, and made soap out of the fat of their bodies and lamp shades out of their skins, was the act of those "supermen" right or wrong, good or bad? Everyone in his right mind will answer that it was evil. But why? Because it is inhuman! But why is it inhuman? The basic dogma of Nazism was the blood-and-soil dogma. Anything that was good and useful for the German "race" was considered morally good. "Now," so the Nazis reasoned, "the extermination of the Jews is good and beneficial to the German race; hence, it is morally good." It would be difficult to find fault with this syllogism, once the premise is accepted. Yet a great many people accept as the principle and basis of all morality just that very premise, *i.e.*, that what is useful is morally good. But if this principle is accepted, its logical consequences should also be accepted and—coming back to our example—its adherents should feel no scruples at washing their faces with soap made of human fat.

One may object that our society does not tolerate such an interpretation. Indeed, our society does, perhaps, condemn such things. But why should our society be the measuring stick of good and evil? In the East, a society is being formed in which many things that we call evil are considered desirable, and vice versa. If society is its own moral standard, why are the concepts of our society superior to those of the other one? If our concepts of good and evil have only a relative value, they may come some day to mean the very reverse of what they mean at present. Perhaps the present man will some day change into the superman of Nietzsche, who preached the transformation of all values, and to whom mercy, loyalty, and fairness were immoral weaknesses and hatred, sin, and pride, moral greatnesses.[1] Thus far, man has not reached that stage of evolution; and hatred, sin, and pride still make neurotics out of many people, including Nietzsche.

The only reasonable answer to the questions presented above is that no system of moral rules will stand the test unless it is based on objective and absolute principles. This is the Catholic position.

Granted that God from eternity has established the standard according to which rational beings should in time regulate their moral conduct, one naturally asks how He made the moral norms known to mankind. God promulgated His law by creating man after His own image, *i.e.*, by giving man a rational nature. Because man is a creature endowed with reason, he participates in a finite and analogical fashion in the divine reason, and this participation enables the human mind to arrive at essentially the same ideas concerning good and evil as those which the divine mind expresses in the eternal law—with the proviso, however, that the human mind is not led astray by adverse influences, of which we shall speak presently.

God's eternal law, as made known to man through his nature as a rational being, is called the *natural law*. Metaphorically speaking, it is said that the natural law is written in the human heart. The pagan writer

Cicero calls it *nata lex,* the inborn law. This does not mean that man possesses ready-made innate ideas and judgments about good and evil, but it does mean that man has a natural, inborn aptitude to grasp the main obligations of the natural law through experience. This aptitude to recognize through experience the dictates of the moral order is the basis of human conscience. The proviso indicated above—that the human mind *if it is not led astray* can arrive at essentially the same ideas concerning good and evil as those which the divine mind expresses in the eternal law —is an important one, for history has given abundant proof that man is capable of misunderstanding and distorting the principles of the natural law even to the point of denying the very existence of an objective moral order. Despite his rational nature, man has proved himself capable of forming an erroneous conscience. A comparison of the moral teachings of the various races and peoples all through history shows at first glance a great variety of views concerning what should be called good and what evil. To be sure, there is common agreement with regard to the fundamental moral principles. There is in the first place the most fundamental and simplest rule of the entire moral system, *viz.,* that there is a difference between good and bad, or in other words, that not everything is allowed. There is also a common appreciation of the value of life, property, and truth and a certain reverence for parents and matters of sex. Some of the principles of the natural law may be found obscured almost beyond recognition, but a more detailed study of certain customs will often reveal a trace of the moral law. For instance, in some primitive tribes the sons consider it an act of filial piety to kill their parents before they grow too old or too sick. This seemingly immoral act, is after all, the result of a strange interpretation of the law expressed in the commandment "Honor thy father and mother," for those people believe that a person continues life in the beyond in the same state of health and vigor in which he leaves the earth. They therefore kill their parents in order to guarantee to them a good life in the hereafter.

To what are these deviations from the natural moral order due? One may mention a variety of influences, but they all fall into the two main groups of constitutional and environmental factors, which will be treated in some detail in the section on conscience.

Under the influence of these factors, variations and distortions of the natural law were sure to arise. God therefore revealed His will by positive revelation. This revealed law is called the *positive divine law.* It comprises both a renewal and a supplement of the natural law. God promulgated the positive laws from the beginning of the world in the primitive revelation given to the protoparents of mankind. Then, after deviations and deflections from the natural law had prevailed, God had pity on mankind and, wishing to restore the law in its pristine purity, free from distortions, He renewed and supplemented the positive divine law later in history, once as the old law through Moses and once as the new law through Christ. The law of Sinai is an explicit statement concerning the natural law known as the Ten Commandments and contains, moreover, the positive law of the Sabbath and ceremonial, legal, and civic precepts. The law of the Gospel reiterates the Ten Commandments, stresses love, and commends the evangelical counsels, but abrogates the complicated ceremonial and legal precepts of the Old Testament.

To round off the picture, there are the *human laws,* the laws defined by legitimate human authority, either ecclesiastical or civil. A human law may be a more definite statement concerning the principles of natural or positive divine law, or it may embody the consequences logically derived from those principles. In either case the human law is subordinate to these general principles, and its precepts, even though they may add to these principles, have binding force only as long as they do not contradict the natural and the positive divine law. When speaking of the law in the following pages, the authors have in mind primarily the natural and positive divine law, for the ethical personality as a rule feels its obligations more strongly than those of the human laws.

An outline of the fundamentals of the Catholic system of morality seemed necessary, because the purpose of this book demands such a frame of reference. As is quite obvious, this system is based on reasoning, revelation, and history. It clearly advocates an unchangeable objective norm of morality, a position that should be kept constantly in mind if the attitude of the Catholic Church in moral matters is to be understood.

CONSCIENCE

The preceding section pointed out that God has established a set of objective moral rules by which man is bound to regulate his conduct. Therefore, it is evident that God must have given to man a power which enables him to know the law and which guides him in moral matters. This power which resides, as has been seen, in man's very nature as a rational being is called moral consciousness. This is the consciousness a person has about the moral value of certain acts. Man is aware of himself and the outside world, he perceives objects, thinks, reacts emotionally to certain events, feels an urge to do things, etc.; these are examples of states of immediate consciousness. Likewise, a human being is aware of the moral value of his own and of others' conduct. For instance, a person hearing or reading about a hideous crime may be filled with disgust; in such a case his moral consciousness is aroused and "speaks." Again, disgust for the lies in international politics or for the way the Mindszenty trial was conducted, admiration for the gesture of certain saints who liberated Christian slaves by taking over their places—all such responses show that the moral consciousness is awakened.

It appears from these examples that human nature is such that it responds with an approving or disapproving attitude when it is confronted with actions, types of behavior, and events which are contingent upon moral values, *i.e.*, which either are or are not in accordance with the objective norm of morality.

When a person applies his moral consciousness to his own acts, one speaks of conscience. The genuine phenomenon of conscience appears only when a man is to make a decision between what is objectively a morally good and a morally bad act, or between a better or less good act. In such a situation, conscience may appear—and speak—before and after the decision.

Before the decision, a man's conscience tells him what is his duty and what is unlawful, and thus makes him realize that he is faced with a conflict. Here conscience appears as a rational judgment which states whether the act the person has in view is good or bad. But there is more: conscience may also stimulate, counsel, exhort to do what is right; it may warn that what seems to be a pleasure or a profit is evil. Moreover, there may be a natural attraction for what is good and an aversion for what is wrong. In this manner, antecedent conscience acts as a moral guiding power that prepares the decision. The decision itself is an act of the will, and since the will in normal cases is free, it is possible to choose against the exhortations of conscience.

After the decision has been made and the act decided upon has been accomplished, conscience appears once more. It then is called consequent conscience. It appears in the form of a judgment, stating that whatever was done was right or wrong, and this judgment is accompanied by feelings of approval or disapproval. The boy scout who has performed his noble deed of the day and the man who has given a substantial donation to a worthy cause may feel quite satisfied with themselves, but the girl who has consented to certain advances of her suitor may suffer pangs of conscience, remorse, and guilt. Conscience then appears as an approving or disapproving agent.

The foregoing analysis shows how conscience works. Now, Catholic moralists have made an attempt to define conscience according to its main function. The majority of them, following the lead of St. Thomas Aquinas, see in conscience primarily a function of the intellect and define it, accordingly, as a dictate of practical reason. Others, however, hold that conscience is not only a function of intellectual understanding, but that feeling and will, too, meet in conscience—in other words, that conscience is the expression of the entire ethical personality. The authors do not intend to take sides here in this psychologically interesting controversy. It suffices to say that all Catholic moralists hold that conscience is rooted in man's nature as a rational being. Some may give a more nativistic, others a more empiristic, interpretation of the origin of conscience, but all agree that conscience is not solely the product of experiential and environmental influences. However, they admit at the same time that environmental as well as other factors largely contribute to the right or wrong development of conscience.

In describing the functions of conscience, the authors purposely used often the auxiliary verb "may." Conscience *may* perform the functions of a guiding power through its judgments, exhortations, warning, approval, disapproval, etc., and as a matter of fact conscience *does* perform these functions provided it is properly formed. In that case one speaks of a *true* or *correct* conscience, *i.e.*, a conscience that reacts in conformity with the objective norms of morality as they were laid down by God in the natural law and revealed by Him in His positive divine law. A true conscience, when faced with moral problems, responds readily and gives a clear-cut answer in accordance with the objective standard. Those who possess such a conscience and act accordingly are said to be conscientious.

But the proper formation of conscience is lacking in many people, either through their own fault or otherwise. In that case conscience does not react in conformity with the objective standard; it may present a caricature of the law, or it may fail to "speak" and may appear dead. One then speaks of an *erroneous* or *false* conscience.

As has been seen, history offers ample proof of the distortion of the human conscience, particularly when it is left to its own devices. Anyone can find countless examples of erroneous conscience in his everyday contacts with the people of his surroundings, and the formation of such a false conscience is due to exactly the same causes as those distortions which we witness in history.

An erroneous conscience may reveal itself either by an excess or by a defect of conscientiousness. Some people are, or seem to be, excessively conscientious. Overconscientiousness should not be confused with a tender or delicate conscience. The latter takes even slight sins for what they are, an offense against God, and therefore avoids them. In itself, it is not at all the same as a scrupulous conscience, but in persons so disposed it may pave the way to it, as may be gleaned from the lives of several saints who became scrupulous at one time or another.

A form of overconscientiousness is the *rigorous* conscience, which belongs to those who stick to the letter of the law and refuse to admit a reasonable interpretation of it. This is the type of conscience that may be found among formalists, sticklers, puritans, and fanatics. When people of that type try to impose upon others the burdens that they impose upon themselves, they may become a nuisance; they are found among the bigots. But still more obnoxious is the pharisaic conscience of those people who feel obliged to "bind together heavy and oppressive burdens, and lay them on men's shoulders, but not with one finger of their own do they choose to move them" (Matthew 23:4); they are the hypocrites clever in inventing sophisms to exempt themselves, the sanctimonious, the dissemblers, the pious frauds, the insincere given to duplicity and lip service.

The extreme form of overconscientiousness is the *scrupulous* conscience. This is the morbid condition of psychoneurotic personalities who are always uncertain about moral obligations, forever fearful of decisions, continually in doubt as to whether they have fulfilled their duty, and therefore continually reproaching themselves for not having done so. This type of conscience has a psychopathological basis, and it will be dealt with in Chapter 19 of this book.

On the other hand, the conscience of many people shows a defective formation. Here the *lax* conscience is encountered. Laxity of conscience is very common and is found in people who are habitually inclined to take liberties with the moral law, *e.g.*, with regard to sex, alcohol, or business ethics. They minimize moral principles, and if their conscience remonstrates, they easily find a pretext or subterfuge to dull its reproaches. This type of conscience is, for instance, frequently found in extrovert personalities, who readily make decisions without properly reflecting, in contrast to introverts, who are more inclined to develop a scrupulous conscience because they feel unable to solve their doubts. A lax conscience develops almost of necessity in persons who do not believe in an objective standard of morality. A person who holds that he himself is the final norm by which to govern his conduct in moral matters can be expected to establish somewhat elastic rules, which will easily reflect his own inclinations. A lax conscience is often due to willful neglect, such as neglect of religious training, but a person may also be the victim of environmental, especially educational, influences beyond his control and thus develop a lax conscience in good faith.

By continually smothering the voice of conscience, a person may succeed in making it practically inaudible, and in that way a lax conscience may gradually develop into a *blunted* or *dormant* conscience. This is a condition in which people may reach the point of confounding right and wrong. They consider themselves as above the law, not recognizing any distinction between good and evil; the only law they follow is the law of caprice, and the only limitation they may impose upon themselves is that of staying out of the hands of the police. Such a condition may be due to a personality structure, such as is found in the cynic, the megalomaniac, and Nietzsche's superman. It may also be due to the lack of moral training and the pernicious influences of environment. Many children—and not only those in the slums—receive no moral or religious education; they just grow up and increase the ranks of the lost generation.

How do these different types of conscience come into existence? The examples cited make it clear that the factors that contribute to the formation of conscience are the same as those which go into the making of a personality. Some of the kinds of conscience mentioned are apparently due to constitutional factors, while others are due to environmental factors; *e.g.*, a certain temperamental type seems primarily to account for a cynical conscience, and a scrupulous conscience is often the result of events and experiences that occur during a person's life. However, it would be more accurate to say that the components of a man's physical and psychic native endowment, including his native intelligence, account for the matrix, the groundwork, of his moral consciousness and conscience, and that this original structure develops under the influence of three kinds of factors—environment, will, and God's grace. In other words, the ethical personality develops along the same line as the personality in general. For that reason, a man's conscience may be described as the expression or "voice" of his ethical personality.

The influence of both the original constitutional make-up and the environmental factors that contribute to the formation of man's ethical personality can be modeled for the better or for the worse by his will, for man is not just the sport of these factors. The formation of his conscience depends to a large extent on what a man does with and to himself and on how he reacts to the factors that influence him. By the same token, the reaction of his will determines also his responsibility in the formation of his conscience; *i.e.,* his own willful cooperation or lack of it decides whether he is guilty or not in the formation of an erroneous conscience. To be sure, the influences that befall him may be so strong that they may impair or abolish his freedom of will, but this is certainly not always the case. For instance, a lax or dormant conscience may be due to the voluntary neglect of religious duties. Some persons may have had in their youth an active and correct conscience, but at a certain period of their life, let us say during adolescence, they stayed away from church, refused to receive the sacraments, and continued to live in a habitual state of sin. At first the conscience protested, but in the long run it gradually weakened and finally fell asleep. This deplorable condition then became habitual because of willful neglect to foster conscience. To understand the river, look at the brook.

There is more: divine grace, too, aids in the formation of conscience. God does not refuse to help a person who earnestly strives to build up a correct conscience. On the other hand, a Catholic who neglects his religious duties and never asks God to make him see what is right will become spiritually tepid and will easily become lax in moral matters, not only as the natural result of habit formation but also as the result of the lack of supernatural grace.

This exposition of the kinds of conscience that may develop in a person makes it clear that conscience is far from being an infallible guide in the interpretation of the objective norm of morality; when it comes to distinguishing between objective good and evil, conscience often is seriously mistaken. Some psychoanalysts have stated that conscience is often far from reliable as if it were a major discovery; they forget that Catholic moralists have held that view for ages past and have pointed out that conscience may fail, partly because of ignorance resulting from original sin, and that it may even make a person mentally sick, as in the case of scrupulosity.

So, conscience is not always a dependable interpreter of the law. Yet, despite all its shortcomings, conscience is the subjective norm of our moral conduct. This means that a man must obey the directions of his conscience, regardless of whether it be true or false, because conscience is the only means that an individual possesses for becoming aware of the objective orders of the Lawgiver. A man with a false conscience, be it strict or lax, "would act wrongly if he did not act according to the conscience which he has, since it is quite impossible for him to act according to a conscience which he ought to have but does not now possess." [2]

However, this rule is valid only when two all-important conditions are fulfilled. The first condition is that a person act in good faith, *i.e.*, that he have not willfully neglected the right formation of his conscience.

The second condition is that his conscience speak with certainty. The distinction between a certain and a doubting conscience cuts across the various divisions of conscience mentioned earlier, with the exception of the scrupulous conscience, which is always doubting. A true conscience, as well as the various types of the erroneous conscience, may or may not have the quality of certainty attached to it. A man's conscience is *certain* when his opinion about the morality of a given concrete act is such that he has no fear of being mistaken. Certainty is, of course, a subjective state of mind, and one may acquire a subjective state of certainty although he is objectively mistaken; in other words, a conscience that is certain may be true but also it may be erroneous. A person with a *doubtful* or *dubious* conscience is one who cannot make up his mind as to the line of conduct he should follow because he realizes that his conscience may be in error.[3]

Now the rule stated above, that a person must obey the dictates of his conscience, requires as a necessary condition that it speak with certainty. One is not allowed to follow his conscience as long as it is in practical doubt.

Provided that these two conditions are fulfilled—*i.e.*, that a person act in good faith and that his conscience be certain—he is bound to follow his conscience and he is morally responsible for his actions in the same measure as his conscience tells him. If his conscience is ignorant of the law, that law, morally speaking, does not exist for him; if his conscience gives a false interpretation of the law, he must follow the erroneous pathways marked by it; if his conscience minimizes or aggrandizes an obligation, that obligation decreases or increases for him in the same proportion.

This exposition may be summarized as follows. The rules of morality are not derived from conscience, but conscience presupposes an objective law. Conscience is not itself the law, for it is not autonomous. It imposes obligations, however, not in its own right but in so far as it is the herald of the Supreme Lawgiver. The formation of conscience is influenced by various factors, constitutional as well as environmental, which may produce, and often do produce, a conscience that gives a distorted picture of the law. Nevertheless, because conscience is the subjective norm of an individual's moral life, each man is bound to obey the dictates of his conscience, provided that it speaks to him with certainty and that he has done his honest best to keep it straight despite the influences that may lead it astray. It is the task of the moralist to help a man to rectify his erroneous conscience. And because an erroneous conscience frequently has strong repercussions on a person's mental health, the psychiatrist, too, should contribute to the straightening out of such a conscience so far as it falls within his realm.

MORAL RESPONSIBILITY

According to many psychiatrists, the aim of psychotherapy is to educate the patients to become responsible individuals. Although it is sometimes hard to find a clear definition of responsibility in their writings, they seem to mean that a responsible person is one who is able and willing to face reality, who no longer looks for escape mechanisms, who has outgrown his childish attitudes and is willing to meet his obligations and duties as a mature person should do. The opposite of responsible would be irresponsible, a term which is then taken as somewhat synonymous with careless, infantile, and unreliable.

Responsibility evidently includes moral responsibility also. A person is said to be morally responsible when he is assumed to be able to fulfill the obligations of the moral law and, consequently, must be reputed guilty and amenable to punishment when he runs counter to these obligations. In brief, moral responsibility is a man's capability of moral guilt. In order to judge a man's capability of making himself guilty by transgressing the prescriptions of the law, the psychiatrist needs the information of the moralist, and the latter can learn from the psychiatrist in deciding the extent to which certain pathological conditions may reduce a person's responsibility.

The correct understanding of moral responsibility should be linked up with our discussion of conscience in the preceding section, for conscience is the ultimate subjective norm of morality. The factors that decide moral responsibility are to be found, in the first place, in the very formation of conscience. Every man may form, as has been seen, either a true or a false conscience. In case he has formed a false or erroneous conscience, be it rigorous or lax, he is not responsible for the formation of it, when he has formed it in good faith, as the victim of influences beyond his control. But the man who has willfully neglected to form a correct conscience is responsible for the formation of such a conscience and, theoretically speaking, for the mistakes it makes. Hence, the source of responsibility resides in the will.

On the other hand, let us consider the condition of a person who has formed a true conscience or an erroneous one in good faith. It has been shown that the function of conscience, be it true or false, is preparatory to a decision which a person's will may make in moral matters. But, since a man's will is free, he may decide either according to, or against, the directions of his conscience. If he decides according to the direction of his conscience, be it true or false, provided it speaks with certainty and is formed in good faith, he is doing the right thing. In the case of an erroneous conscience, his action may be objectively wrong, but he is subjectively not responsible. For instance, in the extreme case cited previously, the pagan tribesmen who kill their parents to secure them a better hereafter objectively commit a sin; but, if they act in good faith, they are subjectively not guilty. To use another term, they commit a material, but not a formal, sin.

But if a person makes a decision against the warnings and remonstrations of his conscience, again regardless of whether it be true or false, he is doing wrong and is subjectively guilty of sin, even though his action may be objectively right. The reason for his being so responsible is that his will decides against the dictates of his conscience, the subjective norm of morality. Hence, again, the source of responsibility resides in a man's will.

And, indeed, the problem of responsibility practically coincides with the problem of free will. Formal sin depends upon the decision of one's will, for, as St. Thomas says, "Sin consists essentially in an act of the free will." [4] The possibility of formal sin presupposes the use of reason; *i.e.*, the sufficient use of reason is the basic prerequisite of the freedom of will; again, Aquinas says: "The root of all freedom is in the intellect." [5] Therefore, the masturbation of an idiot is no formal sin to that person himself. Hence, briefly, formal sin requires freedom of will, and the necessary condition of freedom is the use of reason.

There is a great deal of misunderstanding about the Catholic doctrine of the freedom of the will. Freedom of the will means freedom of choice between motives, a motive being any objective that the mind grasps as good or desirable. The Catholic position is one between indifferentism and determinism. Catholic moralists do not say that freedom of choice is arbitrariness, as if the will could choose arbitrarily without being influenced by motives—that would be the position of indifferentists or indeterminists. They hold that a man cannot choose without motives. But they also reject the opinion of the determinists, who hold that the will, while weighing the motives, is so influenced by one motive that it cannot choose the other motive.

Let us suppose that a person, after weighing in his mind two types of motives, reaches the conclusion that one of them is the more desirable and more attractive. One might say that it would be foolish not to decide accordingly and to choose the less attractive motive. However, that is precisely what Catholics hold—*viz.*, that a person can decide for a less attractive motive. And, as a matter of fact, man often commits this "foolishness," for instance, when he makes a decision in favor of an unpleasant duty as against an alluring pleasure. And the determinists must admit from their own experience that such a decision often happens, and apparently they do admit it. Why, then, do they deny freedom?

Most of the arguments of the determinists are based on an assumption taken either from metaphysics or from science, and run as follows: Man *is* not free, because he *cannot* be; and there can be no freedom, because (*a*) man is a machine (the metaphysical assumption), or (*b*) freedom of action is against the law of conservation of energy (the scientific assumption).

Hence, freedom is denied not on a factual basis, but on aprioristic grounds. It would seem more in keeping with the scientific approach first to consult the facts and after that to consider how possible objections can be met. Freedom of the will must logically be inferred from the facts of everyday behavior. For instance, a man holds himself and other human beings responsible for what he and they do; but such a conviction would not make sense if all were predetermined to do what they do. The main psychological argument is based not on inference but on the direct evidence of interior experience. When a man is faced with a decision, he is convinced that, when he chooses one motive, he could have chosen the motive attracting him to the other side. This is a fact of immediate consciousness. Of course, one may pretend with the behaviorists not to be interested in the data of consciousness, but anyone who denies the immediate evidence of consciousness may as well deny that he is conscious of seeing the paper on which these words are printed.

Once the freedom of choice is established as an ultimate fact of consciousness, one may consider the difficulties that some writers raise on the basis of the philosophical or scientific assumptions that have been mentioned. A good rejoinder to the metaphysical assumption is the simple inversion of that argument: if the facts prove that man is free, it follows that he is not a machine. And as for the assumption taken from science, freedom of choice does not violate the law of conservation of energy, because an act of the will does not create new energy but only directs existing energy and modifies its quality.

But there still remains an objection to be answered. The usual repartee of the determinists against the interior evidence of being free is that it is an illusion. They maintain that a person may think that he acts freely, but, in reality, his action is predetermined. For instance, they will admit, as has been said, the obvious fact that one may choose an unattractive objective instead of a seemingly more desirable motive, but they add that in such a case the person was compelled to put duty before pleasure because of his habit formation or some other such factor.

Now, one should never be too generous with references to illusions when it comes to explaining facts, for those who are may themselves be the victims of an illusion. But Catholic moralists would agree that there are factors that may cause certain motives to influence a person so strongly that his freedom of will is impaired. They agree that in concrete practical cases the human will is not always as free as it appears in theory, for free will may be limited by a number of factors that constitute as many intrinsic determinants of liberty. Such factors may color a certain motive and give it such a weight that it determines a person's decision and subsequent behavior.

The main difference between the Catholic system and determinism is, of course, the fact of will. But, granted that a human being has a will, the difference narrows down to the following. According to the determinists, certain factors *always* determine a person's actions, even though he may labor under the illusion that he himself decides. The Catholic position is that man's will *may* be determined by several kinds of factors.

What are these factors that limit the control of the free will and at times may determine its exercise? Once more, two large groups may be distinguished—*viz.*, constitutional and environmental factors, or, as they are sometimes called, internal and external factors. Some religious sects such as the Gnostics, the Hussites, and the Calvinists add a third kind of factor —*viz.*, God's grace, which of necessity moves certain persons to do good and thus predestines them to eternal salvation. Catholics, too, hold that divine grace motivates but they believe that it does not force the recipient. However, these theological considerations scarcely fit into the framework of this book.

Constitutional factors result from native dispositions, both psychic and physical. For the purpose of this book, it makes little difference whether these dispositions are hereditary or not. St. Thomas clearly indicates that a man's biological dispositions may favor his morally good tendencies when he says: "Some people by their own bodily constitution are disposed to chastity or meekness and the like." [6] But this obviously holds for evil tendencies too. Biological dispositions influence a person's conduct during certain periods of his physical development. For instance, during the period of adolescence and sexual maturation, the inner restlessness, the lack of balance, and the passionate impulses may seriously impair the free exercise of the will in both boys and girls. In a later chapter it will be shown how the involutional period may also influence a person's mind.

Not only during particular periods but all through life, one's temperament may play an inhibitory role in the full development of one's freedom of action. Temperament, as has been seen, is largely constitutional and includes a man's motility, vitality, and emotionality. The amount of vigorous and vital activity is partly the result of a general condition of the organism—*i.e.,* of the health of the person. The lack of energy or "pep," as a permanent attribute of a personality or during sickness, may seriously affect one's will power in such a way that sins of omission, for instance, are not, or not completely, imputable. Lack of energy and a resulting fear of responsible activity is a characteristic feature of neurasthenics; they find it hard to reach a decision, and even when they have reached it, they shrink from action.

Emotional conditions, especially, may create actual or habitual obstacles to free choice. It suffices here to cite a few examples, for there will be ample opportunity to come back to this point in the various chapters of this book. There is, in the first place, fear. Fear is a disturbed condition of the mind caused by real or imaginary danger, and such a condition may be momentary or permanent. Sudden danger may so overwhelm a person that it deprives him momentarily of the use of reason. Now, the use of reason is the essential prerequisite of any voluntary activity. Hence, such a fear may suspend the free will. Freedom is also seriously impaired in the lasting condition of fear, which is called anxiety, and this impairment extends to the compulsory thoughts, feelings, and actions that are thrust upon a man because of his morbid condition of fear. The same considerations hold for rage and its permanent counterpart, the morbid condition of hostility and aggressiveness, and for sadness and its pathological partner, depression. All emotions—or, as the Scholastics call them, passions—form a source of partial or complete determination. Men are often blinded by passion; *i.e.*, passions impede the use of reason. Hence, mental blindness makes a decision impossible. Consequently, there is often little moral responsibility when, for instance, a person kills someone in a sudden fit of rage. When the use of reason is not entirely suspended, passion may greatly diminish the guilt of an evil act. Of course, it should not be forgotten that a person may still be responsible for the evil consequences of a sudden fit of passion because he did not avoid the occasion that he knew would stimulate his rage or sexual impulses.

The other main group of conditions that influence and sometimes determine a man's freedom of action derives from environment. Evidently, environment plays a role only in so far as its influence is, so to speak, assimilated into the psyche. Again, a few examples will suffice. A youngster educated in a communist milieu will, of necessity, have a different outlook on life and society from a youth reared in bourgeois surroundings. In both cases their desires and ideals will have a strong impact on their minds, and these ideals may well determine their conduct.

Suggestion forms another frequent limitation of voluntary control. The curve of suggestibility, which follows the normal curve, indicates that some people are highly suggestible and, therefore, can be easily induced into actions without much resistance of the will. When suggestion is combined with threats, it may result in moral pressure, which, in the last analysis, is based upon fear. Mentally weak persons, people with a weak will readily fall victim to moral coercion, but so may otherwise normal people. Only too often moral pressure is exerted on persons who are economically dependent; *e.g.*, by terrorizing organizations or by political parties. How far such influences impair freedom and moral responsibility is often difficult to decide, but there can be no doubt that the pressure may be so strong as to annul the resistance of the will.

The various experiences that befall an individual during his lifetime, from early childhood on, may create psychic traumas and conflicts, and these, in turn, may cause in persons with a certain predisposition pathological conditions like depression and compulsion, which have already been mentioned, as well as other forms of neurotic or psychotic disturbances. All such mental and emotional disorders form more or less serious impediments of control of the will.

A special form of interference with free-will activity is found in habit formation. A habit consists in a tendency and readiness of acting acquired by frequent repetition, as is clear in the case of the alcoholic. This is a special form of impediment, because it is not to be put on the same level as the other impediments that have been mentioned. Whereas fear, rage, moral pressure, etc., directly affect the will, habit itself is formed through cooperation of the will, at least in most cases. True, habits may be formed in persons who lack the exercise of will power, such as idiots. They may also be the result of some pathological urge, which itself may be a more or less strong determinant of voluntary action, as is the case with many alcoholics. But, in most cases, the first steps in habit formation are due to the choice of the free will; *i.e.*, in many cases a person could have prevented his evil habit if he had controlled himself. Perhaps no one has expressed this better than the German poet Hebbel when he wrote: "The one I am sadly salutes the one I could have been."

However, once a habit is formed, it may become second nature and diminish accountability. How far a habit can impair free will varies from person to person and from case to case, but it may be laid down as a general rule that the just appraisal of the degree of imputability depends upon the efforts an individual makes to break with his habit.

After this brief review it may be concluded that, although in abstract theory the human will is free, in concrete practice there are many forms of encroachment upon that freedom. Now, the freedom of the will is ultimately the basis of moral responsibility, and therefore the intrinsic determinants of liberty mean as many limitations of responsibility.

To be sure, the objective norm of morality is strict and definite; the Catholic moralist calls a sin a sin, and mortal sin a mortal sin; but he also has an open eye for the foibles and weaknesses of the sinner. There is so much ignorance, error, bias, and prejudice, so much thoughtlessness and downright stupidity, there are such strong biological and psychic obstacles interfering with man's freedom, that many people do not know what they are doing or only realize afterward what they have done. In other words, many people act in a manner which is objectively reprehensible, but for which they are subjectively not, or not fully, responsible because their freedom of action is impaired or destroyed.

Among the conditions that impair the exercise of free will, mental and emotional disturbances have been mentioned. Some psychiatrists seem to interpret this to mean that the mentally ill are not responsible for their acts, in other words, that they cannot sin. And some of the mentally ill themselves express the same opinion after their own fashion by saying, "I can do as I please, because I am insane anyway." This opinion is false. It cannot be established as a general rule that all mental patients are morally irresponsible. Such a rule certainly does not hold for the psychoneurotics, and neither does it hold in its generality for the mental defectives and psychotics. Each case must be judged individually.

True, there are conditions where all responsibility is abolished, as with idiots, with most imbeciles, and with some psychotics in the final stage. It is also true that modern psychiatry rejects the older opinion that a mental patient can be ill only in one particular point; rather, it considers a mental disorder as affecting the whole personality. That does not imply, however, that the individual's reason and will are always so affected that he is freed from all responsibility. The majority of the mentally ill combine relative responsibility with relative lack of responsibility. They may not be responsible for a certain type of actions, but they are responsible for those types which are not directly connected with their syndrome; they may not be responsible during certain periods, but they are relatively responsible during those periods in which they are comparatively free from acute attacks of their sickness.

It is, finally, true that mental, and especially emotional, disturbances often entail a morbid tendency to commit certain sins. However, a morbid tendency does by no means always imply determination, because the term "morbid" is not equivalent to the term "uncontrollable." This point can be clarified with an example: Some people suffer from bulimia, a morbid feeling of hunger, but no physician would advise such a patient to give in continually to that craving. Likewise, a morbid tendency to morally reprehensible acts should be checked, and in many cases can be checked. In fact, self-control greatly enhances a patient's chances for recovery. The aim of modern psychiatry is precisely, as was said in the beginning of this section on responsibility, to educate the patients to develop into responsible persons. But how can this aim be achieved if the patient will not cooperate? Cooperation, however, supposes a certain amount of will power. Hence, psychiatrists themselves admit in practice that the mentally ill are not completely devoid of will power.

In brief, if the degrees of responsibility of the mentally disordered were to be represented by means of a curve, one end of the curve would represent those who are completely, or almost completely, responsible; the other end would represent those individuals whose responsibility is entirely destroyed; and in between the two extremes we would find the great majority of persons with a reduced responsibility, which would allow for endless variations.

In this section the authors have endeavored to clarify their position concerning moral liberty and determination. At this juncture, one might ask where the demarcation line falls between full freedom and complete determination. The answer is that no such line exists. Qualitative things can never be measured with a quantitative yardstick. Where is the demarcation line between normality and abnormality? The psychiatrists will admit that there is none, because there is a gradual and imperceptible transition from what is certainly normal to what is certainly abnormal. Instead of speaking of borderline cases, it would be more exact to speak of borderland cases. In between the two extremes is a large margin of no man's land. The same holds true for the difference between freedom and determination. On one side is the free land of democracy; on the other side is the slave state; and in between is contested territory. A large percentage of those who dwell in the borderland is made up of seminormal individuals. They certainly cannot be exculpated from all responsibility by way of a general rule; but, whenever there is serious doubt whether an act, committed in seminormal or abnormal conditions, is free or not, the rule of Catholic moralists is very lenient. When the act is sinful, it must be reputed involuntary, because a man is innocent until he is proved guilty, but when the act favors the agent, it is to be considered free and therefore meritorious.[7]

NOTES AND REFERENCES

1. Nietzsche, Friedrich, "Also sprach Zarathustra": "Evil is man's greatest power. Man must grow better by becoming more wicked, that is what I teach. The greatest wickedness is necessary to make the best superman. . . . Indeed, I teach you to become supermen! The superman gives meaning to the world. . . . At one time the offense of God was considered the greatest offense. But God has died and with him the offenders. . . . 'Nothing is true, everything is allowed,' thus I said to myself. 'To live as I please or not to live at all,' that is how I will it."
2. Davis, Henry, "Moral and Pastoral Theology" (New York: Sheed & Ward, Inc., 1935), Vol. I, p. 67.
3. Catholic moralists are wont to enter into lengthy discussions about another type of conscience, *viz.,* the probable conscience. The controversy involves the problem of what degree of probability an individual should reach before he can safely follow the directions of his conscience. Although important for

the moralists, this problem has less importance within the framework of this book.

4. *S. Theol.* I, II, Q. 77, a. 6, *corp.*
5. *De Verit.*, Q. 24, a. 2.
6. *S. Theol.*, I, II, Q. 51, a. 1, *corp.*
7. PRÜMMER, D. M., "Manuale theologiae moralis" (Freiburg im Breisgau: Herder, 1928), I, 61. On the moral responsibility of the mentally ill, see BRITT, R. E., Moral Limitations in Mental Disease, *Linacre Quarterly*, October, 1947, pp. 16–25; SIMONART, P. C., The Imputability of the Mental Patient, *ibid.*, pp. 8–15.

Chapter 3

DEVELOPMENT OF THE CONCEPT OF MENTAL DISORDERS

Although the story does not always make edifying reading, a very brief historical sketch of the development of ideas concerning mental disorders and treatment of the mentally ill may help to shed some light on present-day concepts and therapy.[1]

From early Greek times—to limit the discussion to the Western World—the demonological or demoniacal concept of mental diseases prevailed. The mentally ill were thought to be under the influence of gods or demons who supposedly manifested their power over them by throwing them into trances and transports of ecstasy and by granting to them the gift of visions and prophecy, as in the case of the Pythian oracles.[2] Because of the belief that demons caused them to behave in a queer, unreasonable fashion or threw them into convulsions, the victims were held in reverential awe by the onlookers. For that reason, epilepsy was called the "sacred disease" *par excellence.*

In recorded history one of the first to combat the notion that mental disorders were induced by demoniacal influence was Hippocrates (460–357 B.C.), the father of medicine and, in many respects, the founder of psychiatry. By means of clinical and anatomical observations, he came to the conclusion that mental disorders not only could be explained in a perfectly natural manner but should be explained on an organic or somatic basis. By exposing the brain of an epileptic, he showed that there was very little of a sacred nature about epilepsy and that it was simply due to a diseased condition of the brain. He held infectious and toxic conditions of the body to be responsible for certain delirious states, and he stressed the same somatic origin for other mental disorders; *e.g.,* he linked up anxiety states with an excess of bile, manic conditions with an excess of blood, and depression with an excess of black bile. It is, of course, of no importance whether the so-called humoral theory be true or false; the point of interest is that an attempt was made to explain mental disorders on a natural, somatic basis.

In ancient times, some of the more outstanding physicians, like Galen, followed Hippocrates' lead. However, the great majority of the laity, together with many medical practitioners, continued to look upon mental diseases from the demonological viewpoint. Although it cannot be denied that some cases of insanity are due to genuine possession, the demoniacal concept was certainly exaggerated. During the earlier centuries of the Christian era, this concept was displaced by the belief that God permitted the insane person's mind to be bemused as a punishment for his sins and that, therefore, only through prayer and sacrifice could his mind be returned to a normal state. This was a rather common view among the general population, but, again, there were many who expressed a more sensible notion. In the later Middle Ages and in the Renaissance, the demoniacal view reappeared in a more virulent form, giving rise to violent reactions in the form of bloody persecutions against the insane. Since these poor people were believed to be either possessed by the devil or given to witchcraft, both Catholics and Protestants vied with each other in exterminating them [3]—an un-Christian movement of mass neuroticism, which the book "Malleus maleficarum" ("The Witches' Hammer") written by two German Dominicans toward the end of the fifteenth century, did much to stimulate. The more sensible of the physicians—Paracelsus and particularly Johann Weyer (1515–1588),[4] whom Zilboorg considers the father of scientific psychiatry—protested against such inhumane behavior and pleaded for the giving of medical treatment to the so-called witches. But their voices were as "the voice of one crying in the desert" (Isaiah 40:3).

It was a very long time before the general trend of thought turned in the right direction. Finally, however, after the English Hippocrates, Thomas Sydenham, gave an accurate description of mental diseases in his "Processus integri" (1692), a change slowly began to appear in the ideas of the general public on the nature of insanity. Although little or nothing was done at first to mitigate the sufferings of the insane or to treat them as human beings, they were no longer burned at the stake, save in exceptional circumstances. Nevertheless, they were still treated as wicked, dangerous criminals. Kept in almshouses and dungeons without light or sunshine, chained to the walls, poorly fed, and denied the means of keeping warm in the winter, these unfortunates were usually attended by keepers who, often from the ranks of discharged prisoners and the lower classes, neglected to supply their charges with even the most important hygienic necessities. If the patients were "fortunate" enough to receive any treatment, it consisted in exsanguinations and drugging. Moreover, they were considered an object of public entertainment: just as today parents and children go to the zoo on Sunday afternoons, so in those days they visited the asylums for the mentally sick, paid a small fee, and spent an enjoyable day viewing the inmates.

It took another century for the idea that the insane were ill and not wicked to penetrate fully into the public consciousness. This change of ideas was achieved by Philippe Pinel (1745–1826), director of the Bicêtre and, later, of the Salpêtrière (the two insane asylums in Paris), who was greatly helped in his endeavors by his assistant and successor, Jean Étienne Dominique Esquirol (1772–1840). Pinel's "Traité médico-philosophique sur la manie" (1801) is considered the turning point in the history of psychiatry. In other words, it is no more than a century and a half ago that the modern era of psychiatry began.

While correcting antiquated notions about mental diseases, Pinel initiated at the same time the humanitarian movement in treating the insane. Upon his instigation and under his direction, jails were changed into hospitals and jailers into nurses, shackles were removed from the patients, and physicians were trained. Continuing the work of his master, Esquirol distinguished himself by drawing up the plans for the construction of completely new and suitable institutions for the care of the insane.[5]

The new ideas concerning the nature of mental disease and the treatment of the mentally ill spread rapidly throughout Europe and the rest of the civilized world. The problems that faced the new psychiatry concerned the classification of mental disorders and their etiology and pathogenesis; once the cause was known, the problem of the type of treatment arose.

The Germans particularly, with their typical Teutonic gift for order, contributed toward the solution of the problem of classification. One of the first in this field was W. G. Griesinger (1817–1868); but his followers began to exaggerate, and soon the number of divisions and subdivisions of mental disorders ran into the hundreds. Finally, Emil Kraepelin (1856–1926) put the matter of classification on a solid footing. In the Heidelberg Clinic, Kraepelin originated descriptive psychiatry and systematized clinical psychiatry as it is known today; he analyzed and compared data carefully and advocated the long-range study of every mental case in order to obtain a complete evaluation of the disorder. In that manner, he arrived at a classification covering some twenty types of mental diseases, a scheme that formed, and still forms, the general basis of the ones subsequently presented, although a certain tendency away from exact classification may be observed at the present time.[6]

However, the problem about the origin and the cause of mental disorders was more important than classification. To disprove the old demonological view, Pinel and his followers concentrated their efforts on showing that insanity was related to some brain disease. Indeed, the surest way to combat the "spiritual" explanation of mental disorders as advocated by the demon-and-spirit view, seemed to be to show the material, organic basis of these diseases. Besides, it is altogether in line with the physician's thinking to look for a cause in the patient's body for any disease he meets.

But there was another reason why certain people were so anxious to find a physical cause for mental disorders. The nineteenth century, particularly its second half, was the heyday of materialism. If it could be proved—so the materialists argued—that every mental disease was related to a brain disease, it would follow that the materialistic thesis was correct, *viz.*, that mental processes—or, more briefly, that mind—is matter. The authors do not intend to discuss materialism here, yet they wish to point out the fallacy of such an argument. There can be no doubt that in man, as he is now living on earth, the brain is the organ of his mind, either directly or indirectly. But this premise does not at all warrant the conclusion that mental activities are therefore nothing but a product of the brain; still less does it warrant the conclusion that the human mind is the same as the brain.

Whatever the various reasons may have been, psychiatrists made every attempt to find a definite somatic cause for the different types of insanity. Griesinger maintained that every mental disorder was a brain disease, and Kraepelin, too, always felt that something pathological should, and would, be found in the brain to account for a mental illness. Kretschmer's energetic attempt to correlate mental disorders with a specific body build or physique offers a further illustration of the tendency to give a somatic basis to mental diseases. These examples make it clear that there was a general tendency among psychiatrists to relate mental diseases with some somatic feature, be it the brain or any other characteristic of the body; and as a matter of fact, as anatomical and neurological research progressed, one type after another of insanity was found to have a physical basis.

Although the trend of thought in the last century was generally in the direction of a physical explanation of mental disorders—in some circles it still is—a reaction against this notion gradually set in. An increasing number of psychiatrists began to voice doubts as to whether all forms of mental disorders were due to somatic or physical causes, and the question was raised whether certain psychological factors might not be responsible for them. Could it not be that worries, tensions, economic stress, life difficulties, acute emotional shocks, and prolonged emotional strain actually did account for certain forms of mental diseases and abnormal behavior? Emotions involve, of course, a bodily disturbance, but the cause of an emotion is to be found in man's inner experiences. The cause of a man's emotional conditions, either acute or prolonged, is to be found in an intellectual insight into his present condition and in memories of past experience. When a person faces imminent danger, when he feels unable to attain physical or moral security, when he sees his aspirations thwarted and his ideals crumble, his mind may well become emotionally upset. Now, these and similar conditions are of a psychic nature; therefore, the problem arose whether such psychic factors might not upset the mind to such an extent as to cause or precipitate its disorganization. It is to be expected that in Pinel's time an affirmative answer was given somewhat hesitatingly, because the concept of psychologically determined disorders looked almost like restoring the old "spirit-and-demon" view. Nevertheless, even then Esquirol, unable to find a somatic cause for all mental diseases, suggested the idea that psychic factors might be accountable for them. And once the era of the demoniacal view had definitely come to a close, more and more psychiatrists began to feel free to look for psychological explanations. Around 1840, Moreau de Tours began to interpret certain mental cases in psychological terms.

At this point, a little digression is in order to show how the view that certain mental disorders are brought about by psychic factors received support from other quarters. While the battle was raging concerning the proper concept and treatment of the insane in the strict sense of the word, similar problems arose with regard to those conditions which are now called the psychoneuroses. But there was one interesting difference: the former problems started with questions about the nature of insanity and, as a consequence, led up to questions about its treatment; but the latter took an opposite course, for the questions about the nature of treatment of neurotics arose first, and once these questions were settled, the nature of the disorder seemed also to have been decided.

Although the story goes farther back, it may be taken up with the time when Franz Mesmer (1733–1815) came into the picture. Mesmer effected some sensational cures with mentally and emotionally unbalanced persons, and he himself accounted for his curative power by what he called animal magnetism. According to his philosophy of nature, the world was permeated by an ethereal fluid which was supposed to act like a magnetic force. Now Mesmer believed that he and certain other persons were particularly gifted with the power to collect this magnetic force either into their own bodies or into some object, *e.g.*, a tub containing iron filings. And when this force passed from the magnetized body or object into the patient's body, his body too was supposed to become magnetized, and in that way the patient was cured of his ailments. Likewise, other Mesmerists effected cures by throwing the patient into a sleeplike state, which we now call hypnosis, and which the Mesmerists also ascribed to the passing of magnetic forces. Hence, the conclusion that the Mesmerists drew was that the cures were obtained by physical means acting upon the patient's body.

However, doubts arose as to the truth of the conclusion, and commissions of physicians and scientists were set up to investigate the nature of the cures. The commissions declared the cures genuine enough, but considered them to be due, not to any form of magnetism, but to the patient's "imagination"—*i.e.*, to the influence of suggestion. To prove this point, one of the members of the commission, Benjamin Franklin, then Ambassador of the United States to France, used a very simple test: he told some patients to stand under certain trees which he declared to be magnetized, and these good people were cured just as completely as those who were standing under trees "magnetized" by the Mesmerists.[7] This test made it pretty clear that the only sensible conclusion was that not physical but psychic devices were responsible for the cures; at present, one would say that the cures were due to psychotherapy. It was to be expected that Mesmer's physical explanation of the cures fell into disrepute and was replaced by the psychological explanation, particularly through the later work of James Braid (1795–1850), who used mere suggestion to induce hypnotic trances.[8]

The decision about the nature of the treatment of neuroses implied, of course, a very important corollary, *i.e.*, the decision about the nature of the disorders themselves. This corollary was clearly brought into the open in the famous controversy that went on in the eighties between the Nancy and the Paris schools of psychiatry. On the surface, the controversy looked as if it were a revival of the question of the nature of hypnosis, but, in reality, it was a dispute concerning the nature of neurotic conditions, particularly that of hysteria. Liébeault and Bernheim, representing the Nancy view, defended the thesis that hypnosis is a condition due to suggestion—in other words, a condition due to psychic causes. But then, it was argued, if neurotic conditions could be treated effectively by psychic means, the conditions themselves must be of a psychic nature. On the other hand, Charcot (1825–1893), director of the Salpêtrière at Paris, argued precisely the other way around. Charcot could not believe that hysteria—or, for that matter, any other mental disorder—was purely of a psychic nature. He, the greatest neurologist of the nineteenth century, who spent all his life in the study of the nervous system, was convinced that hysteria must have a physical basis in that system. Granted this premise, which Charcot was never able to prove, it followed logically that hypnosis, which apparently cured hysterics, was also a physical phenomenon. But then Charcot had to fall back on some sort of Mesmerism or magnetism to explain the nature of hypnosis.

In the course of time, the number of those who adopted Charcot's viewpoint dwindled rapidly, and the psychic character of both hypnosis and the disorders it was supposed to cure was recognized. These disorders, therefore, were no longer called neuroses but psychoneuroses.

This event marked another important turning point in the development of the concept of mental diseases. It meant, pathogenetically speaking, that not all forms of mental disorders have a somatic basis, but that some have a psychic origin; in other words, to borrow two terms used by Thomas V. Moore, some are organogenic and some psychogenic. The latter are supposed to comprise, in the first place, psychoneurotic conditions, but they probably include also some forms of insanity or psychosis, such as schizophrenia, paranoia, depression, etc. True, many psychiatrists, hesitant to subscribe to the psychogenic nature of these psychotic conditions, have always hoped, and still hope, to find an organic basis for them—which is, of course, a praiseworthy enterprise. The failure thus far to find such an organic basis is well expressed in the "Standard Nomenclature of Disease and Standard Nomenclature of Operations," edited by E. P. Jordan and published by the American Medical Association (Chicago, 1942), which presents the psychogenic disorders under the cautious heading of "Disorders without clearly defined tangible cause or structural change." At the present time, there are still writers who reject the psychological point of view for all mental disorders, including the psychoneuroses. But, now that Freud's ideas have become universally accepted, these so-called biologically orientated psychiatrists form a minority.[9] And, indeed, Sigmund Freud, more than anybody else, has contributed to the recognition of the psychological viewpoint concerning mental patients.

Freud's background was such that he seemed predestined, so to speak, to become interested mainly in the neurological, somatic aspects of mental disorders, for in his early years he lectured on nervous diseases, was one year a pupil of Charcot in Paris, and then taught neuropathology at Vienna. Yet, surprisingly enough, Freud's lifework was entirely concerned with the psychic aspects and the psychotherapy of mental disorders through developing his psychoanalysis. However, here a word of caution must be put in to prevent misunderstanding. When Freud speaks of the psychic origin of mental disorders, he certainly means that they cannot be demonstrably traced to a brain disease; in other words, he opposes psychic to somatic. On the other hand, to Freud, a full-fledged materialist, psychic is not opposed to physical, for he conceives of the psyche in terms of some energy, comparable to physical energy.

At present, it is not the authors' intention to explain Freud's system at length; this will be done in Chapters 8 and 9. The point is that psychoanalysis did much to dispel the notion of the somatic origin of all mental disorders.

One might say that the psychoanalytical view is, after a fashion, a return to the demonological concept of mental disorders. The statement must be taken with a few grains of salt, but the two views have in common the fact that not all mental diseases have a somatic basis. While in older times the mentally ill were believed to be possessed by spiritual forces in the form of demons, Freud held that at least some of them are possessed by demons of another kind—the unconscious drives. The difference is that the wicked spirits of old operated from outside the patient's psyche, while in Freud's system they operated from within it.

The present-day concept concerning the origin of mental diseases is that, theoretically speaking, they may be caused either by mental or psychic causes, in which case they are termed psychogenic, or by bodily or somatic causes, in which case they are called organogenic. Practically speaking, the two kinds of factors often intermingle and aggravate one another in producing a mental disorder. Besides, when speaking of organic factors, one should think not only of brain diseases in the strict sense, but of many other bodily conditions that have an influence on the mind and may eventually condition a mental disorder. If a man has a boil or a toothache, his mind is affected and hampered in action. Any physical disease leaves its imprint on the mind. This was the basic idea of Adolf Meyer's psychobiology.[10] Meyer contended that a psychiatrist in evaluating a patient's mental disorder should take notice not only of his mental symptoms but also of his physical development and the organic diseases he suffered during his lifetime. These organic conditions, Meyer argued, influence a person's mind precisely because he is a personality; *i.e.*, a patient is not only a body or only a mind but a personality composed of both. For instance, when an individual is plagued all his life by one physical disease after another, or even by several at one time, he may well develop a schizoid personality.

The most striking examples of organic conditions resulting in psychic disturbances are the accident neuroses. A fracture of the leg may disturb a patient to such a degree that he hesitates to use his healed leg in a normal manner because he is afraid that any kind of exertion may result in another fracture. A workman injured by some machine on which he has been working for years may become afraid to work with the same machine although he is perfectly cured. The automobile driver who has had a car accident often feels unable to drive again. A person who applies for a life insurance policy and is told of a too high blood pressure may change his whole life to escape sudden death. Any kind of acute or chronic disease, even though not dangerous to life, may, in certain persons, result in a psychic disturbance which they will be unable to overcome without psychiatric help. Naturally, it is understood that a certain predisposition is necessary to cause such disturbances. Nevertheless, now that the psychic basis of many mental disorders has been recognized, there may be observed at present a tendency among certain groups to approach a "mental case" solely from the psychological angle—in other words, there is a danger that possible organic aspects will be neglected.

Psychiatry is regarded with antagonism in some circles, and there is some justification for this feeling. The radio, the movies, the theater, and the modern novel all use psychiatric problems to entertain people in a pseudoscientific manner which is very often basically wrong. The use of nonscientific methods of pseudo psychiatry in treating abnormal behavior has often caused mistrust, skepticism, and suspicion against psychiatrists. The attempts of certain groups and schools to participate without medical knowledge in the treatment of mentally disturbed people have increased this distrust in the mind of the general public. Those dealing with the emotional problems of others should have the training, the knowledge, and the facilities necessary for giving a thorough physical examination to their clients and should be able to recognize organic disease if such be involved in the disturbance under study. Whenever seriously disturbed people are examined, the services of a competent physician should be included in the investigation and consultation. Such cases as that of a person who was "successfully" treated for anxiety and other nervous symptoms and then died shortly afterward from cancer bring discredit to psychiatry and psychiatric work.

This should not be regarded as an affront to psychologists and psychiatric social workers, who are doing an outstanding job in handling emotionally and mentally deranged people under the proper supervision of qualified physicians and psychiatrists. But it is important to emphasize that, when one is dealing with so-called mental cases, the entire personality of the patient, both physical and mental, should be examined.

NOTES AND REFERENCES

1. For collateral reading on the history of psychiatry and related sciences, the following may be recommended:
   ARGEL, SAMUEL Z., "Psychiatry, Today and Tomorrow" (New York: International Universities Press, 1946).
   MENNINGER, W. C., "Psychiatry, Its Evolution and Present Status" (Ithaca: Cornell University Press, 1948).
   "One Hundred Years of American Psychiatry," edited by the American Psychiatric Association (New York: Columbia University Press, 1946).
   RAY, MARIE B., "Doctors of the Mind, the Story of Psychiatry" (Boston: Little, Brown & Company, 1942).
   SELLING, LOWELL S. "Men against Madness" (New York: The New Home Library, 1942).
   SEMELAIGNE, RENÉ, "Aliénistes et philanthropes" (Paris: Steinheil, 1912).
   ZILBOORG, GREGORY (in collaboration with George W. Henry), "A History of Medical Psychology" (New York: W. W. Norton & Company, 1941); *id.*, "Mind, Medicine and Man" (New York: Harcourt, Brace and Company, Inc., 1943).
2. Because the Pythias in Apollo's temple at Delphi were probably hysterical women, some writers, such as Babinski, have suggested use of the term "pythiatism" instead of "hysteria."
3. See ZILBOORG, GREGORY, "The Medical Man and the Witch during the Renaissance" (Baltimore: Johns Hopkins Press, 1935).
4. See BINZ, CARL, "Doktor Johann Weyer" (Bonn: Mareus, 1885).
5. At about the same time, the ideas concerning mental defectives and their treatment were radically changed. Until the beginning of the nineteenth century, the mental deficients received neither protection nor care. A change for the better in the attitude toward these unfortunates was largely due to the incessant work of the Frenchman Édouard Onésimus Séguin (1812–

1880), who developed a method for the education and training of the feeble-minded. In 1848, Séguin came over to the United States where, with the financial support of a Massachusetts schoolteacher, Dorothea Dix, he began to establish institutions for mentally deficient children, a movement which rapidly spread over other countries.

6. Kraepelin's textbook "Lehrbuch für Psychiatrie" (Leipzig: J. A. Barth, 1913) is considered the most comprehensive study of clinical psychiatry up to that time.
7. See MURPHY, GARDNER, "An Historical Introduction to Modern Psychology" (New York: Harcourt, Brace and Company, 1929), pp. 134–145.
8. Braid changed the name of artificially induced sleeplike states from "mesmerism" to "hypnotism"—a term which, around 1880, was changed into the present term, "hypnosis."
9. See MOORE, THOMAS V., "The Nature and Treatment of Mental Disorders" (New York: Grune and Stratton, 1944), pp. 1–3.
10. An exposition of Meyer's views, which have been scattered in many articles, may be found in MUNCIE, WENDELL, "Psychobiology and Psychiatry" (St. Louis: The C. V. Mosby Company, Medical Publishers, 1939). See also LIEF, ALFRED, "The Commonsense Psychiatry of Dr. Adolf Meyer" (New York: McGraw-Hill Book Company, Inc., 1948).

Chapter 4

THE PSYCHOSOMATIC CONCEPT OF DISEASE

The preceding chapter dealt with the evolution of concepts concerning *mental* disorders. But also the present time is witnessing some rather drastic changes in our concepts of bodily or *somatic* disease. For a long time, the traditional opinion of the medical men was to consider bodily diseases as having an exclusively organic origin, and the psychic, particularly the emotional, side of illnesses was almost entirely neglected in medical research circles. This tradition was strongly corroborated by the findings made in the medical laboratories. However, some hundred years ago a reaction set in, and in recent times the trend toward emphasizing the emotional factors in the causation of bodily diseases has become very clear.

It has been found that many so-called purely somatic diseases are due, in part or wholly, to psychic factors, such as ideas, wishes, and particularly emotions. In other words, the mental condition of a person has a great deal to do with his physical well-being and may cause organic dysfunction. Under normal conditions, man's vegetative life is not noticeably influenced by emotions. Everyone is, of course, familiar with the fact that emotions have a repercussion on the body: people laugh when something amuses them, cry when they are sad, blush when they are embarrassed. But sometimes emotional states may cause more intense reactions; *e.g.*, a person may experience vague pains or acute abdominal distress during conditions of fear or anger, or he may develop a headache after a particularly exciting experience; unpleasant emotional experiences may take away his appetite, cause insomnia, and result in palpitations of the heart and disturbances of digestion and elimination. Everybody is cognizant of these facts. However, it has been found that emotional states may affect the vegetative system still more violently, so as actually to bring on or to aggravate serious organic diseases. One disease after another, such as heart diseases, high blood pressure, asthma, and hay fever, to quote only a few, has been discovered to be influenced by emotional factors. Hence, in such cases not only should the body of the patient be examined, but a thorough investigation into his mental condition is of equal, if not greater, importance. This means that attention should be paid to both the somatic and mental aspects of the case—in other words, to the patient's entire personality.

The statement that psychic factors intervene in the production of somatic diseases expresses the fundamental concept of *psychosomatic medicine*. Psychosomatics and psychobiology share the common thesis that all illness affects the entire personality, but the two theories attempt to prove this thesis from different angles. Whereas psychobiology states that somatic conditions influence the mind, psychosomatics maintains that mental conditions influence the body.

Although the term "psychosomatic" is rather recent in origin, the general ideas underlying psychosomatic medicine have been known for over two thousand years. Plato, in one of his dialogues, put these words into the mouth of the Thracian king, Zamolxis: "This is the reason why the cure of many diseases is unknown to the physicians of Hellas, because they are ignorant of the whole which ought to be studied also, for the part can never be made well unless the whole is well. . . . This is the great error of our day in the treatment of human bodies, that the physicians separate the soul from the body." [1] The idea that the king wished to convey to his contemporaries was that, because of the intimate relationship between mind and body, the former influences the latter even to the extent of producing organic diseases. The man in the street has, from the earliest times on, felt this influence almost instinctively and has tried to explain it in his own naïve way by telling his physician that under the stress of emotion he felt "lumps in his throat," that his heart "jumped" or "stopped," that his "stomach dropped," and that he was "paralyzed with fear" or "blinded with rage" or viewed the world "with jaundiced eye." Furthermore, there have always been religious sects that strove to cure the diseases of the body with psychological devices. But, by and large, the medical profession failed to appreciate the medical significance of emotional and other psychic experiences on the body. True, all through history there have been exceptions. The family physician of old was unconsciously a master in dealing with psychosomatic disturbances; knowing the emotional states and the life history of his patients, he was able not only to treat physical illness but also to understand that many of their symptoms were of emotional origin and to treat them accordingly. Nevertheless, scientific research was missing up to the second quarter of the last century, when the American surgeon William Beaumont recorded the first scientific observations about

1826.[2] As more and more facts were gradually observed of bodily functions being disturbed by emotional conditions, the groundwork was laid for the psychosomatic approach in medicine. Research in the field of psychosomatics was considerably advanced by Pavlov, W. B. Cannon, and Franz Alexander and his collaborators. Walter C. Alvarez showed the influence of emotions on the digestive tract. Harold G. Wolff and his associates established the influence of personality disturbances on the gastroduodenal and cardiovascular functions, and the relationship between those disturbances and resistance to infection; moreover, they evinced the correlation between the basic pathological mechanisms of chronic posttraumatic headaches and those headaches which follow stress and untoward life situations.

The Second World War contributed greatly to making physicians and the general public better acquainted with the psychosomatic concept of disease. In the United States, a large percentage of men were turned down by Selective Service because of psychoneurotic disorders, and an even greater percentage were discharged from military service for the same reasons. These, together with a large number of psychoneurotic casualties from the war zones, have made thousands of physicians aware of the great importance of psychological factors in producing bodily disorders. Many cases are known of soldiers developing such somatic conditions as gastritis, stomach ulcers, and hypertension while in service, and being cured almost instantaneously after they were returned to civil life.

The principles of psychosomatic medicine may be illustrated by reviewing the main types of disturbances to which emotional conditions may give rise.[3] Any emotional tension may affect the functions of the vegetative system, the kind of effect being dependent on the person's life history, his constitution, and his environment. Some degree of tension, within reasonable limits, is required to meet the daily routine of living and to face the challenging situations that often arise. This tension may be regarded as both beneficial and stimulating and is reflected in a sense of well-being, alertness, and efficiency in work. When the usual situations and the strain of the day are over, the tension is reduced, leaving the individual relaxed and satisfied with his achievement. However, tension may be increased to a pathological degree if the individual's capacity is not great enough to cope with the speed and pressure of daily work. If elements of insecurity are present in the situation, and if the demands of the situation involve conflicts that the individual cannot meet or solve, pathological tension is reflected in the mind and body. Some of the more common psychological symptoms are "feeling jittery," restlessness, anxiety, and worry. The more common somatic manifestations include insomnia, nausea, sweating, and trembling. This tension may be harmful and exhausting to the extent of reducing or blocking the individual's efficiency. Not only may pathological tension represent an overt reaction to the factors mentioned above, but it may also be the beginning of a more serious pathological condition, or may manifest itself as a part of an already existing condition. If these tensions are not adequately relieved, they accumulate and so affect the cortex as to produce mental disturbances and, chiefly through the autonomic nervous system, further affect the physiological constitution as to produce somatic symptoms; thus, misdirected emotional energy may exert harmful influence on organs and tissues.

The way in which the vegetative system is influenced by both body and mind may be illustrated by an example. A man may perspire in summer when it is very hot and humid; he may perspire in the same way in winter if confronted with difficult examinations at school, or if attacked by a robber at night. In both cases, the physical symptoms are the same, but the causes are different; in the first case the cause is somatic, in the second case, mental.

History books are full of examples of psychosomatic diseases due to tension. British Prime Minister William Gladstone developed a "diplomatic cold" whenever he faced a political difficulty or a distasteful debate. Elizabeth Barret, browbeaten daughter of a tyrannical father, was a bedridden invalid for twenty years but was cured almost overnight to the point of leading a reasonably active life when, at the age of forty, she met and married Robert Browning.

Hysterical conversion phenomena are basically caused by repressions. But the mechanism involved in hysterical conversion is fundamentally different, both psychologically and physiologically, from the mechanisms of other emotional disturbances. Hysterical conversion relieves emotional tensions in a symbolic way—*e.g.*, through paralysis, blindness, or loss of voice. The emotional tensions created by some conflicts are converted into such symptoms because they appear to the hysteric to solve the conflict.

The chief emotion causing cardiovascular disturbance is hostility. A connection has been found to exist between feelings of hostility and essential hypertension, anginal pain, and disorder of the heartbeat. Hostile impulses appear to set off, in certain instances, epileptic attacks. There is evidence, too, that hostility is a factor in the causation of headaches. The hostility, in most cases, arises from rebellion against domination and protest against work and responsibility; it may also arise from a constant struggle with a situation of an emotional nature where neither solution nor retreat seem possible.

Many cases of high blood pressure are seen only in the office of a general physician, who usually has not sufficient time to treat them with time-consuming psychiatric methods. One of the authors of this book has personally talked with "untreatable" hypertensives for many hours, finding that with easy relaxed conversation the blood pressure dropped 20 to 60 points and more during a period of less than two hours. The following is an interesting case:

§ A patient who was under psychiatric care for about four years was suffering from high blood pressure, which apparently was caused by an emotional condition. The patient, an easygoing man, had a higher than average position. However, his tremendously ambitious wife, who was always socially active and on the go, neglected to provide for her husband the serenity and peace that he so much longed for. The patient's condition appeared well under control as long as the treatment lasted, but after four years it was interrupted by the psychiatrist's entering the armed forces. The patient regarded this interruption as another attack on his personality and was forced to seek the help of another physician, who informed him that his condition was "beyond psychological approach." He underwent a bilateral sympathosectomy, which resulted in the reduction of his blood pressure to a normal level, mainly because he was bedridden for nearly half a year and had all the comfort and care that he wanted. When his therapist returned from service and saw the patient again, his condition was just as it had been before the operation—a fact indicating that as long as he lives under the same environmental situation his condition will remain unaltered.

Of the respiratory disturbances, asthma and hay fever are the ones that at times seem to be caused by psychic factors. The emotional factors in asthma have been worked out in considerable detail. According to a prevailing theory, such patients defend themselves against fear of separation, or estrangement from their mothers or mother substitutes. They feel that such a situation would be intolerable. If they feel threatened by too suddenly having to deal with a separation, they react with a cry, which is repressed and which comes to expression as an asthma attack. The following case illustrates the results of overattachment of a mother to her child:

§ A forty-year-old woman had her first asthma attack on the cemetery grounds at the burial of her only son. She was a Catholic woman, married to a Protestant husband, and had only the one child; she suffered severely from feelings of guilt, due to the practice of contraception. She regarded the death of her only son as a temporal punishment from God. The walls of her home were covered with pictures of her dead son, reminders that caused her to have almost continual attacks of asthma. When she was in the hospital, or out with friends, or on a vacation, the asthma attacks ceased; but, as soon as she reentered the old environment, the attacks resumed. Her condition grew progressively worse, and she died ten years later of a bronchial condition.

Compared with asthma, few studies of the specific psychic factors involved in hay fever are available. However repressed sexual curiosity has been reported as a cause of hay fever. Strong visual sexual curiosity being repressed, there is thus stimulated an intense olfactory activity, which, in turn, affects the nasal mucosa and determines the site for the symptoms of hay fever.

Chronic urticaria, or hives, seems to be related to the longing for love, especially when such a feeling is being constantly aroused and continually frustrated. The specific emotional factors of these skin disorders have not been clearly established, but exhibitionism, the tendency to self-punishment, and heightened skin eroticism have been noted as auxiliary causes in some cases.

There is little doubt that emotional tension can influence the physiology of the skin and so produce symptoms. This fact is illustrated by the following case:

§ Mrs. P. was referred for psychotherapeutic treatment. She was a tall, good-looking woman who lived with a rather diffident husband and her own mother. Her face, when she was first seen, was covered with a rash similar to acne in appearance. When asked about her complaints, she said that her doctor had mentioned that a psychiatrist might be able to cure her condition, adding, with a laugh, that she was not at all nervous and certainly not insane. She further stated what later proved to be very important—that her condition started on a certain Sunday about six months before; previously, her unblemished countenance had always been considered an asset to her appearance. She remembered the day so well because she was unable to return to work on

Monday on account of her appearance. In the following psychotherapeutic sessions, she became tense, often complained of choking sensations in her throat, and was frequently unable to speak. She finally related what she had previously forgotten: that she had had intimate relations with one of her married coworkers. On the Friday previous to the rash breaking out, this man had told her that their intimacy must cease since he loved his wife and she should love her husband. Feeling unable to return to work, where she would meet the man who had refused her, she promptly developed the skin disorder. After relating this story, she felt relief, and her skin blemishes disappeared in about two weeks.

Nocturnal enuresis has been found to result typically from fear of the parent of the opposite sex, the fear being generated by hostile feelings or by traumatic sexual experiences, whether seductive or rejecting. As a possible cause of urinary urgency and frequency, competitive and ambitious impulses have been reported.

Among the best known psychosomatic diseases are peptic ulcers. Nervous diarrhea and constipation belong in the same category. The fact is—as has been proved by frequent observations—that gastrointestinal disturbances are often the result of emotionally toned impulses and strivings. How this happens is a matter of speculation. The following theory makes an attempt to give an explanation on the basis of association.

From birth on, receiving food has been associated with receiving love, because in the nursing situation feeding is directly connected with maternal love and care. Thus, the process of eating and the subsequent process of digestion has taken on an emotional meaning; *i.e.*, the desire for food has become associated with wishes for care and love and with desires and impulses of various kinds, such as cravings for recognition, sexual desires, and aggressive impulses.

Several writers believe that an explanation of the phenomena of gastrointestinal disorders is found in the light of the above theory. People whose wishes and desires are quite satisfied feel their appetite increased; *e.g.*, they may eat unusual amounts of food after a good bet or a successful speculation in the stock market. It has also been observed that those who, in a more or less aggressive way, are striving to attain some hotly desired objective develop bulimia, or morbidly exaggerated hunger. On the other hand, when, for some reason, cravings for love or recognition are frustrated or certain impulses are inhibited, the result may be dysfunction of the gastrointestinal processes. In some cases, a person not only may lose his appetite or find his digestion disturbed, but he may also find that reversed peristalsis occurs and the food is regurgitated (nervous vomiting). In this connection, the remark has been made that the first "hunger strike" was engineered not by organized labor but by babies.

§ One patient, a very ambitious man, was rather successful, but he did not think that he received enough appreciation for the work that he did. The result was that he wanted several times to quit his job; however, his wife would not let him do so. The striking fact in his case was that he was very careful to live on a milk-and-cracker, salt-free diet for five days a week; but on Saturdays he went out with his wife and ate a hearty steak dinner with French fried potatoes and several highballs, a meal that would have killed him on any other day of the week. This is a typical example of how dissatisfaction or craving for recognition similar to love would permit a man to eat only on such days as he did not have to return to work.

Frustration of the desire for recognition or love seems to be also among the factors that produce peptic ulcers. Ulcers originate when the hydrochloric acid in the gastric juice partially perforates or "eats into" the stomach lining. It is not known why this acid does not affect the wall of the living stomach under ordinary circumstances; none of the many theories advanced to explain this fact is satisfactory. What is known is that an excessive amount of gastric juice may cause stomach ulcers. This is particularly true when the excess of hydrochloric acid is only moderate; when the excess is considerable, it may also cause ulcers, but often it produces only symptoms of gastritis, hyperacidity, etc., without causing anatomical changes in the stomach lining.

Now, in earlier times, stomach ulcers were considered due to purely anatomical and physiological factors. This belief has now greatly changed. Pavlov and many others have established experimentally the fact that stomach ulcers may be caused by psychic influences. A common theory holds that the psychic factors causing stomach ulcers are frustration of the desire for recognition, worries, and nervous tension. As a matter of fact, it has been found that stomach ulcers frequently occur in ambitious, hard-driving people like our modern businessmen, and for that reason Hartman considers peptic ulcers the typical disease of our Western culture.

Stomach ulcers are especially frequent in persons whose cravings for recognition, approval, success, and admiration are continually blocked and in those who are similarly frustrated in their longings for love, care, and dependency. This frustration may be due either to external circumstances or to internal conflicts that arise within the person, *e.g.*, because he denies, out of moral or other considerations, satisfaction to his impulses and cravings.

More recently, clinical observations have shown that there are other emotional conditions that may cause stomach ulcers, and the psychoanalysts mention anxiety and stress. This fact is illustrated by Riley, who reports that "the number of ulcer perforations in London, Bristol and Liverpool during the periods when air raids were frequent increased by as much as one-third to six times the usual number of cases." [4]

Presupposing the association theory that was outlined previously, it is believed that the psychic conditions mentioned stimulate the stomach to secretion of gastric juice and to motility just as the desire for food does. Only, in the former case the stimulation goes on constantly, and it is this constant stimulation of the stomach that may eventually cause an ulcer formation. The general mechanism that causes ulcers seems to be that the psychological conditions produce physiological dysfunction, which leads to structural damage. The process is not known in detail, but Alexander suggests the following causal chain: emotional stimulus → stimulation of subcortical centers → disturbance of the autonomic innervation of the organ → dysfunction of the organ → hypersecretion, hypermobility, alteration of the blood supply → chronicity and structural damage.[5]

§ A thirty-five-year-old teacher asked for an appointment to discuss his gastritis and ulcers of the stomach. He had conferred with many physicians and had been in hospitals of sound reputation several times for periods of observation. Though he had been told that his condition seemed to be of a nervous nature, he looked upon himself as mentally and emotionally well balanced. He seemed to entertain a hardy skepticism about psychiatrists and psychologists in general.

He was tall in stature, and a quiet, friendly, serious person who described in a matter-of-fact way his physical complaints and the way he maintained the diet necessary for his condition. About his early childhood, he related that he came from a family of artists whose financial condition had always been poor. His father was a conservative and rigid disciplinarian, absolutely intolerant of any kind of modern art. The patient recalled being rather crudely mistreated as a child because of bed wetting; he was often treated with suspicion and frequently spanked without any serious reason. He had always been an outstanding student during his school years, and had been at the head of his classes; notwithstanding this fact, however, he was continually threatened with withdrawal from school because the father thought that a boy of sixteen should also contribute financially to the support of the family.

The patient had guilt feelings about early masturbatory habits. While still a high school student, he first noticed that he had stomach disturbances which could not easily be explained. To overcome somewhat these physical disturbances, he thought it would be helpful to marry; his bride was a college girl who proved to be far below his intellectual standing. Both families objected to the marriage, and a certain familial antipathy was carried over into the husband-wife relationship, resulting in almost daily arguments and bickerings in their home.

At the time of consultation, the patient was known as an outstanding research worker with a remarkable memory and was striving ambitiously for recognition in his profession. He was restlessly and anxiously striving toward his ideal of success. He regarded his wife as affectionate and sentimental to a maudlin degree. He felt that she enjoyed him only as a sexual partner, with no proper appreciation of his intellectual ability, and, at the same time, he refused to let her participate in his intellectual life and learnings, since he looked down upon her as his inferior.

The patient had an almost universal hostility toward, and mistrust of, all his superiors. He thought that he was merely being used by them to advance their positions without his receiving any proper credit for his accomplishments. He was apparently a competent teacher and research worker. He had changed his positions frequently. He explained that he was always happy and comfortable at the new place for about a year; after that, as he had not realized fully the success he had anticipated, his ulcers seemed to become very much aggravated and he felt forced to resign and seek a new field for his endeavors. The ulcers invariably disappeared for a time, and then, again, after he had been at a new place for a year, the ulcer distress reappeared.

Here we have a case of one who, from early childhood on, had striven anxiously for the recognition that he had never fully received in the degree he desired. He had suppressed his yearning for love and affection and apparently had sublimated it for a desire of professional recognition. His married life was not a success, though his wife loved him in a simple physical way—a way that was inadequate for him since here, too, he wanted recognition for himself as an intellectual success. Therapy was carried on for only a short time with this patient, and a favorable degree of self-understanding and evaluation of his over-anxious strivings was developed; this insight led to an alleviation of his condition to such a degree that he was able, at least, to make radical changes in his diet.

It has long been known that emotional tension can cause diarrhea and colitis. Recently, it has been concluded that mucous colitis is a physiological disorder of the colon brought about by the action of the parasympathetic nervous system, and that the common source of the parasympathetic overstimulation is emotional tension. Some specific characteristics of the personality, such as sensitivity, overconscientiousness, and dependence on the opinions of others, appear to predispose people to the development of these tensions. An ulcerative colitis is also considered by many to develop in certain cases as a result of emotional tension. Persons with psychogenic diarrhea are those who, when faced with responsibility, usually want to get rid of it; when such a person forces himself to face it, he develops diarrhea. According to one theory, hostile impulses that cannot be expressed by physical attack on environment are expressed by activities of the bowels, instead. Thus urges to give, to produce, or to make restitution are not accepted, and the bowel movement is substituted; eliminating and rejecting reactions are supposed to be substitutes for wishes to be rid of disagreeable situations or impulses. In psychogenic constipation, it is the inhibitory forces developed later, and not the original impulses of earlier life, that are productive of the disorder. It is caused by refusal to give, by inhibitions, and by hostile aggression. It also results from feelings of being rejected and unloved, from distrust and dependence. The defecation becomes so closely associated with inhibited, hostile, soiling impulses that it is also inhibited. The emotional attitude is "acted out" by the bowels as though the excrement were a possession. Whatever the value of such theories may be, the fact is that psychic conditions may cause the above organic disorders.

In conclusion, it may be said that, although it remains obviously true that the diseases mentioned in this review may have a physical cause, it also is true that they may be primarily due to mental factors. In fact, Dr. Daniel Blaine, Medical Director of the American Psychiatric Association, has been quoted as stating that "emotions influence all illnesses, not just the few that have popularly been called psychosomatic illnesses."

The interrelationship between the psychosomatic disorders and the endocrine system is the topic of increasingly important studies. In this respect should be mentioned the research done by Hans Selye, W. Alvarez, T. Reichstein, Edward Kendall, and Louis Starrett. It has long been known that emotions affect endocrine functions, as is seen in the case of thyroid disturbances and diabetes. Conversely, the influence of endocrine functions on emotional life has been demonstrated ever since Marañon. A recent confirmation of these relationships is found in research work on cortisone and adreno-cortico-tropic hormones (ACTH). Cortisone produces a wide variety of psychological responses, ranging from mild excitement to psychoses. It has also been stated that the administration of cortisone has beneficial effects in cases of rheumatic fever and perhaps other rheumatic disorders, as osteoarthritis. These results have raised intriguing questions with regard to the field of psychosomatics. For, if rheumatic fever may be regarded as a psychosomatic disease, it should be expected that cortisone would also contribute to curing other psychosomatic diseases such as skin disorders, bronchial asthma, and hay fever. Furthermore, if cortisone does indeed cure such diseases, this result may give a clue to the problem of the origin and development of psychosomatic diseases. Thus far all that is known is that, as a matter of fact, certain psychological conditions such as worry, strain, and fear do cause somatic disorders; but it is not known why this is so. Why do these conditions cause somatic diseases in one individual and not in another who is plagued by seemingly the same or even greater worries? Could it be that the former individuals suffer from certain endocrinal abnormalities? An abnormal endocrinal function might aggravate the effect of the emotional stimuli to which an individual is subject and at the same time have a detrimental somatic effect. An anomaly in the cortisone production might perhaps give the solution to the problem of the psychosomatic relationship. Only further research will give the answer.

The psychosomatic concept of disease involves, of course, some consequences regarding treatment. If the physician is unable to find an organic basis for the complaint of his patient, he should never make the statement, "There is nothing wrong with you," as there is not only a possibility of some organic difficulty not yet detected but also a strong chance that the patient's troubles may stem from a mental source. "Psychosomatic" patients—if this term may be used—do not just imagine their ailments: they may be seriously, and even fatally, ill. Even though there is no organic indication, it must be remembered that the patient would not complain of symptoms unless he actually felt something was wrong. The ancient Latin axiom, "*Mens sana in corpore sano,*" cannot be repeated too often. It is impossible to draw an arbitrary line between the organic and functional disorders, and there is no room at all for the statement that the patient's complaint is imaginary or is plain, simple malingering. A patient's complaints and feelings are always realities, whether or not organic pathology is able to explain such complaints.

Most important for the psychiatrist is to make the patient talk about his actual life situation and the manner in which he reacts to it. It is not enough to ask, "Are you worried about something?" Nine times out of ten the answer will be "No," in spite of the fact that everyone has problems that may disturb his bodily functions. The patient may feel that his particular problem has no bearing on his symptoms, when it may have everything to do with them although he is unaware of the connection. A significant clue for finding the real source of the disturbance can be found by encouraging a discussion of problems centering around personal relationships and personal experiences.

Making the patient talk is usually best accomplished indirectly, rather than by direct questions. The sooner one can persuade the patient to speak about his "other trouble," the sooner the cause of the "present trouble" comes to the fore. The greater the success in switching the conversation from symptoms to personal affairs, the sooner one hits upon the real trouble disturbing the patient. Therefore, he should be encouraged to talk about himself as a person, rather than as a medical case. In adults, domestic problems and business can play a large part in functional disturbances. In the young, unmarried person, family relationship, choice of a career, religion, and sexual problems are broad topics for discussion.

When the physician finds something in the emotional life of the patient that is apparently causing the illness, it is a great help to the patient to know that the illness is not organic, but due to his emotional life. It is usually easy to make the patient realize that a connection between emotional states and organic conditions frequently exists, by simply referring to certain examples, *e.g.*, by showing that such physiological conditions as goose pimples, blushing, and perspiring are often the result of psychic causes. The patient then may readily understand that, if he cannot find an outlet for tension of emotional origin by word or action, the body will find some means of expressing this tension through a kind of "organ language."

For example, if a patient cannot swallow satisfactorily and no organic cause can be found, it may mean that there is something in his life situation that he "cannot swallow." Frequently a feeling of heaviness in the chest indicates that the patient has a "load on his chest" that he would like to get rid of by talking about his problem.

The knowledge that his organic symptoms derive from a mental cause will save the patient unnecessary trouble and sometimes expensive medical or surgical treatment. Often, just talking out the problem with the physician will alleviate the symptoms. As long as the proper relationship exists between the physician and the patient, there need be no fear on the part of the patient that confidences will be misused or revealed, since the physician observes the inviolability of "privileged communications." In all cases, physicians should learn to pay attention to what their patients worry about, to watch for their signs of anxiety, and be ready to show the patients the kind of treatment and behavior that will help them recover their emotional balance. Once the real cause of the trouble is known, the most important part of the treatment consists in teaching the patient how to react properly to the life situation that has brought about the trouble.

When it is found that emotional factors are associated with actual organic disease, it is unlikely that too much attention can be paid to these factors. It is unfortunate that the feeling persists that physical findings are sufficient to account for the illness. Psychiatrists should not be considered as treating only mental and emotional conditions to the exclusion of organic diseases, but the understanding of an illness and treating sick people consists of something more than the knowledge of organic disease. It necessitates looking upon illness as an aspect of the total person. Such an approach can be applied to a wide variety of ailments. The day is at hand for the final outmoding of the "either-or"—*either* the mind *or* the body—concept in diagnosis; in its stead must be placed the question, "How much of the problem is emotional, and how much is physical?" This is truly the psychosomatic concept of medicine.[6]

Medicine has made rapid progress in dealing with diseases due to microbes and other physical pathogenic agents from the environment. In the last few decades, the sulfa group, penicillin, and other drugs have performed an almost miraculous feat in combating many bacterial diseases. As in every outbreak of war, a great upsurge of disease was expected when the Second World War began; but, with the miraculous louse-killing DDT, typhus and malaria were checked. Sulfadiazine checked meningitis, and malaria was controlled by Atabrine. Looking at infectious and contagious diseases, the medical profession may well be proud of what has been accomplished in the past decade. But the recognition of the psychic nature of many diseases marks no less a progress.

Psychosomatic incidents seem to be more noticeable in highly industrialized nations like the United States than in other countries. Why had China no hypertension until recently? In the remote parts of China and in Tibet, for example, there is a virtual absence of hypertension, appendicitis, peptic ulcers, and colon disturbances. Perhaps the people of those countries know better how to control properly their emotions than Americans do. Whatever the reason, the fact is that one of the greatest health problems in the United States is the rising incidence of chronic diseases; chronic rheumatism, heart diseases, high blood pressure, hay fever, asthma, and many contributory diseases rank highest in producing mortality. A characteristic of these chronic diseases is that they are generally psychic in origin.

In earlier times, it was thought that chronic disease was a peculiarity of old age alone. That this is not so is proved by the U.S. Public Health Service statistics, which show that half of those with chronic diseases are under forty-five years of age, and 16 per cent are below twenty-five. Such chronic diseases create serious social and financial problems. A million people die every year from these disorders that are essentially emotional in origin. This means a mental-hygiene problem, and one of the surest means of solving this problem consists in prevention; *i.e.,* in the early recognition and treatment of emotional difficulties in children. In this respect, besides the physician, the parents can do a very important job by inculcating healthy mental attitudes in their children. The growing importance of guidance institutes and child centers of specially trained psychiatrists promises a solution to the problem. If carried out properly, the mental-hygiene movement, especially among children, may prove to be the greatest step the United States has ever made to improve the health of its people.[7]

It is obvious that the psychosomatic principles of research and treatment are closely related to the philosophical problem concerning the relationship between mind and matter or soul and body. Physicians can perfectly well go on treating their patients according to their psychosomatic principles without concerning themselves with this thorny problem. But since nature often passes nurture, it happens that physicians like to browse round this problem. Hence, a little discussion of the relationship between psychosomatics and the mind-body problem may be in order.

In the authors' opinion, the psychosomatic concept of medicine forms a strong confirmation of the scholastic concept of man. As was explained in Chapter 1, according to Catholic philosophy, man is composed of two realities, body and soul; but these realities are so united as to form one integrated person—so much so that all his reactions, whether they are of a psychic or a physical nature, are reactions of the whole person. This view finds excellent proof in psychosomatic observations and practice. For it is found that whenever the mind is affected, the body, too, suffers; and an affliction of the body has its immediate repercussion on the mind; hence, too, the subject of medical treatment is not only the mind, nor the body alone, but the whole personality.

As is well known, even to those who are only superficially acquainted with the mind-body problem, many other solutions have been presented. But none of them fits the findings of psychosomatic research. These findings certainly cannot be reconciled with psychophysical parallelism, which, taken in the original and strict sense, knows only the coexistence of psychic and physical phenomena in man without admitting any influence of either group of phenomena upon the other.

It would also be very difficult to reconcile the psychosomatic concepts with Descartes' interactionism. Psychosomatics clearly shows that bodily diseases affect the mind of the patients. This is a fact; but interactionism is unable to explain the fact, because it never could solve satisfactorily the question of how the body acts upon the spiritual soul. Omitting the more fantastic solutions, like those of Malebranche and Leibnitz, which nobody takes seriously, the only alternative to the scholastic position is the monistic view, the thesis that body and soul are one and the same thing. This is the position taken by the editorial staff of *Psychosomatic Medicine.*

The editors, in an introductory statement published in the first issue, declare that they "take it for granted that psychic and somatic phenomena . . . are probably two aspects of the same process." [8] This is, of course, Gustav Fechner's standpoint, and since Fechner's solution is based on materialistic monism, it follows that the editors take the materialistic interpretation of the mind-body problem for granted. Why they take for granted precisely this solution among the many other solutions is not explained. Anyway, in reply to this statement, given without any evidence, it suffices to answer, according to the rules of sound logic, that the falsehood of materialism may equally well be taken for granted. Speaking of logic, the editors do not seem to have any too clear an idea about it. Precisely seven lines before they state that psychic and somatic phenomena are probably two aspects of the same process, they announce "the thesis that there is no logical distinction between 'mind and body,' 'mental and physical.'" Do the editors really mean to use the term "logical"? Obviously, there is a logical distinction between two aspects of a thing. At the most, one may doubt whether there is a *real* distinction between mental and physical. It all goes to show that the editors are somewhat confused about matters philosophical, and it also emphasizes again the age-old truth of the proverb that the cobbler should stick to his last. Neither the physician nor the psychiatrist need dig into philosophical issues, for he can very well engage in research and cure his patients along the lines of psychosomatic medicine without deciding the nature of the psyche and the soma. However, if he ventures into philosophical ground, he should show at least a rudimentary knowledge of logic and realize that, in debated philosophical problems, nothing is taken for granted.

NOTES AND REFERENCES

1. Quotation by KATZENELBOGEN, SOLOMON, Psychosomatic Medicine, *Diseases of the Nervous System,* Vol. 4 (1943), No. 11.
2. BEAUMONT, WILLIAM, "Experiments and Observations on the Gastric Juice and the Physiology of Digestion" (Plattsburg, N.Y., 1833), p. 18.
3. Some further interesting case histories may be found in MOORE, THOMAS V., "The Nature and Treatment of Mental Disorders" (New York: Grune and Stratton, 1944), pp. 72–76; *id.*, "The Driving Forces of Human Nature" (New York: Grune and Stratton, 1950), pp. 178–230.
4. RILEY, IAN D., Perforated Peptic Ulcers in War Time, *Lancet,* Oct., 1942, p. 485.
5. ALEXANDER, F., C. BACON, H. B. LEVY, and G. W. WILSON, The Influence of Psychological Factors upon Gastro-intestinal Disorder: a Symposium, *Psychoanalytic Quarterly,* Vol. 3 (1934), pp. 501–588.
6. The following list of some of the major works on psychosomatic medicine may be of help for further consultation:

   ALEXANDER, FRANZ, "Psychosomatic Medicine" (New York: W. W. Norton & Company, 1950).

   ALEXANDER, FRANZ, and THOMAS MORTON FRENCH, "Studies in Psychosomatic Medicine" (New York: The Ronald Press Company, 1948).

   BINGER, CARL, "The Doctor's Job" (New York: W. W. Norton & Company, 1945).

   DUNBAR, FLANDERS, "Synopsis of Psychosomatic Diagnosis and Treatment" (St. Louis: The C. V. Mosby Company, Medical Publishers, 1948).

   HINSIE, LELAND E., "The Person in the Body" (New York: W. W. Norton & Company, 1945).

SLAUGHTER, FRANK G., "Medicine for Moderns" (New York: Julian Messner, Inc., Publishers, 1948).

WACHTEL, CURT S., "The Idea of Psychosomatic Medicine" (New York: Froben Press, Inc., 1951).

WEISS, EDWARD, and SPURGEON ENGLISH, "Psychosomatic Medicine" (Philadelphia: W. B. Saunders Company, 1948).

7. ODENWALD, ROBERT P., The Spiritual Development of the Child, with Emphasis on Problems of Maladjustment in Children and the Emotion of Fear, *The Journal of Child Psychiatry,* Vol. 2, Section 2 (1951), p. 161.
8. Introductory Statement, *Psychosomatic Medicine,* Vol. 1 (1939), p. 1; see also ALEXANDER, FRANZ, Fundamental Concepts of Psychosomatic Research, *Yearbook of Psychoanalysis,* Vol. 1 (1945), pp. 257–266.

Chapter 5

THERAPEUTIC METHODS OF PSYCHIATRY

The ultimate aim of all psychiatric procedures is to cure mental disorders or to improve the condition of those who suffer from them. In view of this final aim, therefore, all psychiatric methods are a form of psychotherapy, a term which means treatment of the mind. However, the different ways of arriving at this end may be divided into two large groups. The first group of techniques includes those procedures which are applied directly to the patient's body in an attempt to improve his mental condition. They comprise the various forms of organic or somatic treatment of mental disorder. The other group includes those methods that the therapist uses in an attempt to affect the mind, *i.e.*, the psyche, of the patient directly; these procedures are psychotherapy, in the strict sense of the word. For the purpose of this book, it suffices to give a summary of the procedures of somatotherapy, whereas psychotherapy will be dealt with in some detail.[1]

ORGANIC TREATMENT—SOMATOTHERAPY

The types of organic treatment fall into two classes: surgical and nonsurgical.[2]

Surgical procedures involve operations on the brain and are obviously indicated in the case of brain tumors or injuries. Two other frequently used procedures are lobectomy (the removal of brain substance) and lobotomy (the incision of brain substance). In lobectomy the skull is lifted and the frontal part of the frontal lobe excised. In lobotomy, performed under local anesthesia, the brain matter of the frontal lobe is penetrated (through a hole drilled in the skull) by a leukotome passed through a cannula, and the frontothalamic fibers are severed.

Transorbital lobotomy, as performed by Fiamberti and revised by Walter J. Freeman, is a simple and safe form of lobotomy. After the patient receives electroshock treatment, the upper eyelid is lifted, a special instrument is inserted in the nasal part of the orbit of the eyes, and the thin orbital bone is cut through by a knife. Inserting the leukotome to a depth of about five centimeters, the surgeon severs the frontothalamic fibers as in the usual lobotomy.

The indications for this process should be carefully evaluated in each case; it is not so much a question as to what diagnosis is made, *i.e.*, from what type of disorder the patient is suffering; rather, the question to be settled is whether lobotomy might improve the patient's condition in such a way that he does not have to be institutionalized. Remarkable success has been reported in the use of this measure; many extremely excited individuals, like those suffering in the greatest degree from fear and anxiety, have been enabled to relax and to perform routine duties. However, it is still a matter of debate as to precisely what produces the beneficial effects of this surgical procedure.

Since not all of the effects of prefrontal lobotomy are equally desirable, the question has arisen whether such an operation is justified from the moral standpoint. On the debit side of the operation, it must be admitted that it is a grave mutilation of the patient—a mutilation that is irreparable and that results in undesirable secondary effects, such as disturbances of the association of mental images, defective synthesis of thought, and a change of personality. After lobotomy there may appear alterations that make the patient intellectually dull and listless. He lacks energy, and his lackadaisical behavior makes him act somewhat like an automaton. His emotional life seems to be impaired, and inhibitions seem to be removed. Sometimes he shows incontinence, regression in the sexual life, lack of appreciation of the gravity of personal situations, and, often, little remorse.

On the credit side, it has been found that very often lobotomy relieves the patient of his disabling symptoms and returns him to a more normal state than he enjoyed before. If he was institutionalized, he may be able to return home, lead a tolerable life with his family, and even make himself useful. Such a patient seems to be relieved of his feeling of fear, anxiety, guilt, and nervous tension; he seems to be a happy individual and may even remind one of a slightly inebriated person. As for the so-called change in personality, which would seem to be the most important objection to lobotomy, it must be remembered that there are two kinds of personality: the empirical and the metaphysical personality. "Empirical personality" means the more or less organized total of traits or characteristics as they appear in a man's behavior. If the operation results in a change of personality, it affects the empirical personality. But it does not affect the person in the metaphysical sense of the word, *i.e.*, the bearer and substrate of those traits and characteristics. After the operation the patient remains the same person that he was before the operation. The phenomena mentioned on the debit side have been regarded by some as indications that lobotomy interferes with the freedom of the will. But the patient's freedom of will in his psychotic state before the operation is usually handicapped to a greater extent. Besides, it should not be overlooked that many of the evil effects that appear immediately after lobotomy are considerably diminished following a period of convalescence on account of the mysterious *vis medicatrix et regulatrix naturae*.

Catholic moralists hold that lobotomy is permissible if the required conditions are fulfilled. The main conditions are that a serious and chronic disturbance be proved, that no other less drastic therapeutic methods be available, and that the probability of harm is outweighed by the probability of benefit. The above discussion makes it clear that, when the first two conditions are fulfilled, the third will often be accounted for, too, but the fulfillment of the first two often leaves much to be desired. For instance, those under eighteen years of age, who present behavior or delinquency problems should not be subjected to such surgical treatment, since these problems in young patients can be successfully treated by other methods. The growing popularity of the operation and the sensational publicity given to it in popular magazines has already stimulated the making of irresponsible and extravagant demands. It has been noted that some patients, especially those with masochistic tendencies, have asked for lobotomy, and that not infrequently the basic motive for such requests seems to have been the patient's desire to be relieved of the responsibility of cooperating with therapy.[3]

Nonsurgical organic treatment comprises two groups of techniques: those which effect a shock in the organism, and those which do not. The purpose of shock or convulsive therapy is to cause a shock to the nervous system or to the brain. The most widely used methods of convulsive treatment, at the present time, are chemotherapy and electric-shock treatment.

The forerunner of today's convulsive therapeutic methods is to be found in hydrotherapy. "Water treatment" consists in continuous warm or cold baths, or wet packs, in order to diminish motor restlessness and produce rest and sleep. A prolonged warm bath—lasting perhaps two hours—results in hyperemia of the skin; the blood volume of the central nervous system is decreased, the respiration becomes deep and slower, and the muscle tone and reflexes are diminished. This method is very helpful to relaxation, especially with elderly patients, and it may relieve the physical tension of the patient suffering from insomnia, headaches, psychosomatic rheumatic pain, and similar troubles. On the other hand cold baths and cold wet packs cause a shock reaction and may, therefore, be compared with electric or other shock treatments. As a consequence, public opinion, regarding such therapy as inhuman, rejected it. Among some psychiatrists, too, hydrotherapy is considered questionable in result. A definite contraindication to its use is extreme anxiety, inasmuch as an anxious patient may consider such treatment to be not a therapeutic method, but a punitive and constrictive measure or a method of getting drowned.

Modern convulsive treatment aims at provoking convulsions of the organism by pharmacological means or through electroshock. The use of chemical substances, such as insulin and Cardiazol, forms the *chemical or pharmacological type* of shock treatment. Insulin, used on the comatose level, has a favorable result on such mental disorders as schizophrenia, catatonia, and intensive anxiety conditions in some psychoneuroses. This convulsive therapy is initiated with a dosage of 12 units of insulin, given usually intravenously. The amounts given are increased by 5 units daily until the comatose state is achieved. In producing seizures by means of insulin, the blood-sugar level falls; Georgi mentioned that it is restored from blood in the brain cells. The use of insulin has one special advantage: with the feeding of ordinary sugar or with injections of glucose, the effects of the treatment can be offset at once. The Cardiazol method, in which the blood sugar rises, is no longer used to induce seizures.

The other form of convulsive therapy, *electric-shock treatment* is valuable in cases of depression, especially those of involutional melancholia, and for slight prepsychotic conditions. The results seem, sometimes, miraculous. However, some claim that shock treatment, especially that of electric shock, is not of permanent value and produces symptomatic effects only. Besides, psychotherapy must usually be used to supplement the effects of the artificially stimulated convulsions produced by shock.

Since insulin treatment requires trained personnel and a certain length of time for its administration, electroshock treatment is the more practical treatment in some diseases. Since it involves fewer risks and complications, it does not necessitate institutional care and may be used, therefore, as an office procedure.

With regard to the organic nonsurgical forms of treatment that do not effect a shock, the *pharmacotherapeutic* methods should be mentioned. This treatment consists in the administration of drugs, such as sedatives. It should be noted that any pharmacological method, aside from its efficacy, has also a psychodynamic effect, which depends upon both the way in which it is applied and the relationship existing between the patient and the physician or nurse.

Herbs and drugs have always been used to quiet excitable and nervous patients. The two most outstanding drugs are barbiturates and bromides, which act as depressants of the central nervous system. In small doses, as they are commonly administered, they may be regarded as sedatives and hypnotics, having a negligible action on bodily functions.

Barbiturates in large doses were used for prolonged sleep treatment in the 1920's and 1930's. They are still used as anticonvulsants in the control of epileptic fits or eclampsia. Phenobarbital and other derivatives of barbituric acid, such as Luminal, Veronal, and Medinal, have been the most commonly used sedatives. In moderate to large doses, they are to some degree dangerous, since they have a cumulative effect. Suicide attempts with these drugs were, and still are, common, but some effort to decrease materially the number of such attempts has been made through recent legislation that outlaws the purchase of these compounds without a medical prescription.

In the modern advance of pharmacology, there has been developed a new group of fast-acting barbiturates that have proved very useful in the treatment of mentally ill people. These barbiturates—Nembutal, Seconal, Pentothal Sodium, and especially Sodium Amytal—are used orally, intramuscularly, and intravenously in a specific technique called narcoanalysis or narcotherapy.[4]

Barbiturate narcosis, effected for instance through the intravenous injection of Sodium Amytal, is being employed as a means of producing sleep and rest in maniacal states. But its chief effect is of a psychodynamic nature, inasmuch as it is a means of establishing contact with hitherto more or less inaccessible patients. After administration of the drug, the patient's ease of expression is facilitated; otherwise solemn, inhibited, depressed, or suspicious persons converse spontaneously and easily reveal their problems, anxieties, and painful memories. In that manner the therapist obtains the information he needs and is also able to impart the advice the patient needs.

Closely related to hypnosis, narcotherapy has the advantage that it can be used also with patients who cannot be hypnotized. The technique is relatively easy. As in all mental diseases, a thorough physical examination is necessary. The patient is informed about this kind of treatment and is required to give—if at all possible—his consent.[5] The injection is given very slowly, 1 cubic centimeter per minute. During this injection, the patient counts or the therapist talks with him until the patient's counting or answering is confused. The dosage needed varies from 7½ to 15 cubic centimeters. Afterward, the discovered material is discussed with the patient.

During the Second World War narcotherapy was used somewhat extensively, and with great success—in breakdowns, in depressions, and in related conditions. At the present time, methylamphetamine hydrochloride or Benzedrine in tablet form is used for those conditions.

Recently a new kind of treatment for psychoneurotic patients has been publicized. It is called carbon dioxide therapy. Ladislas Joseph von Meduna of the University of Illinois uses a mixture of 70 per cent oxygen and 30 per cent carbon dioxide administered through an ordinary anesthetic mask to render the person unconscious. His theory is that the reaction of carbon dioxide upon the brain cells causes a more normal threshold of sensitivity. He believes that this method is effective for anxiety, inferiority complexes, and homosexuality and claims 68 per cent success in its use. However, it is not generally accepted, and further research and observation are necessary to prove his claims.

PSYCHOTHERAPY

The authors wish to make clear that in their discussion of psychotherapy they are speaking only of cases that can be treated outside a mental institution, and their remarks are aimed at giving the nonprofessional reader a general understanding of psychotherapy.

In every case of a mental disorder, one is confronted with the important question of whether such a person should be treated at home or in an institutional setup. The patient who presents a threat of danger to himself or to his environment must be institutionalized. Such cases will not be discussed in any detail here except to say that the decision to institutionalize a patient is not always an easy decision to make, especially when the psychiatrist is confronted with the father, mother, wife, or relatives of the patient. It is almost impossible for one having emotional ties with the patient to have any insight into the mental disturbance of the patient.

Psychotherapy is the treatment of mental disorders by making an appeal to the psyche of the patient. It consists of a psychological approach to the complaints of the patient regarding his mental or physical disorder. Of necessity, a full understanding of the patient's complaints requires not only a description of his illness, but also an insight into his interpersonal relationships with his wife, his siblings, other relatives, and the persons with whom he associates. His life history, his economic status, his religion and faith, and his relation to society and to the state—all play an important part in his present condition.

In a sense one may speak of psychotherapy whenever one human being tries to help another by some psychological approach. In almost any relationship where one person through sympathy, understanding, and patience is trying to help another, one may say that there is a kind of "psychotherapy" taking place in a very broad sense of the word. The father with his child, the priest with his penitent, the nurse with her patient—all are trying to help others, to make them happier, to increase the well-being of their lives. Obviously, the professional psychotherapy of the psychiatrist is very different because he uses many devices unknown to the layman, but in so far as psychotherapy is an art of dealing with human beings, it is based on the same basic concepts of sympathy and understanding.

However, this patient-physician relationship is not like that of friends and partners, but rather like that of two persons of whom one, in despair, has come to get help, and the other is willing to give help. This relationship is similar to the father-child relationship, the father (or physician) being the stronger, and the child (or patient) being the weak one. In this relationship, the patient may honor his "father," or, more often, show repressed feelings of hostility toward him. Yet, the child trusts the superior intellect of the father, and the patient trusts that the physician can help. The establishment of mutual trust enables the physician to influence the mental and emotional functions of the patient. The therapist must show sincere sympathy; the patient must be made aware that the therapist feels for him, because this sympathy is one of the first conditions to a feeling of security. Of course, this sympathetic attitude should be coupled with a certain reserve which observes the necessary distance, a condition that is met in an almost perfect way in the confessional. Moreover, the therapist must be able to employ empathy, the art of projecting himself into the life history and the personality structure of his patient. This brief description of the basic prerequisites for successful psychotherapy makes it clear that psychotherapy not only requires skill which can be learned, but also involves an element of art that scarcely can be taught. Not everyone is capable of exercising the required sympathy and empathy, even though he may be trained in psychology and psychiatry. A psychiatrist may have all the diplomas in the world and still may not be able to help people. One therapist will achieve better and more lasting results than another in the counseling and advising situation, in the application of suggestion, or in analyzing a patient, because one is better equipped than another to establish a satisfactory interpersonal relationship. A failure to achieve results may be due either to the therapist or to the patient.

The personality structure of the therapist is sometimes a barrier to the efficacy of certain psychotherapeutic methods. It is not enough that the therapist have the desire to exhibit his sympathy; at times, he just lacks the capacity, or rather the flair, to reach his patient mentally. It happens, too, that the therapist may be perfectly capable of sympathy, but not in that particular case. Differences of sex, nationality, and race, and at times the difference in age, may make a mutually sympathetic understanding and cooperation difficult to achieve. Furthermore, in cases where it is hard for the therapist to project himself into the personality structure or the cultural background of his patient, empathy with the patient's philosophy or ideology is sometimes still harder. This is, for instance, the reason why certain non-Catholic therapists fail with Catholic patients.

On the other hand, the personality structure of the patient may also form a barrier to efficient cooperation. If sympathy is the basis of psychotherapy, the patient must react with sympathy. But here, too, are limitations. The enlisted man may sometimes feel it hard to meet the physician-officer with sympathy; many a Catholic may find it easier to open up to the priest than to the psychiatrist; and certain individuals, such as those with narcissistic personalities, are hardly able to reveal themselves or to show any real sympathy at all. These are the limitations inherent to the psychotherapeutic situation, regardless of whether the therapist is a psychiatrist, a pastoral counselor, or any other type of therapist.[6]

Since psychotherapy is based on rapport, the sympathetic bond between the therapist and the client, it often is of no avail in the treatment of psychotics, because many of these patients are so far out of contact with reality that rapport cannot be established.

Psychotherapy aims, in the first place, at an empathic understanding of the patient's personality. Therefore, it is necessary for the therapist to have extensive knowledge of the dynamics of personality in general and of his client's personality specifically. Since all personalities are different and even unique, there is no detailed program of rigid techniques of psychotherapy that can be executed in uniform style on each patient, such as there is, for example, in surgical operations or in the treatment of pneumonia. However, the initial stages of psychotherapeutic interviews conducted with adults usually follow the same pattern. The therapist patiently listens to the complaints of this patient, who speaks of his feelings—his fear, his anxiety, hostility, jealousy, and suspicions. From the first moment when the patient enters the office, transference begins. If the physician is a good listener, the patient is able to reveal more and more material of mental and emotional significance. In the therapeutic sessions, the patient relives his past experiences and conflicts, which may go as far back as his early childhood, focusing upon the psychiatrist as the object of those conflicts; the patient then usually feels better, since he is able to talk about himself and his problem. In every session, more and more mental and emotional material slowly appears, and it is the physician's task—as with a jigsaw puzzle—to fit the many pieces into a whole, and thus to come to an understanding of the personality of the patient. The further progress of the interviews and the kind of treatment to be used are determined by the goal that the therapist wants to attain and by the theoretical concepts of psychopathology to which he adheres.

The goal of psychotherapy is, of course, to cure the patient's troubles. There are two ways of doing this. One way is evidently to remove the cause of the difficulty and reintegrate the patient's personality structure; hence this approach is called causal or integral therapy. Inasmuch as it aims at giving the patient an insight into the cause, it goes also by the name of insight therapy. The main form of causal therapy is analytical or depth therapy, with its various schools and techniques.

The other approach does not go all the way down to the bottom of the trouble but is satisfied with relieving the patient of his symptoms. For that reason it is called symptomatic; other terms that seem to cover wholly or partially the same type of treatment are nontechnical or palliative therapy. None of these terms is fully satisfactory, but for lack of a better term the name "symptomatic" will be used.

An example taken from the field of physical ailment may illustrate the distinction. When a person has received a wound in his hand and it has become infected or badly swollen, the physician may advise him to apply hot or cold compresses or some salve to relieve the pain and to take aspirin for keeping down the temperature. He may also build up the body resistance by prescribing bed rest or vitamins and the like. In treating the patient this way, the physician hopes that for the rest nature will take care of itself, and in many cases nature does. This might be called symptomatic treatment. But it also happens that the body defenses, even though reinforced, are apparently not strong enough to overcome the infection or the swelling. In that case the doctor may resort to surgery in the hope of removing the source of the infection, or he may find that the delay in the healing process is due to the patient's general organic condition. He may discover that the body resistance is lowered because of a heart disease or arteriosclerosis. In such a case the physician will try to treat the deeper lying cause, and hence the therapy would be causal.

The same two approaches are found in psychotherapy. When the patient arrives at the psychiatrist's office, the first thing he does is to complain about certain disagreeable experiences. He may feel depressed, or he may find it difficult to resist the foolish urge to wash his hands continuously, or he may be afraid of himself because he feels like throwing himself in front of a passing automobile. These complaints concern his symptoms, and the latter evidently have a cause. The patient usually cares little about that cause as long as the physician can rid him of the unpleasant effects. But the therapist's attitude is different.

The therapist may take either one of two roads to free the patient of his troubles. One avenue open to him is the attempt to discover the cause of his troubles. When probing into the matter, he often will find an entire chain of causes. Could it be, the psychiatrist may ask, that the suicidal tendencies of his patient derive from an urge to self-punishment? But then, what is the cause of that urge? Perhaps a feeling of guilt. Suppose the patient is himself a physician who confesses to be tortured by self-reproach because some years ago he was called to one of his own patients but refused to go and found out the following morning that the patient had died. But, the psychiatrist will argue, such feelings of remorse scarcely would create suicidal thoughts in a normal person. Hence is there not a deeper lying cause of which the patient is not now aware and which is connected with some happenings in the patient's lifetime? When the therapist pursues this investigation down to the final cause, we have causal therapy in the strict sense. While disclosing the cause of the trouble, this treatment strives to give the patient insight into the significance of his disturbance, not only intellectually but—a more important matter—emotionally as well. And while giving the patient an understanding of the psychodynamics that account for the particular development of his personality in view of his life history and environment, causal therapy trusts that it removes the influence of the cause itself. In brief, causal therapy claims to remove the liabilities that prevent the patient's normal adjustment toward reality. To achieve these effects, this kind of treatment requires usually a great deal of time—the so-called long-term therapy.

Symptomatic therapy starts from the obvious assumption that every person, unless totally diseased, has at his disposal a certain amount of psychic resistance, analogous to the body resistance that we mentioned in our illustration of the infected wound. This psychic resistance is rooted in the individual's immanent striving toward self-development. Now the patient's trouble—whatever its cause may be—has disturbed this immanent regulatory power; in other words the balance is broken between his resistance and what he has to bear. Hence the therapist endeavors to build up the patient's psychic defenses, to give the constructive, positive assets that are present in the patient a chance to exert themselves. For instance, the therapist may agree that the patient has suffered many frustrations, but tell him not to forget the many positive values such as his family, his profession, and his religion which make his life worth living. A person who suffers from a feeling of inferiority because of his small stature may be told to accept the fact squarely, but to compensate for it by developing the valuable capacities he possesses. True, this kind of therapy fails to give the patient an insight into the real cause of his symptoms, but by tipping the balance in favor of the power of natural resistance, it may well relieve him of his symptoms and adjust him more satisfactorily to the realities of life and environment. Whereas, as we said, causal therapy strives to remove liabilities, symptomatic therapy aims at restoring and building up the constructive assets of the patient.

This exposition makes it clear that the two procedures often complete one another. As a matter of fact, it will be seen later in detail that a causal method that would aim at nothing but imparting insight to a patient, without developing his constructive potentialities, would be rather sterile. On the other hand, the symptomatic procedures involve at times a causal element. Since often a chain of causes is present, symptomatic therapy may concentrate upon one or another cause, without going into an analysis of the deeper lying causes. In the example of the physician with the suicidal tendencies, the conscious neglect of his medical duties that he presents as the reason for his suicidal thoughts is probably not the real cause. But the therapist may center his attention on that point and, using the technique of assurance, create in the patient a condition of psychic tranquillity favorable to restoring his mental equilibrium.

Nevertheless, the symptomatic methods are sometimes bitterly criticized. The critics are the "perfectionists" who consider a patient cured only when he arrives at a perfect insight as to the cause of his unhealthy condition and in that manner is brought to a complete change in his attitude toward life. The assumption is that the real cause of mental disorders must always be of an unconscious nature. Hence the main critics are found in the ranks of the analysts or depth psychologists. They reject symptomatic therapy as patchwork and are not content until they have dug deep into the patient's psyche and have discovered sadistic tendencies, narcissism, an Oedipus complex, a seductive mother, and the rest of libido's retinue.

Many a psychiatrist will counter with the obvious remark that no long-term depth therapy is known which discloses the cause of mental disturbances in all instances. Despite all theories, we often fail to know the etiology and pathogenesis of mental diseases. Some analysts may claim that the cause of a neurosis can always be found. Be that as it may, it is surely questionable whether depth therapy is equally successful in the treatment of psychoses.

This general remark only shows that causal therapy has its limitations. The authors do not maintain—far from it—that where depth therapy fails, symptomatic therapy could be successful, but there are reasons to believe that the "ideal" treatment, taken in the sense of the analysts, is in numerous instances quite unnecessary.

It may be found that the probing into the depths of a client's psyche with its prolonged sessions is in certain cases hardly worth while because simpler and less time-consuming methods may help the patient to readjust himself sufficiently by relieving him from his symptoms. Hence, if simpler methods for whatever reason bring relief, it is only reasonable to apply them. After all, the patients do not care about the theoretical fights or the professional jealousy among psychiatrists: what they are looking for is some relief and the possible removal of their troubles.

§ Tommy, ten years of age, was brought to the clinic by his mother, a somewhat tense and restless woman, who was visibly disturbed by her son's conduct. The boy was the youngest of four children. His sister, the eldest, and two brothers had always excelled in their studies.

According to his mother, Tommy constantly sought attention. Every night his sister helped him with his lessons, but her efforts were fruitless. Tommy was failing in all his fifth-grade subjects. His mother complained that he was lazy in school, disturbed other pupils, would not concentrate, disobeyed his teachers and parents, and had become a show-off. He teased the younger children, whose companionship he sought in preference to that of children his own age. During the day, he indulged in sweets, and at dinner, he would not eat what was set before him. At night, he often screamed in his sleep, was enuretic, and wanted to crawl into bed with his mother and father. The mother had tried all kinds of punishment: whipping, scolding, depriving of pleasures. Nothing helped.

A battery of achievement tests revealed part of the reason for Tommy's behavior characteristics. He was found to be working on a third-grade level in reading, spelling, and arithmetic. This was two years below his present grade placement—sufficient reason for his current failure! His I.Q., as derived from the Revised Stanford-Binet, was 80. Tommy's mental ability was more like that of an eight-year-old boy in the third grade than like that of a boy of ten years in the fifth grade. Achievement tests established the fact that Tommy was performing up to his apparent native capacity. Pressure of his sister's coaching and his mother's critical urging served only to initiate an emotional reaction which resulted in behavior disorders.

The basic desires, rooted in the nature of every man, were frustrated in Tommy. His desire for success could not be satisfied because, no matter how hard he tried, he could not produce the results that others demanded from a boy of his chronological age. His desire for response, to love and to be loved, was thwarted by the critical attitude of his teachers, parents, and siblings. His desire for recognition as an individual remained unfulfilled, because he was unfavorably compared with other pupils and with his more fortunate brothers and sister. The result was that Tommy's security was shaken. As a consequence, fears, enuresis, night terrors, hostility, rebellion, and all the other negative symptoms of his behavior pattern arose. If he could not have success, there was little motivation for interest and effort in school even if his mother did call him lazy. If he felt unloved, he would seek attention by showing off or crawling into bed with his parents. If he was not recognized as an individual, he would win singularity by teasing the little children of the neighborhood.

A series of play-therapy sessions to release Tommy's pent-up emotions, an intelligent program of action for his parents, and an adjustment program in school soon brought about favorable changes in Tommy's behavior. Here we seem to have a case of causal treatment, but it would be questionable whether any type of depth psychology could have added anything to Tommy's readjustment; in fact, some people wonder whether such a treatment would not have done more harm than good.

There are also instances in which the so-called "ideal" treatment is impossible for a simple, down-to-earth, practical reason which, however, is very conclusive and frequent. The great majority of the mentally ill never approach a depth therapist because they cannot afford to go through the process of long-term therapy for lack of time or for financial reasons. But many of them may profit by a less time-consuming treatment. Of course, the difficulty will be in any case to find a psychiatrist willing to help them, for the equally practical reason is that the docket of most therapists is filled to capacity.

Special Therapy. After having discussed the general classes of psychotherapy, this section concludes with a brief exposition of methods used for special groups of people.

In child psychiatry, most of the therapeutic methods available for adults are impracticable or inefficient. Among those techniques to which younger children who manifest emotional disturbances or behavior problems respond favorably, individual *play therapy* occupies an important place.[7] In a room equipped with various kinds of toys (a family of dolls, a furnished doll house and school building, modeling clay, finger paints, sand box, ships, guns, telephone, etc.) a child may play with any kind of toy he wishes. Psychotherapy with children stresses the present without overlooking the past and assumes that the main factor of disturbance is present in every undertaking of the child. While playing, the child may release his tension by being offensive, hostile, resistant, or submissive in the presence of a permissive adult therapist.

For instance, it may be found that in the play situation the child constantly throws the mother-doll in a corner and apparently refuses to play with it. When he is asked whether he likes his mother, the answer will almost invariably be, "Sure," but for the therapist the child's behavior is significant, and he will frequently find that in such a case unconscious or unformulated hostility toward the mother is at the bottom of the child's troubles. Play therapy, therefore, is a form of causal treatment.

The child's expression in play is one part of the therapeutic procedure. The other part is the child's relationship with the therapist, and this is of maximal importance. This relationship is something new to the young patient, inasmuch as he meets for the first time with an adult who will accept him as he is and is not patently trying to change him. Certainly the therapist sets certain limits, he lets it be known that he refuses to be domineered, but on the other hand he will not domineer either and does not become emotionally involved in any doings with his patient. This attitude of the therapist makes the child gradually realize that he is a person with a certain amount of independence and it makes him feel that he is responsible for his actions. In that manner the child can grow, but although the therapist will help and guide him, he must do his own growing.

Most psychiatric treatment of children is carried on in the setting of a child-guidance institute, where psychiatrists work together with child psychologists and social case workers. Because of the availability of facilities and because of the research that is continually being fostered, such a clinic is most effective if it is affiliated with a university.

Other techniques of therapy employed by the psychologist depend upon the child's individual needs. Sometimes retarded skills in the classroom may result in emotional disturbances. In these instances, the retardation must be corrected; *e.g.*, when a child is way behind his age in reading, remedial reading has a therapeutic value. In other instances the environment must be manipulated by removing pressures in school or at home; *e.g.*, by changing the parents' attitude toward the child.

Group therapy appeals to the positive social forces of emotionally disturbed patients. While such patients easily withdraw from social relations because of their maladjustment, it has been found that they function relatively well, when placed in a properly selected and carefully guided group. Success of the therapy, therefore, depends largely on the selection of the members of the group. For instance, it would be useless to bring together a number of withdrawn schizophrenics. Only such patients should participate in the group who prove their ability to deal with one another, and in that case the intragroup relations have a beneficial effect on the individual. For an effective functioning of a psychotherapeutic group the number of members should not be less than four or five, and should not exceed six or eight patients. Group therapy is the only available method for certain types of patients, but, whenever possible, group therapy should be combined with individual psychotherapy.[8]

Psychodramatic therapy is supposed to be a means for cathartic release through the patients' acting out emotions and thus developing spontaneity.[9] In *bibliotherapy* the patient reads a book recommended to him, and then discusses it with the therapist. *Occupational therapy* and the recommendation of specific hobbies pertain to the same category, and are often used as a means for sublimation.

At this juncture a brief recapitulation may help to clarify the sequence of the three following chapters, which will deal with the psychotherapeutic techniques specifically. The present chapter outlined the two main divisions of somatotherapy and psychotherapy. The latter were further distinguished into two groups, the causal and the symptomatic procedures. The reader will have understood that this distinction may serve as a working basis but possesses only a relative value, because the two procedures sometimes overlap; it is, therefore, difficult to squeeze all therapeutic techniques into either of these pigeonholes. This is notably the case with the counseling technique, for counseling as it has developed may presumably partake of some of the aspects of either symptomatic or causal therapy. For that reason the chapter on counseling will be inserted between the chapter that surveys the commonly accepted forms of symptomatic treatment and the one that deals with the main types of causal therapy.

NOTES AND REFERENCES

1. For the convenience of the reader, a selected list of works on psychiatry and psychotherapy is presented here:

ALEXANDER, FRANZ, "Fundamentals in Psychoanalysis" (New York: W. W. Norton & Company, 1948).

BENTLY, M., and E. V. COWDRY, "The Problem of Mental Disorders" (New York: McGraw-Hill Book Company, Inc., 1934).

BILLINGS, EDWARD G., "A Handbook of Elementary Psychobiology and Psychiatry" (New York: The Macmillan Company, 1948).

BLEULER, E., "Textbook of Psychiatry" (New York: The Macmillan Company, 1934).

DALBIEZ, ROLAND, "Psychoanalytical Method and the Doctrine of Freud" (New York: Longmans, Green & Co., Inc., 1941).

DOLLARD, JOHN, and N. E. MILLER, "Personality and Psychotherapy: An Analysis in Forms of Learning, Thinking, and Culture" (New York: McGraw-Hill Book Company, Inc., 1950).

DUNBAR, FLANDERS, "Synopsis of Psychosomatics, Diagnosis and Treatment" (St. Louis: The C. V. Mosby Company, Medical Publishers, 1948).

HENDERSON, D. K., and R. D. GILLESPIE, "A Textbook of Psychiatry" (New York: Oxford University Press, 1948).

HUNT, J. McV., "Personality and Behavior Disorders" (New York: The Ronald Press Company, 1944).

HINSIE, L. E., "Concepts and Problems of Psychotherapy" (New York: Columbia University Press, 1934); *id.*, "Visual Outline of Psychiatry" (New York: Oxford University Press, 1941); *id.*, "Understandable Psychiatry" (New York: The Macmillan Company, 1948).

LEVINE, M., "Psychotherapy in Medical Practice" (New York: The Macmillan Company, 1942).

MASSERMANN, JULES H., "Principles of Dynamic Psychiatry" (Philadelphia: W. B. Saunders Company, 1946).

MENNINGER, KARL A. "The Human Mind" (New York: Alfred A. Knopf, Inc., 1941).

MOORE, THOMAS V., "The Nature and Treatment of Mental Disorders" (New York: Grune and Stratton, 1944); *id.*, "Personal Mental Hygiene" (New York: Grune and Stratton, 1944).

MUNSIE, W., "Psychobiology and Psychiatry" (St. Louis: The C. V. Mosby Company, Medical Publishers, 1939).

NOYES, ARTHUR P., "Modern Clinical Psychiatry" (Philadelphia: W. B. Saunders Company, 1947).

ODENWALD, ROBERT P., The Importance and Function of Child Psychiatry, *Medical Annals of the District of Columbia*, Vol. XIX, No. 7, July (1950), p. 368.

ODENWALD, ROBERT P., and JOSEPH A. SHEA, Emotional Problems of Maladjustment in Children with Reading Difficulties, *American Journal of Psychiatry*, Vol. 107, No. 12, June (1951), p. 890.

OVERHOLSER, WINFRED, and WINIFRED RICHMOND, "Handbook of Psychiatry" (Philadelphia: J. B. Lippincott Company, 1947).

STRECKER, EDWARD A. "Fundamentals of Psychiatry" (Philadelphia: J. B. Lippincott Company, 1944).

STRECKER, EDWARD A., and KENNETH APPEL, "Discovering Ourselves" (New York: The Macmillan Company, 1947).

WHITE, ROBERT A., "The Abnormal Personality" (New York: The Ronald Press Company, 1948).

2. A good survey of nonpsychological methods may be found in KALINOWSKI, L. B., and P. H. HOCH, "Shock Treatment and Other Somatic Procedures in Psychiatry" (New York: Grune and Stratton, 1946).
3. A more detailed discussion of the present problem may be found in O'BRIEN, P., Prefrontal Lobotomy: Its Present Moral Aspect, *American Ecclesiastical Review*, Vol. 119 (1948), 196–201; BIHLER, HUGH J., *Conference Bulletin of the Archdiocese of New York*, Vol. 24 (1947), pp. 86–92.
4. See HORSLEY, J. S., "Narcoanalysis" (New York: Oxford University Press, 1938).
5. Since the use of narcotic drugs interferes seriously with the patient's freedom of will, it is obvious that from the ethical standpoint this method cannot be used for the purpose of analysis without the consent of the patient. This consent may perhaps be presumed, because the patient, coming to the therapist for treatment, seems implicitly willing to reveal as much of his inner life as the physician needs for that treatment. However, great caution must be recommended. See GÉRAUD, JOSEPH, Procédés actuels d'investigation de la conscience, *L'Ami du Clergé*, August, 1948, pp. 515–518; Narcotherapy in Catholic Hospitals, *Hospital Progress*, Vol. 29 (1948), pp. 107–108; KELLY, GERALD, Current Theology, *Theological Studies*, Vol. 8 (1947), p. 104.

6. See Carp, E. A. D. E., "Grondslagen van Psychotherapie" (Lochem: De Tijdstroom, 1946), pp. 54–68; Hinsie, L. E., *op. cit.*
7. For a presentation of the practical application of play therapy, see Axline, Virginia Mae, "Play Therapy" (Boston: Houghton Mifflin Company, 1947); Axline, V. M., and C. R. Rogers, A Teacher-Therapist Deals with a Handicapped Child, *Journal of Abnormal and Social Psychology,* Vol. 40 (1945), 119–143; Allen, F., "Psychotherapy with Children" (New York: W. W. Norton & Company, 1942).
8. Group Therapy: a Symposium, *Sociometry,* Vol. 8 (1945), 251–542.
9. Moreno, P. L., "Psychodrama" (3 vols.; New York: Beacon House, Inc., 1945).

Chapter 6

SYMPTOMATIC METHODS OF PSYCHOTHERAPY

Although the chief forms of symptomatic procedure have a value proper to themselves, they involve also a common element that is of great importance in psychotherapy, *i.e.*, the element of suggestion. For that reason, they will be considered here particularly from the suggestive angle.

The suggestive techniques are sometimes called simple methods, and it is true that they are relatively simple in comparison with other types of therapy. It therefore happens that nonpsychiatrically trained persons feel quite well equipped to try out these methods. However, a word of caution should be sounded, for these techniques require more training than would at first seem necessary, and an individual who is not familiar with the implications of these methods may meet with unexpected and unpleasant experiences. One of these implications is that the suggestive situation, like any other psychiatric situation, creates in the patient a feeling of dependency on the therapist. This dependency may have unpleasant consequences for the untrained therapist, inasmuch as he may find his time wasted by dependent individuals who wish to maintain a schedule of frequent letters, calls, and visits. This is only one of the reasons why even the so-called simple methods require considerable training.

What is suggestion? The usual definition as proposed, for instance, by Liébeault and Bernheim and repeated by many others, consists in enumerating its characteristics: an image, idea, belief, decision, or plan of action induced into an individual's consciousness from the outside, ordinarily by another individual, but sometimes by means of a lifeless object, is accepted by the individual and translated into action. The description is correct so far as it goes, but it is lacking in the one point that makes a definition definitive—it fails to mention the essential characteristic, the psychodynamics, of the suggestive procedure.

Wundt, von Schrenck-Notzing, and others believe that suggestion operates through a narrowing of consciousness. This may be true in some cases, as in hypnotic suggestion, but in most other cases this characteristic is absent.

An interesting and acceptable interpretation is presented by Carp.[1] It sometimes happens that the suggestee offers a psychic resistance to the suggested idea, but in most instances the idea is adopted without being called into question. This uncritical acceptance seems to be the key to the understanding of the essentials of suggestion. It would seem that the suggested idea penetrates the individual's mind without being fully perceived and takes hold of his mind before he is completely conscious of it. In other words, the suggestee adopts the idea passively and subconsciously, and afterward the subconscious suggests the idea to his full consciousness. In that sense, Coué was right when he said that suggestion is always a form of autosuggestion. Of course, the very fact that the suggestee subconsciously accepts an idea calls for an explanation. It seems that such acceptance is possible in those cases in which there exists a special relationship, a rapport, between the suggestee and the one who makes the suggestion. And, as we saw previously, precisely such a rapport exists in the therapeutic situation.

Suggestive procedures not only are applicable in the case of mental disorders, but also are often quite effective in what used to be considered purely bodily illness. This latter fact is, of course, well known, and it is mentioned only as confirmation of the truth of psychosomatic concepts.

The mental illnesses that deserve consideration for suggestive treatment are the neuroses of milder and less complicated nature. It has been noted, for instance, that many of the so-called war neuroses respond favorably to suggestive methods.

It should be observed, of course, that a suggestive procedure that would be applicable in every case simply does not exist, and the choice between the different kinds of methods is determined by a great many factors.[2]

Suggestion is usually considered under the forms of autosuggestion and heterosuggestion. *Autosuggestion,* strongly advocated, for instance, by Coué [3] and Baudouin, consists in the endless repetition of short formulas, in the belief that people are capable of helping themselves. The method is simple and, for that reason, is sometimes discredited by those who prefer more sophisticated methods. Nevertheless, the method does work with some people, particularly with neurotics of the narcissistic type.

Narcissism is a form of egoism. The personality of the narcissist centers so much around his own self that he is more or less hostile to the outer world. He finds it hard to adapt himself to other people, as if he is afraid to lose his own cherished self in contact with others. Even though he may mix with other people, he lives psychologically in a sort of isolation. He is incapable, to a certain degree, of sympathy and love, and therefore it is difficult for the therapist to establish a sympathetic rapport between himself and the narcissist. These general characteristics reveal themselves also with regard to his own body; in sexual matters, too, his interest is mainly concentrated on himself. Those psychoanalysts who trace every psychic phenomenon back to a sexual origin believe that all the characteristics of the narcissistic personality are the result of fixation of the individual on an early level of sex life in which the sexual object remains the self.

The main narcissistic types are the autists who build up a dream world of their own, because their experience of objective reality is insufficient, some hysterics whose typical characteristic is preoccupation with themselves, and also some individuals given to masturbation. According to Freud, narcissism may be an important factor in the development of homosexuality. The narcissist finds, according to this view, a pseudo identification of himself in a person of the same sex and therefore may find narcissistic satisfaction in homosexual acts.

For these classes of people, autosuggestion may be of value, precisely because of their narcissistic attitude; because they stave off the external world, because their psychic life centers around the self, they feel a tendency to rely not upon any outside help but only upon themselves. The autosuggestive method meets this demand, for it suggests that the patient is able to help himself and forces upon the patient the idea that he is self-sufficient to overcome his troubles. The method is remarkably efficient in some cases. What the patient needs is somebody whom he trusts—as much as he can trust anybody—who points out the method to him. Sometimes the reference to a book will do.

Finally, a word should be said about the suggestive power of *prayer*. The Catholic believes, of course, in the supernatural power of prayer and does not doubt in the least that many sick people have been cured, even miraculously, through the fervent and insistent prayers that they themselves, together with their relatives and friends, sent up to God. But aside from that fact, there is also in prayer a natural element that is due particularly to autosuggestion. This holds true for both "Catholic" and "non-Catholic" prayers. There is no question but that Christian Scientists with their "treatment" with prayers have helped people and, for a time, have made them function better as human personalities. The practice, however, of relying exclusively on prayer is dangerous: it has sometimes impeded medical help for individuals who could have been cured, or cured more rapidly, if the onset of their disease had been treated by medical or professional personnel. After all, there is at least a grain of truth in the old saying that God helps those who help themselves, and prayer presupposes a willingness on the part of the suppliant to act in support of his prayers.

Usually, it is said that there is no essential difference between heterosuggestion and autosuggestion. The above discussion makes it clear that, if there is no essential difference, there exists at least a considerable difference of degree. Heterosuggestion works with persons who are suggestible. Now, suggestibility is distributed according to the normal curve, and narcissistic personalities find their place in that part of the curve which represents very low suggestibility.

Heterosuggestion is attributable, at least initially, to factors other than those coming from the suggestee himself. When the suggestive influence derives from another person, we speak of verbal suggestion. But often the very situation in which the patient is placed may have suggestive power. In this respect each of the somatotherapeutic methods that we have previously mentioned involves an element of suggestion.

Pharmacological and medicinal methods include such an element particularly with regard to the *administration of the medicine*. Although the statement that the efficacy of medicine is, in 99 per cent of the cases, due to suggestion is obviously not meant to be taken seriously, suggestion does play an important role in the way medicine is prescribed or administered. An excellent illustration of this point is the effectiveness of placebos. Placebos are harmless drugs, such as bicarbonate of soda and sugar-coated pills, or hypodermic injections of sterile water. Their efficacy lies mainly in the power of suggestion accompanying their prescription. In giving his medication or injection, the therapist tells the patient of the value of the drug, and the patient is promised relief from his symptoms. The ritual that surrounds the taking of medicine, like the prescription that the pills should be taken three times a day at a fixed hour, the encouraging words of the nurse at the time of the injection, and the rest of the ceremonial, contains a suggestive element. The less the name or the taste of the medicine is known, the better it works. Even the color plays a role; aspirin may be dispensed in white, red, or green tablets, and it is remarkable to see that sometimes the colored pills have better success than the white ones. On the other hand, although a patient may be feeling fine because of the prescription given him by his physician, a peevish remark of another physician about its uselessness may destroy the entire effect.

The different types of *cures,* such as a rest cure, water cure, open-air cure, diet cure, diathermy, sunbath, ultraviolet-ray cure, etc., may have valuable physical effects. But these effects are often reinforced and sometimes surpassed by the effects due to suggestive factors. The rest cure or a trip abroad, for instance, removes the patient from his disturbing environment, from the pressure of work, and from the emotional conflicts in his family. A change of environment makes some of the neurotic factors temporarily inactive. In this manner, the vicious circle of the environment getting on the nerves of the patient and the patient getting on the nerves of his environment is broken, and the improvement may continue after the patient returns home. Since the cure relieves the patient, for the time being, from his duties and obligations, he may feel that he can indulge, so to speak, in his neurotic condition without being a burden to his environment. This temporary relief of guilt feelings, too, may continue.

The cases in which the suggestive power of medicine or cures score good effects are quite numerous. The most important application is found in the field of functional disturbances of a neurotic nature.

The *isolation method* offers another example of the suggestive power of the surroundings. Isolation in a room, sometimes without light, is conducive to becoming quiet. It is occasionally applied in wartime on patients suffering from strong tremors; it also showed good results when prescribed for soldiers suspected of malingering. It may be used in cases of depression and neurasthenic exhaustion, and may be indicated in connection with hysterics because it counteracts their morbid drive to talk about their experiences and sufferings with other people.

Electric-shock therapy, too, contains an element of suggestion. The suggestive influence of electric treatment increases in proportion to the mysterious and important-looking features of the apparatus that is used. Cases of hysterical aphonia are sometimes treated by passing an electric current through the throat; now it has happened that, after the electrodes were placed on both sides of the neck, the patient received his voice back although no current passed through because the apparatus failed to work.

The use of electrotherapy is, in many instances, only an aid to verbal suggestions. Although a rather rough method, it was used in some armies during the First World War when a great number of neurotics had to be made serviceable in a short time. Kaufmann and Kehrer worked out the method in detail. It is based essentially on suggestion, due to authoritative, dictatorial orders and loud commands that are given in a military fashion, and to intimidation. Besides, painful electric shocks are applied so as to reinforce the suggestion. The patient is introduced into a dark room and notified in a stern voice that he will be freed from his troubles by means of a painful electric shock. Although this peculiar technique has given some satisfactory results, the cure is sometimes worse than the disease because acute heart failure occasionally occurs.

It matters little whether one agrees with this method, which seems to be better suited to a medieval torture chamber than to modern psychotherapy; the interesting point is the idea behind the technique. Since the neurotic condition is brought about by an emotional shock, the purpose of the method is to restore the patient's mental balance through another shock, this time caused by suggestive orders and fear. Since the patient has partially escaped from reality into his neurosis, the intent of the method is to make him face reality again by means of a sheer biological urge for self-preservation.

For the sake of clarity, these points may be enlarged upon a little. The method is indicated in cases of hysterical reactions due to emotional trauma, *i.e.*, a shock caused, for instance, by acute fear or terror. Such reactions can occur anywhere, but they are particularly frequent during war. Some writers believe that half the war neuroses belong to the group of hysterically fixated fear reactions. The trauma may cause a chronic condition of emotional tension, and this mental condition may produce physical manifestations, the so-called conversion symptoms. Some of these symptoms are perspiration, tachycardia (*i.e.*, excessive heartbeat), continuous muscular spasms or tremors, tics or spasmodic twitching of the face, insomnia, confusion, stupor, and apathy.

In the initial stage, the symptoms are relatively mild, but after these reactions have lasted for some time, they may become fixated; technically speaking, they gradually become hysterized. They are put into the service of the half-conscious, or even unconscious, instinctive drives of the personality, and the drive that predominates is, of course, the instinct to seek safety and protection. This is the transition period. And in this transition period, the patient's will can sometimes bring him back to normal. Therefore, in this phase, the authoritarian-suggestive method, either with or without the aid of electric shocks, can often be a decisive factor.

However, when the second phase has set in, the technique has much less chance to succeed. In this second phase, when the reactions have become deeply rooted in the personality, there is conversion hysteria in the strict sense of the word. At this time, the symptoms are, for instance, strong tremors, adynamia (lack of normal strength), real stupor or partial unconsciousness, hysterical inability to stand (astasia) or to walk (abasia), etc. With the onset of this phase, the chances for a speedy recovery by any method have passed.

The use of electric stimulation has found another application in the distraction method. Mohr and Oppenheim employed this technique on patients suffering from pains of a psychogenic nature. By applying painful stimuli to other places on the body, they attempted to distract the patient's attention from the painful spots of which he complained. But distraction of attention can be obtained by less drastic devices, and one of the most commendable is to keep the patient busy. The value of occupational therapy is partly due to distraction of attention, a method that succeeds well with hypochondriacs, neurasthenics, and some hysterics.

Somewhat related to the distraction method is the method of purposive overlooking. This method deserves more attention than it is usually given. To overlook does not mean to ignore the complaints of the patient in an arrogant way, to belittle him or deride him. On the contrary, the physician takes serious cognizance of the patient's complaints and shows it by examining him. However, after the examination, the physician acts as if he pays no further attention to the patient's complaints, but concentrates all his attention upon such matters as the individual's mental attitude, his plan of life, and his affective life. This treatment presupposes, of course, a previous insight into the individual characteristics of the patient. The treatment is comparable in a way with the distraction method, inasmuch as it distracts the patient from his morbid concentration upon his neurosis, but it avoids the danger that sometimes accompanies the distraction method. In fact, when the therapist—as well-meaning people are apt to do—advises the patient to look for diversion and relaxation, the patient may easily get the impression that the adviser does not take his complaints seriously and perhaps thinks them imaginary. In that case the effect may be just the opposite to the one desired; the advice, which the patient interprets as an evaluation, may reinforce the patient's urge to justify himself, and that urge may result in an accentuation of his neurotic phenomena. The overlooking method can be used freely in geriatrics, where age would make it very difficult to proceed with other types of psychotherapy.

§ A woman seventy-seven years of age came for treatment, complaining of pericardial discomfort, pain in the bladder region, a fear that her breasts were shrinking (a normal process at this age), and a "ball sensation" in the throat. She had gone to many physicians: some examined her urine; she was fluoroscoped and x-rayed; and always she was told that it was her age and that no serious disease was present. Most physicians did not bother with her at all, depending upon her narrative. The patient took rest cures and went from one married child to the other, but she was always, and rightly, afraid that she was a burden.

With the therapist overlooking all her complaints and concentrating on her egocentric attitudes, she slowly improved. In several sessions, she gladly talked about her happy past and her husband. Complaints were not mentioned, and she received a lot of encouragement, with the result that she improved and kept consistently away from doctors for several years.

That *surgical operations* may carry the power of suggestion is illustrated by the following case:

§ A forty-five-year-old woman thought that she had some intestinal obstruction or cancerous tumor. Married to a completely disabled veteran, who later died from progressive paresis, and troubled because her only son was not the person that she wanted him to be (although he really tried to help his mother whenever he was able to do so), she felt frustrated and depressed. Physical examination by physicians and hospital observation were negative in result. Nevertheless, the patient was dissatisfied with herself and the world, and, thinking that the Veterans Administration didn't treat her as well as she would be cared for by a private physician, she continued to complain.

At last, a surgeon agreed to an exploratory laparotomy. The patient submitted rather apprehensively to this procedure; however, she seemed more relaxed and hopeful. As was expected, the operation revealed no sign of an organic disease or physical disturbance.

She recovered slowly; but the astonishing thing was that she became free of symptoms and showed no signs of fear and anxiety. Years later she was still enjoying a perfect recovery.

This case of suggestion through surgery was given only to show the power of suggestion. It may be frankly stated that this method is bad medicine and unethical, and must, therefore, be condemned in the strongest terms.

All these methods involve elements of suggestion, which are inherent in the patient's very situation. In addition, *verbal suggestion* may be employed. The main forms in which verbal suggestion appears are systematic reassurance, encouragement, and persuasion.

Reassurance consists in putting a person's mind at ease, and as such it has been used since the beginning of mankind. As a therapeutic technique it should be given in a systematic way; *i.e.*, it should be adapted to the case and to the personality of the patient. Hence, systematic reassurance presupposes the study of the patient's personality in order to approach him in the best way. Reassurance, like the persuasion technique, is not exclusively based on rational motives and logical arguments that would show the patient how unreasonable his neurotic attitude is; on the contrary, it contains a great many "irrational" elements, based as it is on the rapport or identification of the patient with the therapist.

Reassurance is indicated in cases of anxiety; it scores success in cases of neurasthenic and hypochondriac depressions, especially those which develop out of masturbation conflicts. Sometimes it is also effective when the neurotic condition has resulted in functional disturbances such as cardiac, circulatory, and respiratory disorders.

The power of reassurance is particularly important in quieting down the pangs of conscience which, when exaggerated, may create depression and anxiety conditions. It should be emphasized here that, often enough, persons who suffer from pangs of conscience are perfectly conscious of some guilt. Now, when real guilt is involved, this should be acknowledged without glozing over the truth, but acknowledgment of guilt can well be reconciled with reassurance. On the other hand, the reassurance method falls short of the mark when anxiety is due to an unconscious cause. However, even then reassurance may succeed temporarily at least, in so far as it effects in the patient a condition of mental tranquillity and in that manner weakens the influence of unconscious guilt feelings. Reassurance works somewhat like opium; but, as with opium, the dose of suggestion must be continually increased if one wishes to achieve the desired effect. Hence, sooner or later, one arrives at its limit of service.

Of course, the method is applicable also in cases where no guilt feelings are involved. Here is such a case in which the reassurance technique was repeated at certain intervals and worked quite satisfactorily, whereas other techniques might have failed:

§ A sixty-six-year-old man was bedridden most of the time. When he woke up in the morning, he could not at once sit up, as he was told he might get a heart attack. Someone had to lift him up inch by inch—a feat that he described as his first "physical workout" of the day. He could walk only very slowly and had to rest after a few steps. According to his history, he had been told that he had a "coronary occlusion" and therefore had to take it easy; otherwise, he would die suddenly.

He was hospitalized and given a thorough physical examination, including an electrocardiogram. The reports were negative. The patient always carried with him nitroglycerin tablets, of which he took eight to fourteen daily. Repeated reassurance helped him to leave the hospital one morning and not to return that evening. Further reassurance helped him to resume his former regular eight-hour workday. He liked riding in his car and soon enjoyed driving it two hundred to three hundred miles daily. Most of the time, he felt fine and "newborn," and enjoyed living. His only requirement was monthly checkups, which were, naturally, continuous assurances.

In this case, reassurance was of the utmost help. Psychotherapy in an analytic sense was not initiated in view of the patient's age and the fact that he had no understanding of psychotherapeutic procedures.

Since reassurance plays an important role in conditions of a very different nature, *viz.*, in cases of incurable sickness, either physical or mental, a little digression is in order. Theoretically, there are two possibilities: either the patient realizes the seriousness or hopelessness of his condition, or he does not. In practice, however, many patients do realize their condition but play the ostrich with themselves and hope against hope.

If the patient is fully convinced of the hopelessness of his fate, reassurance would be sheer farce; in that case, the only thing left to do is to induce him to practice resignation and submission. If he does not realize his condition or pretends not to do so, the approach to be taken by the physician is different from that of the priest.

Most physicians consider "truth fanaticism" a medical crime. It is their job to keep their patients not only alive, but also in as good a shape, physically and mentally, as they can. And it is definitely true that the revelation of the naked truth has a bad effect on most patients, mentally as well as physically. Patients, especially those who say that they want to know the bare truth, more often than not collapse altogether when their wish is fulfilled.

So for the physician—*casu quo* for relatives and other lay people—there is only one avenue open: reassurance. And this reassurance has a remarkable effect on the patient, even in those cases in which the patient, after all, realizes very well what is in store for him. Even in that case, reassurance given by the "man who knows" creates some sort of "depersonalization." The terrifying images of suffering and death are suppressed or rather nullified. It is as if the patient no longer suffers his own sufferings, but rather observes them from a distance. There is suffering, to be sure, but this suffering is not a menace for the patient directly. Reassurance causes the patient to pass from the subjective to the objective attitude. The physician—*casu quo* others—is perfectly entitled to produce this condition in his patient, *i.e.*, to create a kind of gap between the patient and his suffering.

But the case is different for the priest, who, although also concerned with the patient's physical well-being, is, however, first and foremost interested in his soul. The priest, too, will try to keep up the patient's hope of recovery. Even when he administers the last sacraments, he will reassure him by pointing out that one of the graces of Extreme Unction may be restoration of the person's health. But there are cases in which the priest can no longer keep silent. For instance, when the patient, although in a really critical condition, refuses to receive the sacraments, the priest, as a last resort, is obliged to tell him the truth. But then again, much depends upon the way it is said. It may be added that there are patients who, having no fear of death and being well trained in the theology of their faith, prefer to receive Extreme Unction before it reaches the status of being a "last resort." But these patients, too, as prepared as they may be, should be told that they are dying, when the time comes.

Closely related to reassurance is *encouragement*. Some analysts seem to believe that courage is only a form of overcompensated cowardice. This is certainly not always true; many people are courageous by nature. Besides, it is a strange thing to define a virtue by its opposite vice. It should be granted, however, that sometimes a courageous attitude is due not so much to nature as to suggestion. Under the influence of suggestion, the thought of danger and the fear of it are suppressed or nullified. The effect of encouragement will depend largely on the personality and the prestige of the individual who tries to inspire the patient. Encouragement is indicated when one is dealing with persons who show little life energy.

Although persuasion dates back to the time when Eve urged the apple on Adam, the elaboration of the *persuasion method* as a technical form of therapy goes back to P. Dubois, a psychotherapist at Geneva at the beginning of this century.[4] The method makes an attempt, by means of reasoning processes, to show the patient how unreasonable and senseless his neurotic attitude is. Before using his therapy, Dubois first explained to the patient the possible cause of his condition. According to the then prevailing opinion, the causes of neurosis were considered to be predominantly biological, such as exhaustion, nervous strain, accumulation of harmful metabolic products, etc. For the use of the method, it matters little whether that opinion was right or wrong, for the prestige of the physician is usually sufficient to make the patient accept any explanations; what is interesting to note is that Dubois, by employing a psychotherapeutic method on what he considered an organogenic disease, applied the concepts of psychosomatic medicine.

Dubois scored considerable success. At the present time, several authors still use his method; for instance, Carp [5] gives several examples of cases in which the method may be used to good advantage. It works particularly well in those cases in which the neurotic condition is caused by feelings of guilt. Hence, the method may be effective when one is dealing with conditions of hypochondriasis or neurasthenic depressions, which often are accompanied or caused by sexual sins; *e.g.*, a frequent application of the method is found in cases of depression caused by masturbation conflicts. In addition, favorable results have been reported in mild compulsion cases, in some cases of erotic perversion, and with some alcoholics.

The applicability and value of the persuasion technique is decided not only by the nature of the condition involved but also by the patient's life period. The best results are obtained with adolescents, because they are still accessible to persuasion, for at that age the personality structure is not yet consolidated. The method gives diminishing results as life proceeds, and its use becomes doubtful about the time of the climacterium, when the personality structure is, so to speak, set. Whenever formal sin is the cause of the psychiatric condition, the persuasion method should of course not aim at reasoning away the sinfulness of the patient's act, but only at showing the unreasonableness of his neurotic attitude. An example is the following case:

§ A twenty-year-old medical student had been masturbating since the age of twelve years. Being a devout Catholic, he regularly went to confession, where he was admonished and was warned of the danger of habit formation and of being unable to perform his marital duties later.

He became confused and thought that he could not concentrate and had lost his former brilliant memory. With girls, he was apprehensive and shy, and gradually he retired more and more from people. His masturbation practices became almost a compulsion, and he was told to get the help of a psychiatrist. By that time, he thought that his faith had been shaken, and he was doubtful that the medical profession was his proper vocation.

At the beginning of treatment, it was suspected that this might be a case of possible psychosis. However, it was found that this possibility could be ruled out. Since only a limited time was available for treatment, the persuasion method was used. The psychiatrist made the patient realize that his misgivings about the effects of his sinful behavior were unfounded and that his attitude was unreasonable. Although the dynamics in this case were only superficially investigated, the persuasion method helped him to continue his work. It was later discovered that this short treatment was successful for at least one full semester.

Some physicians accomplish favorable results by using the persuasion method in connection with their knowledge of analysis; the result is the analytically orientated persuasion method. It is not necessary that the patient be analyzed in the technical sense of the word, for it suffices that the therapist, because of his analytical training, have a fairly good insight into the causes of the patient's condition.

The persuasion method may be classified as a "rational" method and therefore well suited to "rational" cases. For instance, in the case history just given, the patient's feeling of guilt was rational in its origin although it took an irrational form. Nevertheless, although the persuasion method may be called rational, the suggestive element in the method appeals to personality factors other than pure reason. When a person accepts an insight based on reasoning, it is not the intellectual element alone that turns the scale, but in the final analysis, some irrational (*i.e.*, emotional or affective) element brings about the decision. In the therapeutic situation, this irrational factor is due to the rapport between therapist and patient, and therefore the personality of the therapist is of the greatest importance.

That same irrational element is often enough the decisive factor with regard to the convictions held by normal individuals. It is highly questionable if our taking sides in freely debated discussions is exclusively determined by rational considerations. We find an excellent example among Catholic scholars. The adherents to one or another view in the famous controversies among the various schools of scholastic philosophy or in the opposing opinions of theology may believe that they are motivated exclusively by intellectual arguments; but their adherence to a particular school or view is at least equally determined by irrational factors, such as the religious habit they wear or the suggestive power of their former teacher. In fact, sometimes the very tone of their arguments betrays the emotional origin of their convictions.

NOTES AND REFERENCES

1. CARP, E. A. D. E., *De suggestieve behandelingsmethode en het suggestieve element in de psychotherapie* (Lochem: De Tijdstroom, 1939), pp. 7–18.
2. An excellent survey of the suggestive methods may be found in CARP, *ibid.*, pp. 41–80. We express our indebtedness to this work.
3. COUÉ, EMILE, and J. LOUIS ORTON, "Conscious Auto-suggestion," 1921.
4. DUBOIS, P., Ueber Suggestion und Psychotherapie, *Schweizer Corresp. Blatt.*, Vol. 3 (1900); *id.*, "Die Psychoneurosen" (Bern: 1910).
5. CARP, *op. cit.*, pp. 50, 78.

Chapter 7

COUNSELING

Counseling is a discussion about a problem between two people, one of whom is supposed to know something concerning that problem, whereas the other knows little about it or is in doubt, but is sincerely willing to be enlightened. This is the definition of St. Thomas Aquinas,[1] and it is broad enough to cover the various counseling procedures that will be discussed here. Aquinas also points out what would now be called the psychodynamics that induce a person to seek counsel. This is, in the first place, hope for a satisfactory solution of the problem, because no one seeks counsel when he is definitely convinced of the impossibility of a solution. But a still more powerful motive to look for counsel is fear inflicted by the difficulty of a situation and by the lack of confidence in one's own powers.[2]

Counseling is being used in a great number of circumstances that have little or nothing to do with mental health, but it may obviously also be employed as a psychotherapeutic technique. If so, it is in most cases related to symptomatic therapy. Such is, for instance, the case when a vocational counselor advises an emotionally blocked client about the abilities of which that person is himself unaware. However, in recent years some types of counseling have developed which claim to partake of the nature of causal treatment. Such is the claim of nondirective counseling.

TYPES OF COUNSELING

There are numerous possible ways of carrying on counseling—ranging from an informal chat over coffee and cigarettes to the more formalized series of conferences, with or without psychological testing, in a professional or academic setting. In all these, the interview between counselor and counselee is the backbone of the process.[3]

The counseling interview differs from other types of interview in its purpose and function; hence, its dynamics will develop and proceed accordingly. The counseling interview, ideally, should result in one or all of the following accomplishments on the part of the counselee or the counselor or both: (*a*) a deeper knowledge of the counselee; (*b*) a clearer appreciation of the counselee's basic problem; and (*c*) progress toward the solution of the problem.

All approaches to any kind of effective counseling require "rapport" between counselor and counselee. Rapport refers, as we have seen, to that harmonious and sympathetic relationship between counselor and counselee wherein the counselee feels that he can work toward a solution of his problem. Rapport implies that the counselor is genuinely interested, friendly, understanding, sympathetic, and uncritical; that the atmosphere of the interview is unhurried, confidential, and comfortably free of interruptions; that the counselee is respected and accepted by the counselor; that he can feel free in expressing the attitudes and emotions surrounding his problem; and that he, not the counselor, will ultimately be responsible for any final decision regarding his future.

Granted rapport, the procedure of the interview will depend largely on one's "philosophy" of counseling. There are various approaches possible to the counseling interview, but no one approach has been found empirically to be universally effective, and no professionally recognized approach seems to be totally without merit.[4]

The major approaches currently used, in some form or other, will be briefly classified and described below. The reader will realize that such a brief description can hardly hope to do justice to the respective approaches, and at best can only hope to highlight the essential points of contrast.

The *benevolent-dictatorial approach* is used where the counselee is extremely dependent and, at least temporarily, is psychologically incapable of making decisions. This approach is sometimes useful and even necessary, especially when a decision cannot be postponed and cannot be made by the counselee alone. In such a situation the counselor becomes a figure of authority and is accepted as such by the counselee, who is relying completely upon the counselor. The dynamics of counseling here include strong advice, even threats, and authoritative appeal to the counselor's experience.

The *supportive approach* is based upon the establishment of an emotional relationship between counselor and counselee, where the emotional transference to the counselor is strong. Praise and affection are freely given to the counselee for good decisions and actions; kindly but firm disapproval, for undesirable actions. This approach to the counseling interview is sometimes useful as a temporary measure to weather a difficult storm, to combat groundless fears, and to provide the counselee with security in making necessary decisions.

The *traditional approach,* or so-called *directive approach* emphasizes the appeal to reason. Counselor and counselee are more or less equally active in the counseling process, but the counselor is regarded as expert in certain areas where the counselee needs help. The counselee makes all the decisions, but subtle direction can be given by the counselor, who will not hesitate to manipulate the environment where such manipulation seems feasible in working toward a solution. Directive counseling has been termed "eclectic" because it uses all possible means—case histories, psychological tests, diagnoses, the experience of the counselor, etc.—to further the solution of the counselee's problem.

The so-called *nondirective approach* stresses the feelings and attitudes of the counselee. This approach has been called "client-centered": the counselor has, externally, a more or less passive role in the counseling process; he introduces no new ideas and keeps the responsibility for the direction of the interview in the hands of the counselee. The following are among the basic postulates of nondirective counseling:

1. The counselor operates on the principle that the counselee is responsible for his own adjustment and has within himself the drive to become psychologically mature and properly self-directive.
2. To allow this drive of the counselee to become operative, the counselor creates a permissive atmosphere wherein the counselee has complete freedom for self-expression or for maintaining silence.
3. The limits set to this permissive atmosphere are simple, minimal, and are on behavior only, not on the expression of attitudes or feelings.
4. The counselor maintains complete acceptance of emotionalized attitudes, especially by prudent use of reflection of the counselee's feeling.
5. Negatively, the counselor does nothing to indicate approval or disapproval or to hinder the counselee from achieving clarification of his own feelings, with the subsequent development of insight into the nature and source of his problem.

The nondirective type of counseling is strongly advocated by C. R. Rogers.[5] Rogers' work consists of an elaboration of Freud's principle of passive release therapy. This therapy refuses to make use of those mechanisms that at one time were supposed to be valuable in counseling, such as persuasion, advice, suggestion, and supportiveness, and it operates on the basic assumption that the individual has an inherent capacity to work out for himself an adequate solution to his problem. In his latest work

(1951) Rogers puts less emphasis on the significance of insight and stresses the therapist's empathic identification with the client as of primary importance for a successful therapy. It is not enough that the therapist understand how the patient feels—that would be the intellectual approach—but he must make the patient feel that he goes with him through the same experiences. In other words, Rogers now emphasizes what was recognized decades ago, as the basic prerequisite for successful psychotherapy. But, whereas there is a difference of accent as to the prerequisite, the main scope of Rogers' client-centered counseling remains the same: all the therapist has to do is to release the inner forces that are supposed to be at work in the individual and, after that, let him choose his own way of becoming a responsible person.

Nondirective counseling has lately acquired a considerable number of followers. However, strong reservations must be expressed concerning its use. Client-centered counseling may be indicated when the subject matter of the counseling interview is morally "neutral." For instance, it may be used in the case of vocational counseling or personnel guidance, except perhaps in the case of religious vocation, in which more often than not concrete advice is required. Even in so-called "neutral" cases, however, its use seems to be quite limited; *e.g.*, it would be interesting to see how far industrial counselors would get with purely nondirective counseling when trying to settle a dispute between labor unions and the managers.

But the procedure takes on a very different aspect whenever religious and moral elements are involved, as is often the case when counseling is employed for therapeutic purposes. Client-centered counseling contains the essential weakness which is inherent in any inner-release therapy and which will be discussed in the chapter on the evaluation of depth psychology. It would be merely utopian to believe that the "releasing of inner forces" is all that is needed to make an individual a morally healthy, responsible person. But there is more, and that is the basic assumptions underlying this kind of therapy and the implications derived from those assumptions.

In the first place, client-centered therapy, as set forth by Rogers, is based on the belief that man is basically good. Catholics, too, hold that some positive, constructive elements may be found in every man, but they also hold that, as a result of original sin, man is inclined toward evil and that man, left to himself, is only too prone to follow his evil tendencies because his intellect is darkened and his will is weakened.

Secondly, client-centered therapy, again as advanced by Rogers, is an antiauthoritarian system, *i.e.*, it is based on the assumption that the source of valuing things lies exclusively in man himself. Man does not admit any authority outside himself, as he is the shaper of his own destiny. If we push this principle to its logical conclusions, it would follow that man is a law unto himself, both in moral and religious matters. In other words client-centered therapy refuses to admit an objective norm of morality and disposes of the authority of God. In the final analysis, it makes man his own God. It should be emphasized that these principles and implications are inherent in the system itself.

Obviously no Catholic can accept such implications. Carl Rogers, himself doubtful about reconciling his system with Catholicism, has expressed in oral communication his concern about the Catholic followers of his therapy. He said that either Catholics do not grasp the implications of client-centered therapy, and in that case they will necessarily do superficial work, or they do grasp those implications, and in that case it is difficult to see how they can avoid a serious conflict with their belief. It would seem that these words epitomize, better than any lengthy discussion, the very serious objections that should be advanced against client-centered therapy from the Catholic standpoint.[6]

BRIEF REVIEW OF A COUNSELING PROCESS

Without necessarily advocating an eclecticism, this section will list a few of the interviewing skills which, along with others, can well be utilized, depending on the circumstances, in facing some of the problems of the counseling interview.

Initiating the Interview. The counselor must be concerned here with establishing the rapport mentioned above. If the counselee seems reluctant to inaugurate the discussion of his problem, the counselor must be patient and, by impersonal questions or comments, give the counselee ample opportunity for assuming at least minimal responsibility for directing the interview toward his problem. The counselor should avoid the pattern of questions or statements that can evoke only a "yes" or "no" answer; he should get the *counselee* to talk.

Conducting the Interview. There are a number of positive and negative skills that will serve to keep the interview flowing in such a way that the counselee will be able to work toward his solution both during the interview itself and even *after* the interview has been concluded.

1. The use of silence; the counselor should not be alarmed at the silences that are apt to occur in any interview. Silence is not necessarily a sign of

sterility of thought or feeling but, on the contrary, can be indicative of deep and useful thinking. The counselor should interrupt a silence only to encourage the client to express himself more fully, and he should interject his own comments only when he knows that the silence is paralyzing instead of stimulating the counselee.

2. The counselor should avoid giving the impression of cross-examining. If it is necessary to get information through questioning, it is wise either to spread the questions throughout the interview, or if possible to have someone else obtain the needed data, perhaps before the interview. The counselor who asks many questions is apt to give the impression that he merely needs the answers to his questions in order to amalgamate from them the solution to the counselee's problem.

3. The counselor should not "steal" the conversation from the counselee. Most people stumble or fumble for words when speaking of personal problems. For the most part, they should be permitted to fumble. The counselor might find that, in trying to help the counselee express himself by suggesting the apt word or phrase, he has sidetracked the counselee's thinking. The counselee should do most of the talking, if possible.

4. The counselor should accept, and make clear that he accepts, the counselee's feeling. The counselor must strive to make clear that he is maintaining—at least for the purposes of the interview—a nonjudgmental attitude toward the counselee, so that the latter will feel free in expressing himself *completely* concerning his problem. Otherwise, the opportunities for valuable insight and clues are lost both to the counselee and to the counselor.

5. The counselor should encourage further expression of feeling through a neutral, nonevaluative reflection of the feeling (not the content) of what the counselee says. There is danger here of merely "parroting" the verbal content, or of merely paraphrasing the verbal expression of the counselee. This skill requires of the counselor that he develop keen sensitivity to the feelings of others, and a certain amount of expertness in recognizing the "clues" to feelings that may be better revealed by gestures and physical attitude than by words.

6. The counselor should avoid creating problems. A problem usually exists for the counselee only when he himself is aware of it. If the counselor suspects that the basic problem has not been touched, he can only furnish the atmosphere in which the counselee will develop the insight needed to detect the real problem and to bring it into the open for con-

sideration. In the counseling interview, one can rarely "force the issue" with success.

7. The counselor should diplomatically establish and observe reasonable limits. Limits can have a stimulating and therapeutic influence upon the counselee; often when a counselee notices that time is running out, he will present highly significant material. Both the counselor and the counselee should know beforehand how long the interview is to last and, by implication at least, the limits of mutual responsibility, the extent of aggressive action permitted the counselee, etc. The responsibility for observing the limits set is that of the counselor.

Concluding the Interview. A useful way to conclude the interview is to get the counselee to summarize what has taken place, or what he "got out" of the interview. The counselor should conclude the interview with relaxed graciousness, making sure that the counselee knows that the counselor is accessible for future interviews.

The above remarks on interviewing skills are not presented as a complete "set of rules," but are suggested as some of the major, practical implementations of the basic principle of all good counseling: to help the counselee, in the light of honest self-evaluation, to make his own decisions.

VOCATIONAL COUNSELING

Professional counselors, apart from psychiatrists, are classified into a few groups according to the subject matter with which they deal or the area in which they specialize. Thus, we hear of vocational, industrial, legal, educational, pastoral, and marriage counselors.

Pastoral counseling will be taken up in Chapter 12 and marriage counseling in Chapter 24. Here a brief discussion of vocational counseling will be added because of its preventive character in connection with mental health. The choice of the right vocation may prevent many personality problems and much mental grief. As a matter of fact, vocational dissatisfaction hampers the happiness of at least one-third of the workers of the United States.[7]

The choice of a vocation is a problem that quite often, fortunately or not, resolves into some kind of a decision simply by pressure of time or by force of circumstances. It is this element of haphazardness that vocational counseling seeks to eliminate.

Vocational counseling may be described from a functional viewpoint as a process of helping an individual to evaluate properly his total self, with all his assets and liabilities, to the end that he may make a successful vocational choice.

A successful vocational choice means much more than mere occupational choice or job placement. It implies, first of all, to borrow a phrase from Harry E. Jager, *vocational adjustment,* which involves every attribute of the individual: "not merely his hand or brain, but also his personality and physical organism, his home conditions, his personal relationships and his inner life." [8] The same all-inclusive view of adjustment is adopted with reference to students by the 100 selected counselors whose work and views were carefully studied and reported by Rachel Dunaway Cox.[9] These counselors found that successful adjustment to educational development involved almost every conceivable level of the student's life: adjustment to the family group and to the school environment and associates, physical and mental conditions, the complete background of experience. Secondly, successful vocational choice means a success more broad than the earning of a good salary, the winning of prestige, or advancement to top positions.

A vocation is etymologically (hence, originally and radically) a calling —a calling to something and, as used here, to one's lifework. A calling implies a relationship; someone is called by someone to something. The "something" is, of course, the lifework. The "someone called" is the person with the vocational problem. Who or what is the "someone calling"?

The Christian philosopher here steps aside from the modern beaten path and ponders basic truths. He acknowledges a personal, intelligent Creator Who is so interested in the world and its creatures that He has an individual plan of happiness for every rational being He sends into the world. Man has one basic purpose—vocation, if you will—in life, and that being fulfilled, vocational success and happiness are assured. Man was created to praise, reverence, and serve God, and by this means to save his soul. All other purposes in life are but means—subsidiary and complementary—to this basic purpose. If this basic vocation is being fulfilled, one's life is a success. The saving of one's soul may be considered the ultimate goal in life; one's praise, reverence, and service of the Creator become, then, the roadway to that goal, and one's individual vocational choice is one's individual, personal, concrete way of praising, reverencing, and serving God.

Unless one conditions his vocational choice (the same is true, *pari passu,* of vocational counseling) by the basic desire to fulfill God's Will, complete vocational happiness and success will not be attained. As a corollary to the above, Scripture presents us with the first rule of thumb for vocational thinking: "Seek ye first the Kingdom of God, and all these things shall be given to you" (Matthew 6:33, Luke 12:31). A wise student of the human heart put his finger directly on the source of much vocational unhappiness and discontent when he made the observation that many first choose, *e.g.*, to marry, which is but a means and a subsidiary vocation, and only secondarily to serve God in the married state, which service of God is the end, the basic purpose, and vocation of the rational being. Such people make of the means an end, and of the end a means.

The above point is worth emphasizing, because a principle that is much stressed in the psychological field today is the fallacious one that every individual must have his needs satisfied according to self chosen and subjective norms. The fact that the "needs" are often bizarre, if not abnormal, should alert us to the fact that such an individual's choice mechanism is not operating in a healthy atmosphere, and therefore cannot readily be trusted to make the choices that will be ultimately and genuinely successful.

At the same time, it should be emphasized that the authors are not advocating that responsibility for vocational choices be left to someone other than the individual concerned, nor are they maintaining that all vocational indecision or dissatisfaction is a symptom of emotional disturbance.

Vocational indecision does not necessarily indicate any significant mental or emotional instability, and in adolescents it is quite a normal occurrence. This view is supported by the observation of those who have worked extensively in the field of vocational counseling.[10] Some cases of indecisiveness may be due to phobias or obsessions, but in such cases the individual's life is pretty well shot through with indecisiveness. He simply cannot decide things for himself. He has just as much difficulty in choosing a necktie as in choosing a career. Such a type of indecisiveness enduring with any degree of permanency is relatively rare in adolescence and should be dealt with by a psychiatrist if possible.

The ordinary type of vocational indecision, however, is, as has been said above, a normal occurrence during adolescence. It is an indication that new powers and energies are being developed, new horizons are opening, new desires and aspirations are being felt. The adolescent is aware of these changes and cannot interpret them. He feels "different" from what he was formerly; he is more prone to recognize himself as a personality *sui juris,* and subconsciously, if not consciously, he wishes to publish his own personal declaration of independence yet fears the responsibility entailed.

Such vocational indecisiveness, if not unduly prolonged, can be most healthy and protective. The individual recognizes that he is in a state of flux and therefore does not wish to commit himself to a final decision until he and his world and the reciprocal relationships involved—the "phenomenological self"—have become more stabilized.

For many individuals, such indecision is resolved, wisely or not, either by time or by circumstances, or its resolution can be comfortably postponed. But for many others, the indecisiveness cannot be long prolonged. Certain decisions, *e.g.*, whether or not to take premedical studies, whether or not to be a priest, or a nun, must be made at a certain time and usually cannot be delayed. Such harassed individuals will turn for counseling and help to the person they think most competent to help them; this will often be their pastor, confessor, teacher, or principal.

Vocational counseling is concerned primarily with helping the individual, in the light of proper self-evaluation, to make and carry out vocational choices that will lead to a completely happy life here and hereafter. This definition is not restricted to religious vocational counseling, nor does it exclude that field.

Vocational counseling is not a substitute for a sense of responsibility; its essential function should be to so help the individual that he will be able to make his own choices. No vocational counselor with a conscience will ever presume to make the choice for anyone. Vocational counseling is not vocational dictation.

Depending upon how the vocational counselor has organized and delineated the scope of his functions and services, it may be necessary for him personally, or for some one of his associates to whom he refers the counselee, to have at hand some of the sources and references on occupational, educational, and related information. The collection, organization, and use of such information can be a specialty in itself. Even keeping abreast of occupational literature is itself a complex occupation. The type of information to which the counselor may have to refer will warrant a special library annex. A valuable booklet on selecting, organizing, and using occupational materials in a guidance program is published under the auspices of the Occupational Information and Guidance Service, Office of Education, of the Federal Security Agency.[11]

As regards specific occupational choices, when the counseling process is drawing to a close and the counselee seems to be approaching a decision, it is wise to bear in mind that, in connection with vocational choices of a nonreligious character, one should not be looking for the one and only specific job that is to be fulfilled by the counselee for life; the old idea of each square peg in its square hole is not strongly adhered to today. Counselors look more to fields of interest wherein there is a certain amount of flexibility and adaptability. This protects the counselee from preparing for only one job, working at it for years, losing it, and then being at a complete loss as to what to do.

The discussion thus far has dealt with vocational counseling as it may take place almost anywhere and at any time. It would seem that the ideal place for vocational counseling should be the secondary school, where our youth spend most of their adolescent years. Yet, less than one-fifth of our secondary schools have any kind of adequate guidance or counseling program.[12] True, the Catholic high schools are working zealously to provide spiritual training for many of our future citizens, and their educational standards are among the highest in our country. But in the field of guidance may not the question be raised of how adequately they are helping our young men and women choose that work in life wherein they can find temporal as well as eternal happiness? The average person spends as much time at work as in sleep; a well-chosen occupation can give perfect expression to man's basic work in life—to praise, reverence, and serve his Creator—and can fulfill in happiness the most fundamental needs of every man, the perfection of his own unique personality in work. A comment made by a supervisor of public school counselors, would seem to indicate that the Catholic schools are losing out on opportunities to help our youth as much as possible. "Catholic schools," remarks this supervisor, "have always rated fairly high in informal guidance programs, but very poorly on formal programs of guidance."

It is not enough to designate a not-too-busy faculty member as "Student Counselor," and then trust to his (or her) personal zeal and ingenuity to help several hundred students solve their vocational problems. Many Catholic institutions are now sending their members to the fields of higher education to receive the specialized training required for a counselor's position. They would do well to send even more of their priests, Brothers, and Sisters into the field of professional psychology and counseling. Perhaps it will not be too difficult, with their Catholic heritage of educational standards and zeal, to baptize "profane" psychology in their classrooms. The authors advocate that every school have a professionally trained counselor (or counselors!), who will possess the competency and training to establish a formal guidance program, including a well-organized testing bureau.

The help that can be given the counseling process by psychological testing must not be overlooked. For the scope of this discussion and the present purposes of this book, psychological testing will be treated in Chapter 13. One need be neither overskeptical nor overenthusiastic about psychological tests. It may be that more harm is done by the misinterpretation of test results than by overcredulity in the tests themselves. The comment of David Rapaport is worth recalling: "Psychological testing [often becomes] a pragmatic procedure protected by a thin veneer of statistical respectability, and hardly in touch with the psychological reality of the problems it tackles." [13]

If one uses psychological tests, he should be thoroughly familiar with the tests in question. Test names and test titles are not always accurate guides to their functions. Granting the validity and reliability of the tests, the counselor will always keep in mind that the test "measures" normative behavior—the behavior of the group upon which the test is standardized—and hence measures individual behavior only in so far as the individual conforms to the behavior patterns of the normative group. One definite help, then, to be gained from tests is that they can furnish clues that will direct the alert counselor along unsuspected avenues of investigation.

Certainly a formal guidance program, cooperatively administered, can inject new vitality into the life streams of a school. Besides providing counseling, the guidance program can help every teacher perform his or her task more efficiently and more easily, by detecting, *e.g.*, the sources of academic failure. In numerous ways it can furnish information needed for the occasional revision of the curriculum or the administration of the school affairs. There is no reason why the work of the student counselor should exist in a vacuum or be isolated from the rest of the educational program.

Whether or not the school or institution has a formalized guidance and counseling program, the young person wrestling with vocational indecision should have someone available who can sympathetically and constructively help him to work through his vocational problem. A vocational problem for an adolescent and young adult can assume gigantic proportions, nor does every youngster find it easy to speak to just any elder about his vocational hopes and fears, his doubts and ambitions. It is one of the basic functions of the school to ensure that somehow or other even the timid adolescent has an easily accessible source of help.

Throughout the counseling process, the counselor, in whatever way he can, should help the counselee to the maturity of assuming responsibility for making his vocational decisions and for the execution of them. No one will deny that our present era of refined comfort and advanced civilization, ready to advance even farther under the impetus of atomic energy, has brought in its wake certain psychological disadvantages. Description of our modern hypertension and excessively stimulated sex consciousness may be omitted, but it seems important to mention the lack of one characteristic that is too often minimized in our humanitarian day—a sense of individual responsibility. Frequently, one hears exhortations on society's duty toward this or that unfortunate individual; and truly the healthy or wealthy community does have an obligation of charity toward the sick and suffering of its members—of such is the Mystical Body of Christ. But there is a gross neglect of the basis for this communal charity, *viz.,* the obligation of the individual to the community. These two obligations are reciprocal and mutually complementary: the society toward the individual *and* the individual toward society. The former without the latter is fatuous paternalism; the latter without the former is totalitarian slavery. In this country today, there is a danger that the individual's duty to society is being minimized altogether too much.

Whatever approach to vocational counseling is used, counselors have the common endeavor of helping to produce Christian citizens who have a mature sense of responsibility: *citizens* who will recognize that they have duties as well as rights; *Christians* who choose this or that vocation not merely because by it they will achieve wealth or a great name, but because through it they will fulfill their eternal vocation, their eternal peace of soul.

NOTES AND REFERENCES

1. S. *Theol.,* I, Q. 22, a. 1, 1; I, II, Q. 14, a. 1, 2; II, II, Q. 52, a. 33.
2. S. *Theol.,* I, II, Q. 44, a. 2, 3.
3. This discussion on counseling was written by Rev. Albert F. Grau, S.J., with the exception of the evaluation of nondirective counseling.
4. Darley, John G., "The Interview in Counseling" (Washington, D.C.: U.S. Department of Labor, Government Printing Office, 1946).
5. Rogers, Carl R., *Counseling and Psychotherapy* (Boston: Houghton Mifflin Company, 1942); *id.,* "Psychotherapy," in Dennis, W. A., *et al.,* "Current Trends in Psychology" (Pittsburgh: University of Pittsburgh Press, 1947), pp. 112–117; *id.,* Some Observations on the Organization of Personality, *American Psychologist,* Vol. 2 (1947), 398–468; *id.,* "Client-centered Therapy: The Current Practice, Implications, and Theory" (Boston: Houghton Mifflin Company, 1951).

6. In view of what is said in the text, it is difficult to agree with Charles A. Curran, who made an attempt in his "Personality Factors in Counseling" (New York: Grune and Stratton, 1945) to demonstrate that the principles of nondirective counseling are in harmony with the principles of scholastic philosophy.
7. Ruch, Floyd L., "Psychology and Life" (New York: Scott, Foresman & Company, 1941).
8. Jager, Harry A., The Guidance Program Broadens Its Base, *Occupations*, Vol. 17 (1949), pp. 469 f.
9. Cox, R. D., "Counselors and Their Work" (Philadelphia: Archives Publishing Company of Pennsylvania, 1945).
10. Super, Donald, "Appraising Vocational Fitness" (New York: Harper & Brothers, 1949), pp. 3 f.
11. Greenleaf, Walter J. "Guide to Occupational Choice and Training" (Washington, D.C.: Superintendent of Documents, Government Printing Office, 1947).
12. Jager, *op. cit.*
13. Rapaport, David, The Psychologist in the Clinic Setting (symposium), *American Journal of Orthopsychiatry*, Vol. 18 (1948), pp. 492 ff.

Chapter 8

DEPTH THERAPY

As was pointed out previously, depth psychology comprises the main forms of causal, integrative psychotherapy that aim at reaching the root of neurotic disorders. In popular language, all these forms are sometimes covered by the word "psychoanalysis." However, the orthodox Freudians claim that this name should be reserved to their system; on the other hand, several other systems of depth therapy prefer a different name, just to distinguish them from Freudian psychoanalysis.

There are, of course, as many definitions of depth therapy as there are systems, theories, schools, or groups. By way of example, Alexander's definition is presented here: "Any therapy based on psychodynamic principles which attempts to bring the patient into a more satisfactory adjustment to his environment, and to assist the harmonious development of his capacities. All forms of therapy, however flexible, having this basis and this goal, may be considered psychoanalytic." [1] While all types, groups, schools, and systems of depth psychology have in common the fact that they intend to explore the depth of the patient's psyche, they also show differences. In some cases, these differences between the rival systems are more or less nominal; in other cases, they are real, comprising differences of methodology or even differences of the underlying philosophy and ideology. Most of these schools or groups are strongly organized after the pattern set by Freud, who, right from the start, developed a clannish organization in his school. Of course, many psychiatrists practice depth therapy, even though they are independent of any organized group; they consider it to be not inconsistent professionally to have recourse to a certain eclecticism.

The character of this book permits only a brief summary of each of the main groups. These summaries will omit as far as possible the esoteric terminology of certain analysts. A new tribe of nominalists has sprung up in the field of science, particularly in the field of psychology and psychiatry. The introduction of a few new terms, preferably of Greek derivation, is sometimes heralded as a major contribution and deemed sufficient to serve as a new theory.[2] However, the multiplication of terms and the tendency toward logorrhea does not always seem to increase the clarity of the exposition, and it is doubtful if it contributes much to the main purpose of all therapy, that of curing a sick person. In this respect we might recall Goethe's word that "*in der Beschränkung zeigt sich erst der Meister*—restraint is the sign of the master." Aside from an undue worship of words, one finds also in the various "schools" of psychiatry a rather frequent disregard for scientific evidence. Anecdotal evidence, instead of empirical findings, is sometimes being used as the basis of theories. Too ready acceptance of hypothetical symbols and mythological figures of speech serves to complicate the semantic problems of psychiatrists and particularly depth psychologists. Naturally, this situation makes for confusion, obscurity, misunderstandings, and mistrust. More and more voices, including some from among the depth psychologists themselves, are being raised in favor of clarity and a common language and against the would-be technicality, sophistication, and word-cult.

PSYCHOCATHARSIS

Historically, modern depth therapy goes back to the Viennese school of psychoanalysis founded by Sigmund Freud (1856–1939). A brief note on the early historical development of Freud's idea is probably the best introduction to an understanding of the psychoanalytic movement. Freud started his psychotherapeutic work on neurotic patients, mostly hysterical women, in collaboration with Joseph Breuer; the two partners at first used the psychocathartic method of treatment.

Psychocatharsis, the forerunner of psychoanalysis proper, is a technique enabling the patient to express his pent-up emotions fully by reliving hurtful or disagreeable experiences of the past and thus to "get them off his chest." It is a simpler form of treatment than psychoanalysis and is not so ambitious as to aim at the reintegration of the patient's personality, since it does not dig as deeply into the psyche. It does not enlarge upon the mechanisms and dynamisms of transference and repression but simply speaks of forgetting unpleasant experiences, and it knows nothing of ego, id, superego, ideal-ego, super-id, unconscious guilt, infantile longing for death, castration complexes, father-images, etc. Nevertheless, it may be said that psychocatharsis is analysis in an embryonic form.

The psychocathartic technique requires the patient, after relating an account of his life history, job, and family, to give the therapist a complete report of his complaints, his thoughts, mental images, fantasies, conflicts, wishes, desires, and memories. It often happens in the course of the interviews that the patient, wittingly or unwittingly, omits mentioning just those memories and mental conflicts which might be important for an understanding of his neurotic phenomena. Hence, the therapist should frequently repeat the advice that everything may be significant and that the patient, therefore, should report everything that comes to his mind. It would, however, be tactless to torture the patient from the very beginning with painful questions that go—as the therapist may believe—right to the point. And it would be naïve and harmful to give the patient an "insight" into his condition by forcing upon him some sort of schematic explanation of his complaints according to the physician's own theories.[3]

Much patience and tact are required to bring the client to a frank confession of all his experiences, and one can expect him to be quite reluctant at first. The therapist will be able to break down this resistance only by being tactful and by winning the patient's confidence. This confidential relationship between patient and therapist is the basis of the transference phenomena that are considered so important in psychoanalysis proper.

The psychocathartic procedure may be accompanied by light hypnosis. In fact, Breuer's treatment consisted in hypnocatharsis. Freud later rejected hypnosis as being inadequate. At the present time, however, hypnosis has been reintroduced as a therapeutic aid because it enables the therapist to use his power of suggestion; it is used in acute cases and is most valuable in some forms of hysterical behavior. Lately hypnosis has also been used in the technique of hypnoanalysis, which is a mixture of psychoanalysis and hypnosis.

The aim of the cathartic method, with or without hypnosis, is "abreaction." The reproduction into full consciousness of memories, representations, and emotional experiences makes the patient face them as they are. He will realize that they are less harmful than he imagined. He is made to reactivate and actually relive the psychotraumatic events of past life that were forgotten, suppressed, and not completely digested. Lived through again, the original experiences become "abreacted" together with the emotional component that caused the neurotic state.

In that manner, psychocatharsis has a purifying effect on the human mind; hence, the very name: κάθαρσις—purification. In his theory of tragedy, Aristotle expressed the same idea by pointing out that the arousal of pity and fear had a purifying effect on the audience.

Even though psychocatharsis supposedly fails to reach all the way down to the very roots of neurotic phenomena, the method often gives satisfactory results, especially when followed up by reassurance and other suggestive techniques.

Because of its purifying effect, psychocatharsis has been compared with confession. As a matter of fact, if confession, as it is known in the Catholic Church, can be compared with any therapeutic method, it is rather with psychocatharsis than with psychoanalysis.

FREUD'S PSYCHOANALYSIS

Since psychocatharsis scored good therapeutic results by exposing hurtful, forgotten, unresolved emotional experiences of past—mostly adult—life, Freud, in the period of his earlier work, was led to believe that these experiences were the cause of neuroses. But he was struck by an intriguing feature. Although forgotten, these experiences apparently were still active and able to exert so much influence on people's behavior that this influence could make them sick. The status of psychic material—thoughts, drives, memories, feelings—which is not actually conscious and yet influences human behavior might be called preconscious. In order to become conscious, such latent, peripheral mental contents needed only reactivation by way of recollection.

This discovery set Freud to thinking and led him to the concept of what is popularly called "the unconscious." Breaking with Breuer, he started his own theory of psychotherapy, which he called psychoanalysis. If the human mind, he theorized, harbors preconscious material, *i.e.*, contents that are forgotten and yet dynamic, it may well harbor completely unconscious contents which cannot be remembered by any direct way of recollection but which still exercise influence on our behavior. Once embarked upon this idea, Freud found, of course, what he sought and then laid the cornerstone of psychoanalysis.[4] His studies centered around these questions: How can we reach "the unconscious"? What is this unconscious material? What is it that keeps it from becoming conscious? In answering these questions, Freud built up the psychoanalytic movement, which began as a therapeutic method but soon developed into a full-fledged theory of individual mental life, and finally into a philosophical system embracing—at least in words—all the cultural contributions of mankind, such as social institutions, art, and religion.

In order to bring the unconscious mental material to the surface, Freud discarded—as has been said—hypnosis and devised two new techniques, those of free association and dream analysis.

Dreams are of basic interest to Freudian psychoanalysis because, as

Freud expressed it, they are the "royal road that leads to the unconscious," *i.e.*, dreams are supposed to reveal repressed material. But they often do so in a symbolic and distorted form. For dreams are incoherent and often violate the rules of probability as to time, place, and circumstance. As Freud observes, the dream resembles schizophrenia in that the word-image is divorced from the object-image. Hence, in order to discover the "latent" content, the dream should be analyzed. This is accomplished by the association technique and the interpretation of symbols. Some portions of the dream may be related to the previous day's happenings, but Freud maintains that, when one applies the free-association technique on the dream contents, they often prove to refer to experiences of the remote past. Therefore, Freud would present a certain dream item and request the subject to elaborate on it with everything that came to his mind; the subject was urged to hold nothing back, regardless of whether it made sense to him or not. With regard to the interpretation of symbols, Freud starts from the hypothesis that all dreams are attempts to wish fulfillment —wishes that concern biological drives, such as hunger, thirst, comfort, and particularly sex.

In later years, Jung considerably expanded the technique of free association by preparing in advance of a session with a subject a list of a hundred words. According to this procedure, word after word is presented to the subject who is asked to say the first thing with which he associates the word when he first sees it. Reaction time is measured, and exceptionally long reactions, lasting three seconds or more, are supposed to be significant. Therefore, the words leading to these long reactions are called critical words, as they appear to be related to memories which, for one reason or other, seem to be blocked. Besides, an unduly high percentage of peculiar, so-called individual, responses may be indicative of some mental disturbance. A standard list of such association words, widely used in the United States, is the one devised by Kent and Rosanoff.[5]

After collecting the data by means of his techniques, Freud proceeded to interpret them in the light of the theories that he gradually developed. The cases of hysterical women that Freud studied in the beginning of his career seemed to convey the impression that the preconscious contents of the mind which caused neurotic disturbances were practically always of a sexual nature. This idea impressed him deeply. However, when he started probing into the unconscious depths of the mind, he found that not only adult experiences but also early childhood experiences are often the cause of neurosis. In order to fit this discovery into his early conviction that neurosis had always something to do with sex, he was forced to broaden his concept of sexuality. And that he did to excess by formulating his libido (sex in a very wide sense of the word) theory. Although it is hard to find in Freud's works a consistent and clear-cut definition of this force, it certainly is closely related to the pleasure principle, which he considers the most basic psychodynamic force in human life. "In the psychoanalytic theory of mind," Freud says in "Beyond the Pleasure Principle," "we *take it for granted* that the cause of mental processes is automatically regulated by the pleasure principle." Hence, Freud takes for granted Epicurean or, rather, hedonistic philosophy. But in the hedonistic system the sex impulses play a large part. As a matter of fact, although libido, according to Freud, may manifest itself in the most sublime forms of love or in intellectual interests, any manifestation of it is, in the final analysis, derived from the sex instinct.

Sexual pleasure is not limited to that which the adult derives from the activity of the genitals, but, according to Freud, also includes childhood sexuality. The child, and even the infant, may experience sexual pleasure which centers around the oral, urethral, and anal zones. Thus, it may happen that eating, urination, and defecation have a sexual meaning, or as Freud put it, become "eroticized." According to psychoanalytic theory, the growing individual first passes through the period in which his sexual longings are directed toward the parents (the oral phase), then through the period in which he finds sexual gratification from his own body by masturbatory activities or from the same sex (the urethral or narcissistic and the anal phase), until, finally, the libido takes on its mature and normal form by settling on the opposite sex.

However, during the sexual development of the growing child to adolescence and adult age, various important complications may arise. In the first place, the child and the adolescent may repress or suppress his sexual impulses, and such repressions and suppressions may later be the cause of serious neurotic disorders, as will be explained hereafter.

Further, the normal development may be blocked by the process of *fixation*. The individual's psychosexual development may become arrested at the earliest stage of parent-attachment; in that case, the so-called *Oedipus complex* may develop. Sometimes the individual may revert from the normal to an earlier phase of the libido; this is called *regression*. The psychoanalysts cite as an example of regression to the oral phase the case of alcoholics.

The Oedipus complex—the Electra complex is the feminine equivalent

—is named from a Greek legend in which Oedipus unknowingly kills his father and marries his own mother, with dire consequences. In the old Greek plays, this behavior was represented as coming about through the blind determination of fate. Oedipus, the son of Laius and Jocasta, King and Queen of Thebes, is exposed as a suckling because an oracle had informed the father that his son, who was still unborn, would be his murderer. Oedipus is rescued and grows up as a king's son at a foreign court until, being uncertain of his origin, he, too, consults the oracle and is warned to avoid his native city where he is destined to become the murderer of his father and the husband of his mother. On the road leading away from his supposed home, he meets King Laius and, in a sudden quarrel, strikes him dead. He comes to Thebes, where he solves the riddle of the Sphinx who is barring the way to the city. Thereupon he is elected king by the grateful Thebans and is rewarded with the hand of Jocasta. After he reigns many years in peace and honor and begets two sons and two daughters by his unknown mother, a plague breaks out, and the consulted oracle reveals the tragedy.

In the psychoanalytic sense, the Oedipus complex is a sexual attraction of the child to the parent of the opposite sex, though it is not quite clear why analysts regard this phase of the child's life as an origin of guilt in later life. Many psychoneurotic symptoms and sexual aberrations are regarded as being caused by an unresolved Oedipus complex.

Conflicts are also caused by the *castration complex,* which means that boys are afraid of being castrated; they have a fear of losing the penis as a source of erotic pleasure. This fear is regarded by Freud as a general fear resulting from childhood deprivation of pleasure when, for example, the child was weaned from the breast or from the bottle. The castration complex is supposed to play a role in the life of girls, too, but evidently in a different way. According to Freud, the girl, not having a penis, either assumes that she must have had one and lost it, or, since the clitoris seems to have a function similar to the penis, the child expects that the clitoris will later grow into a penis.

The castration complex has been attacked more than any other concept in Freud's psychoanalysis. What is more, the very concept of the libido as being the only driving force of human nature has always been met by considerable doubt, even among Freud's first disciples. The libido concept was the bone of contention that sent Alfred Adler from Freud's flock to start his own system, which proclaimed that the will-to-power or self-assertion is the most fundamental human drive. Shaken by this opposition,

Freud, in "Beyond the Pleasure Principle," proposed two classes of basic driving forces: eros and thanatos.

Eros, the life instinct, involves self-preservation and coincides to a considerable extent with libido. *Thanatos,* the death instinct, is the tendency that man shows to turn against himself: like all living beings, he gradually tends toward the nonliving state. If this tendency assumes catastrophic proportions suicide results.

Into this division Freud fits the sexual perversions of *masochism* and *sadism.* Although some people like to punish or maltreat themselves even to the point of self-mutilation, few people go so far as to destroy themselves by suicide. Hence, in psychoanalytic terminology, thanatos is impeded or inhibited by eros. Besides, the death instinct may turn from inflicting pain on one's own person to inflicting it on others, and then sadism appears. But few sadists go so far as to kill their victims; hence, again the death instinct is opposed and softened by eros. Therefore both kinds of perversions result from a mixture or fusion of the two primeval drives.

Freud's attempt to meet the opposition against the monopoly of the libido by introducing the death instinct has not proved popular. Even among the psychoanalysts there are few who believe this a felicitous finding. It is true that some persons suffering from endogenous melancholy sometimes exhibit a suicidal drive; moreover, some conditions of constitutional depression, as it appears in old age and during the critical period of puberty, may present symptoms of a death tendency. But such cases are far from being a sufficient basis on which to claim the existence of a universal death instinct as the counterpart of a life instinct.

Several writers, therefore, believe that if Freud's mysterious and unattractive thanatos means anything, it simply coincides with aggression turned against one's own self.[6] This concept of aggression has drawn considerable attention in the later development of psychoanalysis.

When Freud tried to free the mind's unconscious libidinal contents, which were supposed to be the cause of the individual's mental troubles, he found that he had to overcome a certain resistance on the part of the patient. Hence, there seemed to be a force that impeded the entry of the unconscious, mostly sexual, contents into consciousness. Since the unconscious contents were presumed to be of an immoral, libidinous character, the repressing force seemed to act as the guardian of morality, and Freud, therefore, gave it at first the name of *censor.*

Introducing new terms and enlarging upon the concept of repression, Freud presented in his "The Ego and the Id," a topographic-dynamic view, dividing the human psyche into three departments, the id, the ego, and the superego, each of which influences the others. The *id* is the sum total of innate, instinctive strivings, for the most part of libidinal nature, blindly seeking satisfaction; it is the primary reservoir of energy, supplying the driving force of mental life and motivating the individual to do "what he wants, when he wants." The *ego* is the phenomenological center of the human personality, the conscious part of the human psyche, the source of synthesized perception, conscious thoughts, conscious feelings, and voluntary movements. The *superego* is a new name for what Freud previously called censor. Hence, the superego is the mentor, the watchman of morality, the subjective moral norm. To avoid misunderstanding, a brief description of its functions is *à propos*.

In the first place, the superego fulfills the role of what in common language is called the conscience, which passes judgment on our conscious thoughts, feelings, and actions; hence, this function is of the conscious level. Many psychoanalysts soft-pedal this important role of the superego, but several present-day analysts clearly state this function.

However, the psychoanalytic concept of the superego is larger: it also comprises an important unconscious component. The superego is supposed to repress, prohibit, postpone, and direct the inadmissible wishes, desires, and drives which make up the id and therefore are not conscious. All, or practically all, these activities take place on the unconscious level.

Since one of the most important functions is repression, this concept requires some clarification. Repression is not the same as suppression. *Repression* is the process of inhibition that keeps the unconscious mental contents outside the sphere of consciousness. To a large extent this process is unconscious. But it happens that some of those unconscious contents which are unacceptable to the recognized ethical or social standards of the individual—*e.g.*, bad thoughts and desires—succeed in penetrating into consciousness. If they do, the individual may do one of three things: he may nurture them; he may sublimate them by directing the energy attached to them into constructive channels; or he may suppress them—*i.e.*, dismiss them from consciousness. Likewise, he may suppress painful, unpleasant experiences or memories. Hence, the process of *suppression* takes place on the conscious level. Because the suppressed material once has been conscious, it is pushed back into the preconscious sphere rather than into the unconscious sphere of the mind. Suppression, particularly when it takes place under emotional strain, may cause mental trouble. Whereas suppression is a defense mechanism of the mind operating on the conscious level, repression is the primary defense mechanism of the mind operating on the unconscious level. In his autobiography, Freud showed that he was quite proud of the discovery of unconscious repression, for he wrote that this process was "a novelty and nothing like it had ever before been recognized in mental life."

At this juncture, one may well ask what reasons psychoanalysts have for postulating the existence of an agency that operates outside the conscious sphere to repress, oppose, postpone, or direct unconscious drives and desires. Their answer is that the acceptance of a repressing force, unconsciously operating on unconscious drives, explains the otherwise mysterious origin of many neurotic reactions.

The instinctual drives, hidden in the unconscious reservoir of the id but ever claiming satisfaction, constantly clash with the repressing force that opposes their entry into consciousness. Hence, there originates an intrapsychic, unconscious conflict whose exact nature the individual does not know. But, as a result, he exhibits abnormal or socially unacceptable behavior. Such conflicts, when not solved satisfactorily, may cause psychic maladjustments or neurotic conditions. The psychoanalysts therefore conclude that, in order to understand the pathogenic elements in the origin of neurotic disturbances, it is necessary to admit the existence of an unconsciously dynamic id clashing with an unconsciously operating repressing force.

Just because the superego represses the id's strivings that continually try to hew their way through to the conscious ego, the ego's integrity is endangered. Then the ego becomes the battleground, so to speak, between the id and the superego. However, for the most part, the ego is not conscious of the conflict itself, but may become conscious of its effects, *i.e.*, of the smoke and the fumes, figuratively speaking, that ascend from the battlefield and make the ego mentally sick. By way of illustration, we may take the diseased functioning of conscience in compulsive neuroses, *e.g.*, scrupulosity. According to the psychoanalytic explanation, such a condition is understandable if one assumes that one of the roles of the superego is that of self-punishment and penance on the unconscious level.

The fact that the censor or superego functions even during dreams was one of the main arguments that Freud used to show the unconscious character of the processes just mentioned. Inadmissible desires emerging from the unconscious may sometimes reach the level of consciousness in dreams, but it must be that they can do so only by outwitting the censor, because they present themselves in the disguise of symbols.

Obviously, this explanation of the origin of neurosis is more penetrating than the one Freud advanced in the first part of his career when he applied the psychocathartic method. At that stage, he considered the cause of neuroses to be the suppression of hurtful experiences. Later, without repudiating this opinion, he conceived the basic reason for neurotic reactions to be principally the conflict between the repressing force and the unventilated, unconscious thoughts and desires.

Of the greatest importance for the understanding of Freudian psychoanalysis is the way Freud and his followers explain the origin of the superego. Whereas the id and the ego are inborn, the superego is acquired or rather superimposed upon the psyche. The superego derives in the first place from a process of introjection; in other words, the individual incorporates into his own mind the moral and social standards which his parents and teachers taught him in his youth and which society teaches him all through life. The individual identifies himself with the persons he admires and loves, particularly his parents, and this self-identification induces the growing personality to forbid and command himself all those things that previously his environment had forbidden or commanded him. It should be noted, too, that the persons—his parents, particularly—who inculcate the individual with moral precepts are objects of love. And since all love is one way or other libidinal, the superego owes its origin in the final analysis to the libido.

The idealization of other persons as the source of the superego is reinforced by the idealization of self. The individual loves himself, but he feels that self with all its imperfections is hardly worth loving. Therefore, he sublimates his love of self, as he visualizes himself as the perfect self that he should or might be. In that manner, the ego-ideal comes into existence as a component of the superego. Again, it should be noted that love of self is the narcissistic form of the libido; hence, again, the ego-ideal is a product of the libido.

Although many psychoanalysts use the terms "superego" and "ego-ideal" interchangeably, others prefer to give them a differentiating connotation. Alexander, for instance, uses in his earlier work the term "superego" to indicate the unconscious component and ascribes to this force the function of watchdog, which warns the ego not to submit to the demands of the id. On the other hand he prefers to employ the term "ego-ideal" for the conscious component, to which he ascribes the positive functions of controlling and directing the instinctual drives toward constructive goals.[7] To complicate matters still further, some writers suggest that the more unconscious irrational component of the superego should be called super-id.

The Freudian explanation had its repercussion on the conception of conscience. If conscience may be considered as the rational, conscious component of the superego, it follows that conscience, too, comes into existence according to the psychoanalysts through the introjection of the parental figures and the creation of an ego-ideal. This means that conscience is the purely subjective product of the individual. Moreover, the superego or ego-ideal is not only the subjective norm of morality, but, for Freud and most psychoanalysts, it is the only norm. There is no objective norm of moral behavior. This very important point will be taken up again in connection with the evaluation of depth psychologies.

The superego concept has not only a theoretical value in the explanation of the dynamics of the human personality, but also a practical application in the psychoanalytical techniques. These techniques are, of course, ultimately based on the rapport between the analyst and the analysand, but in psychoanalysis this relationship takes on a special aspect. Whereas in psychocatharsis and other types of psychotherapy it is enough that the patient regard the therapist as the knowing, benevolent, powerful, expert helper in distress, psychoanalysis confers upon the analyst a still more important role. To arrive at any satisfactory analysis, the physician must become in the eyes of the patient the representative of the superego; because the superego is the introjected image of the parents, the physician thus represents the patient's parents. This process of the patient projecting upon the analyst his superego and the parent-image constitutes *transference* in the analytical sense of the word.

The analyst represents the loving, helpful parents (positive transference) as well as the forbidding and commanding parents (negative transference), and the patient should respond with the corresponding love or fear. Psychoanalysis considers the transference phenomena as crucially important, because it aims at a change of the superego which, by virtue of its harsh dictates, is supposed to be the main cause of the patient's troubles. But this change can be effected only by the physician's taking over, at least temporarily, the role of the superego, because by doing so, he will be able to weaken the harsh demands of the superego. Later in the treatment, this parent-regarding attitude of the patient must gradually be broken down, because the patient must learn independence.

Overlooking at first the emotional factors in the relationship between psychiatrist and patient, Freud came only later to a realization of its importance. In more recent years, the transference technique has, in certain psychoanalytical quarters, become so important that it almost supersedes the exposure techniques, *i.e.*, those which attempt to uncover the subconscious contents of the patient's mind.

Since psychoanalytic theory holds that neurotic disturbances are due to the blocking of vital drives (libido) by a repressing force, it follows that the primary goal of Freud's psychoanalytic therapy is the release of these vital (libidinal) energies and the recognition of their right of existence. This therapeutic approach is sometimes called the inner-release approach. Chapter 10 will take up the question of whether the inner release approach is a satisfactory therapeutic procedure.

Freudian psychoanalysis has become popular. The main reason for that popularity is that its therapy often succeeds. The "new psychology" introduced by Wundt and at first greeted with enthusiasm has caused ever more disappointment. The laboratory psychology never became popular. Who but a few professional psychologists is interested in the Weber-Fechner law, the phi phenomenon, the conditioned responses of the white rat, or the gamma hypothesis? Factorial analysis certainly produced important results, but it has been said that it threatens to degenerate into a mathematical hide-and-seek game of nonexistent factors whose nonentity is cloaked in an unintelligible name before which only the finder stands in reverent awe. The most promising and most practical methods of psychology are without doubt the testing methods; they have proved to be of great practical value, though some people feel somewhat disappointed in them because they believe that the testing techniques have not yet solved satisfactorily the most important problem of all psychology, personality.

Psychoanalysis and other depth psychologies, on the other hand, precisely claim to reveal the innermost dynamics of personality. Moreover, these types of psychology have been shown to score successes, regardless of whether their theoretical concepts are right or wrong. By introducing the unconscious, they reintroduced consciousness—a concept that the behaviorists had thrown out of psychology.

The danger inherent in the Freudian system is its sensational appeal to sex-minded people. It threatens to become too popular, inasmuch as it seems to turn into some sort of parlor-psychology. The untrained seem to gather from it only one lesson; *i.e.*, that one should refrain from all moral inhibitions lest he become neurotic. Parents are afraid of imposing any discipline on their children lest they might create repression. When someone mispronounces a word, he is supposed to have a complex. And no longer does anyone simply forget something; he is repressing it, preferably for libidinal reasons. Much of this is due to a gross misinterpretation of the analytic systems; however, it is true that several of these systems do include basic errors, as will be seen in the chapter on evaluation.

ADLER'S INDIVIDUAL PSYCHOLOGY

Alfred Adler (1870–1937), one of the early associates of Freud and one of the first to deviate from the master, gave his system the name of "individual psychology." [8] He differs from Freud in regard to the philosophical basis as well as in regard to the methodological approach. The basic driving force of human nature is not the libido, according to Adler, but the will-to-power. He, therefore, traces the origin of neurotic and even psychotic disturbances in an individual back to an exaggerated, but frustrated, drive to dominate. This is particularly true with individuals who suffer from corporeal inferiority, either organic or functional. The feeling of inferiority and lowered self-esteem may drive such individuals to overcompensation and a fight for self-assertion. When the struggle for superiority overtaxes the individual's psychic strength, when his superiority proves to be a fiction but he desperately holds on to the fiction, he may fall victim to depression, rebellion, hostility, and aggressive tendencies. The will-to-power, however, is not restricted to those who suffer from bodily inferiority but is a universal tendency; hence, neurotic reactions may also appear in a person whose bodily condition is quite normal but whose urge to dominate is too intense or frustrated.

Adler's therapeutic approach, too, is very different from Freud's original ideas about therapy. The aim of individual psychology is decidedly psychagogic or reeducative. Adler feels that it is not enough to show the patient what is wrong with him by unfolding the snares of the urge-to-power, but he advises him that he cannot disentangle himself unless he reeducates himself with the assistance and under the guidance of the analyst. Adler, therefore, tries to foster in his patients feelings of fellowship to the neglect of egotistic drives to power. Self-assertion and will-to-power are not wrong in themselves, on condition that they are used in the interest of the community. Hence, environmental factors occupy an important place in Adler's program.

Although Adler's power-principle is more fundamental than Freud's libido principle and Adler's therapy is more helpful than Freud's, the Adlerian movement has not been perpetuated in the form of a school;

nevertheless, Adler's ideas have been incorporated into several other systems of depth psychology.

JUNG'S ANALYTICAL PSYCHOLOGY

Carl G. Jung (1875–), another of Freud's early pupils, is the founder of the Zurich school of depth psychology that he himself calls *analytical psychology.*[9] The reasons why Jung left the Freudian mother church are, like those of Adler, both theoretical and methodological, but Jung's theoretical objections go deeper than Adler's and concern one of the fundamental problems of philosophy.

Freud's philosophical outlook—his outlook on life and personality not excluded—is mechanistic, whereas Jung's is finalistic, teleological, or—as those who suffer from teleophobia prefer to say—functional.

According to mechanists, one knows a thing when one knows what it is made of; hence, all one has to do in order to understand a thing—life and psyche not excluded—is to analyze it, breaking it down into its component elements. The sum total of these elements will give the complete picture of that thing.

The finalist, or functionist, holds that the mechanical composition of a thing leaves the picture incomplete and that it should be supplemented by knowledge of the purpose of that thing—*i.e.*, what it is for, what it intends to do, what function it serves.

The opposition of these two philosophies may be illustrated by an example. Suppose Roger Bacon, or St. Albert the Great, or any one of their contemporaries who liked to play with mechanical toys, came upon a modern tank in medieval Oxford or Paris. They might break up the machine so as to see what the elements were that went into the making of it. But all their tiresome work of reducing the machine to its constituent parts and subsequently reassembling them would not reveal the kind of monster they had come upon, unless they knew what it was made for. They would miss its meaning unless they knew its purpose.

Now Jung, in contrast to Freud, holds that the meaning of life, and particularly of the human psyche, is also to be found in its function or purpose. This conviction is reflected in his concept of analysis.

He calls analysis in the Freudian sense causal analysis, but he points out that this gives only a retrospective understanding of the human psyche, because Freud, analyzing the present condition of a person, discovers only what the *past* has made of him or what he has made of himself in the *past.* Jung concedes that the picture of a human personality as it came about through the events of the past is of great importance. But it is not enough. Equally important is a functional, prospective understanding of a personality, *i.e.*, the knowledge of what the psyche is aiming at in the *future*.

"A person is only half understood," Jung says,[10] "when one knows how everything in him came about. Only a dead man can be explained in terms of the past; a living one must be otherwise explained. Life is not made up of yesterday only, nor is it understood nor explained by reducing today to yesterday. Life has also a tomorrow and today is only understood if we are able to add the indications of tomorrow to our knowledge of what was yesterday."

Where does Jung find "the indications of tomorrow"? He believes that his functional analysis finds the elements of prospective understanding in the collective psyche.

Jung has considerably extended the concept of the unconscious psyche. Freud was mainly concerned with the individual unconscious, *i.e.*, the repressed libidinal drives; Adler was mostly interested in the personal urge to power. According to Jung, these individual drives are but two among many others. In his view, the unconscious also comprises supra-individual contents. Terming the totality of these contents the collective psyche, Jung included in it the primitive animal drives and all the experiences of the human species from its very beginning; the collective psyche harbors, so to speak, the history of mankind. Jung considers the existence of the collective psyche to be borne out by the fact that its elements, as they reveal themselves in dreams, myths, and legends, show a striking similarity among the most heterogeneous peoples and races.

These archaic residues, as found in the collective psyche of every individual, are called archetypes; they are the unconscious fundamental strivings, thoughts, impulses, and dispositions which form, so to speak, the reservoir of man's psychic potentialities or dynamics. His immanent striving toward self-development in connection with external factors will actualize some of these potential dispositions, but others will remain unconscious. In this fact, Jung finds the explanation of the origin of both neurosis and psychosis.

The psychosis is, according to Jung, a regression of the person back to the primitive stage of the collective psyche. When the mind turns insane, it retraces in reverse order the stages of development of the animal race. This regression does not stop at the infantile level of the human species but proceeds all the way down the phylogenetic ladder to the most primitive stage.

As for neuroses, Jung, in contrast to Freud, refuses to believe that they spring from a conflict between unconscious libidinal impulses and an unconscious moral censor. For Jung, neurotic behavior is due to a kind of lopsidedness in the actual development of the potentialities of the collective psyche. When certain potentialities are developed at the expense of others, which should have been developed so as to counterbalance the former, the personality lacks harmony, balance, or synthesis; and this lack of synthesis may result in neurotic behavior. Overdevelopment of libidinal tendencies at the expense of moral constraint, overdevelopment of the will-to-power at the expense of social feelings, unilateral emphasis of cognitive life at the expense of affective life, undue accentuation of extrovert at the expense of introvert traits—all such disturbances in the course of the natural development of the psyche may create neurotic and psychotic conditions.

As the collective psyche offers the explanation of the origin of neuroses, it likewise gives us the elements of treatment. If lack of synthesis is the cause of neurosis, resynthesis should be the aim of psychotherapy. Although an individual has actually developed exclusively extrovert traits, yet introvert traits have maintained themselves in a simple form on a primitive level of the psyche. The impulses, thoughts, and dispositions of the unconscious which were neglected or not properly utilized should be activated and employed in the service of the individual's future, more harmonious, development. These contents of the unconscious are not only signs of past experiences (as Freud thought in his dream symbolism) but also (in Jung's view) indications of what the individual is able to do in the future. In this manner, the archetypes become symbols that point the way for further development. How do we know which archetypical potentialities are hidden in a particular individual? Jung's answer is that they reveal themselves in his dreams.

Jung gave a new impetus to the interpretation of dream symbolism. Comparing the contents of the dream with the primitive thinking of humanity as it appears in myths, legends, and primitive rituals, he thought that he was observing a great likeness. He therefore concluded that the dream is a primitive form of thinking, for as soon as consciousness is reduced, primitive thinking in its archetypical form takes over, and this reduction of consciousness occurs in the dream. He found a confirmation of his concept in the fact that the thinking of those whose consciousness is impaired, as in the case of psychotics, takes on a very primitive or archetypical form.

Jung declares that whenever psychic harmony or balance is broken, the individual strives toward restoring that balance in his dream thinking. It is therefore the task of psychotherapy to interpret the symbols (archetypes) of a patient's dreams in order to show him which potentialities he harbors in his unconscious psyche. Among these dream symbols Jung also finds religious symbols. His attitude toward religion differs greatly from Freud's. Whereas for Freud religion is an obsessional neurosis that humanity should outgrow as soon as possible, Jung believes in the function of religion. However, it would be an altogether mistaken notion to think that Jung considers or uses religion in the same sense as the priest or the theologian does.[11] Jung professes to have no interest in the question of whether religious dogmas are true or false, whether God exists in reality or not; he is interested only in the psychological value of religion. By analyzing his patient's collective psyche and by interpreting its dream symbolism, he claims that he finds moral concepts; he finds also that the Deity exists as an archetypical image in his patient's psyche, and he turns these symbols to good advantage in the treatment.[12]

This exposition of Jung's system discloses that he strongly emphasizes the value of psychosynthesis. Whereas Freud expects all salvation from mere analysis, Jung holds that in most cases analysis will not yield lasting results if it is not followed up by a rebuilding process based on the materials that the analysis has laid bare. And he finds, too, among these materials, elements that bear a moral and religious label. But then the aim of psychotherapy takes on the character of a radical change.

RANK'S WILL THERAPY

Otto Rank (1884–1939), also one of Freud's original disciples, left the Freudian group in the twenties. He himself avoided choosing a special name for his ideas, but others sometimes refer to them as Rankism.[13]

Rank's theoretical deviations from Freud concern the origin of neurosis. Rank emphasized, much to Freud's dislike, the birth trauma as the important cause of neurotic reactions. At the moment of birth, the child leaves the "pleasurable situation in the womb" to start a new type of life which is painful in many respects. This change leaves a trauma in the child's psyche, and Rank believed that neurotics are persons who in their childhood did not succeed in overcoming the birth trauma.

From the standpoint from which this book is written, Rank's practical therapeutic innovations are of greater interest. Aside from minor variations, such as advocating briefer methods than Freud used, he considered the will as a very important factor in psychotherapy.

It happens that mental patients sometimes come for help to the physician without actually wanting to get well; they would rather hang on to their neurotic condition. Wilhelm Stekel even considered most neurotics to belong to that type, but the data of other psychiatrists contradict Stekel's generalization. Rank was one of the very first to call attention to the patient's will to health (*Gesundheitswille*) and to make use of it in the therapeutic procedure. He agreed with Freud that analysis helps to make the patient understand his condition, but he held that the patient is far from being cured by simply submitting to analysis and leaving the entire treatment up to the analyst. Rank believed that in many cases the patient's personal effort to take himself in hand will turn the trick, but he knew that the therapist has to help him to make that effort, because experience tells us that even though the patient may have come to the physician with a sincere willingness to get well, this will to health gradually will fade during the treatment. The patient, in other words, projects his own will onto the analyst, confident that he, the expert, will take care of everything. Rank's therapeutic aim, therefore, was to break down this projection and to stimulate the patient to help himself. Abstracting from the question whether or not Rank regarded the will as a spiritual faculty, the main point is that he did not reduce the will to a sexual drive, as Freud did. Will activity, Rank said, is not sexuality as psychoanalysis assumed, "but an actually anti-sexual tendency in men which we have characterized as a voluntary control of the instinctive life." [14] By assigning to the will the function of controlling instinctive life, he obviously opposed the latter to the former. Hence, Rank also disagreed with Jung, who derives every striving toward a goal from the unconscious psyche.

Rank's therapeutic ideas have penetrated into many psychoanalytic circles. Naturally, since most psychiatrists are afraid of anything that smacks of the will, they rather avoid the term "will therapy," but they apply the technique just the same. In so doing, however, they deviate from orthodox Freudianism.

EXISTENTIAL ANALYSIS

Under this name a new type of depth psychotherapy has gained a number of followers in Europe in recent years. One of its strongest supporters is

Viktor E. Frankl, professor of psychiatry at Vienna.[15] Although these analysts are closer to Jung than to Freud, they go far beyond Jung.

They maintain that existential analysis, by using such techniques as free association and dream interpretation, is able to discover the spirit—*i.e.,* moral and religious thoughts and values—even when treating irreligious people who are, or profess to be, unconscious of such values. Even though these values are at times hidden deep down in the unconscious, the existential analysts strongly emphasize the fact that they should be interpreted as belonging not to the Freudian id or the Jungian collective psyche, but to the unconscious forces of the ego. According to their theory, not only the instinctive, but also the spiritual, life may be unconscious. They also hold that people sometimes become mentally disturbed because they fail to realize, or have repressed, these unconscious values within themselves. Hence, in such cases the task of psychotherapy is to make the patient conscious of these forces. Whereas psychoanalysis is only concerned about making the unconscious id conscious, existential analysis aims at bringing to the conscious level something very different—man's own spiritual existence. Such analysis further maintains that the spiritual can be neither derived from, nor reduced to, the instinctive life of the id. Time and again, the existential analysts argue against Freud that the instinctive id is not the only source of psychodynamics in man, because they refuse to be deluded into the belief that man is a sublimated animal as long as they can prove that he hides within himself a repressed angel.

They stress the unitary character of human personality as being equally important. Freud's lasting contribution was, they concede, that he ventured, in an age of prudery, to show that sexual instincts are among the most important factors in the psychic life of man and that they may greatly disturb the human psyche. Freud's most fundamental mistake, however, was to view a person as a machine, a set of mechanisms, and to consider the psychoanalyst as a technician or mechanic who is supposed to mend these mechanisms when they function badly. Because of his mechanistic view, Freud depersonalized the unitary human being: he atomized it. He never ceased analyzing: he broke down the id into several drives, these in turn, were reduced into partial drives, and he ended by thinking that he found a number of components in each partial drive. Likewise, he atomized the ego into various ego-drives. Freud made a schizophrenic out of every individual by assuming him to be just a sum of split personalities. Existential analysis, on the other hand, holds that the human being is a unit; even though it may possess components, they are bound together by the spiritual ego. Its main thesis is "I *am* a person, and I *have* an id," and they add "I *have* a conscience."

For the existential analysts, the existence of conscience is the stepping-stone to arriving at man's religious nature. They oppose conscience to consciousness by saying that, whereas we are conscious of what is, conscience is concerned with what must be but is not yet. Now, the anticipation of what later must be, requires intuition. Therefore, conscience is an intuitive function, *i.e.*, it acts on the irrational level. Hence, they agree with the psychoanalysts that conscience, the superego, the ego-ideal, involves irrational unconscious elements. However, they disagree with both Freud and Jung in holding that conscience cannot be derived from either the id or the ego. Psychoanalysis has made the attempt to reduce conscience—according to its terminology, the superego—to the id, because the origin of the superego is due to an introjection of the parental image and the parental image itself is supposed to be a product of the libidinal id. The existential analysts find this explanation utterly contradictory: the superego cannot be derived from instinctive life, libidinal or other, because it is inconceivable that the instinctive drives repress, censure, or sublimate themselves.

Going a long step further, the existential analysis rejects any subjectivistic or psychologistic interpretation concerning the origin of conscience. One cannot derive the superego from the ego because, again, it is a sheer contradiction to assume the ego to be its own lawgiver or be responsible to itself. How, then, do the existential analysts explain the origin of conscience? Before answering this question, they first point out where and how they find conscience. They hold that the "voice of conscience" is often revealed by the interpretation of the dreams of their patients (*existenzanalytische Traumdeutung*). They consider it a mere prejudice to assume that every dream implicitly contains some infantile sexual elements. On the contrary, the existential analysts claim to show that, in a considerable number of dream cases, the most natural interpretation is that the dream reflects the voice of conscience. The irreligious person, according to existential analysis, is one who denies or fails to appreciate the transcendental character of conscience. He, too, *has* a conscience, and deep down in his psyche he feels responsibility. But he does not worry, at least apparently, about the origin of conscience. Whenever he hears its voice, he tells himself that it is just something that he himself has built up in himself. However, one may well ask whether his assumption is correct.

After having established conscience as a psychological phenomenon, the existential analysts start to reason about it. The very function of conscience is its censor function; it exhorts man to obey its voice. But it does not make sense that one should obey himself. Therefore, conscience must be something superior to man. The individual hears and perhaps listens to the voice of conscience, but conscience does not derive from him; it transcends human nature, it derives from a superhuman source. Conscience cannot be explained unless we take into consideration its transcendental character. The existential analysts feel unable from their own standpoint to decide what the nature of this superhuman source is, but they surmise that it is God, *i.e.*, a personal God.

Thus, the ethical problem turns into a religious one, into the problem concerning man's relationship to God. With regard to religion, the existential analysts once more disagree fully with Freud and Jung. They fail to see on what grounds psychoanalysis contends that God is a mere father-image. It is true that, ontogenetically and biologically speaking, the father is the first in the life of the child, but the psychoanalysts have no reason whatever to stop at this point. The fact that the father is biologically the first in relation to the child does not disprove in the least that God is ontologically the first in relation to the child and the father too. Existential analysis therefore states that God is not a father-image but that the father is an image of God, and that the proof of this statement lies in the fact that an unprejudiced analysis of the unconscious depth of a man's psyche reveals his relation to God. Even when treating persons who profess to be decidedly irreligious, the existential analysts find what they call unconscious religion. By this they mean an unconscious relationship to God. They use here the term "unconscious God" (*der unbewuszte Gott*). This somewhat cryptic term does not imply that God is unconscious of Himself but that an individual is sometimes unconscious of his relation to God. So the existential analysts conclude that there is something like unconscious religion.

Since Jung also found religious elements within the sphere of the unconscious, there exists a point of agreement between him and existential analysis. But that is as far as the agreement goes, for the latter completely rejects Jung's concept of religion. Existential analysts point out that Jung and his followers consider the unconscious religious elements as ultimately belonging to the domain of the id; as the Jungians speak of the sexual and the aggressive drive, so they speak of a religious drive. According to them, these religious elements are inborn in man, since all the so-called archetypes of the collective psyche are innate, hereditary residues.

The existential analysts find fault with each one of these Jungian statements. First, they deny that the religious elements belong to the id, as we have seen. Second, because religion is within the sphere of man's most personal decisions, it cannot originate in a collective unconscious. Finally, religion cannot be inborn because it is nothing biological. Looked upon from the purely natural standpoint, it presents itself to the individual in the form of admonitions, examples, and ceremonies of his environment.

The existential analysts are convinced that in many cases mental disturbances are due precisely to unconscious or repressed religion. Their standpoint is that of Freud, but in reverse order. When Freud says that religion is the universal compulsive neurosis of humanity, the existential analysts maintain that compulsive neurosis is often diseased religion, and they give numerous examples of case histories to bear out the statement. They find, in many cases, a deficiency in the neurotic individual—*i.e.*, they find that his relationship to things transcendental is disturbed or repressed—and they believe that the individual's unrest and neurotic symptoms are signs of this disturbance.

On the basis of the premise thus far laid bare, existential analysis sees its task in making the neurotic person conscious of his responsibility. Of course, responsibility does not make sense unless the person knows for what he is responsible, and to whom. In other words, existential analysis aims at making an individual conscious of his human destiny, the meaning of his existence, for responsibility is precisely one of the main attributes of human existence. The very meaning of a human being consists not in being driven by some id, but in being a responsible person. Because the final scope of this psychotherapy consists in making an individual conscious of the meaning of his existence, it is called existential analysis. It should be added that this system remains solely on the empirical level and avoids the metaphysical implications of existential philosophy.

The reader may have noticed that the authors have described existential analysis with a good deal of sympathy, and indeed, while certain points may not be acceptable or may be expressed in an obscure way by the defenders of the system, it yet contains many valuable elements.

DEPTH PSYCHOLOGY IN THE UNITED STATES

Although there are a small group of Jungians and a few Rankists among the depth psychologists in the United States, the great majority profess themselves to belong to the Freudian school, and the majority of these profess to be orthodox. The question is sometimes raised as to how orthodox an analyst, or a group of analysts, is. From the standpoint of this book, it is of little importance to know how far an analyst or a group of analysts is allowed, in theory or practice, to deviate from Freud before being branded as heretical. Besides, the authors would scarcely be in a position to decide the question. It would need some sort of an infallible Freudian pope to define the true Freudian gospel or to pronounce the anathema over a heretic.[16] Yet psychoanalysis, as it exists at present in the United States, presents many variations and dissensions from the original Freudian system. In the first place, there are many instances in which Jungian and Adlerian elements have been incorporated into the Freudian system. It may be debated whether this incorporation is that of a simple addition or an assimilation. Some may call such modifications a sign of progress; others may call it eclecticism. Moreover in several groups one finds a tendency to reject or mitigate the very basis of Freudian psychoanalysis, *i.e.,* the libido theory. These newer orientations, under the influence of anthropology, sociology, and behavioristic psychology, stress the importance of the environment in the formation of personality and character. Personality dynamics, they hold, are not only to be found in the instinctive id, but also—and perhaps even more so—in environmental factors, particularly interpersonal relations. By the same token, they pay less attention to Freud's libido and its infantile sexuality in the production of neurotic personalities. Instead of stressing internal conflicts arising from the clash between the libido and the superego, as Freud did, they lay greater stress on external conflicts. By these, they mean conflicts that may arise between a person and his social or cultural surroundings. They therefore see the main reason of neurosis in a person's inability to adapt himself satisfactorily to his environment. It may be noted in passing that the choice of the term "external conflict" is not particularly fortunate. It may well be that the cause of a person's conflict is partially due to external circumstances, but that does not make the conflict itself external; the conflict that makes a person neurotic is itself obviously internal. The facts just mentioned make it clear that there are groups of analysts who seem to dissent considerably from Freud. The majority of American analysts, however, still strongly advocate the libidinal-conflict theory as the cornerstone of psychoanalysis. The following pages will give a brief description of some of the main groups of psychotherapists in the United States.

Several writers are mentioned as the spokesmen of the more orthodox psychoanalysts, among them Karl A. Menninger. And the preceding chapter cited the group of analysts who, under the leadership of Carl Rogers, advocate nondirective therapy. This group may probably also be called "orthodox," inasmuch as it carries out Freud's inner-release program almost to the letter.

The Association for the Advancement of Psychoanalysis was initiated by Karen Horney. When she left Europe, Horney was an orthodox psychoanalyst, but after arriving in America, she gradually began to cast off or to reform several traditional Freudian theories and practices.[17]

When speaking of basic anxiety, Horney traces it back to an infantile origin. However, she does not interpret this origin in the sense of the Freudian infantile sexuality, but rather along the lines of interpersonal relations. In his long, helpless, insecure infancy and youth, the child has acquired an attitude of dependency on parental love and care. In later life, society takes over the place of the parents, and unless an individual is able to establish a satisfactory social adjustment, he may fall prey to his infantile sense of helpless insecurity. Clearly, in this view the libidinal factor in the causation of neuroses recedes into the background; the repression of psychic material into the unconscious is considered only of secondary importance and psychoanalytic theory becomes, so to speak, desexualized. According to Horney, not all neurotic trouble stems from within and sexual conflicts are only one side of the picture.

Since Horney and her group consider interpersonal relationships as the basic cause of neurotic behavior, they feel that the treatment, too, should concentrate on an exploration of these relationships rather than on an endless probing into the depths of the individual's unconscious.

A summary of Horney's psychotherapeutic orientation may be seen in this quotation: "I do not consider it justified to focus our attention on childhood in a sort of one-sided fascination and to consider later reactions essentially as repetitions of earlier ones. . . . When we realize that great import of cultural conditions on neuroses, the biological and physiological conditions, which are considered by Freud to be their root, recede into the background. The influence of these latter factors should be considered only on the basis of well established evidence." [18]

It is worth while to note that Horney in her later work ("Our Inner Conflicts") considers not only social factors but also moral factors as contributing to mental difficulties. Whereas so-called external conflicts are due to lack of cultural and social adaptation, inner conflicts may be due to ethical problems.

It seems to be customary in a survey of contemporary American depth psychology to give a more or less prominent place to Harry Stack Sullivan.

Sullivan and his followers split from the Horney group and, after merging with the William Alanson White Psychiatric Foundation, formed the Washington School of Psychiatry. This group, too, stresses the importance of interpersonal relations in the production of neuroses, and it is hard to find significant differences between the Washington School and the Horney group, as far as theory goes. In practical matters, the former shows an interesting deviation from the Freudian closed-shop policy, since it admits among its ranks a few nonmedical analysts. Sullivan's reputation seems to be mostly due to his work with schizophrenics.[19]

Franz Alexander and Thomas M. French, the leaders of the Chicago Institute for Psychoanalysis, are best known for promoting psychosomatic medicine. They consider psychosomatic disorders to be an indication of neurotic conditions, and they hold that neurosis is the result of the individual's inability to adapt himself to his environment. Hence, Alexander, like Horney, stresses the importance of the individual's psychic relations to his environment in the production of neuroses. Also, the Chicago group stands with Horney on the same side of the fence that separates the American analysts with regard to the very important problem of inner-release therapy. The Chicago school no longer emphasizes digging into the patient's unconscious and unfolding hidden material as the most important aim of psychotherapy. Rather, they aim at reeducating the patient, and in doing so, they particularly stress the great value of the transference relationship between doctor and the patient; they use this relationship as the most valuable factor of psychotherapy.[20] Alexander agrees with Horney and other psychiatrists that an adult may become a neurotic when he perpetuates the form of dependency that he used as a helpless child. Now, a number of analysts have drawn the conclusion that all forms of dependency in adult behavior are unhealthy and lead up to neurosis. They therefore use the transference phenomena of the therapeutic setting to first bind the patient to the psychiatrist and then gradually wean him away from all forms of dependency so as to make him what they call a self-sufficient person. Alexander and his followers, however, refuse to believe that all dependency is neurotic; on the contrary, they hold that people are in need of certain dependencies just to keep them normal. They, too, exploit the transference situation; however, they do it not only to show the patient where his sense of dependency is wrong, but also to educate him to healthy dependency.

Milton R. Sapirstein has ably summarized the latest development of psychotherapy, as may be gleaned from the following quotation: "If we were to reconstruct the history of the analytical movement, we could subdivide it into three major phases. The first period was concerned with the mechanism of flight or withdrawal, based essentially on a study of the unconscious. These investigations, while fruitful, have about reached the point of diminishing returns from a research point of view. The second phase was concerned with ego psychology and the efforts of the human being to attain a higher degree of self-sufficiency and creativity. The third phase, which has barely begun, is the evaluation of healthy dependency phenomena as a crucial mechanism of normal social adaptation. Franz Alexander seems to be writing this new chapter into psychoanalytic history with his recent works." [21]

It is evident that this latest attitude of psychoanalysis is a far cry from Freud's. And it is rather amazing to see that it took the analysts so long to come around to this common-sense idea.[22]

NOTES AND REFERENCES

1. Alexander, Franz, *et al.*, "Psychoanalytic Therapy Principles and Application" (New York: The Ronald Press Company, 1946), p. 27.
2. Erich Fromm, in his introduction to Patrick Mullahy's book "Oedipus, Myth and Complex" (New York: Hermitage Press, 1948), has a few edgy words to say about the unfair and sometimes childish rivalry among the analytic groups—words that are well worth reading. See also Standen, Anthony, "Science Is a Sacred Cow" (New York: E. P. Dutton & Co., Inc., 1950).
3. See Carp, E., "De Neurosen" (Amsterdam: Scheltema & Holkema, 1947), p. 280.
4. Freud's original works are collected in "Gesammelte Schrifte" (12 vols.; Leipzig: Internationaler Psychoanalytischer Verlag, 1924–1934). Freud's main works are the following:

"Selected Papers on Hysteria and Other Psychoneuroses" (New York: Nervous and Mental Disease Monograph Series, No. 4, 1920).
"Totem and Taboo" (New York: New Republic, Inc., 1927).
"The Future of an Illusion" (New York: Liveright Publishing Corp., 1928).
"Three Contributions to the Theory of Sex" (New York: Nervous and Mental Disease Publishing Co., 1930).
"New Introductory Lectures on Psychoanalysis" (New York: W. W. Norton & Company, 1933).
"The Interpretation of Dreams" (New York: The Macmillan Company, 1933).
"The Ego and the Id" (London: Hogarth Press, 1935).
"The Psychopathology of Every Day" (London: Breen, 1935).
"An Autobiographical Study" (London: Hogarth Press, 1936).
"The Problem of Anxiety" (New York: W. W. Norton & Company, 1936).
"Moses and Monotheism" (New York: Alfred A. Knopf, Inc., 1939).

"Civilization and Its Discontents" (London: Hogarth Press, 1939).

"Beyond the Pleasure Principle" (London: Hogarth Press, 1942).

"A General Introduction to Psychoanalysis" (Garden City, N.Y.: Garden City Publishing Company, Inc., 1943). A collection of a number of Freud's writings may be found in "Collected Papers," translated by Joan Riviere, Alix and James Strachey (5 vols.; London: Hogarth Press, 1949–1950). A. A. Brill edited "Basic Writings of Sigmund Freud" (New York: Random House, 1938).

5. ROSANOFF, A. J., "Manual of Psychiatry" (New York: John Wiley & Sons, Inc., 1927), pp. 547–620.
6. See FLUGEL, J. C., "Man, Morals and Society" (New York: International Universities Press, 1945), pp. 101–102.
7. ALEXANDER, FRANZ, "Psychoanalyse der Gesamt-persönlichkeit" (1927). Translation: "Psychoanalysis of the Total Personality" (New York: Nervous and Mental Disease Monograph Series, No. 52, 1930).
8. Adler's main works in English translations are the following:

"A Study of Organ Inferiority and its Psychical Compensation" (New York: Nervous and Mental Disease Monograph Series, No. 24, 1917).

"The Neurotic Constitution" (New York: Moffatt, Yard & Co., 1917).

"The Practice and Theory of Individual Psychology" (New York: Harcourt, Brace and Company, Inc., 1924).

"The Education of Children" (London: George Allen & Unwin, Ltd., 1930).

"Social Interest: A Challenge to Mankind" (London: Faber & Faber, Ltd., 1938).

"Understanding Human Nature" (New York: Greenberg: Publisher, Inc., 1946).

9. Jung's main works (English translations) are as follows:

"Psychological Types, or the Psychology of Individuation" (New York: Harcourt, Brace and Company, 1926).

"Psychology of the Unconscious" (New York: Dodd, Mead & Company, Inc., 1928).

"Two Essays on Analytical Psychology" (New York: Dodd, Mead & Company, Inc., 1928).

"Modern Man in Search of a Soul" (New York: Harcourt, Brace and Company, 1933).

"Psychology and Religion" (New Haven: Yale University Press, 1938).

"The Integration of the Personality" (New York: Rinehart & Company, Inc., 1939).

"The Psychology of the Spirit" (New York: The Analytical Psychology Club of New York, Inc., 1948).

10. JUNG, C. G., "Collected Papers on Analytical Psychology," translated by C. E. Long (London: Ballière, Tindall & Cox, 1920), p. 385.
11. A wrong interpretation of Jung's ideas on religion may be found in WITTCUT, W. P., "Catholic Thought and Modern Psychology" (London: Burns, Oates & Washbourne, 1943). The author, who, at the time he wrote the booklet,

was a Catholic priest, performed some strange acrobatics to make a Thomist philosopher out of Jung.

12. Jung, "Psychology and Religion." A good exposition of Jung's concepts of religion and soul may be found in Schaer, H., "Religion und Seele in der Psychologie C. G. Jungs" (Zürich: Rascher Verlag, 1946), translated by R. F. C. Hull, "Religion and the Cure of Men's Souls in Jung's Psychology" (New York: Pantheon Books, 1950).
13. Otto Rank published two works in collaboration with others; they are (in English translation) Rank, O., and H. Sachs, "The Significance of Psychoanalysis for the Mental Sciences" (New York: Nervous and Mental Disease Publishing Co., 1915); and Ferenczi, S., and O. Rank, "The Development of Psychoanalysis" (New York: Nervous and Mental Disease Publishing Co., 1925). His own major works published after he left the orthodox Freudian group (also in English translations) are "Modern Education" (New York: Alfred A. Knopf, Inc., 1932); "Will Therapy" (New York: Alfred A. Knopf, Inc., 1936); and "Truth and Reality" (New York: Alfred A. Knopf, Inc., 1936).
14. Rank, "Will Therapy," p. 227.
15. Frankl's main works are the following:
    "Aerztliche Seelsorge" (5th ed. Vienna: Franz Deuticke, 1942).
    "Trotzdem ja zum Leben sagen" (2d ed., Vienna: Franz Deuticke, 1947).
    "Zeit und Verantwortung" (Vienna: Franz Deuticke, 1947).
    "Ein Psychologe erlebt das Konzentrationslager" (2d ed., Vienna: Verlag für Jugend und Volk, 1947).
    "Die Existenzanalyse und die Probleme der Zeit" (Vienna: Amandus-Edition, 1947).
    "Der Unbewuszte Gott" (Vienna: Amandus-Edition, 1948).
16. Gregory Zilboorg seems to be asking for some such infallible authority in an article entitled Present Trends in Psychoanalytic Theory and Practice, *Yearbook of Psychoanalysis,* Vol. 1 (1945), pp. 79–84. Zilboorg deeply regrets the "acute dissensions and schismatic undulations" in the psychoanalytic movement and therefore raises the cry, "Back to Freud!" But since Freud's system is notoriously open to many different interpretations, it would be interesting to know who might be the genuine and infallible interpreter of the real Freud.
17. Horney's main works are the following:
    "The Neurotic Personality of Our Time" (New York: W. W. Norton & Company, 1937).
    "New Ways in Psychoanalysis" (New York: W. W. Norton & Company, 1939).
    "Self-Analysis" (New York: W. W. Norton & Company, 1942).
    "Our Inner Conflicts" (New York: W. W. Norton & Company, 1945).
    "Neurosis and Human Growth: The Struggle toward Self-realization" (New York: W. W. Norton & Company, 1950).
18. Horney, "The Neurotic Personality of Our Time," Introduction, p. vii.

19. Sullivan's main contributions to the field of psychiatry are as follows:
Socio-Psychiatric Research: the Implications for the Schizophrenia Problem and for Mental Hygiene, *American Journal of Psychiatry,* Vol. 10 (1931), pp. 977–991.
"Conceptions of Modern Psychiatry" reprinted from *Psychiatry, Journal of the Biology and the Pathology of Interpersonal Relations,* Vol. 3 (1940), No. 1, and Vol. 8 (1945), No. 2.
Sullivan's writings are obscure and apodictic. An illustration of his phraseology may be found in his attempt to give a definition of the very nature of man ("Conceptions of Modern Psychiatry," p. 14). Sullivan says that he disagrees with Aristotle's definition—by the way, the present authors would like to know where Aristotle teaches that man is a creature of instincts—he disagrees with William McDougall, with the medievals and Otto Rank, with Bacon, Alfred Adler, Alfred Korzybski, Compte, De Gobineau, and Hitler, and, as if this were not enough, he disagrees also with Freud and Jung. The amazing thing about this sweeping statement is that it covers no more than exactly eight lines, without a shadow of proof. Perhaps one might apply here the remark which somebody once made concerning Macaulay: "I wish I could be as sure of one thing as T. B. Macaulay is about everything." Anyway, after watching this iconoclastic assault on some of the greatest thinkers of mankind, one is, of course, anxious to learn what man is. Dr. Sullivan then imparts to his readers that man is the tangible substrate of human life. If this so-called definition has any meaning, it simply means that a concrete living man is a concrete living man. Was it really necessary to kill off a number of celebrities before finally telling this self-evident truth?
20. Omitting Alexander's articles, some of which he wrote in collaboration with other authors (W. Healy, H. Staub, G. W. Wilson, C. Bacon, H. B. Levy, M. Levine, W. C. Menninger, and others), we quote here his main books:
"Psychoanalysis of the Total Personality" (New York: W. W. Norton & Company, 1930).
"The Medical Value of Psychoanalysis" (New York: W. W. Norton & Company, 1932).
"Our Age of Unreason" (Philadelphia: J. B. Lippincott Company, 1942).
ALEXANDER, F., and W. HEALY, "Roots of Crime; Psychoanalytic Studies" (New York: Alfred A. Knopf, Inc., 1935).
ALEXANDER, F., *et al.,* "Psychoanalytic Therapy: Principles and Application."
21. SAPIRSTEIN, MILTON R., "Emotional Security" (New York: Crown Publishers, 1948), p. 82.
22. For the gradual development of psychoanalysis, see THOMSON, CLARA, "Psychoanalysis: Evolution and Development" (New York: Hermitage Press, 1950).

Chapter 9

EVALUATION OF PSYCHOANALYSIS

Among the general public there is a rather widespread tendency to identify psychiatry with analytical or depth psychiatry and more specifically with Freudian psychoanalysis. The man in the street almost immediately associates psychiatry with Freud and his system. This attitude is unfortunate, and false besides, for depth psychology is only one section in the psychiatric town and in that section psychoanalysis is only one avenue, even though it may be a broad one. Because of this misconception, it sometimes happens that the stigma that some people feel should be attached to psychoanalysis is affixed to psychiatry as a whole.

It would seem like carrying coals to Newcastle if one were to set out to prove the right of psychiatry to existence. Psychiatry is admittedly that branch of medicine which is focused upon the nature and treatment of mental disturbances. Such disturbances range from full-fledged psychoses, which usually demand confined institutionalization, to partial disturbances of the mind, which are generally called psychoneuroses and which represent the cases most frequently treated by the private practitioner in the office situation. Obviously, no one could object to a physician's attempts to heal an upset and distracted mind or to help another person over a particularly trying emotional experience which has caused certain psychic or even physical disorders. There is nothing mysterious or magical about such a procedure. It is an endeavor that is as old as the human race and is perhaps most simply exemplified by the picture of a loving father holding and comforting his sobbing child. Hence, there is evidently no need for a justification of psychiatry, but that branch of it which is called the analytical movement seems to call for an appraisal.

Since the opposition to, and resentment of, the broad field of psychiatry is centered in Freudian psychoanalysis, and since the latter not only was the starting point of the analytical movement or depth psychology but also continues to be the cornerstone upon which many present-day analysts build their system, the present discussion will be limited mainly—but not exclusively—to Freudianism.[1]

Is Freudian psychoanalysis acceptable to the Catholic? Since the Catholic Church existed for quite a few centuries before Freud appeared on the world's stage, a fair question would seem to be: was the Catholic doctrine acceptable to Freud? Because Freud considered all religion an illusion, the answer is negative. Such an answer would seem to settle the problem. However, it is not quite settled, for opinions vary concerning the extent of the incompatibility between the Catholic and Freud. It would be somewhat natural to answer Freud's disparaging remarks about everything religious in the same vein and simply reject his entire "creation," and this is what some Catholics seem rather inclined to do, for they find little to commend in Freudianism. On the other hand, others feel that we ought to distinguish between different aspects of it; usually, they distinguish between Freudianism as a system and Freudianism as a therapy. In the authors' opinion, one should look upon it from three angles and distinguish between (*a*) the philosophical foundation of Freudianism with its religious and moral implications, (*b*) the psychological concepts, hypotheses, and theories involved in it, and (*c*) the therapeutic value of its methods. To be sure, the three viewpoints hang together closely; yet, it seems that there are sufficient grounds for distinguishing between the systematic, psychological, and therapeutic aspects in order to arrive at an adequate and fair appraisal.[2]

THE PHILOSOPHICAL AND RELIGIOUS IMPLICATIONS

A man's outlook on life is inspired by his answer to two questions: What is God? And what is man? The answer to these two basic questions decides the solution of all philosophical, religious, and moral problems and therefore may well color many of man's scientific attitudes. It also marks the demarcation line between Freud and those who believe in him, and those who believe in the Catholic position on these questions.

What is God? According to Freud and his followers, God is not an objective reality but a subjective idea; they concede that God exists, but only as an idea in the mind of man. The Freudians present several hypotheses in order to explain how this idea came into existence in man's mind. It may come about, so they say, as a displacement of a man's attitude toward his parents. In his early years he pictured his parents as two external figures, on whose goodness, wisdom, and power he relied, and now in later years, in order to recapture that same sense of security, he conjures up in his mind the picture of another dominating and all-wise figure, projects it outside, and calls it God. Another so-called explanation is to consider the idea of God as an external projection of the internal superego. Since the superego is a part of man's psyche, God becomes, in this "interpretation," a part of the person himself. By way of some sort of proof, it is pointed out that in that manner one can readily understand conditions of religious exaltation and mysticism, because the mystical union between God and man is nothing but a kind of fusion between the ego and the superego.

Such, and similar, concepts of God entail, evidently, a radical transformation of the concept of religion. If God is a projection of the superego, with the latter itself being a product of sublimation, it is understandable that religion, too, should be conceived of as the product of sublimation. And indeed, religion is just that, in the eyes of many depth psychologists.

It goes without saying that such ideas are altogether unacceptable not only to Catholics, but to anyone who believes in the real existence of a personal God. It is this freebooting in the philosophical and religious field that has made psychoanalysis objectionable to many people, Catholic and non-Catholic alike. It is a hopeful sign that at least some of the present-day analysts feel the same way. Not all do, however, for there are some analysts who believe that the objections of the faithful to religious ideas of psychoanalysis spring from resentment and that this resentment is inspired by fear, fear that psychoanalysis is undermining religion because it has revealed, so they say, the real motives, such as projection and sublimation, that produce religious beliefs.[3] These analysts may be sure that Catholics, in repudiating the religious tenets of psychoanalysis, are driven by no deep-seated resentment or fear—no more than when they combat any other philosophical or religious falsehood. Driven only by the desire to defend the supremacy and honor of God, and to defend truth, logic, and common sense, they maintain that this part of psychoanalysis, which claims to contain a religious credo, is false because it violates truth, logic, and common sense. They maintain further that, as far as this part is concerned, a good Catholic cannot be a psychoanalyst and a psychoanalyst who subscribes to these religious extravagances cannot be a Catholic.

For this reason, it is difficult to see how Liebman, who professed to be a faithful Jew, elevated, in his "Peace of Mind," Freud to the rank of a prophet. If he subscribed to the psychoanalytic thesis that God is a creation of the human mind, he could not call himself a believer; and if he was really a believer, he could not admit the psychoanalytical concept of God.[4]

What is man? A bisexual animal, Freud says. The Catholic philosopher agrees with him that man is an animal but adds that he is an animal endowed with reason and that this qualification differentiates him essentially from the brute. Freud himself had foreseen this answer, for somewhere he makes the statement that the clergy will never admit that man and animal are essentially the same. Indeed not! And not only the clergy, but millions of people with them, hold that both faith and reason are able to show that man possesses a spiritual soul, which, because of its spirituality, can never be the product of any kind of evolution, but is created by God. It is due precisely to the spiritual nature of the human soul that man is endowed with the two powers, reason and will, which, again because of their spiritual nature, can in no way be explained by purely physiological mechanisms. This is the position of the Catholic psychologist, a position that he substantiates with solid proofs. He therefore rejects the opposite opinion of the Freudians, which, it should be added, is not borne out by factual evidence but is simply taken for granted as the consequence of materialistic prejudice. Man is not an animal *only;* this statement marks the first cleavage between the Catholic and anyone who subscribes to the Freudian definition of man.

A second chasm separates the Catholic from Freud and his followers when they define man as a bisexual animal. Omitting for the moment the prefix bi-, one finds that according to the Freudian definition the most essential driving force of human nature is sex.

Freud viewed his thesis that man is just a sexual animal as a major discovery. He wrote that in the history of mankind there have been only three important discoveries: the first was that of Copernicus and Galileo, who proved that man's dwelling place was not the center of the universe; the second was that of Darwin, who humiliated man a little more by robbing him of his privileged position as the king of creation and putting him on the animal level; and, finally, the third was Freud's own discovery, which deprived man of the last remainder of his pride by revealing that he is just the sport of the basest instincts—of which, moreover, he is often not even conscious. May Freud's gloating over man's humiliation be attributed to a sadistic trend in his own character?

What evidence does Freud offer to prove his theory of pansexualism? The only answer consists in explaining in a few words a peculiar twist in the Freudian way of thinking. According to Freud, the only evidence in favor of his doctrine lies in *accepting* his doctrine. This holds true not only for his views on pansexualism but for any of his statements. The only way to believe fully in Freudianism is to accept it. The paradoxical reason for this attitude is as follows. It is a dogma of orthodox psychoanalysis that no one can pass a true judgment on the value of the system unless he himself is analyzed, for as long as a person remains unanalyzed, a large number of unconscious drives and complexes are active in him and influence his conscious reactions, including his judgment. Suppose one has some doubts or misgivings about the Freudian system; he may find several points unlikely, childish, exaggerated, fantastic, ridiculous, offensive, or immoral. But if he has not been analyzed, any of these statements is necessarily prejudiced because it is the product of the working of the unconscious drives within him.

Any other theory or system can be judged and evaluated according to more or less objective standards. Not so orthodox Freudian psychoanalysis; one has to belong to its inner circle in order to form a just appraisal of it. Suppose a Catholic invited a non-Catholic to join the Church. The latter would rightly request that the former first prove that his is the true church. If thereupon the Catholic were to reply: "Sorry, I cannot prove that to you, unless you first join us," we would have an imaginary case comparable to Freud's attitude toward disbelievers.

The authors personally know several people, mostly physicians, who have been analyzed either by Freud himself or by one of his first apostles and who therefore belong to the innermost circle. Hence, their judgment ought to be infallible. Nevertheless, many of them refuse to subscribe to Freud's system, taken as a whole. They may see several good points in the system, but they fail to swallow it hook, line, and sinker. The answer of the orthodox die-hards would certainly be that these critics never were, and never could become, real adepts because their criticism shows that there was still some unconscious resistance left, despite the analysis. Such an answer, of course, does not confute the critics but closes the door for any further discussion.

Well, let us leave the door closed. It seemed desirable to point out this dogmatic attitude for three reasons. In the first place, it shows that one cannot argue with the die-hard Freudians. In the second place, it shows that those who believe in psychoanalysis, but are not real Freudians, do not belong to the "mother church" but are psychoanalytical protestants. In the third place, it shows that a believer, regardless of whether he is a Catholic or Protestant, never can be a full-fledged Freudian—he may be an analyst but not an out-and-out Freudian. For the Freudian dogma insists that a believer never can be fully analyzed; he never can become the complex-free personality that an ideal analysis would require, because his mind will always harbor some complexes; there will always remain in him a resistance against some of Freud's dogmas so that he will, according to Freud, always remain prejudiced.

The above picture does not apply to all analysts and not even to all present-day Freudians, but it does apply to the master and his immediate disciples, who formed a perfect clan with a rigorous discipline which did not tolerate any divergent opinion. It was precisely this rigorous dogmatism that repelled some of Freud's first adepts, and one of the main stumbling blocks that caused the dissidents to leave the "mother-church" was Freud's pansexualism.

As was seen in the previous chapter, Jung kept the term "libido" but interpreted it no longer in the sexual sense; rather he saw in it the general drive to live, some sort of an *élan vital*. Adler rejected the libido completely as the basic driving force of human nature and claimed that the root of all our unwholesome drives is self-assertion—in other words, pride. Adler's doctrine was Freud's upside down. Whereas Freud would interpret the longing for superiority as a sublimation of the sexual libido, Adler explained the sexual libido in terms of the will-to-power.

The present time is again witnessing a healthy change in attitude, as may be evidenced by the following quotation taken from Karen Horney: "Sexuality is an important domain in our life. . . . But the one-sided emphasis that Freud has given sexual factors may tempt many people to single them out above others. . . . To be straight in sexual questions is necessary; but to be straight only with them, is not enough." [5] At the 1948 convention of the top United States scientists in Chicago, Orval Hobart Mowrer of Harvard University assured the psychiatrists that Freud's emphasis on repressed sexual energy had put them on the wrong track. Thus, more and more psychiatrists come to realize that not all man's basic instincts are of a sexual nature. There are all kinds of drives in man, both wholesome ones and unwholesome ones, too. The latter eventually cause mental disorders, but many of them have little or nothing to do with the sexual instinct. Man may be driven by ambition, aggressiveness, revenge, jealousy, selfishness, longings for recognition, fame, and wealth—to mention only a few of the driving forces. But applying the age-old rule of sound logic that a gratuitous assertion should be met with a gratuitous denial, one can refuse to consider any of these drives as a sublimated form of sexuality until psychoanalysis has unmistakably proved that it is.

The Catholic attitude toward Freud's pansexualism is clear: sex certainly plays an important role in man's life, but it is not the only, and not even the main, driving force. The Catholics, quite understandably, prefer following the Master of Nazareth to the Master of Vienna. Some Pharisee once asked Christ, "Master, which is the great commandment in the Law?" Jesus did not point out the sixth and the ninth commandments, which have to do with sex. Instead, "Jesus said to him: 'Thou shalt love the Lord thy God. . . . This is the greatest and the first commandment. And the second is like it: thou shalt love thy neighbor as thyself' " (Matthew 22:36–39).

Catholic theology as well as scholastic philosophy teaches that love is the basic driving force in man. Man is driven by a great number of impulses, drives, instincts, and strivings, but there is one common element in them all. Whatever the human mind is aiming at, it is, in the last analysis, seeking something that will fully satisfy it. And this something is the infinite good, God.

It would take this discussion too far afield to explain here the sublime doctrine of man's natural desire for God; it suffices to say that the Supreme Good is the end at which man is forever aiming, consciously or unconsciously, in order to achieve real happiness, and that, therefore, the quest of God is the most fundamental driving force of human nature. Here may be quoted a passage from St. Augustine's "Confessions," that unsurpassed book that contains the most profound self-analysis ever made: "To Carthage I came, where there sang all around me in my ears a cauldron of unholy loves. I loved not yet, yet I loved to love, and out of a deep-seated want, I hated myself for wanting not. I sought what I might love, in love with loving, and safety I hated, and a way without snares. For within me was a famine of that inward food, Thyself, my God; yet, through that famine I was not hungered; but was without all longing for incorruptible sustenance, not because filled therewith, but the more empty, the more I loathed it." [6]

A final remark concerns the prefix in the term bisexual in Freud's definition of man. If man is not by definition a sexual animal, he is a fortiori not a bisexual animal by definition. There are, of course, persons who are both heterosexual and homosexual. There is, perhaps, in man's youth a period in which the qualification might apply, although most of the facts that are brought forth to prove the point show rather that children are asexual, *i.e.*, that sex means nothing to them.

Summarizing, it may be concluded that Freudianism as a philosophical and religious system is unacceptable to Catholics, and therefore any theory that logically derives from Freud's philosophical premises is equally unacceptable. Why make a psychiatric system the substitute of philosophy, theology, anthropology, and what not? By way of contrast, Adolf Meyer's psychobiology may be considered. Few people would object to his system, precisely because it refrains from any claim to a philosophical evaluation of man's ultimate nature and destiny. Yet Meyer's approach to mental disturbances represents a psychiatric technique that is just as specific and differentiated as Freud's psychoanalysis, and, since Meyer's technique scores results at least as good as Freud's, it is highly questionable if Freud's philosophical ballast contributes anything to an efficacious treatment of mental disorders. It is understandable, therefore, that the opposition to Freudian psychoanalysis is directed toward the latter's philosophy and naturally to those theories which logically derive from its philosophical premises.

Realizing this, several other systems of depth psychology reject wholly or in part Freud's philosophical principles. An example is the case of the existential analysts, who simply stick to facts without browsing around in a territory that they rightly consider irrelevant to psychiatry. Whenever during analysis they find moral or religious elements in their patient's mind, they do not fly off on a pseudophilosophical tangent, but take them as psychological facts and interpret them according to the mental make-up of the patients.

THE PSYCHOLOGICAL CONCEPTS AND THEORIES

The philosophical and religious concepts of depth psychology, whether presented in the form that Freud gave it or in any similar form such as those in which it may be found in some contemporary schools of depth psychology, are unacceptable to the Catholic mind because these systems deny, ignore, or misrepresent the very bases of Catholic religion and philosophy. This is the conclusion reached in the preceding section.

Now, in the Freudian system there is found a body of theories that are immediate corollaries of his philosophical premises about the nature of God and man; *e.g.*, his theories about infantile sexuality, the Oedipus and castration complexes, derive directly from his pansexualism. Also among these are his belief in the antisocial nature of the human instincts, his denial of free will and original sin, his replacement of the moral law with the principle of reality, the theory about the death instinct, masochistic tendencies, etc.

These and similar concepts, hypotheses, and theories are inextricably linked up with Freud's materialistic, deterministic, and hedonistic philosophy and for that reason are unacceptable to the Catholic patient and therapist alike. Some of these theories, like those which deny the free will or the moral law, must be repudiated completely. With regard to others like the libido, the Oedipus complex, the death instinct, Catholics do not maintain that they never play a role in the origin or development of mental disorders. To be sure, just as the sex impulse may so strongly influence some people's minds and behavior as to create psychic conflicts, so traces of certain complexes are found in some individuals, but it is a gross exaggeration to generalize these concepts as if they express the very nature of man. When, for instance, Nunberg, an orthodox psychoanalyst, says that the Oedipus complex forms the nucleus of all neuroses, there seems to be very little evidence to support such a statement.

As has been said, Catholics reject, either wholly or in part, these opinions. It is certainly gratifying to see that they are joined by the defenders of other systems of depth psychology and even by a number of analysts who profess to be Freudians. When one examines the concepts of Freud's system that those writers repudiate, one finds a surprisingly large number of precisely those items which directly derive from Freud's *Weltanschauung.* To recapitulate, Adler, Jung, and Horney object to the supremacy of the libido; Rank reestablished, at least in practice, the importance of the will; hardly anyone has much use for Freud's death instinct; many consider the Oedipus complex of little help; and an ever-growing number of analysts deviate one way or another from Freud's antireligious attitude.

But what about the concepts and theories that seem to be of a purely psychological nature, such as—to mention only the main ones—the theory about the existence of unconscious mental activities, the psychodynamics of conflict, the concepts of repression and resistance, the methodological notion of transference, and the interpretation of neurotic conditions? It is necessary to say that such concepts *seem* to be of a purely psychological nature, because it is precisely the crux of the whole problem, whether there are in the Freudian and other analytical systems purely psychological concepts, *i.e.*, concepts that can be divorced from the analysts' philosophical principles. It certainly is true that many depth psychologists make the divorce quite difficult, because only too often their psychological theories are heavily clouded by philosophical prejudices, and this is particularly true in the case of Freud. One is frequently unable to find out what is fact, what is psychological theory, and what is philosophical assumption in his writings. Nevertheless, it seems to the authors that the question can be raised whether a divorce or at least a "separation from bed and board" can be rightly effected—in other words, whether resistance, repression, fixation, regression, etc., are really active in man's psyche or are only hypothetical artifacts, and whether theories like those concerning the origin of neuroses are well founded in facts, apart from any philosophical consideration.

There are certain authorities, Catholics as well as non-Catholics, who feel that the psychoanalytic theories cannot be separated from their philosophical bases. If one holds to that view, and if he rejects those bases, it is only logical that he will also repudiate the theories. But there are also authorities, again Catholics as well as non-Catholics, who believe that a separation is feasible. In that case, the decisive factor in evaluating the psychological theories and concepts of the analysts is exclusively the answer to the question, whether the analytical theories are psychologically well substantiated. In that case, they can and must be judged on their own merits. If the answer is satisfactory to a scientific mind, no one will raise objections, be he Catholic or not. But then it also follows that, granted the possibility of separation, it is rather inane to ask what one as a Catholic thinks of those analytical theories. Granted the possibility of separation, as a Catholic he thinks of them just as much and just as little as when he is confronted with the question of whether Hering's or Helmholtz's theory of color vision is correct.

All this is, after all, quite obvious, but it appeared to the authors of this book to be not redundant to expatiate on this point, were it only to present their own standpoint. They thoroughly repudiate, of course, the analysts' philosophical and religious extravagances and also admit that it may be difficult to draw, in the Freudian system, the boundary line between philosophy and psychology, but they believe that there are a number of psychological theories and concepts that can be separated from Freudian or other analytical philosophies, even though they were first presented in the framework of these systems. By way of examples, a few of the most important psychological concepts of depth analysis may be reviewed.

The basis of any system of depth psychology is of course the existence of what is popularly called the unconscious. The problem of the unconscious does not concern the question whether there exist in the human mind unconscious contents and dispositions. This is undoubtedly a fact, for—to mention only one example—the human mind harbors innumerable memory traces which remain unconscious until the moment they are, for one reason or other, revived. But the question is whether any such unconscious elements, even though they remain unconscious, can be active in such a way that they influence a person's conscious mind and behavior. Now, a great deal of evidence points out that one must admit in the mind the existence of dispositions and experiences that are not just static but dynamic in nature; they may reveal their activity in certain conscious symptoms like depression or anxiety, although the source of these disturbances may remain hidden to the patient.[7]

It has been said that the doctrine of unconscious active elements of the mind is not original to Freud. In fact, references to such unconscious mental elements can be found, for instance, in the works of some Greek psychologists, of St. Augustine, of Juan Vives, and of Leibnitz. The dynamisms of the unconscious mind were surely not unknown to Pierre Janet. But the honor of having properly formulated and systematically exploited the doctrine of the unconscious in the explanation of psychoneurotic disturbances goes to Freud.

The term "the unconscious," is used here simply as a collective noun to indicate the sum of dispositions, experiences, and memories of the mind. By "mind" is meant the soul as the subject of mental life. But only a small part of man's mental life is conscious, *viz.*, those contents which every single moment stand out clearly in consciousness, surrounded by a fringe of mental contents of which the individual is dimly aware. The greater part of man's mental life is unconscious, some of it seemingly inactive, and some of it apparently active.

All the systems of depth psychology are concerned with the active influences of the unconscious mind. There are many patients who are unaware that unconscious experiences or strivings are the source of their symptoms. They are, of course, very conscious of their disability, like compulsions or depressions or scrupulosity, but they do not know the source of their sufferings, just as they fail to know the source of their dream material. This, however, does not mean that all mental or emotional troubles spring from unconscious sources. Many persons are well aware, either fully or in part, of the cause of their disturbances, but although they may understand it intellectually, they are unable to digest the traumatic experience emotionally. It has become fashionable, even among the general public, to exaggerate altogether the role of the unconscious. Analysts themselves recognize this danger, and some of them sound the warning that much of what is called unconscious is really preconscious or unformulated.

Granted the existence of unconscious dynamics, the question has been raised whether it is ever possible to be sure that unconscious motivation does not interfere with an individual's free will and hence limit his moral responsibility. In other words, some writers hold that the existence of unconscious motivation contains an objection against the freedom of the will not only in the case of abnormal persons but also in the case of normal ones.[8]

Yet, there is a great difference between abnormal and normal people with regard to unconscious motivation. It never should be forgotten that the existence of unconscious dynamics is inferred from the existence of reactions of which the individual is perfectly conscious. For instance, in the case of a compulsive patient, the compulsion may perhaps be unconsciously motivated, but the patient is quite aware of the compulsion itself. He may feel unable to resist the strength of the compulsion, but that very inability to resist puts him precisely in the class of abnormals. The case of normal people is entirely different. A normal person may perhaps also be influenced by unconscious motivation to perform a certain act. But, when such unconscious dynamics rise above the conscious level, he has it in his power to decide freely whether to yield to the motivation or not. *What* motivates him may be unconscious, but he is conscious *that* he is motivated to do something. Granted, for the sake of argument, that a well-balanced person may be motivated by an unconscious drive, he is able to freely decide before he acts, just because he is normal. In fact, the less clear a normal person is in his own mind about the source of certain motives, the less he will feel inclined to accept them. Of course, here as elsewhere, it is necessary to recognize the existence of the "borderland" between apparently normal and apparently abnormal individuals.

Presupposed that the mind harbors contents that are somehow barred from consciousness, there seems to be a force that is opposed to the entry of these contents into consciousness. Now, one need not be a psychoanalyst to admit the existence of such blocking force or resistance. Resistance is the reluctance or inability on the part of the patient to admit his troubles fully to the psychiatrist, and in that sense resistance is a natural phenomenon which the psychiatrist can expect from every patient. It is a kind of defensive or protective mechanism; the patient protects himself, as a child seeks to protect himself against the painful or unpleasant influences of his early environment. The patient is willing enough to complain about his mental, emotional, and even physical symptoms that make normal social life impossible or difficult for him, but he feels reluctant to face those aspects of his troubles which reflect their root, even though he may be dimly aware of their existence. And the reason is clear: no one wishes to admit frankly that he has personality faults like immaturity, childishness, and insecurity, and all people are reluctant to discuss unpleasant or personal offensive experiences. In that sense resistance is encountered in any treatment situation.

In the previous paragraph it was assumed that, although the patient resists disclosing fully his troublesome experiences and conflicts, he is somehow aware of their cause, and that will be often the case. Sometimes, however, the source of the patient's anxieties, worries, fears, and longings may be completely hidden to him. And when the psychiatrist discloses to him the real origin of his symptoms, the patient may again react with a strong resistance. At any rate, the first objective of psychotherapy is to remove resistance, because as long as the patient resists facing the source of his troubles, he resists efficacious treatment. It is of no help to the patient for the physician to understand the cause of the patient's mental or emotional disturbance—the patient himself must understand and admit the cause. This insight will be brought about by free association of thought, the revival of childhood memories, and other devices that will reveal more and more of the origin of the patient's symptoms. When the patient, with the help of the psychotherapist, no longer attempts to resist facing the naked truth, a very important goal has been reached and the process of analysis itself has come to an end.

It is clear that the term "resistance" is used here in a broad sense, including under it everything that interferes with the process of analysis. Now it cannot be denied that Freud and other depth psychologists have contributed greatly to an understanding of the nature, the source, and the dynamism of resistance—a contribution that gave rise to the concepts of suppression and repression. No doubt, suppression plays an important role in mental and moral life, and as for repression it is interesting to note that some Catholic authors have made an attempt to give Freud's theory of repression a Thomistic interpretation.[9]

No one will object to the thesis that the cause of neurotic disorders is often to be found in the conflict or clash between the repressing force and instinctual drives. It has been repeatedly pointed out that, from the descriptive point of view, there is little difference between Aquinas' notion of the passions and Freud's idea of instincts, irrespective of the underlying philosophy. And as far as the conflict is concerned, both St. Paul and St. Augustine indicate the ambivalent character of man's nature in their description of the conflict between the "old and new man," the struggle between the sensual and rational natures. Man is indeed the battleground between his lower and his better self. Now, it serves little purpose to squabble about the name of the better self, whether it be called censor, superego, ego-ideal, or what not. One may perhaps agree that not only conscious but also unconscious elements go into the making of that better self, but many people, and not only Catholics, will feel reluctant to accept the psychoanalysts' definitions of the concepts just mentioned, because they feel that these definitions are too vague, hypothetical, or metaphorical. Many will feel even more reluctant to admit Freud's departmentalization of a human person into three sections, the id, the ego, and the superego. And Catholics will disagree fully with Freud's attempt to explain the origin of the better ego—call it, if you wish, the superego—as being, in the final analysis, the result of libidinal drives.

It was mentioned previously that Freud in the earlier part of his career completely overlooked the importance of transference. Yet transference is undoubtedly a process of basic importance to any kind of psychotherapy. Transference is a natural phenomenon in many situations. As an example, consider the mother of a mentally deficient child, who constantly blames the schoolteacher for the child's inadequacy in school achievement. The mother is unable to accept the real fact squarely, and so she transfers the blame for the child's poor achievement to the teacher. Likewise, in psychotherapy, the patient, when reliving the emotions connected with certain actions of his earlier life, unconsciously refuses to accept these past actions as part of his own doing and actually passes the responsibility for them on to the psychiatrist. In view of this fact, the psychoanalysts' description of transference as the process whereby the patient projects his "superego" onto the analyst might perhaps be accepted in a metaphorical sense.

Transference is obviously related to resistance, because whenever something is missing in the relationship between the patient and the physician, it is due to some resisting force in the former's mind.

Sometimes the remark has been made that transference is a dangerous instrument, because an unscrupulous therapist might take advantage of his patient's emotional reactions. Such things may happen, of course, but this kind of danger is not limited to psychiatry and may crop up in any relationship between physician and patient.

Analysts are wont to present their therapeutic successes as an argument to prove their concepts and theories. Their ideas must be right, so they reason, because they work. The answer to this pragmatistic way of thinking is that good results do not necessarily prove the truth of a theory. As was seen in Chapter 3, Mesmer effected remarkable cures with his psychoneurotic patients—cures that he ascribed to the influence of ethereal fluids and animal magnetism. The cures were found to be quite genuine, to be sure, but few people nowadays will admit Mesmer's elaborate theory.

A pari the cures effected by the analysts do not necessarily bear out the theoretical implications of their system.

THE THERAPEUTIC VALUE

There can be no doubt that psychoanalysis and other depth psychologies have considerable success in helping the mentally sick, especially the neurotic. Even those who would call psychoanalysis an error admit that it scores practical successes. Of course, no form of depth psychology is a panacea against all disorders. When it comes to explaining the cases in which no recovery sets in, one encounters again that peculiar twist of mind, especially frequent with psychoanalysts, which has been mentioned before. In cases in which no success is obtained, they often refuse to attribute the failure to the fact that possibly the method might not be reliable or that the theory behind it might not be applicable to the case, but, more often than not, they blame the patient himself; the patient, they say, unconsciously refuses to be cured because he sees a greater advantage in staying sick. Now, it is true that there are neurotics whose condition is kept up, if not caused, by an unconscious desire to remain sick because of some advantage, as in the case of war neuroses, compensation neuroses, and some forms of hysteria. But, although these things happen, it would seem that the analysts take things a little too easy if they attribute all failures to the unconscious drive to remain ill. Some psychiatrists point out that there is a great deal of catharsis and suggestion involved in any form of psychoanalysis, and those authors believe that many cures can be explained by these factors rather than by analysis proper. The mere fact that a person is allowed and encouraged to express himself as fully and as frankly as possible in the presence of a man he trusts is in itself an excellent means of relieving this person from his troubles. Other results may be due to suggestion. A system that looks quite complicated, that bristles with mysterious terms, and that, besides, is widely publicized is well suited to the exercising of a suggestive power upon many people, even in our somewhat sophisticated age. Also, a therapy for which people pay such high fees simply must be effective, in the eyes of the public. Another fact that proves the suggestive power of analysis is that the analyst himself must believe wholeheartedly in the efficacy of his method. There is a case of a psychiatrist who had been trained in Freudian psychoanalysis and practiced it with pretty good results. When, later, he got acquainted with the teachings of a different school of analysis, he began to compare both schools with a more critical eye and felt that he was no longer so certain about the choice of the right method. The result was that the number of his cures dropped.

Although admitting that probably not all cures effected in the analyst's office are due to his analytical method, one must recognize fully that this method is valuable in many instances. What, then, is this method? The primary aim of all methods of depth psychology consists in giving the patient an insight into his condition by revealing to him the deep-seated reasons of his personal difficulties. The analysis of his inner life may bring to light that early experiences, unresolved dependencies, unconscious conflicts, sexual drives, or hostilities have their impact on his present disturbance. In simple words, the first step in the analytical procedure is to bring the root of the patient's troubles to the surface and make him realize what is wrong with him and what is the origin of his difficulties. There can be little doubt that this method has a powerful therapeutic value. When unconscious or half-conscious drives and conflicts are brought into the open, *i.e.*, when they become fully conscious, the patient no longer is intrigued by the mystery of his own behavior. Why he is as he is, is no longer a puzzle for him. However, at this juncture a very important question arises. Is mere analysis of a patient's disturbed mind enough to cure him? Is the mere knowledge of how his troubles developed sufficient to make a new man out of the patient? The earlier and several present-day psychoanalysts think that mere analysis is enough to change a mentally ill man into a healthy individual, and even to change a sinner into a saint. However, other depth psychologists are not so optimistic about the value of analysis alone, but feel that often advice and guidance is required for full and permanent recovery. Because of the importance of this problem and the implications involved in its solutions, it will be discussed in the next chapter.

This evaluation of psychoanalysis, up to this point, may be summarized as follows:

1. The philosophical and theological assumptions of Freudian psychoanalysis are at direct variance with the Catholic doctrine. Hence, Catholics take exception to the philosophy that gradually has been tacked on to the psychoanalytic therapeutic technique—if the term "philosophy" can be properly attributed to the often vague, fantastic, and unscientific hypothetical and imaginal mental wanderings that characterize the doctrinal aspects of Freudian psychoanalysis about the nature of God and man. Orthodox Freudianism is atheistic, and there is no difference between the Darwinian fundamentalists and the orthodox school of psychoanalysts in

so far as both claim a materialistic interpretation of man, with complete disregard of the spiritual soul.

2. The psychoanalysts have formulated a number of concepts and theories that are intended to describe or explain the dynamisms of the human individual. Since some of these psychological theories are aprioristic derivations of the Freudian philosophy of life, they should be judged by the same criteria as the underlying philosophical premises. But other theories and concepts are not necessarily connected with those premises and should therefore be evaluated by the same criteria by which any other hypothesis in psychology is to be tested; they are acceptable in so far as they can stand that test.

3. Freudian psychoanalysis started as a method with which to cure mentally sick people, and Freud achieved good results with his technique of analyzing the mind of those patients before he had developed his various theories about mental dynamisms and before he had constructed his *Weltanschauung*. This very fact proves that the analytical technique can be disconnected from its philosophical superstructure. It shows by the same token that a psychiatrist may very well use the analytical method without advocating in the least the Freudian philosophy of life and those theories which necessarily derive from it. Hence, there is no inconsistency in a Catholic psychiatrist's opposing and criticizing the doctrinal content of Freudian psychoanalysis, while at the same time defending and using its therapeutic technique. In the hands of a trained and experienced practitioner every type of sound psychotherapy is a valuable asset in the treatment of his patients, and the Catholic psychiatrist considers analysis a helpful method; in fact, many Catholic practitioners claim that their analytical treatment has been instrumental in bringing people back to the Church.[10] Although recognizing the abuses that have characterized the work of many psychoanalysts precisely because they mix method with philosophy, Catholic psychiatrists look upon analysis of the mind as a valid means of serving their anxious, disturbed, and neurotic fellow men. They feel that it would be incongruous, for example, to refuse the use of an effective make of safety razor because it was invented by an atheist. Likewise, they see nothing wrong in using an efficient psychiatric technique even though it has been offered to the world by one who, in his research on man's nature, lost sight of God Who gave him the perspicacity for inventing that technique.

In the light of these considerations, one understands also the answer to the question of whether psychoanalysis is dangerous to the religious faith of the patient. It is not dangerous but actually an asset when it is administered by a psychiatrist who has his own two feet solidly on the bedrock of Christian philosophy, but it is dangerous, and very much so, when the psychiatrist is guided, not only by the analytical technique, but also by the materialistic philosophy of human nature which Freud championed so ardently.

NOTES AND REFERENCES

1. This chapter and the next formed part of a series of eight lectures, bearing the title "Symposium on Catholic Concepts of Psychology," which one of the authors, in his capacity of consultant in psychology of the National Naval Medical Center, gave in 1948 to the officers of the Naval Hospital at Bethesda, Maryland.
2. An evaluation of psychoanalysis, from the Catholic standpoint, may be found in the following works:

ALLERS, R., "The New Psychologies" (New York: Sheed & Ward, Inc., 1933); *id.*, "The Successful Error, a Critical Study of Freudian Psychoanalysis" (New York: Sheed & Ward, Inc., 1940).

BRUEHL, CHARLES, "Psychoanalysis" (New York: The Paulist Press, 1949).

DALBIEZ, ROLAND, "Psychoanalytical Method and the Doctrine of Freud," translated by T. F. Lindsay (2 vols.; New York: Longmans, Green & Co., Inc., 1941 and 1948).

DONAT, J., "Über Psychoanalyse und individual Psychologie" (Innsbruck: F. Rausch, 1932).

DONCEEL, J., Second Thoughts on Freud, *Thought*, September, 1949, pp. 466–484.

FORD, JOHN C., "Depth Psychology, Morality and Alcoholism" (Weston, Mass.: Weston College, 1951).

GAETANI, F. M., "La Psicanalisi" (Rome: La Civiltà Cattolica, 1925).

MOORE, THOMAS V., "Dynamic Psychology" (Philadelphia: J. B. Lippincott Company, 1926), pp. 253–308.

NODET, C. H., Psychanalyse et morale, *Cahiers Laënnec*, May, 1948, pp. 22–36.

ODENWALD, ROBERT P., Psychiatry and Psychoanalysis, *The Sign*, Vol. 29, No. 8, March (1950), p. 35.

SHEEN, FULTON J., "The Modern Soul in Search of God" (Washington, D.C.: National Council of Catholic Men, 1948); *id.*, "Peace of Soul" (New York: McGraw-Hill Book Company, Inc., 1949); *id.*, "Lift Up Your Heart" (New York: McGraw-Hill Book Company, Inc., 1950).

TESSON, F., Description de la conscience morale et incidences psychiatriques, *Cahiers Laënnec*, May, 1948, pp. 3–21.

3. See FLUGEL, J. C., "Man, Morals and Society" (New York: International Universities Press, 1945), p. 263.

4. One of Liebman's coreligionists, David Daicher, in the February, 1951, issue of *Commentary* called Liebmann's "Peace of Mind" an absurd book.
5. Horney, Karen, "Self-analysis" (New York: W. W. Norton & Company, 1942), p. 295.
6. Saint Augustine's "Confessions," translated by E. B. Pusey, in Everyman's Library (New York: E. P. Dutton & Co., Inc., 1929). See on this subject the excellent work by O'Connor, William R., "The Eternal Quest" (New York: Longmans, Green & Co., Inc., 1947); see also Moore, Thomas V., "Personal Mental Hygiene" (New York: Grune and Stratton, 1945), p. 307.
7. Moore, Thomas V., "The Driving Forces of Human Nature" (New York: Grune and Stratton, 1950), pp. 63–95, presents a clear exposition of the problem and of the evidence of unconscious active mental contents.
8. The reader will find a brief and clear statement of this problem in Kelly, Gerald, Current Theology, *Theological Studies,* Vol. 10 (1949), pp. 84, 85.
9. Duynstee, W., De Verdringingstheorie, beoordeeld van Thomistisch Standpunt, in "Psychoanalyse" (Nÿmegen: Centrale Drukkerÿ, 1935), pp. 32–57.
10. The psychiatrist Dr. Karl Stern, in his autobiography "The Pillar of Fire" (New York: Harcourt, Brace and Company, 1951), in which he describes his conversion from Judaism to Catholicism, claims that one of the turning points of his life has been his personal analysis. Referring to his experiences during the analysis, he writes (p. 154): "Among the numerous things which changed in my life during this time was an extraordinary fact: when I first lay down on the couch I was a convinced dialectic materialist; when I arose from the couch for the last time I was absolutely convinced of the primacy of the Spirit."

Chapter 10

THE PSYCHAGOGICAL METHOD

At the end of the last chapter two views were presented concerning the value of mere analysis. The first view holds that analysis, and nothing but analysis, of a person's inner life is sufficient to rid that person of his mental, and even moral, troubles. This view is called the inner-release view. The other opinion is that analysis by itself is not sufficient to effect a change and should be supplemented by the method of reeducation. For this method the term "psychagogic" has been coined; as the education of children is called pedagogy, so the education of the mind may be termed psychagogy. "Psychosynthesis" is another term, used because it is felt that taking a patient's mind apart by way of analysis is not sufficient, but that the therapist should strive to resynthesize his patient's disorganized mind. In very simple terms, the method consists in offering the patient a new, or better, plan of life for the future or, if one prefers a more formal term, a satisfactory philosophy of life.

Some people have a wrong plan of life. Others do not seem to have any plan: the only one that many people follow consistently seems to be that they act consistently without any plan. Now, it has often been found that the neurotic behavior of patients is due either to the lack of a plan or to the presence of a false, unsatisfactory plan of life. The psychagogical method tries to remedy this condition.

The inner-release view represents the original Freudian standpoint—a standpoint that the founder of psychoanalysis strenuously defended all through his life. His exclusive aim was to make conscious as much hidden psychic material as possible and to decline any outside help from ethics or religion or any other source. He summarized his attitude in the clearest possible way in this one statement, made in "The Future of an Illusion": "Our science [psychoanalysis] is not an illusion. But it would be an illusion to believe that we could get elsewhere what analysis cannot give us."[1] This was Freud's position, and he maintained it, particularly with regard to the therapeutic value of moral and religious principles, to the end of his days.

The inner-release therapy in its pure Freudian form consists in bringing fully to the surface all the ramifications of the conscious and unconscious material of the patient's mind. After doing this the therapist, considering his task terminated, leaves up to the patient the solution of the question of what he is to do about the matter. He refuses to give any direct advice or directions, for he is convinced of the patient's ability to deal effectively with his problems, mental and moral, once he has obtained an insight into the forces that were the causes of his problems. Because the therapist refrains from any direct counseling, his attitude may be called the neutral attitude. This approach may be illustrated by Liebman's description [2] of a married man carrying on an extramarital affair. He went to a clergyman for advice and help, but the interview, which Liebman calls a "confession," failed, and the man fell back into his practice. Liebman considers the interview to have failed because it did not dig deep enough into the person's past and therefore did not disclose the psychogenic roots of the evil. Such a man—whether his case was real or imaginary is not clear—Liebman would advise to try psychoanalysis, and he places the emphasis on mere analysis inasmuch as he tells us that the method of treatment consists solely in revealing to the man the causes of his "neurotic behavior," causes that would be found in his childhood experiences, but that he should in no way be "told what to do or how to act." This method, Liebman holds, would change the adulterer into an exemplary husband. According to the view illustrated by this case, self-control automatically results from self-understanding; yet, age-old experience has taught us that no self-understanding will liberate a person from his sexual yearnings without self-control.

In order to understand fully the neutral attitude of the inner-release therapy, one must remember that, according to a common theory, many neuroses are due to a conflict between repressed desires and a repressing moral force. For the purpose of making the point clear, it matters little at the moment whether this repressing force is called conscience, or censor, or superego, or any other name. Within the framework of the psychoanalytic theory, the therapist, after revealing the dynamics underlying the conflict, is faced with a dilemma: he may put himself either on the side of the censor, or on the side of the the repressed desires and impulses. If he takes the first alternative and advises the patient to obey the dictates of his moral conscience, he would make himself a partner of the repressing force which, according to the Freudian theory, has done so much harm to the patient, and in that case he would expose the patient to the danger of building up new repressions. On the other hand, if the therapist takes the opposite side and advises greater gratification of impulses with disregard for the dictates of conscience, he plays into the hands of the critics of psychoanalysis who object against it on precisely the ground that it undermines conventional morality.[3] As a result, the therapist in either case is faced with supposedly unacceptable consequences. Therefore, rather than face them, the inner-release therapist believes that the only way out is to take a neutral attitude.

Later it will be seen whether the dilemma—which, we should not forget, is a dilemma for psychoanalysts because it follows from their principles—cannot be solved in a satisfactory manner. For the moment, it suffices to consider the merits of the release theory. It has been pointed out already that the practical application of this theory possesses a great therapeutic value. By bringing the conflict to the surface, inner tensions are released, the cause of the patient's condition is supposed to be revealed, and by the same token the motives of his behavior may lose some of their attraction. However, the inner-release therapy involves two inherent difficulties: (*a*) one may seriously doubt that the therapy is as neutral as it is said to be; (*b*) even if it is granted for the sake of argument that the therapy could be really neutral, it is still doubtful whether such therapy is sufficient to restore the patient's health.

In the first place, then, one may entertain serious doubts whether a inner-release attitude is really neutral. During the treatment the patient must obviously get the impression that conscience—the censor—is a psychic force that is not always a very reliable guide, and it must become painfully clear to him that, at least in his case, it has done a great deal of harm. But then, what is more natural than for the patient to draw the conclusion that henceforth he should disregard the dictates of the censor? The therapist may pretend to remain neutral, but this very attitude of neutrality would motivate the patient's decision.

Theoretically one may speak of a neutral attitude. In practice, the inner-release theory is not neutral, because it necessarily raises the question of what should be released. Only the biological needs of man? Biological needs do not exhaust the needs of human nature. There are two selves in man. Which self should be expressed? The higher self with its lofty aspirations toward perfection, or the lower animal self? The best evidence that the release theory never is neutral in practice is found in Freud's own attitude. Freud definitely had a philosophy of life: the Epicurean or hedonistic philosophy, which aims at the egress of the lower self, the expression of biological needs, even though this expression should take place within limits, or—to use Freud's terminology—the pleasure principle should be subordinated to the reality principle.

Since Freud clearly shows in his writings that he considers the moral taboos to be wrong, and since he says that much mental grief and sorrow could be prevented if the rules of public morality were less rigorous, it is probably no rash judgment to surmise that he advanced, or hinted at, the same ideas when treating his patients. If that be true, it could scarcely be called a neutral attitude. Equally unneutral is Stekel's opinion, when he advocates in his earlier books that masturbation should not be considered evil and that homosexual activities should not be condemned. Whether this opinion is expressed in the form of advice or disguised in the form of an insinuation, it certainly is not an opinion that reflects neutrality, and the implication for certain patients is all too clear. True, Stekel in his later works revised his opinion, but not because of moral considerations. It is obvious that not only Catholics but all those who believe in the natural law reject such a "neutral" attitude. Even if it be granted for the sake of argument that the free satisfaction of immoral impulses might help the patient to regain his mental balance, yet sound ethics forbid him to buy his health at that price. But experience tells us that the unhampered gratification of immoral impulses will *not* restore the neurotic's mental health. This was precisely the reason why Stekel revised his earlier opinion. It may be concluded, therefore, that the inner-release therapy is not neutral.

Secondly, supposing that the release therapy does take a really neutral attitude; then, a serious question arises. Is the nondirective analyst really justified in stopping where he does? Presupposing that analysis has given the patient an understanding of his condition and that it has disclosed certain dynamic tendencies operating in the patient, should the therapist leave the patient to work out his own problem without any support, direction, advice, or counsel, from the therapist's side? In by far the majority of cases it will be found that the patient possesses both good and bad potentialities in the therapeutic, social, and moral sense of these words. The neutral-attitude theoreticians would advise to withhold any advice. A recent example is the attitude of Carl Rogers, whose technique has been hailed as a return to the original Freudian inner-release theory. Rogers believes that the therapy will be successful only when the therapist is genuinely willing to accept the patient's own choice, regardless of whether the client chooses "goals that are social or antisocial, moral or immoral," regardless of whether the client chooses "neuroticism rather than mental health . . . , death rather than life." As was said in Chapter 7, this attitude is unacceptable to anyone who believes in the natural law. But apart from this basic objection, and considering the problem from the purely therapeutic standpoint, it is highly questionable whether—as Rogers believes—life will be chosen when the therapist is willing to accept the patient's choice for death, or whether a healthy normality will be chosen when the therapist is willing to accept the client's choice for neuroticism.[4] There are limits to "accepting," as one of Rogers' own collaborators, Thomas Gordon, rightly points out.[5]

Rogers would probably counter with the remark that every patient contains within himself constructive elements. This may well be true, but then the fundamental question still remains whether the patients also possess the capacity to integrate themselves or to develop the desirable tendencies that are beneficial for their well-being without any help or direction. And the answer of a great many analysts is that faith in the patient's abilities in that respect is rather naïve. One of the more recent authors of psychoanalysis, M. R. Sapirstein, offers as his opinion: "Unfortunately for the average patient, the mere understanding of where his machinery has broken down and what his internal conflicts are, may not be sufficient to cure all his difficulties. He may find that although he understands what is wrong with his interpersonal relationships, he is still unable to change." [6] These words mean that analysis is only part of the process and that the analyst should go beyond by outlining for the patient a new and better plan of life. But then it should be frankly admitted that the psychagogical or psychosynthetic procedure means a wide breach in the very structure of the original Freudian methodology.

We find, even among Freud's own disciples, several analysts who abandoned the original inner-release technique as insufficient. Early in the history of the psychoanalytical movement, A. Kronfeld pointed out the necessity of the psychagogical or psychosynthetic procedure. He admitted that he felt happy even (*sic*) when his patients were Catholic or communist, because in that case they offered a positive basis upon which to build a constructive plan of life. Kronfeld condensed his guidance program into one formula, which he expressed in the word "*stärker-sein*"; he advised the patient to "be stronger" also in moral matters.[7] But then it is obvious that the reeducation process comes down to a training of the will.

Several other authors, even though they may not consider the will to be a faculty, admit that there is in man a power or a function that should be reinforced in order to obtain lasting therapeutic results. Otto Rank has been mentioned in this connection, and one may add J. H. Schultz [8] and A. Moll.[9] Summarizing this aim of psychotherapy, Carp says that the pillars upon which the entire psychotherapy rests are (*a*) self-knowledge obtained through catharsis and analysis, and (*b*) training of the will.[10]

To digress a little by way of some concrete examples, it may be said that training of the will is particularly indicated during the period of reconvalescence of patients suffering from traumatic hysteria and in the case of psychopaths. In such and similar cases, what does the advice to "be stronger" imply? In the first place, there is a suggestive element in it, for any advice or admonition coming from the psychiatrist is strongly suggestive to the patient because of the relationship of transference between the two. But the advice to "be stronger" includes much more; it means that the patient should take himself in hand and reform his character, but he can do so only if he strengthens that power in him which we call the will.

Many psychiatrists have a very strange idea about will power, and yet one may truly say that they use it in their therapeutic procedures without knowing it. Some time ago, a well-known New York psychiatrist discussed the problem of the will with one of the present authors. His conclusion was expressed in these words: "Well, if you can call it will, when my patients follow my advice and do what I tell them, it suits me well." And indeed, his presentation might be termed a definition in simple form of the activity of the will. At any rate, this psychiatrist showed by these same words that he did not subscribe to the Liebman recipe of not telling his patients "what to do or how to act." Whatever their theoretical ideas about will power may be, the fact remains that a considerable number of psychiatrists see the strengthening of the patient's will as the first step in his program of reeducation. But, since the will must have an object, the question naturally arises of what the patient's will should be trained for. To this question many psychiatrists answer that the patient should train himself to live up to a more satisfactory plan of life which the psychiatrist should help to outline for him.

There is no doubt that many an outstanding psychiatrist stresses the great importance of a philosophy of life, both for the therapist and the patient. So does Adler, followed by L. Seif.[11] So does Jung, to whose view Von Hattingberg subscribed. According to Jung, a therapy that leaves out of consideration the basic notions of a political, economic, philosophical, and religious nature or purposely disregards recognizing the very real influence of these concepts on man, hardly deserves the name of therapy.[12]

Therefore, Jung's complaint is understandable when he concedes that he is at his wits' end when he has a patient who just does not have any ideal or plan of life, because in that case, as he says, he really does not know what to do with him. The psychagogical method also finds strong advocates in Carp and Hugenholtz.[13]

Among the prominent advocates of psychagogic therapy in the United States should be mentioned Adolf Meyer, Thomas V. Moore, and Erich Fromm. Meyer always insisted that the patient should take an active part in the treatment. The therapist's scope should be to make the patient realize that neither the environmental circumstances, nor the various experiences, organic diseases, or complications that befall him during his lifetime are the sole causes of his mental disturbances, but rather that it is his internal attitude toward these factors that is at fault. Hence, to achieve a lasting cure he should rebuild his personality by adopting a new role in life and by striving toward the attainment of more pertinent values.

Moore pointed out his therapeutic aims by emphasizing the signal importance of a sound philosophy of life for the patient. By a philosophy of life he means "an interpretation of life, a view, provisional at least, of the purpose of life and a body of principles to govern conduct in the more or less serious problems and difficulties of life. . . . We need a philosophy of life in order to deal with life's interior mental problems and to govern our external relations with other human beings." [14] Moore had many followers in Catholic circles; yet, he did not succeed in converting all his collaborators from the old-fashioned Freudian attitude of neutrality to his reasonable and more efficient directive therapy.

Erich Fromm expresses very much the same idea as Moore did, for he holds that what the majority of psychoneurotic patients really need is a reorientation about their own human destiny so as to become aware of the meaning of life.[15] There is, however, an all-important difference between Moore's standpoint and Fromm's. Whereas Moore advocates a philosophy of life in which God holds the central place, Fromm approaches the problem of destiny from a nontheistic standpoint. Among non-Catholic writers who seem to adopt Fromm's ideas but interpret human destiny in theistic terms are Rollo May [16] and Seward Hiltner.[17] The problem of the theistic versus the nontheistic view will be examined in the next chapter.

The above survey clearly shows that many outstanding psychotherapists have turned away from Freud's original "analysis-alone" method. The change is far from general; even though among the orthodox Freudians there is in practice more directive therapy than they wish to recognize, theoretically at least they consider any reference to a philosophy of life as an aimless rationalization which only serves to cover up the therapist's own complexes. Nevertheless, an impressive number of psychotherapists see the fulfillment of their task in making the patient adopt a better concept of life.

A positive philosophy of life supposes some concept or value that holds the position of central importance in one's life. Theoretically speaking, each of the values that may predominate in the life of men might be stressed by the psychotherapists in their psychagogic endeavors. But, as a matter of fact, the literature mentions particularly hedonistic, political, social, moral, and religious values as the aim of psychotherapy.

The authors have previously expressed their opinion that Freudianism is, despite its pretense of neutrality, a *hedonistic*, Epicurean system, and therefore there is no need to come back to it.

Adler and his school see the final aim of psychotherapy in the reinforcement of the patient's *social* interest. The individual should conquer his fundamental egoism, his selfish urge to dominate, and replace his individualistic will-to-power by the will to serve the community. Somewhat the same idea is expressed in the writings of many contemporary American psychiatrists. They assume that most or all emotional troubles of their patients result from their failure to adapt themselves satisfactorily to their social environment. The remedy therefore lies in helping the patient to change whatever is unsatisfactory in his relationship with other people and readapt himself realistically to the society in which he lives. This is the main therapeutic aim of Adolf Meyer and his followers. Harry Stack Sullivan, too, sees the main purpose of psychiatry in giving the patients "an understanding of the social order in which they live." [18]

There can be little doubt that this therapy has its merits, but only up to a certain extent. In the first place, the assumption on which it rests is questionable. Everyone knows from experience that by no means all mental and emotional difficulties are due to unsatisfactory interpersonal relations. In that respect, Adler's view digs deeper into the matter. Moreover, the social-adjustment view runs into practical difficulties because it is based on a relativistic standpoint. What kind of social order should be presented to a patient as the ideal for which he is to work? A capitalistic or communistic, national or international, democratic or authoritarian society? One may advocate adjustment with the "social order in which the patient lives." But it is easy to imagine an individual who lives in a certain social order, *e.g.*, in a capitalistic society or under the Nazi regime, and who has become neurotic precisely because of the pressure brought upon him by that system. One may picture the enthusiasm with which a patient in such circumstances will accept an exhortation to make himself comfortable in the social order in which he lives. It may, therefore, be concluded that the social-adjustment therapy, although not to be rejected, is limited in its scope and applicability.

Still more limited is a therapy that aims at building up *political* values in its patients. Of course, it would be somewhat surprising if there were in the United States a psychiatrist who would tell his patients that their troubles would vanish if they firmly embraced the Republican or Democratic ideals. But in totalitarian states "political" therapists are not an exception. An example was the German psychiatrist Gauger,[19] who saw the purpose of psychotherapy in promoting political ideals in his patients. He tried to instill into their minds the value of blood and soil, national interest, discipline, loyalty, and honor—all very desirable values. But Gauger was living in Hitler's Nazi state, and hence he interpreted these values according to the Nazi ideology. He may well have scored success with some enthusiastic believers in the Third Reich, but what is left to them, now that their entire political world has collapsed? The example shows how relativistic this kind of therapy would be; it would have no permanent value.

An ever-growing number of psychiatrists begin to recognize the significance of *moral* values for psychotherapy. It has been seen previously how Stekel came, through sad experience, to realize the value of moral obligations. Karen Horney believes that a thorough orientation concerning moral problems belongs to the very basic task of psychotherapy. According to J. C. Flugel, morals can no longer be divorced from psychiatry. In the opinion of V. Frankl,[20] ethical values ought to have precedence in the hierarchy of values—*i.e.*, the economic, political, social æsthetic, and other objectives that the patient may consider as his ideal should be evaluated in the light of sound ethics. But then the question arises of what is to be understood by "sound ethics." This is another of the crucial problems that confront the psychiatrist. Vernon Jones[21] complains that teachers have standards in spelling but not in morals. The same complaint cannot be made—far from it—with regard to psychiatrists as a whole, but unfortunately it is true that many advocate relativistic standards of morality.

It may be worth while to take a look at some of these standards. Freud, forgetting for a while his own neutrality principle, would advise the building up of the ego-ideal of the patient—and the ego-ideal is, to Freud, primarily a moral factor that admonishes the individual to adopt the moral standards of his environment. But what right has Freud to look upon the moral standards of one's environment as *the* standards of morality, and what guarantee does he offer that these standards are better and more reliable than those which the patient has thus far made his own and which have been—wholly or in part—the cause of his neurotic condition?

G. Brock Chisholm thinks that present standards of morality are too rigorous and that, because of their rigidity, they form an obstacle to enduring peace and social progress. He therefore suggests that, if ethics is to be of any use to psychiatry, a higher concept of ethics must be built, although he is not very clear about how to achieve this goal.[22] If this suggestion of superior ethics is taken at its face value, the question may well be asked whether it does not lead to Nietzsche's paranoia.

Chapter 2 has shown the incongruity of the relativistic position; here it suffices to show a few applications of the Catholic doctrine of objective morality. There is no special ethics for high society, bourgeoisie and proletarians, for geniuses or exceptionally gifted men like artists. There is not even a special type of ethics for politicians and diplomats; neither is there any for physicians or psychiatrists. The Catholic Church condemns any psychological or psychiatric theory or practice that clashes with the dictates of objective morality.

If there is a conflict between psychiatry and objective ethics, the former must cede the issue. Why? Because ethics deals with one's moral health, and psychiatry with one's bodily or mental health; the moral health is the more important of the two. Suppose a patient is suffering from a conflict between his suppressed desires—perhaps the impulse to practice masturbation, or sexual intercourse outside marriage—and the moral force called conscience. Suppose a physician, on the basis of some theory, would advise that patient to gratify his impulses. The Catholic Church's comment upon such advice is very simple and direct: she condemns it.

Some find the Church's uncompromising attitude difficult to understand; therefore, a comparison may, perhaps, clarify this attitude. Another patient needs a rest, a change of surroundings, and the physician recommends a nice trip abroad. But the patient has not got the money for it. For his health's sake he should get it, one may say, but should his physician advise him to steal the thousand dollars that he needs? Probably not. Stealing is against the law in civilized countries, and the physician's suggestion might bring his patient, and perhaps even himself, into unpleasant contact with the police.

It may be that the first patient, whom the physician has advised to give in to his sexual impulses, stays clear of the police. Nevertheless, there is another law forbidding such behavior. Of course, if one believes that this law is man-made, one may possibly find a loophole for escaping it. But that is precisely the point. The Catholic Church refuses to admit that the law forbidding acts of impurity—to use that old-fashioned word—is a mere human law; she believes that such acts are forbidden by divine law and that God must be obeyed. "*Dura lex, sed lex*—it is a hard law, but it is the law," the old Romans used to say.

Perhaps some might try to rationalize their advice on the basis of this or that analogy. Stealing a piece of bread when a person is starving is not really stealing. Now a patient may be hungry, craving for some sexual satisfaction. Therefore . . . what? No conclusion follows from such an analogy. Snatching a piece of bread when one is starving is not stealing; it is not only allowed but commanded because of the law of self-preservation, which takes precedence over the right to private property. But the gratification of the type of sexual lust of which we speak here remains stealing, whether the person craves for it or not, for such acts are necessary neither for self-preservation nor for the preservation of the species. Other means are available to satisfy or to counteract such cravings: sublimation, character formation, and voluntary control.

What has been said thus far about the value of moral principles in psychotherapy has been from a more or less negative viewpoint; it has been pointed out what a psychiatrist with any respect for the moral conscience of his patients should avoid doing. It is now important to approach the matter from a more positive standpoint. When the condition of a patient involves moral issues, the psychiatrist should be expected in the first place to clarify these issues for him. Every psychiatrist meets patients who are terribly confused concerning such matters, as, for instance, is the case with scrupulous people. Any psychiatrist is likely to be confronted with questions like this: "Do you think, doctor, that I am morally allowed to do such or such a thing?" An example in point is the practice of masturbation. In asking such questions, the patient expects a serious answer, and because of the relationship of trust and sympathy that exists between him and the therapist, he is likely to follow it up. But then it is clear that, if the psychiatrist wishes to give an answer, he ought to know the correct answer so as not to confuse his patient's conscience. Especially when dealing with a Catholic patient, he ought to know what is formally a sin and what is not, and he ought also to know what the extenuating circumstances are that exculpate an individual from subjective moral guilt, although his act might be objectively wrong.

It is no secret at all that the knowledge of Catholic morality among psychiatrists is not always very profound; hence, it is understandable that many of them try to avoid answering such questions. Yet, the patients want an answer. Therefore, instead of simply brushing aside such questions, it would be more beneficial to the patient for the psychiatrist to refer him to a priest. Here, then, we have an example of how a fruitful cooperation could be established between the pastor and the psychiatrist.

The problem about the relationship between ethics and psychiatry concerns not only the clarification of moral issues, but also the correction and guidance of the patient's behavior. At this point, an important question arises. Should the therapist assume a correcting or directing role in moral matters? And here a certain wavering attitude is found among psychiatrists, at least in their theory. Presupposing that they do not belong to the neutral-attitude school, they recognize fully the therapeutic value of moral principles in securing for the patient a better plan of life; but, on the other hand, they do not feel qualified to act as "moralists." In practice, however, they often play a role which, if not that of a moralist, is at least a reasonable facsimile.

In order to understand the psychiatrist's position with regard to the direction and guidance in the patient's reeducation program, let us put the problem on a broader basis and ask whether the therapist is entitled to impose any plan of life upon his patient, regardless of whether this plan is social, or moral, or religious, or of any other type. In practice, the problem will come down to this: is the psychiatrist justified in imposing his philosophy of life? Some therapists may say: "Yes, of course, because the patient should trust the principles underlying my therapy, or else he should leave or never have come to me in the first place." Now, there are many patients, such as those in hospitals, asylums, institutions, and in the armed forces, who have little say in the matter of choosing their psychiatrist. But even apart from that fact, the answer obviously evades the issue. If the psychiatrist's purpose is to free the patient from the consequences of a plan of life which he had adopted but which, because it was not satisfactory, has made him a neurotic, it is clear that a plan of life that is forced upon him may have the same, if not worse, consequences.

The psychiatrist who, consciously or unconsciously, would impose upon his patients his own philosophy of life would trespass the limits of his competence. This is so obvious that it scarcely needs arguing. No one would deem it permissible for a Catholic or communist psychiatrist to force his philosophy of life upon a non-Catholic or noncommunist patient. Such a procedure not only would be unfair, but would probably serve only to confuse the patient still further. But then the same rule may be expected to hold for any other psychiatrist, whether he be a follower of Freud, Adler, Stekel, Jung, Adolf Meyer, William A. White, H. S. Sullivan, K. Horney, Franz Alexander, Levi Bianchini, or anyone else who has devised a psychotherapeutic theory. The German author J. H. Schultz rightly warns psychotherapists, including analysts, not to set themselves up as peddlers in philosophy, as moralists, as pastor-substitutes, or as schoolmasters.[23]

Here again the psychiatrist seems to face a dilemma. On the one hand, he is not supposed to impose on the patient any philosophy of life. On the other hand, after the patient has gained an understanding of what is wrong with him, he is often unable to change unless assisted, and this assistance usually involves some plan for his future life.

The solutions of the dilemma as presented by some therapists are sometimes vague and ambiguous. But most of them adopt, in practice, the following attitude as a solution. While the aim of analysis and catharsis is to give the patient a certain measure of insight not only into the causes underlying his condition but also into the tendencies and potentialities of his personality that are beneficial to his further development, the psychagogical method aims at guiding and directing the patient toward the realization and actualization of these potentialities inherent in his personality structure. In simple words, if the therapist really deserves the name of psychiatrist, he must be able, through analysis and observation, to penetrate into the patient's personality and guide him according to the potencies, ideals, and aspirations that he discovers in his patient's psyche, regardless of whether they are hidden in the depth of his unconscious or are well above the level of consciousness.

Hence, the purpose of the reeducation method is to bring the patient to the realization of those objectives that will make his life worth living—in other words, to revive values to be found within himself. These objectives will never become real values to the patient if they are forced upon him from the outside, but they should be appropriate to his own individual personality, and therefore the patient should discover them himself in himself. The psychiatrist, on his part, having gained a sufficient insight into the patient's personality structure, should be able to assist him in discovering those valuable objectives.

This general principle could and should be applied, too, when it appears that a patient would greatly profit by adopting a sound set of moral rules to govern his conduct. And here there comes to the psychiatrist's attention a fact which is often misinterpreted or ridiculed but which is nevertheless true and has been recognized as true by sound-thinking people since the beginning of mankind. This fact is that the natural law is inscribed in the heart, or psyche or soul or whatever one wants to call it, of all men.

The basic principles of the natural law are made known to each man through the "voice of conscience." This "voice" is in many cases very soft indeed, and it may be scarcely audible. But any unbiased analysis, *i.e.*, any analysis not prejudiced by some preconceived theory about the origin of morality and of conscience, will find traces of the natural law in each man. The only thing required of the therapist is that he recognize conscience as an existent fact and point its value out to the patient just as he might point out any other value that he discovers in the patient's personality structure.

If the psychotherapist is able to strengthen and steady the "voice of conscience," he is doing his client the best possible service. In doing so, he is certainly not taking a neutral attitude, but neither is he acting as a pastor or schoolmaster or moralist. He is acting in perfect line with his own profession, which consists in securing for the patient a future free from mental trouble. For, is it not true that much mental trouble finds its source in a conflict between a person's lower impulses and his conscience? If that is the case, it is altogether within the jurisdiction of the physician to try to avoid future conflicts by pointing out the danger that lies in the gratification of the lower instincts.

This is as far as the psychiatrist should go and, also, as far as he can go. Further discussions about moral matters, such as the origin of conscience and the question whether obedience to the natural law is obligatory, belong not to the physician's province but to that of the pastor.

The attitude of the psychiatrist concerning moral matters may be compared with that of the priest concerning medical matters. Suppose a patient tells the priest that according to his doctor he suffers from—and some unpronounceable name follows. He continues by saying that the doctor prescribed—another mysterious name. The only sensible attitude that the priest can take is to tell the patient to believe the doctor and to take the medicine; if the patient wants to know more about the nature of his ailment or about the working of the medicine, the priest can only refer him to the doctor.

Clearly, the procedure as outlined above is in every respect very different from Freud's technique. In theory Freud laid little stress upon the psychagogical method; his primary aim consisted in making conscious the id, which is basically a negative, destructive force no matter what Freud finally claimed to create out of it. Modern psychagogical therapists maintain that therapy should not insist on making things conscious at any price. And if the therapist aims at making things conscious, he should also make conscious the positive, constructive values that he discovers in the patient's personality, and assist the patient in actualizing these values.[24] Many present-day analysts emphasize that the final aim of psychotherapy consists in the formation of desirable habits in the patient. True, some are rather vague in their definition of the term "desirable habits," but others are quite exact and simply stress the value of good moral habits. Now, it should be remembered that good moral habits are, in theology, called virtues, either natural or supernatural. Hence, it is clear that at least some analysts have come to recognize the significance of moral virtues in psychotherapy.

It is also clear that conscience is after all not such a wicked and harmful force as Freud suggested when he blamed God for having created in man "an uneven and careless piece of work." Certainly, conscience may be formed wrongly, and then it may be the source of emotional and mental difficulties. But God is not to blame for the improper formation, as Freud believed, nor is religion as such to blame, as Liebman says, but the blameworthy factor is either the person or his surroundings.

Conscience, if properly formed, is a reliable guide and is by no means a repressing force only. This brings one back to the dilemma outlined in the beginning of this chapter, the dilemma that drives many analysts to the so-called neutral attitude. They feel that they cannot side with conscience, because it would serve only to build up new repressions; on the other hand, they feel hesitant to advise greater gratification of impulses, because they would then be accused of undermining morality. Unable to solve the problem, they pretend to resort to neutrality. As has been pointed out, this is a dilemma that follows from Freudian premises. Hence, no one else is obliged to solve it for those who created it. As a matter of fact, for the Catholic psychiatrist it does not exist. If it be admitted that conscience *in itself* is not a harmful instrument, the entire dilemma disappears into thin air. Conscience may be harmful when formed in an erroneous way. But then it would be the task of the therapist to re-form it, and if the therapist does not feel qualified to do so, he should accept the cooperation of the pastor.

In this chapter the neutral-attitude theory has been criticized and it has been maintained that it should be—and, as a matter of fact, often is—supplemented by a reeducation program. The various values that may be of help in psychotherapy have been surveyed, and the great significance of moral principles has been singled out. The implementation of these principles will be greatly beneficial to the patient, if they are in accordance with the objective norm of morality. And the therapist will often find these principles in his patients through an unbiased analysis of their conscience. The next chapter will discuss in some detail the significance of religious values in psychotherapy.

NOTES AND REFERENCES

1. *"Nein, unsere Wissenschaft ist keine Illusion. Eine Illusion aber wäre es, zu glauben, dasz wir anders woher bekommen können, was sie uns nicht geben kann";* quoted in SENG, H., Gedanken zum Problem: Psychotherapie und Religion, *Nervenarzt,* Vol. 2 (1929), p. 393.
2. LIEBMAN, JOSHUA L., "Peace of Mind" (New York: Simon and Schuster, Inc., 1946), pp. 31, 32.
3. The dilemma outlined in the text is exposed with great clarity in FLUGEL, J. C., "Man, Morals and Society" (New York: International Universities Press, 1945), pp. 32, 33.
4. ROGERS, CARL R., "Client-centered Therapy" (Boston: Houghton Mifflin Company, 1951), pp. 48, 49.
5. GORDON, THOMAS, "Group-centered Leadership and Administration," in ROGERS, *op. cit.,* p. 356.
6. SAPIRSTEIN, M. R., "Emotional Security" (New York: Crown Publishers, 1948), p. 252.
7. KRONFELD, A., "Psychotherapie" (Berlin: Springer-Verlag, 1924), p. 375: *"Eine solche Ideė des Stärker-seins läszt sich in jedem Menschen aufrufen."*
8. SCHULTZ, J. H., "Die seelische Krankenbehandlung" (Jena: Gustav Fischer, 1930).
9. MOLL, A., "Der Hypnotismus" (Berlin: H. Kornfeld, 1924).
10. CARP, E. A. D. E., "De Psychopathieën" (Amsterdam: Scheltema & Holkema, 1940), p. 462.
11. SEIF, L., Weltanschauung und Psychotherapie, *Zentralblatt für Psychotherapie,* Vol. 7 (1934), p. 193.
12. JUNG, C. G., Geleitwort, *ibid.,* Vol. 8 (1935), p. 3: *"Ein Heilsystem welches dabei die weltbewegenden* 'représentations collectives' *politischer, ökonomischer, philosophischer und religiöser Natur auszer Acht läszt oder gar deren gründliche Anerkennung als bestehender Mächte geflissentlich übersieht, verdient wohl schwerlich den Namen einer Therapie."*
13. HUGENHOLTZ, P. T., "De Psychagogie of re-educatieve Behandelingsmethode" (Lochem: De Tijdstroom, 1946).

14. MOORE, THOMAS V., "Personal Mental Hygiene" (New York: Grune and Stratton, 1945), p. 235.
15. FROMM, ERICH, "Man for Himself" (New York: Rinehart & Company, 1947); "Psychoanalysis and Religion" (New Haven: Yale University Press, 1950).
16. MAY, ROLLO, "The Art of Counseling" (Nashville, Tenn.: Abingdon-Cokesbury Press, 1938), "Springs of Creative Living" (Nashville, Tenn.: Abingdon-Cokesbury Press, 1940).
17. HILTNER, SEWARD, "Pastoral Counseling" (Nashville, Tenn.: Abingdon-Cokesbury Press, 1949).
18. SULLIVAN, HARRY STACK, "Conceptions of Modern Psychiatry" (reprinted from *Psychiatry, Journal of the Biology and the Pathology of Interpersonal Relations,* Vol. 3 [1940], No. 1, and Vol. 8 [1945], No. 2); see also GREEN, A. W., Social Values and Psychotherapy, *Journal of Personality,* Vol. 14 (1946), pp. 199–228.
19. GAUGER, K., Psychotherapie und politisches Weltbild, *Zentralblatt für Psychotherapie,* Vol. 7 (1934), p. 158.
20. FRANKL, VIKTOR, Zur geistigen Problematik der Psychotherapie, *ibid.,* Vol. 10 (1938), p. 33.
21. JONES, VERNON, Ideas on Right and Wrong among Teachers and Children, *Teachers College Record,* Vol. 30 (1929), pp. 529–541.
22. CHISHOLM, G. BROCK, The Psychiatry of Enduring Peace and Social Progress (William A. White Lectures), *Psychiatry, Journal of the Biology and the Pathology of Interpersonal Relations,* Vol. 9 (1946).
23. SCHULTZ, J. H., in Bumke's "Handbuch der Geisteskrankheiten" (Berlin: Springer-Verlag (1934), Vol. 5, Part 1. The psychotherapist is not supposed to be a "*Menschheitsbeglücker, Pastorenersatz, Schulmeister für Erwachsene, Systempropagandist oder Weltanschauungshändler.*"
24. FRANKL, V., "Der unbewuszte Gott" (Vienna: Amandus-Edition, 1948), pp. 44–48: "*Heute dürfen wir nämlich keineswegs mehr auf dem Standpunkt beharren, in der Psychotherapie komme es auf Bewusztwerdung auf jeden Preis an; denn nur vorübergehend hat der Psychotherapeut etwas bewuszt zu machen. Er hat Unbewusztes—und so auch geistig Unbewusztes—nur bewuszt zu machen, um es schlieszlich wieder unbewuszt werden zu lassen; er hat eine unbewuszte* potentia *in einem bewuszten* actus *überzuführen-zu keinem andren Zweck jedoch, als um schlieszlich einen wieder unbewuszten* habitus *herzustellen.*"

Chapter 11

RELIGION AND PSYCHIATRY

The growing interest among psychiatrists as well as the general public in the therapeutic value of religion is rather intriguing to witness. Lectures on this topic are likely to draw large audiences; papers on the subject are being given a place on the program of the meetings of psychiatrists and the associations for mental health; and books discussing the problem are among the good and best sellers. Again, one of the present authors represented the Catholic viewpoint in a group made up of clergymen from the three largest religious bodies of the United States, of psychologists, and of psychiatrists. For some time, this group met monthly under the auspices of what then was called the National Committee for Mental Hygiene in order to discuss the relationship between psychiatry and religion. All this activity goes to show that Freud's expectation about the "future of an illusion" has not come true and that, instead, one might well speak of the illusion of what Freud predicted to be the future.

Freud considered religion to be the universal obsessional neurosis.[1] To the founder of psychoanalysis, religion was a pure fiction, an illusion having no real value and, therefore, an illusion from which mankind should liberate itself and for which psychoanalysis, supposed to be not an illusion but a reality, should be substituted. Freud came to his opinion about religion through his blind belief in the infallibility of his own method. His argument runs briefly as follows. Psychoanalysis has laid bare the real nature of religion by revealing the nature of its object, the divinity. Psychoanalysis has shown that God is nothing but the external projection of the early childhood image of the parent. But, if God does not really exist but is a figment of the mind, then religion is the worship of a fiction and, therefore, an illusion itself.

It is clear that the entire argument rests on the premise that psychoanalysis has once and for all solved the tremendous problem of the existence of God and the origin of religion—a premise that finds few believers outside psychoanalytic circles. The argument boils down to a very simple one. If God does not exist, psychoanalysis may possibly be a substitute for religion; but the fact that Freud and some of his followers make it a substitute for religion does not prove that God does not exist. Freud, of course, was well aware of the fact that mankind as a whole did not accept his dogmatic pronouncements, and his hostile attitude toward any kind of religion is probably explained by this awareness. If he believed that psychoanalysis meant a challenge to religion, he knew also that religion was the chief enemy of his system, for he said, "Of the three forces which can dispute the position of Science religion alone is a really serious enemy." [2] Freud considered this enemy a real danger, because, in brief, to his mind religion makes weaklings out of people.

A very simple factual observation would show that Freud's fear of this danger was slightly exaggerated, to say the least. Long before Freud, millions of people professed one or another form of religion but were, on the whole, no more neurotic than Freud. It would be a somewhat gratuitous statement to maintain that all those millions who "survived" their belief in God were weaklings; their strength and powers did not seem to be paralyzed by their obedience to God.

After seeing that Freud and other analysts have made psychiatry an inextricable tangle of psychology, medicine, ethnology, history, pseudophilosophy, pseudotheology, comparative religion, etc., people asked themselves if it would not be more reasonable to stop arguing about philosophical and theological problems. They wondered if it were really necessary to make lectures about the existence of God and the origin of religion the prerequisites for psychiatric treatment. If some therapist feels obliged to contest religious beliefs, let him put on the cap and gown of a theologian and thus enter the theological arena. However, does he need these impressive paraphernalia also when he enters his psychiatric office in order to treat a poor anxiety patient? Why not put psychiatry back on a factual basis? If Paracelsus returned, he might, perhaps, find reason to repeat his old warning "to forget words and manners and treat your patients."

Of course, religious problems may be at the root of the patient's condition. But is the psychiatrist requested to solve those problems on the theological level? The only thing that seems to be required is that the psychiatrist, regardless of what his own conviction about religion may be, do not brand his patient's religion as an illusion. At times he can use the patient's religious experiences in such wise that they will be helpful for the treatment.

Freud's exaggerated position is contradicted by many psychiatrists, including analysts, who no longer hold that belief in God is an illusion or a danger. One of the first to side with Freud's "really serious enemy" was his own pupil, Carl G. Jung. In his book "Modern Man in Search of a Soul," Jung makes the statement that he would have few patients if people, after passing the age of puberty, lived up to the tenets that the well-established religions have to offer.[3] And in an address delivered to a group of Protestant ministers at Strasbourg in 1932, he expressed an opinion directly opposite to Freud's: "It seems to me," he said, "that the considerable increase in the number of neuroses has paralleled the decrease of religious life." [4]

Jung holds that the chief tenets of religious belief exist as "images" in the collective psyche or, as Klages expresses it, in mankind's primeval original consciousness.[5] The philosopher will ask, of course, how these "images" happen to be there, but for purposes of this book one may well dispense with the question and simply point out that to these authors religious beliefs are not a mere illusion but a fact—a fact, moreover, that may be used to great advantage in psychotherapy.

The existential analysts, too, strenuously defend the same idea. The Viennese analyst, Viktor Frankl, says that many analysts no longer worry in the least about the future of an illusion, but that they have started thinking about the eternity of a reality.

In England, B. G. Sanders recently published an essay in which he compares Freudian psychoanalysis with religion. Flatly contradicting Freud's basic principle, he presupposes that God exists. On that basis, the book is a defense of Christianity against psychoanalysis. On the other hand, Sanders believes in Freud's purely psychological theories, and for that reason he makes an attempt to interpret the Christian religion from the psychoanalytic point of view, or—as he says—"to translate religion into the new language." [6]

To the authors' way of thinking, Sanders even though displaying a keen sense of logic, goes too far in his attempts to interpret Christian experience in the language and thought of psychoanalysis. Although it is true that the semantic differences sometimes handicap the development of mutual understanding between analysts and clergymen, there seems to be little need for translating religion into psychoanalytic language, and besides, in many instances it would probably be downright impossible. One might as well require psychoanalysis to be translated into the terminology of the Christian religion.

In the United States, too, we witness a movement of *rapprochement* between depth psychology and religion. Evidence thereof is to be found in the conferences and meetings referred to at the beginning of this chapter.

Among the writers who, each from his own standpoint, have contributed to that movement, Gregory Zilboorg,[7] Joshua Liebman,[8] Erich Fromm,[9] Thomas V. Moore,[10] and Karl Stern [11] may be mentioned.

William C. Menninger seems to express almost the same idea concerning the value of religion for mental health that Jung does. Menninger, in an address recorded by Lewellen's Productions, had this to say: "Christ Himself, centuries ago, laid down one of the principles of mental health that we now recognize as of paramount importance. Matthew, Mark and Luke all quoted Christ when they said in effect, 'For whosoever will save his life shall lose it, but whosoever will lose his life for My Sake will save it.' That sentence condenses in a nutshell the attributes of the mature individual. Some men can love others enough to derive more satisfaction from that than from being loved themselves. It is still a magnificent precept. If you can follow it, you will never live to make a date with a psychiatrist." [12]

Not all the writers mentioned may hail religion as a friend, but at least they do not ostracize it and they do find religious experiences helpful in their therapeutic procedures. Their number grows measurably when one takes into consideration the view of the many psychiatrists who do not belong to any school of depth psychology. After all, it should not be forgotten that not all psychiatrists are analysts, and still fewer are Freudians.

However, a serious word of caution must be inserted. Although some analysts begin to recognize the therapeutic significance of dependency on what they call, rather vaguely, religion and morality and to consider "religion" as a powerful source of emotional security, the concept of religion as it seems to exist in the mind of many of them is simply that of a tool that they incorporate into their therapeutic devices. What is worse, many of them seem to hope that psychoanalysis by incorporating religion will eventually be able to serve as a substitute for religion or at least to compete with it. In other words, psychoanalysis is to become the "new religion."

It seems, therefore, advisable to the authors to clarify their own position by defining the term "religion," for it is useless to speak of the therapeutic value of religion as long as one has not defined the term. Definition is all the more necessary inasmuch as the word "religion" has many entirely different connotations. At least a half hundred different definitions exist; in fact, Leuba, in 1914, set forth some forty-eight definitions, and others have since been added. Inasmuch as they reflect their formulators' own concepts of religion and of its origin, most of them are tendentious, but here is a definition free from that evil and covering, in accordance with the traditional sense, all the different kinds of theistic religions: "Religion is the sum-total of beliefs, rules of conduct, and rites governing the relations of man with a Power or Powers looked upon as transcendent."[13] This has been labeled a definition of religion in the traditional sense because at one time people considered it self-evident that religion is theistic. If it recognizes one supreme Power, or God, it is called monotheistic; if it recognizes more than one transcendent Power, or God, it is called polytheistic. Pantheism, which identifies the Supreme Being with the universe, may still be called theistic, but then the word is used in a broader sense.

In recent times, the term "religion" has been used with a still broader meaning in certain ideological systems in which the state or the political party is supposed to control the individual's destiny and is, hence, elevated to the rank of Supreme Being. Clearly, in this case, the adjective "theistic" no longer can be applied, and the word "religion" is used in an allegorical sense, in much the same way as when St. Paul says of certain people that "their God is in the belly" (Philippians 3:19). This type of "religion" was met in the discussion of the merits of Gauger's blood-and-soil therapy in the preceding chapter.

The usual consequence of the ideological or political type of religion is that people express their "belief" in one man, the leader, whose dictates they follow with some sort of religious fanaticism. Here, then, a man takes the position of central and supreme importance in the convictions of his followers, and if one still wishes to extend the term "religion" to such an authoritarian man-centered system, one might aptly call it humanistic religion. In other words, it would be perfectly arbitrary to see in humanistic religion the opposite of authoritarian religion.

Yet, this is precisely what some authors are doing at the present. They oppose humanistic to authoritarian religion, and in their eyes humanistic religion means that each individual takes the place of supreme importance, each one becoming his own god. The cultivation of his own personality, his self-realization, the development of his own strength and powers, is the objective of this kind of religion. This religion is the type advocated by Erich Fromm.[14] But one might well ask if the term "religion" is still in order when used in this way. It might be called a philosophy of life, but the claim that it is religion seems to be as confusing as the claim of the Russians that they, too, have democracy. Fromm adds still more to the confusion by saying that his humanistic religion is also theistic, when he actually means by "God" not a person, not a really existing being, but a symbol of man's powers. And the confusion reaches the height of absurdity when he speaks of "religion of no religion." His attempt to find historical support for his thesis in the field of comparative religion, and to show that his "new religion" is really very old, does not make his system a religion. It is a philosophy of life in which, although some moral ideals are advocated, man is the maker of his own laws. How stable such a man-made ethical system is in the long run, is Fromm's problem.

The above digression was necessary in order to point out the demarcation line between theistic and nontheistic religion. In this chapter the term "religion" is used to mean the theistic type, as it is practiced, for instance, by Catholics, orthodox Protestants, Jews, and Mohammedans—with, of course, special emphasis on the Catholic position.

Although Freud was antagonistic to all religions, it may well be that he would find little difficulty in accepting the nontheistic, humanistic kind of religion, for there seems to be little difference between this nontheistic religion and Freud's atheistic philosophy. But, regardless of what Freud would or would not accept, the fact remains that Freud's chief enemy, theistic religion, is still very much alive—certainly the Catholic religion is.

The Catholic concept concerning the origin of religion is clear. Religion is not born out of fear or out of a need of security; it is neither the projection of a father-image nor a common denominator of the teachings of the so-called great religions in the world. Religion is twofold, natural and revealed. The human mind is able to arrive through logical reasoning at the conclusion that God, the Creator of the universe, exists and that, in consequence, He has a right to obedience and to certain forms of worship; this is natural religion. Revealed religion comprises the body of truths that God Himself has taught mankind, either directly or by means of those who spoke in His name. These prophets who are God's mouthpiece are either men or, as Catholics and orthodox Protestants believe, God's own Son, Jesus Christ who took to Himself human nature, while remaining a Divine Person. In so far as that body of teachings contains truths which, theoretically speaking, the human mind could find out by itself, but which are so difficult and obscure that only a few would be able to do so, one may speak of revealed natural religion.

Blaise Pascal has written these profound words: *"Il n'y a que deux sortes de personnes, qu'on puisse appeler raisonnables: ou ceux qui servent Dieu de tout leur cœur, parce qu'ils le connaissent, ou ceux qui le cherchent de tout leur cœur, parce qu'ils ne le connaissent pas encore*—There are only two kinds of people who may be called reasonable: those who serve

God with all their heart, because they know Him, and those who seek God with all their heart, because they do not yet know Him."

Indeed, there are many people who have serious religious convictions, either of natural or revealed religion. Furthermore, many of them live up to their belief in such a way that their convictions regulate and dominate their moral conduct; as Pascal put it, they serve God with all their heart. Obviously, in these cases, religious experiences belong to the person's conscious sphere. To such people, religion is doubtless a strong anchor in life's emotional crises.

There are also people who apparently have no religion whatever; whose attitude toward God is, if not hostile, at least negative. And yet it may be found that, subconsciously or unconsciously, they are longing for "something higher" than what life seems to offer them. These are the ones who would command the interest of the depth psychologist.

If there are any people who belong to neither class, who lack religion and feel no desire to have any, not even unconsciously, it would ordinarily be a waste of time to "try religion" on them.

In the attitude of those "who serve God because they know Him," who not only have serious religious convictions but also try to live up to their belief in practice, there is certainly found a philosophy of life. For, when God holds the position of supreme importance in a person's life, that man has a purpose to live for and therefore understands the meaning of life and his own destiny. Such knowledge, based on deep conviction, is of immense value for mental health, both in the so-called ordinary days of life and in the times of acute emotional crisis.[15] He knows that he is playing a role in the universal scheme of things as planned by the Creator. The role may seem insignificant, but it acquires worth-while significance if one views it as part and parcel of God's plan. This knowledge gives the truly religious man a sense of submissiveness and resignation as well as satisfaction with his lot, peace of soul, and happiness. Modern psychiatry stresses the importance of creative activity. But if one is convinced that he is playing the role that God has assigned him, he will joyfully act his part, be he an artist or a banker or a bootblack.

Perhaps someone may say that nontheistic religion, too, is able to give a meaning to life and to outline for man his destiny. Indeed, a humanistic philosophy of life may well be beneficial to man's health, if it embodies a set of moral principles that are in accordance with the natural law. But again, one may well doubt the stability of a system that sees man's ultimate destiny in man himself. Moreover, that a humanistic philosophy may possess a positive value does not in the least mean that theistic religion has a negative value.

To speak of serving God implies, of course, that religion teaches dependency on God. Now, some psychoanalysts think that this is not a desirable attitude. In fact, one of Freud's objections to religion was precisely that it teaches dependency on an external power, for to Freud and his followers, the supreme good of psychiatry should be to make the patient a mature, independent, self-sufficient person. But this type of psychiatry seems to be decreasing in practice, since psychiatrists are beginning to realize that independence and self-sufficiency may be just as unhealthy and neurotic as some forms of dependency; they have learned by experience that the extremely independent individuals are not the most useful elements in society. To quote M. R. Sapirstein: "More and more, psychiatrists seem prepared to accept the dependencies of religion, social causes and group movements, as healthy and needful, without labeling them 'sublimated homosexuality' to a father figure, or a desire to return to the mother's womb." [16] This is the opinion of a non-Catholic. Catholics hold that the dependency on God is a healthy one because it prevents the individual from becoming unduly attached to, and therefore dependent on, himself, other persons, and things. On the other hand, dependency on God, according to the Catholic doctrine, does not make a weakling out of man, for that doctrine teaches very emphatically that God helps those who help themselves (*"Facienti quod in se est, Deus non denegat gratiam"*). This conviction gives him strength, self-respect, and the proper evaluation of success.

In the light of his own destiny, religion teaches a person to accept frustrations and suffering, and thereby religion is able to dissipate unhappiness. The individual aware of life's basic meaning more readily endures sorrow, grief, the monotony of everyday routine, and emotional crises that otherwise might result in depression. He may see that even suffering serves a purpose, and thus it becomes a constructive element.

Does religion take away life's disappointments, difficulties, perplexities, drudgery, labor, duress, and pressure? Certainly not! But it teaches the individual endurance and resignation, because religion—and religion alone—gives him the answer to the perennial problem of the nature of evil and sorrow. One who does not know why there is evil in the world and why so much hardship befalls him personally, is likely to collapse and fall into depression, and eventually he may be driven to suicide. For those who are tortured by the problem of good and evil there is only one alternative —an alternative strikingly illustrated in the life of the French writer Joris Karl Huysmans, who tried Satanism but finally returned to Catholicism, the faith of his childhood. His friend, Barbey d'Aurévilly, wrote of him: "Only one choice is left to Huysmans, the choice between the revolver and the crucifix." Huysmans chose the crucifix.

As for the duress or pressure that arises from exterior circumstances, it may easily happen that religious leaders, *e.g.*, priests, are able to ease such pressure by modifying the environment; in this respect, they are better qualified than the psychiatrists. Religion, as such, cannot, of course, modify the environment, but it can modify the individual by helping him to adjust better to his environment. Psychiatry can do that, too, but it acknowledges defeat in the face of truly insuperable difficulties coming from without. Now, even in such cases religion may be of considerable help, for there are numerous examples of persons who find sufficient strength in their religion to face, and adjust themselves to apparently insuperable difficulties. However, such cases can hardly be explained from the natural standpoint.

A theocentric plan of life teaches a person to surmount his egocentricity. An example is the notoriously self-centered hysteric, who is well on the road to mental health if he can be brought to an attitude of patiently enduring his sufferings for God's sake instead of making a show of them. The surmounting of one's egocentricity also provides a basis for satisfactory interpersonal relationship and charity toward his fellow men, because respect for persons is grounded in the fatherhood of God instead of in changing human sentiments.

Not infrequently one finds a certain confusion about the respective roles of ethics and religion. The two are not identical. An ethical system is not necessarily a religion, unless one wishes to give to the term "religion" the farfetched interpretation that was rejected in the discussion of nontheistic religion. Such a system easily breaks down when the stress of life becomes really serious, because it lacks a solid basis. On the other hand, every religion worthy of the name includes a body of moral principles which it presents to its followers as the rules that should govern their conduct. Religion is effective in the implementation of moral standards, which, if sincerely followed up, would prevent a great deal of mental and emotional grief. In addition, religion gives the individual the reasons why he should conform his conduct to those standards.

When the authors, in their discussions with psychiatrists, particularly analysts, have compared what the psychiatrists call desirable and undesirable habits with what Catholic ethics and theology call virtues and vices, they have repeatedly come to the conclusion that most psychiatrists lack a correct understanding of the latter. If psychiatrists would learn what Catholic moral theology means by virtues and vices, much misunderstanding could be prevented. For that purpose they would do well to read the clear-cut definitions set forth by St. Thomas Aquinas, particularly in the Second Part of the *Summa Theologica.*

An example of such misunderstanding may be found in connection with the virtue of humility. The reason why some psychiatrists appear to rate humility as of little value seems to be their erroneous definition of that virtue. They believe that the desire that they encourage in their patients to be successfully competitive as a part of their normal self-fulfillment violates humility, even when they insist that the desire be kept within limits, since they are well aware of the fact that the excessive drive for success may become pathological and endanger healthy human relationships. It is hard to see where psychiatry and religion differ concerning the strivings resulting from such a desire when they are considered from the purely natural standard. To be sure, religion forbids pride, the inordinate, excessive striving after one's own excellence and greatness, and vainglory, pride's resultant showing off of one's real, or imagined, greatness. If this drive to appear more than one is, goes to excess, it may well become pathological and the source of neurosis, especially when the drive is frustrated. Now, the opposite of pride is humility, but humility is not what some seem to think it. It is not opposed to moderate self-respect. The humble man recognizes that all that he is and has, comes from God, but he is also convinced that he may use all the gifts and talents that God has given him, not for his own but for God's glory. Real humility does not prevent normal self-fulfillment. On the contrary, Catholic ethics encourages the full development of one's capacities, talents, and skills. In fact, it considers normal self-fulfillment here on earth for the rank and file of people their best preparation for eternal life. And in that sense, Catholic ethics does not prohibit the drive for success, even worldly success, as long as this drive does not become excessive and turn into pride, vainglory, ambition, or presumption. We said Catholic *ethics,* because Catholic asceticism may stress the renunciation of all worldly success; but this renunciation is not the general rule and is advised only to those who wish to strive after higher perfection and are spiritually equipped for such a life.

Another example of misunderstanding is found in the concept of hostility, of which there is so much talk in the more recent psychoanalytic literature. The thesis of the analytic school is that no close relationship exists without a certain amount of hostility, which then is traced back to some hurtful relationship in early childhood. And because the analysts believe that the release of such hostility feelings serves a useful therapeutic purpose, they feel that they should encourage the expression of such feelings during the analytical sessions. For the same reason they look somewhat askance at religion, which—so they suppose—suppresses all feelings of hostility. The supposition is incorrect, because religion does not merely take a negative attitude by suppressing these feelings, but it makes a positive attempt to resolve hostility by the exercise of the opposite virtue; *i.e.*, religion teaches that hostility toward men should be met by exercising the virtue of charity, and hostility toward God by the virtue of religion. As to the latter, feelings of hostility toward God are by no means always evidence of the lack of faith, as some analysts seem to surmise. On the contrary, it happens that such feelings are found in believing and devout people. Another wrong notion found in the writings of psychoanalysts is that hostility toward God is forbidden because it implies retaliation. This is an erroneous idea. Such hostility is forbidden because it is evil. As a matter of fact, psychiatrists ought to be grateful that true religion tries to resolve hostility; for the more religion succeeds in doing so, the less work will they have to do to analyze and release those feelings of hostility. On the other hand, it is understood that religion does not go deeper than the conscious level and does not reach or attack the unconscious source of certain forms of hostility.

Still another example of confusion is found in the concepts of sin, guilt, and guilt feelings. It may, therefore, be valuable to set forth the correct distinctions. Sin and the feeling of guilt do not parallel each other. Sin is a violation of the moral law and, therefore, an offense against the Supreme Lawgiver. Sin supposes full consciousness. This is an important point, because it means that there is no such thing as an unconscious sin and that a purely material deviation from the law, not adverted to as such, is no sin in the formal sense.

Now, if one has committed a formal sin, he is guilty; yet, the feeling of guilt is a subjective phenomenon. As a feeling it is evidently conscious, although it may be vague or confused. But such a feeling may be the result of either conscious or unconscious factors. When a person commits a sin, he knows full well why he feels guilty. But the source of guilt feelings may also be unconscious; in other words, an individual may feel guilty where there does not seem to be any apparent sin. With these distinctions in mind, one is in a position to give an answer to a question that arose among a group of psychiatrists at whose meeting the authors were present: Are guilt feelings always undesirable? Some of those present were of the opinion that all guilt feelings are undesirable; others, that some guilt feelings could be put to constructive use. The authors' answer was that sin itself is always "undesirable," but that when it comes to feelings of guilt, one must distinguish among them. Guilt feelings caused by a formal, conscious sin are a natural phenomenon and desirable because they motivate a man to see his own inadequacy. The realization that he has committed a sin may well create in a person a feeling of humiliation; it shows him his imperfection and limitations, and in that manner guilt feelings may have a constructive character. On the other hand, guilt feelings that stem from an unconscious source are always undesirable. Now, religion has little to do with the latter, because it plays a role only with regard to those guilt feelings that are the result of a conscious sin.

A final question remains concerning sin. If the psychiatrist is not, and should not be, a moralist, what, then, should be his attitude toward sin? The question is important, because wrong ideas about it seem to exist, even among Catholics. Sin, in the sense of an offense against God, should be treated in the confessional, not in the office of the psychiatrist. A comparison may make this point clear. When a physician treats a syphilitic, he does so without moralizing about the patient's previous conduct that has caused the sickness. However, after the man has been cured, the physician might, perhaps, give him a bit of human advice for the future —at least he might, if he has at heart the patient's well-being and not his own pocketbook. A similar condition exists when the psychotherapist is treating a mental case. Suppose that certain activities which ethics calls sinful have made the patient what he is, a neurotic. During the treatment, there will be appraisal of the conflict and of the motivations underlying the man's actions, but it is not within the psychiatrist's scope to enter into a discussion about the morality of these actions. However, although the psychiatrist is not a moralist, this does not in the least imply that psychiatry is divorced from morality in the sense that it may advise or allow immoral practices if it considers them useful or needful for the "self-fulfillment" of the patient.

When the contributions of religion to mental health are compared with those of psychiatry, psychiatrists often make two remarks that deserve an answer. The first remark concerns the nature of the goals and aspirations of psychiatry and religion respectively. Some psychoanalysts hold that the goals and aspirations of psychiatry are usually quite high, and they believe that those set by religion are "much lower and easier of fulfillment." This is really an amazing statement—a statement that no one with even a superficial acquaintance with the teachings of Christian ethics, moral theology, and asceticism would ever make. Psychiatry may set itself various goals, but the all-embracing goal is, probably, to heighten the individual's aspirations for personal fulfillment—but, psychiatry wisely adds, *within limits;* it does not believe that a person achieves his fulfillment by aspiring at goals of a neurotic or infantile nature. What are religion's goals? The Catholic religion teaches that the ultimate end of man is, objectively, God's extrinsic glory, and subjectively, his own eternal happiness. How is he to attain this goal in his present life? By knowing and serving God to the best of his abilities; in a word, by striving after self-perfection. To be sure, this includes, in the first place, spiritual self-perfection, but it includes, too, the perfecting of his nature by the exercise of all its functions, physical as well as mental. The proximate end of a man is the self-realization of all his potentialities: he *must* strive to become a useful person in society, and he *may* strive after recognition, honor, riches, and pleasure, but *within limits—i.e.*, he may strive for them as long as these aspirations do not clash with his primary goal, the service of God, the observance of His commandments, and the welfare of his fellow men. In view of this statement, it would seem that the goal of serious psychiatry and religion may, at times, coincide. But it is false to believe that religion's aims are of a lower order. Since striving toward self-perfection requires an unwavering discipline throughout life, it is hard to understand how anyone would think that the goals and aspirations of religion are set "much lower" than those of psychiatry. As a matter of fact, religion sets them on a higher level.

The second remark, somewhat contradictory to the first, is that psychiatry can, after all, contribute all that religion has to offer. Apart from the simple, pragmatic observation that religion is for the millions and psychiatry for the few who can pay a handsome fee, the Catholic psychiatrists' answer is that religion is no substitute for psychiatry nor psychiatry a substitute for religion.

Psychiatry, including any type of depth therapy, offers methods and techniques for the treatment of the mentally ill. In that respect, religion is no substitute for psychiatry, for the simple reason that religion—at least the Catholic religion—is not a medical system. Religion primarily aims at bringing people closer to God, and by doing so it may secondarily promote their mental health. And this secondary task is mostly of a protective, preventive, and safeguarding nature.

However, once a person has a serious mental breakdown, he may—if he so wishes—go to church and light a candle, but right after that it would be a sensible thing for him to visit the office of a psychiatrist. And then, while the psychotherapeutic treatment develops, the therapist may feel the need of assisting the patient to outline a better plan of life for the future. This plan of life may stress various values that may help to make the individual's life worth living; *e.g.*, as we have seen, it may stress artistic or social values, or even economic or political values. The psychiatrist may also stress the value of religion, and by religion is meant—the demarcation line having been drawn in the beginning of our discussions—theistic religion.

Nevertheless, there are certain things that no psychiatry can ever give. Of these, two points may be considered here. Religion alone (again, theistic religion) can give what the Germans call the "*ruhenden Pol*"—the firmly fixed pole, the Absolute. When God holds the central place in one's life, life's perplexities and emotional crises become relatively unimportant. But no psychiatry can give God to a patient unless he already has serious religious convictions.

But there is more: people who have such serious convictions believe that God assists them in a very personal way. This belief is found among Catholics and Protestants alike and is far from uncommon among the adherents of non-Christian religions. This assistance is called divine grace. And no psychiatrist can give grace to his patients. Many a psychiatrist will shrug his shoulders and say that he does not know what that means. This may well be true, but ignorance gives no one the right to refer to grace as an illusion. It is well to remember occasionally Shakespeare's caustic words: "There are more things in heaven and earth, Horatio, than are dreamt of in your philosophy." Regardless of what grace may mean to the unbeliever, the fact is that it is a very real thing in the minds of the faithful and that it plays a real part in their lives.

Avoiding theological discussions and distinctions, a simple description of what Catholics mean by supernatural grace may help to make the concept at least understandable, if not acceptable. Grace is a supernatural gift of God to man, bestowed for the purpose of helping him to achieve his salvation. This divine assistance illumines a person's reason so that he may see more clearly what is good and expected of him, and it strengthens his will so that he may more readily fulfill his obligations.

Many Catholics may not have a very clear conception about grace, but every good Catholic possesses the basic concept that God helps him in a special way, particularly in times of need, stress, strain, and emotional trouble. This very idea that "God will help me to overcome even that" contributes greatly to producing in him a sense of trust, strength, resignation, and submission, and, if necessary, the capability of starting a change of life.

A few illustrations may clarify what might be called the psychodynamics of grace. It should be understood that supernatural grace does not substitute for, or destroy, the natural powers and functions of man, but, rather, builds upon them. A person during or after prayer, when he "feels better," may see his difficulties in a different light; he may feel deeply sorry for his sins and thereby feel reconciled with God; he may feel a greater love for God; he may see the importance of things eternal and, by the same token, the relative insignificance of earthly things, including his sufferings; his hope may be strengthened so that the future looks brighter; he may feel resigned to accept whatever comes to him; etc. All these thoughts, desires, acts of the will, and aspirations have a reassuring, uplifting effect, even when we look upon them from the purely natural standpoint. But Catholics hold that God influences the soul of a person in prayer in such a way that he not only experiences these thoughts and aspirations, but does so to a higher and more efficacious degree. And everyone will agree that such aspirations have a beneficial effect on one's mental condition and, according to psychosomatics, on his physical well-being, too.

Another illustration is faith. The acceptance of the body of Catholic teachings is, in the final analysis, based on faith. Faith is an assent of the mind based on the authority; *i.e.*, the wisdom and veracity—of another. If the "other" is God, we speak of divine faith. Now, divine faith is a grace; *i.e.*, without a gift from God of His enlightening and helping grace, no man can make an act of faith that is profitable for salvation. And this faith in God is, in the minds of the faithful, a powerful means for overriding doubt, fear, and anxiety.

True faith also inspires hope; the faithful Catholic not only hopes that God will reward him with eternal life but also trusts that God will help him in the difficulties of his earthly life. But again, according to the Catholic doctrine, hope is not only a natural phenomenon, but also a supernatural gift, which the faithful acquire and develop through God's grace.

One of the main difficulties that every person encounters in his present life is the fight to control his animal instincts. Of course, the Catholic Church rejects the "man is only an animal" theory of certain groups of psychiatrists. As long as they adhere to this principle, any further discussion is perfectly useless. Catholic doctrine concedes that man is an animal, but adds that he is "endowed with reason." The aim of the Catholic religion, therefore, is not to kill the animal in man, but so to enlighten and strengthen his higher powers, intellect, and will that man may achieve the purpose for which he is created. And here is another illustration of what is meant by grace. Left to himself, a person would hardly be able to subdue his animal instincts, but if he asks for it, God will help him. A good example is found in the case of the alcoholic who asks the Lord every morning to help him to stay sober that day; he is convinced that, if he succeeds, he owes it to God's assistance, and to the alcoholic this assistance is not an illusion, but a very real thing.

The fact that grace is a reality does not mean that it must be tangible or visible. Except in extraordinary conditions, grace is usually known only by its effects. If one wishes to adopt analytical language, one might say that divine grace usually works on the unconscious level to produce very conscious effects, but that this is an unconscious sphere that is not accessible to psychoanalysis.

A psychiatrist may here remark that he cannot work with such a thing as grace. No, of course not. This is precisely the point that the authors wanted to make clear. In this respect, religion infinitely transcends any type of psychiatry. And it was necessary to make this point clear, because this chapter deals with the relationship between religion and psychiatry.

In a discussion of that relationship, one often encounters the trite objection that religion is, after all, not a perfect guide, because religious people may also become mentally ill. Indeed they do! Before taking up a more detailed discussion, it may be well to repeat the thesis of this chapter: the sincere observance of serious religious convictions and practices protects and safeguards mental health, but religion is not a panacea any more than psychiatric treatment is an infallible means for curing a patient.

The problem may now be considered from several angles. When one has to do with a mental disorder of an organogenic, or endogenous or constitutional, nature, such as certain forms of psychosis, religion can no more prevent its development than it can prevent or cure, *e.g.*, hereditary ataxia. Hence, the problem dwindles down to a consideration of the exogenous and psychogenic disorders, particularly the psychoneuroses.

Now, it happens in some instances that, far from being preventive, the patient's religion is, on the contrary, conducive to the creation of mental disorders. We mean those types of religions that are based exclusively, or almost exclusively, on irrational, emotional elements. Examples in point would be voodooism, spiritism, and mediumism. The treatment of a patient who is the victim of his own religious practices seems to run into a dilemma. On the one hand, the patient's religion—not an interpretation of it, but his religion itself—is supposed to be the cause of his troubles; on the other hand, the psychiatrist is bound to respect a person's conscience in the choice of religion. It is not for Catholic psychology to solve this dilemma, since Catholicism certainly does not belong to the irrational or highly emotional types of religion, but it would be interesting to see how a conscientious psychiatrist would solve it. Anyway, the example shows that not every type of religion is conducive to mental health.

It happens also that an individual may falsely interpret the precepts of his religion. Such a misinterpretation of otherwise perfectly sound rules may lead to such deplorable conditions as compulsions, fixed ideas, and scrupulosity. In that case, not religion, but the peculiar twist in the patient's mind (or, at times even a peculiar twist in the mind of the spiritual adviser) is to be blamed. In that case, the first thing a psychiatrist has to do is to give the patient a correct picture of his own religion. Therefore, the therapist ought to know the teachings of his patient's religion about objective and subjective sin as well as what the limitations of free will are in a mentally sick person. Naturally, there arises the question of how the psychiatrist is to approach his task if he has little knowledge of religion in general and of his patient's religion in particular. The ideal in such cases is usually that the psychiatrist and patient observe the same religion.

Moreover, while it may well be true that a conflict is at the root of most psychoneuroses, it is equally true that not all these conflicts are of a religious or moral nature. For instance, the seed of these conflicts may well be sowed in childhood, an age in which religious convictions are quite unstable or nonexistent. To ask religion to uproot in later life the evils planted in early life would be asking for a kind of miracle.

Finally, once more it must be repeated that the condition for the mental-health value of religion is that people truly live their religion. Perhaps not all people who are supposed to be religious and yet become neurotic have made their religious convictions an integral part of their lives. Some may consider this remark a mere evasion. But Jung, who had some experience in the matter, did not think so, as witness his statement mentioned previously.

Thus far, this chapter has discussed the mental-health value of religion for those persons who have serious religious convictions. What of those who confess to have little or no religion—is a religiously tinted plan of life of any use to such individuals when they are in mental trouble? Often enough, one will find that those who now profess to be without a religion once had one. For one reason or another, they gave it up, but they are quite conscious of the remnants of the old religious education; in fact, that old religion for some mysterious reason may still appeal to them. This holds true especially for Catholics. An example is the case of a sailor of Polish ancestry who appeared to be in a state of severe depression. The man had not practiced his religion for twenty or more years; he had lived a fairly dissipated life and had broken almost all the precepts and commandments except the one forbidding murder. But he confided: "I gave it up, because—you know—it is really too difficult, but in spite of it all, I cannot get away from it." By "it" he meant, of course, the religion of his youth. It may be said in passing that here is another illustration of the dynamics of supernatural grace, for the Catholic explanation of the man's state is that the grace of baptism was still active in him. And it did not take long to find out that what the man really needed to overcome his depression was a return to the faith of his fathers and a practical observance of its moral rules. The only way to reeducate this person to a better plan of life was to rekindle the embers of his earlier religious and moral ideas.

There are also people who never had any serious religious ideas to speak of, and who profess not to feel the need for any religion. These are the people who pose an interesting problem when they come to see the psychiatrist. The psychiatrist, at his wits' end, may decide to advise them to "try religion." Of course, the very idea of "trying religion" is absurd, for religion is not just a pair of galoshes that one puts on because it happens to be a rainy day. If one has neither sincere and honest religious convictions nor a sincere and honest desire for them, he cannot acquire them overnight, no matter how hard he may momentarily try. When dealing with a patient, one should not claim too soon that he lacks all religious aspirations. However, in case the analyst does not find anything that even remotely resembles religion, it would obviously be useless to "try religion."

The reader may remember that the assumption underlying the discussion of both this and the preceding chapter is that the psychiatrist is looking for a plan of life to give the patient in order to secure his future. If the patient does not seem to show any religion, is the psychiatrist to renounce religious values and rely on some social, or vaguely moral, value as the basis of the patient's reorientation? This is one of the most serious problems that confront a psychiatrist who is concerned about the future of his patient, as is evidenced by Jung's complaint that often he did not know what to do with patients who lacked religious ideals that might give meaning and direction to their lives.

At this point, a solution is offered by the existential analysts, whose remarkable work has done a great deal to break down false and prejudiced ideas and to revive very old ones. They maintain, as we have seen, that an analysis unbiased by any preconceived concepts reveals a longing for spiritual values in many individuals. These religious strivings may emerge from the deepest levels of an individual's unconscious, even in persons who reject all religion. Like other strivings, they demand release; in fact, the repression of these longings for something higher may be found to be the very reason for the patients' restlessness and depressions. This standpoint is, after all, nothing new, but it is very remote from Freud's.

The observations of the existential analysts, although expressed in the analytic language, are consistent with Pascal's observation that many of those who do not know God are at least seeking Him. They are consistent with St. Augustine's immortal words: "*Inquietum est cor nostrum, donec requiescat in te, Domine*—Restless is our heart, O Lord, until it rests in Thee." They are also consistent with the age-old adage that "*anima est naturaliter religiosa*—the soul is naturally religious," a truth that Tertullian expressed in an even stronger form. The observations of the existential analysts are, in fine, consistent with the teaching of Catholic philosophy concerning the "eternal quest"; *i.e.*, in a rational human being there is a natural desire for God. Therefore, when treating their patients, the existential analysts do not hesitate to bring these spiritual strivings into the open. They act somewhat like St. Paul, who, after finding in the midst of the Areopagus an altar with the inscription "To the unknown God," began to proclaim to the men of Athens what they worshiped in ignorance (Acts 17:22–31).

But, supposing that the psychiatrist thinks that the revival of religious ideals might be beneficial for the patient, there recurs the same question that has already been presented with regard to the moral values. How is the analyst to approach his task? The existential analyst, like any other psychiatrist, knows that he is not a priest; neither should he, as a physician, attempt to replace, or substitute himself for, the priest. Such an attempt would be beyond his task. What is more, it would serve no curative purpose were he to drive or to stimulate his patient in a religious direction, since an imposed religion is no real religion. Therefore, the patient must decide his ideals for himself. All that the therapist should do is to wait until the latent religious elements within his patient break through spontaneously. Sooner or later, as he knows by experience, they will appear, even with a manifestly irreligious person. When they do, the psychiatrist may help the patient to develop them.

This discussion of the mental-hygiene value of religion leaves little doubt that religion can be useful in preserving mental health or in giving a solid basis for its recovery should it be lost. However, it is wholly wrong to consider religion as the handmaid of psychiatry. Such a notion might arise in the minds of those who conceive of depth psychology as a new form of religion. If analysts wish to make use of religious experiences in the treatment of their patients, it may be all for the better; but they should not presume that psychoanalysis is the yardstick by which these experiences must be measured, nor should they believe that religious and moral convictions and experiences have value only when they can be interpreted in analytical terms, as if that were the only language that counted. Religion has a mental-health value all its own, and had it long before there was any professional depth therapy.

Although psychiatry and religion cannot be compared in many respects, it is quite possible for the psychiatrist and the pastor to work together for the well-being of the people. The work of one may supplement that of the other. The necessary condition to such cooperation is that the psychiatrist consider religion not as an illusion, but as a reality, for simple fairness would forbid him to use an illusion as a means of helping his patients. If religion were an illusion, Freud would have been right in suggesting that it should be stamped out. Since it is a reality, the therapist may make use of it; but, when doing so, he no longer adheres to the gospel of the Viennese master.

This evaluation of the analytical methodology may now be summarized briefly. Although in theory some depth psychologists may advocate a purely nondirective and neutral inner-release therapy, in practice the majority aim at educating their patients to be responsible individuals. Obviously, the term "responsible" makes little sense unless we know for what and to whom we are responsible. An increasing number of therapists consider the task of psychotherapy to be that of making their patients so aware of their responsibility for the fulfillment of certain positive values that purpose is given to their lives. Which values the patient chooses, depends upon his own individual personality structure. It is precisely the task of the analyst to bring this individual disposition to the fore. How far the analyst wishes to go in guiding or correcting his patient's aspirations will greatly depend upon his own principles and personality and upon his own conscience.

Objectively speaking, not all values that a person considers worth living for are to be put on the same plane. Purely hedonistic values will scarcely be found to be beneficial to the individual, and such other values as the social, economic, and political ones have only a relative significance; but moral values are of the greatest importance. To whom is an individual responsible? The demarcation line is here drawn by the individual's positive or negative attitude toward God. If he has a nonreligious philosophy of life, he may feel responsible to society or to his own conscience for whatever value he wishes to realize in his life; if his plan of life is religious, he knows that he is responsible to God. Again, the first attitude has only relative significance; the latter has absolute value.

The relationship between theistic religion and mental health may be summed up in the following statements:

1. Sincere religious convictions are a powerful therapeutic aid to the preservation of mental health, but they do not constitute an infallible panacea.

2. Religious convictions have no mental-health value for an individual unless he makes an honest attempt to regulate his conduct according to his belief.

3. Religion is no substitute for psychiatry: when a person's health has broken down, pious exhortations alone will not restore it, but religion may well provide for a better plan of life in the future.

4. Psychiatry is no substitute for religion, despite the attempts of some "new religionists."

5. Religion may be considered from the natural standpoint and, as such, helpful for mental health as it provides for a stable set of moral principles.

6. The Catholic religion is revealed, supernatural religion; being supernatural, it cannot be compared with psychiatry. However, this fact does not imply opposition: there need be no more opposition between the Catholic religion and psychiatry in the sense of treatment of the mentally ill

than there actually is between the Catholic religion and general medicine.

7. Religion works on the conscious level; analytical psychology, to a great extent, on the unconscious level. There need be no opposition between the Catholic religion and analytical psychiatry so long as the latter avoids smuggling into either its psychological theories or its therapy any philosophical principles that are unacceptable to the former. Freudian psychoanalysis is doing just that.

NOTES AND REFERENCES

1. Freud, S., "Die Zukunft einer Illusion" (Vienna, 1927), p. 48: "*Uns hat sich mit Hilfe der historischen Reste die Auffassung der religiösen Lehrsätze als gleichsam neurotischer Delikte ergeben und nun dürfen wir sagen, es ist wahrscheinlich an der Zeit, wie in der analytischen Behandlung des Neurotikers die Erfolge der Verdrängung durch die Ergebnisse der rationellen Geistesarbeit zu ersetzen.*"
2. Freud, S., "New Introductory Lectures on Psychoanalysis," p. 205.
3. Jung, C. G., "Modern Man in Search of a Soul" (New York: Harcourt, Brace and Company, Inc., 1936), p. 264: "During the past thirty years, people from all the civilized countries of the earth have consulted me. I have treated many hundreds of patients, the larger number being Protestants, a smaller number Jews, and not more than five or six believing Catholics. Among all my patients in the second half of life—that is to say, over thirty-five—there has not been one whose problem in the last resort was not that of finding a religious outlook on life. It is safe to say that every one of them fell ill because he had lost that which the living religions of every age have given to their followers, and none of them has been really healed who did not regain his religious outlook."
4. "*Es scheint mir als ob parallel mit dem Niedergang des religiösen Lebens die Neurosen sich beträchtlich vermehrt hätten.*"
5. Klages, L., "Vom kosmogenischen Eros" (Munich, 1922).
6. Sanders, G. B., "Christianity after Freud" (London: Geoffrey Bles, Ltd., 1949).
7. Zilboorg, Gregory, Psychoanalysis and Religion, *Atlantic Monthly,* Vol. 183 (1949).
8. Liebman, Joshua L., "Peace of Mind" (New York: Simon and Schuster, Inc., 1946).
9. Fromm, Erich, "Escape from Freedom" (New York: Rinehart & Company, Inc., 1941); "Man for Himself" (New York: Rinehart & Company, Inc., 1947); "Psychoanalysis and Religion" (New Haven: Yale University Press, 1950).
10. Moore, Thomas V., "Personal Mental Hygiene" (New York: Grune and Stratton, 1945).
11. Stern, Karl, Religion and Psychiatry, *Commonweal,* Vol. 49 (1948), pp. 30–33.

12. "Meet Your Mind," with Dr. William C. Menninger, Narrator and Technical Advisor, Lewellen's Productions, 1947.
13. GRANDMAISON, L. DE, "L'Étude des religions" in "Christus, Manuel d'histoire des religions," edited by J. Huby (Paris: Beauchesne, 1931), pp. 6–7.
14. Another typical example of the man-made concept of religion may be found in DUNLAP, KNIGHT, "Religion: Its Functions in Human Life" (New York: McGraw-Hill Book Company, Inc., 1946).
15. An excellent description of the value of religion for mental health may be found in MOORE, *op. cit.*, pp. 232–248.
16. SAPIRSTEIN, M. R., "Emotional Security" (New York: Crown Publishers, 1948), p. 82.

Chapter 12

THE PRIEST AND MENTAL HEALTH

In the Catholic Church the care of souls (*cura animarum*) is entrusted to the priests, who work among the faithful under the direction of their bishops and, ultimately, of the Pope, Vicar of Christ on earth. This pastoral care is, first and foremost, of a spiritual nature. The priest's primary task is to bring the people to Christ through observance of the Gospel's precepts, and thereby secure their eternal salvation. This task comprises preaching the Gospel, supervising and giving religious education to young and old, administering the sacraments, assisting the sick, presiding over liturgical ceremonies, and giving pastoral advice and counseling; and the Church lays upon the priest the obligation of praying for the flock in Holy Mass and the Divine Office. In a word, the priest is ordained to serve man in the things that pertain to God. He takes care of the spiritual needs of his parishioners' souls, and if need be, he is doctor of the soul. In all these functions, the priest is dealing with people; the interpersonal relations between the priest and the faithful extend all through the latter's life from the cradle to the grave.

But each one of all these people has his own particular problems. These problems may be of an economic, a social, or a more personal nature, such as emotional and mental problems. Since, among Catholic parishioners the priest is their personal confidant, he is often the first one whom they approach in the crises of life. In this respect, it is interesting to relate the results of an inquiry that Jung made with regard to the question whether people in spiritual distress—the term "spiritual" is used in a very wide sense—"prefer nowadays to consult the doctor rather than the clergyman." The following summary shows the answers to his questionnaire. "Those who decided for the doctor represented 57 percent of Protestants and only 25 percent of the Catholics, while those who decided for the divine formed 8 percent of the Protestants and 58 percent of the Catholics. These were the unequivocal decisions. There were some 35 percent of the Protestants who could not make up their minds, while only 17 percent of the Catholics were undecided." Jung added that the inquiry was restricted to educated persons and expressed his conviction that the uneducated classes would have reacted in a different way.[1] But it is our belief that the reaction of the so-called uneducated classes of Catholics is overwhelmingly in favor of consulting the priest first.

Only a small percentage of the mentally disturbed voluntarily go to see the psychiatrist. Others of them arrive at a kind of compromise with themselves, just hoping that time and nature will take care of their troubles—and they sometimes do. Still others, unable or unwilling to see the psychiatrist, find their way to the rectory. In addition to the latter group, there is the great number of quite normal people who submit their problems to the priest for advice and counseling.

Every period of history has its own problems, but it is probably safe to say that our present complex society creates more mental and emotional problems for people than has been the case at any other turning point in history. Modern society has been unbalanced for some time, and two global wars have done little or nothing to restore the lost equilibrium and give people freedom from fear. The unstable economic and social conditions cause insecurity and unhappiness in the lives of millions of people. Normal family life is threatened by divorce, by contraception, and, in many instances, by the lack of adequate housing. Broken homes have created an upsurge of juvenile delinquency. Unemployment and alcoholism add to a further deterioration of society. And because international, national, and interpersonal relations are strained, very many people are confused and filled with suspicion, fear, tension, and mistrust. All these factors, to which many more could be added, are detrimental to mental health because this external and internal pressure and strain are the cause of much mental suffering, which, often enough, develops into mental disorders. This is evidenced, for instance, by the fact that in the United States a suicide is committed about every half hour. Another illustration is the well-known fact that one-third of all the rejections for military service in the United States were made for mental or nervous diseases, while 44.6 per cent of the discharges given by the army for medical reasons were for mental or emotional disturbances.[2]

Now the Church, although never intended to be primarily an international court of arbitration, has, wherever possible, promoted peace among the people; likewise, the Church, although not primarily a social service agency, has never ceased to prevent social ills by promoting educational and recreational facilities, by seeking to moderate the warring elements in labor unions, and, in general, by exercising an influence for peaceful living. The prevention of national and international conflicts and the re-establishment of a social order offering greater security for individuals would erase the causes of a great deal of mental unhappiness and strain. However, this discussion does not deal with the measures of prevention in the international and social orders but rather with the question of what can be done to help the individuals whose mental health has already suffered or is now being imperiled for any reason whatever. It is true that the causative factors for such suffering may belong to the categories mentioned, *i.e.*, they may be found in the present international and social conditions; but it is also true that the causative factors may belong to more personal categories, *i.e.*, they may be found in the domestic and other interpersonal relations of the individual or in his own personality. Whatever the reason may be, the question is what the priest can do to give such help to his people as to prevent the appearance of mental disease or to restore mental health in the event that disease does occur. It should be emphasized once more that the Church is neither a psychiatric institution nor an association for mental hygiene, nor is the rectory a consultation agency for the mentally unbalanced. Nevertheless, the pastor cannot remain uninterested in the question of the mental health of his parishioners, for mental confusion, instability, and disorder interfere with his people's spiritual well-being. What can priests—operating in their own sphere, using their own means, and relying on the help of their own training—do to improve the mental health of their parishioners?

When speaking of the priest's contribution to mental health, one's thoughts turn first to his function as a confessor. Now, confession in the Catholic sense has a therapeutic value all its own, but it cannot be compared with any other therapeutic device since confession is a sacrament and therefore belongs to the supernatural order. Those who look upon sacramental confession as just another psychotherapeutic device miss its meaning completely. When a Catholic sincerely confesses the sins that are known to him and, after repenting his sins, promising to mend his ways, and accepting the penance imposed upon him, receives absolution, he firmly believes that God has forgiven his sins and is giving him through this very sacrament the grace to lead a better life.

Although confession belongs to the supernatural order, it has psychotherapeutic aftereffects, for it not only rids the penitent of his sins but greatly contributes in most cases to his feeling of security by ridding him of his feelings of guilt. This holds for the average individual. Many a person tortured by guilt feelings due to perfectly conscious sins confides to the priest after a good confession, "If this had gone on much longer, I believe it would have driven me crazy; as it is, I feel much relieved." Hence, confession may help to prevent the occurrence of mental disease.

In this connection, the case of a fallen-away Catholic priest comes to mind. Although a talented man, he had an unbalanced and epileptic personality, and, after apostasizing, he launched attack after attack against the Church. This state of affairs continued for some time, until at length he fell sick with a serious nervous breakdown. One day, he complained to his Protestant nurse that he was utterly unhappy and frightened. Whereupon, the nurse, who knew who he was, flatly told him, "What you need is a good confession." This simple diagnosis opened his eyes; he went to confession, was received back into the Church, and has led a tolerably happy life ever since.

As has been said, a good confession is able in most cases to rid the penitent of his guilt feelings. However, not everybody leaves the confessional in a state of elation, for some, even though they have made a sincere confession, continue to be tortured by feelings of guilt. There are, for instance, the scrupulous, who walk out of the confessional still tormented by feelings of guilt concerning their so-called sins; in their cases, confession should be coupled with a special treatment, which will be discussed in the chapter on scrupulosity. There are also those who are tortured by guilt feelings that do not seem to have a conscious cause but appear to stem from the unconscious depths of their minds; in their cases, confession is restricted to cleansing them from the sins of which they are conscious.

When Christ instituted the Sacrament of Penance, He did not intend it to be a means for healing mental or emotional abnormalities. In receiving the sacrament, the penitent confesses only his sins—and these belong, necessarily, to the conscious sphere alone, for there is no such thing as an unconscious sin in the moral sense of the word. Thus, confession is not a device to dig below the conscious level and therefore does not reach guilt feelings that have their origin in the unconscious sphere. In order to clear up these feelings, psychiatric means, such as analytical methods, for instance, must be used. It would seem, therefore, that confession, particularly the general confession, shows a greater resemblance to the cathartic method than to analytical methods, inasmuch as catharsis in the strict sense of the word does not penetrate below the conscious level of the mind. In addition, both catharsis and confession have a cleansing, purging effect on the individual.

A few other points of analogy between psychotherapeutic methods and confession may be signalized. In the first place, the examination of conscience that precedes the confession is some form of self-analysis, although restricted to the conscious sphere. Again, confession, like analysis, may show a strong element of resistance. Every priest knows how difficult it can be, at times, to make the penitent open up and be really sincere with himself—a fact that may be illustrated by turning once again to the French writer, Joris Karl Huysmans, who narrated the story of his own conversion in his novel "En route." Huysmans related how, during the examination of his conscience, he became more and more horrified by the recollection of his sins. Frightened by the thought of revealing the sordidness of his entire life to another man, he began to shudder and perspire; indeed, he came very close to leaving the place. After much hesitation, however, he entered the confessional, but was only able to blurt out the words: "I have committed every sin, every sin . . . ," and then he cried out: "I cannot. I cannot." But just as he was about to run away, he felt the priest's hand on his shoulder and heard a quiet voice telling him: "You are too excited now; come back tomorrow morning at nine o'clock; I'll be waiting for you." And the next morning the confession succeeded.

It may be said that confession also presents an analogy with the transference phenomenon. However, when the penitent confesses to the priest, he does not see the latter in any of the roles that psychoanalysis ascribes to the analyst. The penitent does not see in the priest a father-image, nor does he see his own ego-ideal, which would have the paradoxical and rather sterile implication that he would confess to his own conscience. Rather, to him the priest takes the place of God, and the penitent knows that he receives absolution in the name of God. Hence, if one may speak of transference reactions in the confessional, they are, for the average penitent, those occurring between himself and God.

It is true that in some instances there may be some transference reactions of an emotional nature on the part of the penitent with regard to the confessor. It has been said that the priest is usually less well equipped than the psychiatrist to handle such reactions. The truth of this remark can be conceded up to a certain extent. The priest is not in a position to make use of the transference phenomenon, as the psychiatrist is; *i.e.*, the priest does not explain or verbalize such reactions to the patient, and should not, for the simple reason that the confessional is not a couch. However, here a serious warning should be sounded with regard to the dangers of transference. Although most priests are quite capable of recognizing the pitfalls of transference, when they are dealing with mental cases in or outside the confessional, it sometimes happens that they are caught unawares and then faced with embarrassing consequences. As an illustration the following case may be cited:

§ A girl, twenty-five years old, had slight psychotic symptoms. She lived a very expensive life, had many men friends, and had frequent sexual relations. Finally she went to see a priest, and in subsequent interviews she expressed again and again her sorrow about her past life under a flood of tears. The priest would then try to quiet her by showing his sympathy and by comforting her in a fatherly manner. This sympathetic approach did help her and made her break with her sexual excesses. But the priest failed to realize that now the girl transferred her feelings of love to him. Of course, as soon as he recognized that he was regarded as a love object by the girl, he interrupted the relationship.

Finally, confession presents a strong psychagogic element, inasmuch as it implies the firm purpose on the part of the penitent to amend his life by avoiding sin and conquering illicit desires and practices. And the admonition of the priest often gives an outline of a new plan of life. The main psychagogic element is divine grace, which helps the penitent to follow this plan of life. But at this point all analogy ceases, for one enters into the realm of the supernatural.[3]

As an objection to confession some writers, who seem to suffer from phobiophobia, declare that confession inspires fear and therefore is undesirable. To this objection we reply that, as we have said before, not every fear is detrimental to a person. The fear of sin and of its consequences is, when properly taught, a wholesome sentiment. It is one thing to cause fright about possible danger and another thing to give instruction with regard to it, even though this instruction inspires fear of the danger. This distinction holds good not only for physical danger, but also for mental and emotional dangers. In fact, psychiatrists themselves warn their public against entertaining certain mental attitudes lest mental disturbances result. Why, then, should it be considered dangerous to issue warnings against spiritual perils?

Obviously, pastoral care extends far beyond the confessional. By meeting personal and social problems constructively, the priest can relieve or prevent a great deal of mental unhappiness. This is true, for example, in connection with his contacts with people on his sick calls, when he gives to his ailing parishioners not only his direct assistance but also the indirect assistance of exerting his influence on the environment and teaching the people involved how to deal with the sick. Common sense tells him that the conventional phrases of consolation and encouragement are only too often hollow and empty; therefore, he should be trained in adapting his words to the particular situation.

Again, he can prevent mental grief by helping to maintain sound family life in his parish or in the sphere in which he works, for family life is still the basis of the community, the state, and the country. Since the first ten years of a child's life often determine the stability of his later life, a happy and healthy family environment is of the greatest importance in his personality development. Now, parents who are dealing with early behavior problems in their children often go first to their pastor for counsel; his advice, therefore, may not infrequently prove to be a decisive factor in preventing later maladjustment.

Nearly as important as the first ten years are the years from ten to fifteen—the time in which the school assumes an ever greater place in the child's life. In the school the child should learn self-discipline, but the process of teaching it to him ought to be impregnated with understanding, encouragement, and love so that he may learn in practice as well as in theory how to live with his fellow men and how to free himself from prejudice. Again, the priest has an important role in promoting and maintaining the mental health of his people, for the realization of these educational objectives will, as far as parochial schools are concerned, depend largely upon the pastor, who, since he cannot give his personal participation in every phase of instruction, should at least exercise care that proper teachers are chosen.

The subject of sex instruction will be treated more fully in a later chapter; in the meantime, it will suffice to remark that a healthy sex education is of great value in promoting the growth of a happy, normal family life and, thus, in providing for the proper mental development of the adolescent. Whenever a priest responds to a request for marriage instruction, he fulfills a task that may prevent a great deal of unhappiness, for marriages often suffer damage and are not infrequently shipwrecked because the partners were not properly prepared for sex experience in their marital relationships. This does not at all mean that marriage counseling deals only with sex instruction. Any constructive marriage counseling stresses the moral values involved in marriage, points out the difficulties that will inevitably occur in the dark hours of life and amid the problems of rearing children, and emphasizes the duty of the parents to give up certain personal enjoyments and to make sacrifices for the proper bearing and upbringing of children.

The pastor may also be called upon in the question of giving sex instruction to children. When the parents are unable or unwilling to impart this instruction, the burden may fall on the priest or on persons whom he designates. And almost every priest will face this problem when dealing with adolescent conflicts. If the priests or nuns who teach the children could have experience in mental-hygiene clinics or could see patients in the psychiatric office or mental institution, they would be astonished at the harm that can be done to children when proper sex instruction is avoided.

In connection with the priest's relationship to his flock, it may be pointed out that it is of great value for the priest to show an understanding of the human personality in his sermons and to use a psychological approach in his preaching. Far be it from the authors to condemn all strong and forthright sermons, but one may well wonder whether some priests fully appreciate how an ill-advised or an angry sermon affects people. Scolding and bitter lamenting about the immorality of the world may change some people, but sermons that make the listeners feel as if they are treated as immature children may set up in them defense mechanisms intended to minimize the priest's words, or even to make them do the contrary of that which the priest tells them to do. Of course, the truth does sometimes hurt, and if certain people cannot stand the truth, it is just too bad for them; but the truth can be made acceptable by the proper approach to the audience. Fortunately, Catholic priests are very well equipped for this task by their seminary courses in homiletics, but some seem at times to forget what they once were taught.

The priest's dealings with people require on his part psychological insight, tact, and very often skill in the art and technique of counseling. This is particularly true in the so-called parlor work, for people come to the rectory for advice in a hundred and one different cases. The people who have marital difficulties, the parents who cannot achieve proper parent-child relations, the woman who faces the change of life, the young engaged couple still unable to marry, the adolescent tortured by temptations of the flesh, the newly released ex-convict, the drunkard who knows that he causes untold suffering to his family, the seekers who have no religion but are looking for "something," the people confused about world conditions, the mother whose son has died in action, and countless others come to the rectory or monastery, looking for understanding and expecting efficient advice and guidance. When confronted with the problems of these more or less normal people, the priest will not forget to advise them to use the supernatural means like prayer and the sacraments, but in addition he should also use the natural means. What these people need is good counseling; therefore, the priest should know what to say and how to say it.

Chapter 7 dealt with the nature of counseling and with its different types—*i.e.*, directive and nondirective counseling. Pastoral counseling is not different, of course, except for the fact that the pastor-counselor always has in view, as his primary aim, to bring the counselees closer to God. After establishing the necessary rapport between himself and the counselee, the priest attempts to understand his client's problem and to help him solve it according to the latter's personality structure, in view of making a better Christian and thereby a better man out of him. Pastoral counseling, therefore, is decidedly psychagogic; it is of such a nature that it should not only help the parishioner with his present problem, but also give him the rules with which he can help himself in similar or even different situations.

Good counseling is, in the first place, an act whose very basis consists in empathy, the feeling into the counselee's psychic condition, and some counselors possess this natural capacity of establishing a rapport between themselves and the counselee in a higher degree than others. But counseling is also a technique that can be learned; common sense, experience, and the reading of pertinent material may help to train the priest for the task of counseling. If the authors may make a suggestion regarding the matter, they recommend that there be inserted into the seminary curriculum a seminar dealing with counseling techniques. In such a seminar, the students, under the guidance and supervision of a trained teacher, would each present a report on how to go about counseling in cases drawn from real life or synthesized from several actual cases, and each report would be followed by a general discussion in which the professor and other students would contribute their suggestions and, if necessary, their corrections.

No one will deny that pastoral counseling is of great importance and that it often takes up a great deal of the priest's time. It has been estimated, for instance, that in military service 75 per cent of the chaplain's work deals with pastoral counseling. However, it is an entirely false notion to think that a priest should be primarily looked upon as a counselor. A church that has little more to offer than counseling service may be called a counseling center, but hardly a church. And a church that advocates nondirective counseling as about the highest goal of its activities either has no principles or is afraid to put them into practice. Most pastoral counseling will necessarily be directive, because most of it deals with problems of a moral or religious nature and the priest, on account of his pastoral function and in view of his primary aim to bring the people to Christ, cannot remain indifferent as to whether the counselee accepts these moral or religious directives or not. As long as no moral issues are involved, some nondirective counseling may be useful, *e.g.*, when the pastor is called upon for vocational counseling; but, on the whole, pastoral counseling will be, for the most part, of a directive nature.

What is more, whenever moral or religious principles are involved, the very concept of counseling, either directive or nondirective, is no longer applicable in the strict sense of the word. Mrs. O'T. tells the pastor that she wants a divorce because she feels that she can no longer live with her alcoholic husband. The priest may summon up all his counseling art and technique to dissuade her, but, in the final analysis, the question of divorce is no matter of counseling and he has to lay down the law. Mr. P. begins to think of his eternal salvation and wishes to return to the Church, but refuses to give up his affiliation with Freemasonry. Mrs. K. is very unhappy and suffers pangs of conscience, but wants to stick to her practice of using contraceptives. Jimmy S. has decided to marry a non-Catholic girl, but she refuses to subscribe to the *cautiones*. In these, and many other such instances, the principles involved are simply no matter for counseling. There can be no minimizing of dogmatic truths or soft-pedaling of moral principles. This fact is, of course, as clear as daylight to the Catholic priest, but it must be pointed out in order to make it also clear in certain non-Catholic circles where the idea seems to prevail that counseling also means merchandising with principles. However, it may take a great deal of counseling to bring about the acceptance of dogmatic truths and moral principles; in such instances the priest has to use all his tact and skill to make the interested parties accept the principles, even though they may hurt.

Thus far, this discussion has dealt with the more or less normal people who come with their problems to the rectory or monastery. It is absurd to think that everyone with a problem needs psychiatric help, even though the problem may upset him. But a fair number of people who do need such help to a greater or lesser degree also appear among the visitors to the parlor. These are the mentally derailed, the profoundly disturbed, those with inner conflicts, the emotionally disordered, the oppressed, the compulsives and scrupulous, the chronic alcoholics, those plagued with sexual abnormalities, and others troubled by a host of varying difficulties.

What can the priest do in such cases? What should he not do? St. Mark (3:14–15) listed the healing of the sick among the apostles' functions: "And He appointed twelve that they might be with Him and that He might send them forth to preach. To them He gave power to cure sicknesses and to cast out devils." And the apostles began to do just that, as the same evangelist says three chapters later (6:12–13): "And going forth, they preached that men should repent, and they cast out many devils, and anointed with oil many sick people, and healed them." It has sometimes been suggested that these words mean that the apostles, and by implication their successors, were to act as medical men. This is not a correct view. Mark's words, according to the Council of Trent, intimated the Sacrament of Extreme Unction, which is described by St. James (5:14–15); furthermore, this healing through anointment was of a miraculous nature. But such healing is very different from exercising the function of a physician. Except in the rare instances where a man has combined the two professions, priests are not physicians—a fact that is very obvious with regard to bodily ailments. Neither are they psychiatrists—a fact that is not always so obvious. However, with regard to the mentally ill, one must keep in mind two facts: the first is that many mentally disturbed persons are first observed by the priest; hence, he is responsible for doing something about them. The second, and more important, fact is that the problem of the mentally disturbed very often concerns a moral or religious outlook on life.

For these reasons, priests should have some knowledge of mental disorders, their diagnosis, and their therapy. The curriculum of the student for the priesthood comprises at least two years of philosophy, including psychology, and four years of theology, and it gives him a solid understanding of the human personality and its dynamics. This knowledge is by no means merely theoretical, for a great deal of moral and pastoral theology deals with practical case work. Undoubtedly, the Catholic priest is well prepared to meet the demands of his work. However, in order to cope with "mental cases" more knowledge is needed of psychodynamics, counseling techniques, mental hygiene, and psychotherapeutic methodology. Now, a course in pastoral psychiatry and psychopathology would impart the necessary basic knowledge of how to deal with the mentally disturbed.

What does "the necessary basic knowledge" mean? It does *not* mean that the successful completion of a course in pastoral psychiatry would qualify a priest to take up practical psychotherapy. It does mean that such a course would achieve some most important and advantageous results.

For one thing, it would take away certain prejudices against psychiatry. Here, a recent case of just such prejudice comes to mind. A young priest who was prefect of discipline in a large high school told a psychiatrist, bluntly, that he did not believe in psychiatry. Now, a better study of the nature of emotional conflicts and of the available methods of solving such conflicts would surely help to prevent the indiscriminate discrediting of psychiatry. But there is more: the study of pastoral psychiatry would give the priest a certain amount of diagnostic skill, which would enable him to differentiate between the tricks of some mentally disordered persons and the supernatural phenomena and gifts that God may bestow on his chosen ones; *e.g.*, it would prevent his falling for the ruses of hysterics who claim to have visions, revelations, and the gift of prophecy. It would also help him to distinguish between purely natural and preternatural phenomena, between a simple case of scrupulosity and deep-seated compulsion, between the latter and hysteria, and between transitory and permanent cases; and it would help him to see when sexual sins are complicated by abnormalities.

Moreover, the study of pastoral psychiatry would give the priest a psychological evaluation of his parishioner's difficulties; *e.g.*, it would help him to realize when a scrupulous penitent has reached the stage at which the feeling of guilt has become a severe neurosis—a stage at which he should indicate the necessity of psychotherapy. Again, a better knowledge of psychic disorders would prevent his advising marriage to cure such disturbances as alcoholism, or shyness, or some phobia. In earlier times, people with certain sexual problems, such as exhibitionism and homosexuality, were told both by priest and by physician that the best thing for them to do was to marry and that marriage would probably cure them. Today, however, no competent physician would ever recommend such a step, and the priest would do well to follow that example.

Above all, a better knowledge of mental disorders will help the priest to comprehend that, under ordinary circumstances and barring the occurrence of a miracle, the recommendation of prayer and the reception of the sacraments is no more sufficient to rid a person of a serious mental disturbance than is prayer alone sufficient to heal a man suffering from diabetes. Priests who understand the emotional disturbances of their parishioners who suffer from phobias, oppressions, or compulsions, know that it is of no help for these unfortunates merely to be told to get on their knees and pray.

In case the priest himself is not qualified to give therapeutic aid to the patient, the latter will almost invariably ask for his adviser's counsel as to what psychiatrist he should seek. Answering this question will be much easier for the priest if he has a sufficient knowledge of the different types of psychotherapy and their underlying philosophies. This background is particularly necessary when the parishioner asks if he might benefit by analysis. In view of the damage done by certain analysts to the faith of Catholic clients, we can well imagine many a priest being hesitant to give an affirmative answer. However, in case he decides that some form of analytical treatment might be beneficial to his parishioner's condition, he ought to know the tenets of the various schools of depth psychology, and, by implication, he ought to know also the affiliation of those psychotherapists with whom he is acquainted.

It goes without saying that no Catholic priest could possibly recommend to his parishioner any therapist who considers religion an illusion, a fiction, or a neurotic reaction to reality, who holds that belief in God is a danger to the individual's mental well-being, who feels that religion interferes with the analytical procedure, or who would in any other way undermine his patient's faith or moral concepts. The survey of the various analytical schools presented in Chapter 8 makes it clear that for these reasons the orthodox Freudians should be ruled out. Likewise, greatest caution is needed in recommending Jungians, for, despite the fact that they are supposed to favor religious values, their interpretation of the origin of religion is fraught with danger. In other systems, the danger of undermining the patient's faith is more remote, but much will depend on the actual practice of the individual therapist.

As we have seen, the priest should never expect the psychiatrist to be a pastor-substitute, but he may rightly insist that the therapist treat the Catholic's religious convictions with understanding and respect and certainly refrain from trying to instill his own philosophy of life in his client. The ideal situation for a Catholic patient would probably be met when the psychiatrist, too, is a believing Catholic, but this condition is not necessarily required. There is a growing number of non-Catholic psychiatrists, including analysts, who sincerely try to meet the requirements outlined above.

Should the priest himself ever make an attempt at psychotherapy? It cannot be denied that some—by no means all—priests show a remarkable skill in dealing effectively with "mental cases." Their success usually concerns the lighter cases and may be due to a certain natural gift of insight into the patient's condition, to experience, and to the precious gift of common sense. However, most cases require more than that; they require a solid training in psychotherapy. Now, the priest-psychiatrist will always remain a rare exception, and for obvious reasons it could not possibly be the intention of the hierarchy to increase the number of these exceptions even though some Catholic patients may believe that the combination of the two professions in one person is precisely what they need.

However, on the other hand, it might be a good thing to have in every diocese a number of clinical psychologists among the clergy. For, although the clinical psychologist is not a substitute for the psychiatrist, yet—as will be seen in the next chapter—his training gives him a basis for the diagnosis of mental disorders and may help him in some forms of psychotherapy.

At this juncture a somewhat delicate question arises. The suggestion has been made that any clinical psychologist should be analyzed; by implication, therefore, a priest who is in training for clinical psychology should also go through personal analysis. In fact, some would go so far as to require such an analysis for all those who are involved in the *cura animarum*—a view that is patently absurd, almost as absurd as the chimerical requirement that all analysts be priests. As for the necessity or usefulness of personal analysis of a priest-student in clinical psychology, this is evidently a matter for the hierarchy to decide.

COOPERATION BETWEEN PRIEST AND PSYCHIATRIST

Inasmuch as the problem of many mentally disturbed persons is, as Jung put it, one of "finding a religious outlook on life," it would seem that the psychiatrist and the priest should assist each other in the solution of that problem. Both are concerned, each in his own field, with the care of souls. This is literally true for the priest, but psychotherapy, too, aims in the last analysis at the care of souls even though it tries to achieve its purpose with scientific means. The therapy of the mind and the care of the soul, far from excluding each other, would seem to complete one another.

Yet, as a matter of fact, despite certain lip service, the present cooperation between priest and psychiatrist leaves much to be desired. For, in this area, too, one finds mutual complaints and recriminations, misunderstanding and distrust. Some psychotherapists complain that the clergy misinterpret their intentions and lack sufficient knowledge to appreciate the aims of psychotherapy. On their side, the clergy retort that, far from misinterpreting the aims of certain forms of psychotherapy, they interpret them only too well; and they openly wonder how there can be any cooperation with those psychiatrists who are determinists, hedonists, and materialists, who have no understanding or respect for the religious needs and convictions of their patients, and who are hostile to any form of revealed religion.

It would be difficult, indeed, to see how any cooperation is possible with a consistent Freudian. Freud himself would have none of it, and he was at least consistent. On the supposition that religion is a neurosis, a clergyman trying to help a neurotic would be ludicrous, for it would mean one neurotic helping another. As long as a psychiatrist believes that the Freudian philosophy is part and parcel of his technique and method, cooperation is out of the question. Cooperation is out of the question, too, so long as a psychiatrist believes that his therapy has all the answers, and therefore makes it a substitute of religion and the moral code. Moreover, cooperation would be impossible with physicians who, when approached on the problem of severe marital discord, suggest divorce as the only possible solution, or who would advise premarital or extramarital sexual relations.

Nevertheless, there are scores of psychiatrists with whom the priest could collaborate fruitfully and who, in their turn, are looking for some form of collaboration. The opposition of the clergy is directed for the most part against Freudian psychoanalysis. But, we repeat once more, psychoanalysis is only one system of depth psychology, and depth psychology is not identical with psychiatry. Many psychiatrists practice some form of analysis, without in the least accepting the philosophy underlying psychoanalysis or that underlying any other form of depth psychology. Some psychiatrists scrupulously refrain from permitting their own convictions in religious or moral matters to influence their treatment. A case in point is the psychiatrist who refuses to accept patients with marriage problems because, since he himself solved his own marital difficulties by obtaining a divorce, he feels disqualified to treat a marriage problem, assuming that he would unconsciously counsel in the direction of separation or divorce. True, there are psychiatrists who have taken their Catholic patients' faith away, but there are also others who make better Catholics out of them by restoring their emotional balance, by making them more sincere and less egoistic.

How can cooperation be achieved? The priest is supposed to be the leader in spiritual things; but, unless he is himself a psychiatrist or clinical psychologist, he is not an expert in mental disorders. Therefore, the man to handle the treatment is the psychiatrist, who, however, may refer the patient to the priest when the case is complicated by problems of moral responsibility. It goes without saying that in the latter case any cooperation that involves the sacramental seal of confession would be impossible. The psychiatrist has to do the spadework; he must help the patient to disentangle himself from his neurotic attitude, give him insight into his condition, clear up the debris, and make him aware of his own potentialities. But, as has been repeatedly pointed out, the ultimate purpose of psychotherapy is psychosynthesis, reeducation; *i.e.*, the patient should be given a new plan of life to prevent his falling into the pitfalls that caused his previous condition. Now, if the patient is a Catholic, the priest can give valuable assistance in formulating the rebuilding program. When this program contains moral, religious, and spiritual values, the roles are reversed, and the priest, as the representative of God, is the expert; therefore, he would participate in such a reeducation program not only as the moral theologian, but also as the dogmatic theologian with the doctrine of divine grace.

Were psychiatrists—and, for that matter, clinical psychologists also—to begin to realize more universally the importance of such a collaboration, the result would be only for the good of the patients. In this respect, Raymond B. Cattell's words, although primarily intended for clinical psychologists, hold equally true for the psychiatrist: "The possibility that the clergyman, rather than the psychologist or the medical practitioner, is the ultimate specialist in human adjustment has been most unscientifically ignored." [4]

In practice, the pastor's opportunity for cooperation will often concern individual cases and involve an individual psychiatrist to whom the priest has referred his sick parishioner. Of course, the ideal condition would be that of priest and psychiatrist belonging both to the same religion, but useful cooperation is also possible when the latter has a different, but positive, religion. Even when the psychotherapist does not seem to profess any religion, cooperation is not necessarily precluded, provided the therapist honestly respects his patient's religious convictions and conscience. On the other hand, any fruitful collaboration requires of the clergyman a certain amount of knowledge of psychiatry and what it can do.

The problem of cooperation may be clarified by a few examples. There is the question of advice with regard to such moral problems as masturbation. If the psychiatrist has come to the conclusion that his patient's practice is compulsive, his stand concerning the patient's responsibility may well contradict the priest's opinion, and this difference may cause great confusion in the patient. It should be noted here that it is by no means always the psychiatrist who takes the lenient attitude in such matters; not infrequently, it is the priest who exonerates the patient of moral responsibility, while the psychiatrist, because of therapeutic considerations, tells his patient that he is responsible for giving in to the practice. One easily sees that some understanding between priest and psychiatrist would be to the patient's advantage. Of course, in such matters the problem of professional secrecy on the one hand and the seal of confession on the other may render cooperation difficult. In many cases, however, the psychiatrist may notify the priest about the patient's condition and about the general line of his own treatment.

A very important task of the psychiatrist is to help persons who suffer from neurotic anxiety and guilt feelings. In case such feelings spring from the realization of objective sin, the assistance of a priest may be of invaluable aid to the psychiatrist in prescribing treatment.

It is true that certain neurotic reactions hide under the guise of religion, but there again it is the priest's task to decide what is true and what is false religion, or, rather, a false application of religion. For instance, the treatment of the scrupulous would undoubtedly require the assistance of the priest.

Once more it should be repeated that the main task in which the spiritual and temporal *curatores animarum* could and should meet is in teaching the patient the meaning of life and existence. In outlining a reeducation program and in helping the patient to adopt it and to put it into practice, the religious leader will be of inestimable value.

The priest's role in a program of cooperation can also be envisaged within the framework of the psychotherapeutic team, which usually consists of a psychiatrist, a social worker, and a clinical psychologist. In institutions, such as homes of correction, reformatory schools, and asylums, the chaplain, too, is often a member of the team; indeed, he should be a member, for his task in such institutions consists not only in saying Mass, administering the sacraments, and preaching an occasional sermon, but also in giving his effective participation in the mental-health program of the Catholic inmates—a participation that can do untold good. In the larger institutions, this role is a full-time job. Yet, some time ago the authors heard that in one mental institution of about six thousand patients, of whom some 50 per cent were Catholic, there was only one priest, and he was on part-time duty because, in addition to his work in the institution, he had to take care of a parish. Under such conditions, his presence could scarcely be of great profit to the patients.

But, if it is recognized that the priest should have a place on the therapeutic team in the institutions mentioned above, it should also be recognized that pastoral assistance is useful on teams operating in child centers, guidance clinics, and mental-hygiene clinics. These agencies usually disregard such assistance, yet these clinics treat many patients who might well benefit by it. With regard to this matter, these words of Raymond B. Cattell are worth considering: "As clinical psychology extends itself to the lesser maladjustments of individuals and the major maladjustments of society, it encounters more and more the importance of values. And if the pride of clinical psychology is followed by a fall, that fall will surely come through failure to realize that adjustment *to* values is one thing and adjustment *of* values quite another." [5]

The priest can also do a great deal of good for the happiness and mental health of his parishioners by working together with agencies for social work, family service, and Catholic charities. An example of this kind of work is the straightening out of marriage difficulties. With both the priest and the family social worker being aware of proven concepts of mental hygiene and personality development, they compose an exceptionally well qualified team to help couples with the problems of their marriage. In one such case, a parish priest labored months to help a couple arrive at a happy adjustment in their marriage. He prayed for them, pleaded with them, did everything that he could to help them; yet, their quarrels and unhappiness remained. With the assistance offered to him by the social worker, a study was made of the marriage and the two lives who were making it. It was found that one of them was a decided neurotic whose neurotic behavior was the basic disturbing component in the marriage. Together, the priest and the social worker worked with the healthy spouse, giving the interpretation, insight, and encouragement that would permit a hopeful acceptance of the situation and, accordingly, an adjustment to the existent circumstances. To the neurotic partner, likewise, insight and help was offered that would occasion the growth of a greater ability and interest in leading a more normal and healthy life.

The content of the specialized courses taken by the social worker in a graduate school of social service is, in some part, covered by the seminary curriculum. At the close of the curriculum and following ordination, every parish priest will find it decidedly advantageous to keep active his interest in the nature and behavior of human personality through reading and study. The young priest still fresh from the seminary has a background intellectually rich for productive labors amid the countless opportunities that will be his to be of genuine assistance to those who come to him for help with their problems. The parish priest has at hand an excellent opportunity to reduce to concrete practice the theory that has been given him in the seminary, for by his priesthood alone he wins the confidence of thousands—a confidence won arduously by others. Truly, it well behooves the young priest to attempt by means of study and application to make valid use of the psychiatric and mental hygiene concepts given him in his seminary curriculum.

Several instances have been cited in which a direct opposition exists between the ideas of religious leaders and certain psychiatrists, particularly those of the Freudian school. This does not mean, however, that opposition to religion is inherent to psychiatry. The priest and the psychiatrist may well meet one another on mutual ground, because psychotherapy is based on the Gospel principle of being a helpmeet to one's neighbor. Each one working through his own means, both priest and psychiatrist help their fellow men to live satisfactory, adjusted lives and to attain the peace of mind that Christ promised to those who follow Him.[6]

If one may believe the old Greeks, there is a certain resemblance between the two professions. Religious leaders, priests, ministers, and rabbis are often called men of God. Now, the Greeks, even before Hippocrates, used to say: "ἰατρός ἰσόθεος ἔστιν—there is something Godlike about a physician." Therefore, if both are "men of God," after their own fashion, it would not seem impossible for the two to cooperate peacefully for the well-being of the people, each laboring in his own field without overstepping the boundaries of the other's territory. For a fruitful collaboration between priest and psychiatrist two fundamentals are required: the priest should have a sufficient knowledge and appreciation of psychotherapy and the psychiatrist should show a sympathetic understanding of the patient's religious and moral needs.

NOTES AND REFERENCES

1. JUNG, C. J., "Die Beziehungen der Psychotherapie zur Seelsorge" (Zürich: Rascher, 1932). The English translation of the essay, under the title "Psychotherapists or the Clergy," is inserted as Chap. XI in "Modern Man in Search of a Soul" (New York: Harcourt, Brace and Company, Inc., 1939), p. 265.
2. The reader will find some significant statistical figures concerning the incidence of neuropsychiatric disorders in the population in MCNEILL, HARRY V., Contemporary Developments in Clinical Psychology, *Proceedings of the American Catholic Philosophical Association,* 1950.
3. For a detailed comparison between confession and psychotherapy, see BOPP, LINUS, "Moderne Psychanalyse, Katholische Beichte und Pädagogik" (Kempten: Kosel und Pustet, 1923); SCHOLLGEN, WERNER, Psychotherapie und sacramentelle Beichte, *Catholica,* Vol. 1 (1932), pp. 145–158.
4. CATTELL, R. B., "The Meaning of Clinical Psychology," in PENNINGTON, L. A., BERG, I. A., *et al.,* "An Introduction to Clinical Psychology" (New York: The Ronald Press Company, 1948), p. 13.
5. CATTELL, *op. cit.,* p. 13.
6. For further information concerning the topics discussed in this and some of the preceding chapters, the reader is referred to works on pastoral psychology and psychiatry. The following list may be helpful:

ALLERS, R., Abnormality: a Chapter in Moral Psychology (nine articles), *Homiletic and Pastoral Review,* Vol. 42 (1941–1942).

BERGMANN, W. (ed.), "Religion und Seelenleiden" (7 vols.; Düsseldorf: Schwann, 1926–1932).

BLESS, H., "Pastoraal Psychiatrie" (Roermond: J. J. Romen, 1945).

EYMIEU, A., "Le Gouvernement de soi-même" (3 vols.; Paris, 1934).

KLUG, I., "Die Tiefen der Seele: moral-psychologische Studien" (Paderborn: Schöningh, 1928).

LACHAPELLE, P., "Psychiatrie pastorale" (Montreal: Beauchemin, 1942), translated by G. J. Brady, "Psychiatry for the Priest" (Westminster, Md.: Newman Press, 1945).

MCCARTHY, R. C., "Safeguarding Mental Health" (Milwaukee: The Bruce Publishing Company, 1943); *id.,* Common Grounds for Psychiatrists and Priests, *Linacre Quarterly,* October, 1947, pp. 1–4.

MÜNCKER, THOMAS, "Der psychische Zwang und seine Beziehungen zu Moral und Pastoral" (Düsseldorf: Schwann, 1922); *id.,* "Die psychologischen Grundlagen der Katholischen Sittenlehre" (Düsseldorf: Patmos-Verlag, 1948).

NIEDERMEYER, A., "Pastoral Psychiatrie" (Paderborn: Bonifacius Druckerei, 1938).

NODET, C. H., Psychoanalyse et morale, *Cahiers Laënnec,* May, 1948, pp. 22–36.

O'BRIEN, PATRICK, "Emotions and Morals" (New York: Grune and Stratton, 1950).

ODENWALD, ROBERT P., Mental Hygiene and the Priest, *The Homiletic and Pastoral Review,* Vol. LI, No. 3, December (1950), p. 235.

RULAND, L., "Handbuch der praktischen Seelsorge" (3 vols.; Munich: Hueber Verlag, 1930–1933), translated by T. A. Rattler, "Foundations of Morality" (St. Louis: B. Herder Book Company, 1936).

SCHULTE, C., "Was der Seelsorger von nervösen Leiden wissen musz" (Paderborn: Schöningh, 1936), translated by C. Tschippert, "Nervous Mental Diseases" (London: Coldwell, 1938).

SINÉTY, R. DE, "Psychopathologie et direction" (Paris: Beauchesne, 1934).

SURBLED, G., "La morale dans ses rapports avec la médecine et l'hygiène" (Paris: G. Masson, 1921).

Among the books written from a non-Catholic standpoint, the following may be mentioned:

BONNELL, JOHN SUTHERLAND, "Pastoral Psychiatry" (New York: Harper & Brothers, 1938); *id.,* "Psychology for Pastor and People" (New York: Harper & Brothers, 1948).

BONTHIUS, ROBERT H., "Christian Paths to Self-acceptance" (New York: King's Crown Press, 1949).

DEWAR, L., and C. E. HUDSON, "Manual of Pastoral Psychology" (London: Allan & Co., 1935).

DICKS, RUSSELL L., "Pastoral Work and Personal Counseling" (New York: The Macmillan Company, 1944).

HILTNER, SEWARD, "Religion and Health" (New York: The Macmillan Company, 1943); *id.,* "Pastoral Counseling" (Nashville, Tenn.: Abingdon-Cokesbury Press, 1949).

OLIVER, J. R., "Psychiatry and Mental Health" (New York: Charles Scribner's Sons, 1933).

WEATHERHEAD, LESLIE, "Psychology and Life" (Nashville, Tenn.: Abingdon-Cokesbury Press, 1935).

WISE, CARROL A., "Religion in Illness and Health" (New York: Harper & Brothers, 1942).

A monthly professional journal called *Pastoral Psychology* is published in Great Neck, N.Y.

For pastoral medicine, the reader is referred to the works of Antonelli, Capellmann-Bergmann, Gemelli, Mulligan, Malley and Walsh, Olfers, Salsmans, Stöhr. See also NIEDERMEYER, ALBERT, "Handbuch der speziellen Pastoralmedizin" (Vienna: Herder, 1949), Vol. I; this work is to consist of six volumes.

Chapter 13

PSYCHOTHERAPY, CLINICAL PSYCHOLOGIST, AND SOCIAL WORKER

In recent years, the question has arisen as to whether anyone outside the medical profession might be qualified to practice psychotherapy.[1] To all except quacks it is, of course, a matter of conviction that both the diagnosis and the treatment of the mentally ill belong in the first place to the province of the physician-therapist; but there are at the present time some people with training in psychology, but not in medicine, who claim to be able to take in hand the diagnosis and the therapy of certain types of mental disorders.

It is readily conceded that they should "render to Caesar the things that are Caesar's" (Matthew 22:21); *i.e.*, the treatment of many cases as well as the decision in many problems concerning these cases should be reserved to the physicians. To mention only a few of such cases, in the care of mental disorders caused by organic conditions, such as toxic poisoning, infection of the central nervous system, and cerebral tumors or injuries, the physician is the only competent authority. Moreover, he is also the only one who can make decisions with regard to functional mental disorders. Functional mental disorders are attributed to psychic malfunction—a subject that is, as yet, only vaguely understood—and may clear up through psychotherapy. Whether the etiology of the functional disorders will eventually be discovered in the blood, endocrines, tissue chemistry, or in any other part of the organism, need not concern us here. The point is that the physician is the only competent authority to distinguish functional from organic disorders; hence, it belongs to the physician's competence to decide whether, in a certain case, psychotherapy is indicated at all. Psychotherapy may be indicated in the treatment of stomach ulcers, asthma, and skin diseases; again, it is obvious that such cases belong solely to the sphere of the physician-therapist. Then, too, he is the only one who can properly treat cases of psychoses.

Those qualified to practice psychotherapy will grant that all such cases —and many more—belong to the domain of the physician-psychiatrist. However, there are some—let us call them "nonmedical"—therapists who claim to be able to diagnose and treat "certain forms of mental disorders," a somewhat vague reference to the milder forms of psychoneurosis. The main reasoning with which they support their claim includes a rather pragmatic observation: the great majority of the physician-psychiatrists are so overburdened with work that they simply cannot handle all cases of mental illness; hence, the "nonmedical" therapists believe it natural and preferable for the milder forms to receive treatment from persons who, even though they have no M.D., are supposed to be properly trained in psychotherapy than for such cases to receive no treatment at all. In addition to making this pragmatic observation, they pose a question which, according to their view, reaches the root of the problem. What is there, they ask, in any form of psychotherapy, including depth therapy, that requires medical training? The essential task of any psychotherapist is to grasp the psychodynamics of a personality, be it normal or abnormal, and to apply this knowledge in individual cases. Is such knowledge and skill, they query, the exclusive privilege of the medically trained mind? Besides, they point out, the problem of who should be allowed to practice psychotherapy is largely an academic problem anyway. As a matter of fact, they say, there are several different groups of people who are engaged in therapy, such as some child psychologists, educators, social workers, the various kinds of counselors (including the pastoral counselor), and the clinical psychologist.

On the other hand, most physicians, hesitant to accept these claims, maintain that the diagnosis and treatment of all the mentally ill should be reserved to the medically trained. They admit at the most that those trained in psychology might engage in some diagnostic and therapeutic work on condition that they keep in close contact with the physician.

It is not the authors' intention to take sides in this controversy. In the first place, it seems too early to do so. And secondly, it would seem to be wise to await the decisions and measures which the lawgivers of the several states and of the nation will eventually take. Nevertheless, because a brief picture of the work done by the "nonmedical" therapist may throw some light on the present problem, it seems useful to give a description and evaluation of the work performed by the members of the so-called neuropsychiatric or psychotherapeutic team. In this chapter, the discussion is limited to the work done by the clinical psychologist and the social worker.

THE CLINICAL PSYCHOLOGIST

Clinical psychology is a war product. Although known in educational circles since the end of the last century (the beginnings are to be found in the psychological clinic founded by Lightner Witmer at the University of Pennsylvania), clinical psychology grew in importance during the First and Second World Wars, particularly after the latter, when the Veterans Administration assigned the clinical psychologist an important role in the neuropsychiatric or psychotherapeutic team.[2]

Diagnostic Task. Since the psychiatrist and the clinical psychologist approach the diagnosis of the patient from a different angle and with different methods, it would seem that the contributions of the two professional workers complement each other.[3] As has been said, all the medical aspects, such as the recognition of organic disorders and the differentiation of functional from organic disorders, belong to the jurisdiction of the psychiatrist. He is trained to discover the functioning, or, rather, the malfunction, of the psychological process. Unless he has been specially trained in the administration and interpretation of psychological tests, the psychiatrist relies on his personal observations and the impressions gathered from interviews and case histories.

The clinical psychologist has other devices at his disposal; hundreds of tests have been devised to measure verbal and nonverbal intelligence, achievement, interests, attitudes, aptitudes, and personality patterns.[4] True, relatively few of these may be found in the average clinical psychologist's armamentarium. Yet, knowing both the validity and the reliability of the tests that he uses, and the nature of the standardized groups used in their construction, he believes himself to be in a position to derive from test data much that will be useful to the psychiatrist. Not that psychological tests replace clinical evaluation, but they contribute information that can help the psychiatrist to make his diagnosis.

The clinical psychologist's first step is to obtain a quantitative analysis of the patient by administering an *intelligence test.* The tests of individual intelligence most constantly employed by clinical psychologists are the Revised Stanford-Binet and the Wechsler-Bellevue Intelligence Scale. The latter is proving very satisfactory for older adolescents and adults; the former is admittedly a good test for children. But, unlike the psychometrician, the clinical psychologist does more than grind out I.Q.'s; he assumes the functions of a qualitative diagnostician.

In the hands of a competent clinical psychologist, these intelligence tests yield more than the number commonly called an I.Q. Close observation of the testee, while he is working on the various subtests, allows the psychologist to form subjective estimates of the individual's powers of attention, manner of solving problems, degree of confidence, security, emotional reaction, ability to form social relations, capacities for self-appraisal, and a host of other factors which, when added to the psychiatrist's professional observations, are valuable in formulating a fuller concept of the testee's personality. Often, these qualitative observations are more important than the quantitative results of the test.

In addition to intelligence tests, *achievement tests* are frequently helpful in diagnosis, especially in child psychiatry. They may uncover the sources of pressure that influence behavior disorders. Some psychologists, unfortunately pressed for time under a heavy case load, streamline this part of their investigation. They may omit achievement tests entirely and rely on the grades of teachers to estimate the basic skills of the child client. In terms of grade levels, achievement tests measure objectively a child's rank in some particular school subject.

When dealing with mental disorders in adults the psychologist uses, instead of achievement tests, *interest inventories* and *aptitude tests* to study occupational areas as sources of trouble. The Kuder Preference Record or the Strong Vocational Interest Blank may help to find out whether a client is really interested in his occupation. Various aptitude tests for specific jobs may be employed to discover whether a client is fitted for work he is doing. Some of these interest inventories and aptitude tests can be helpful to the psychiatrist in treatment of emotional problems stimulated or aggravated by improper vocational placement.

While the preceding types of tests may give the clinician already valuable insight into the psychodynamics underlying the client's reactions, this insight is completed by administering the so-called *personality tests.* There are three kinds of personality tests, each calculated to yield a distinct set of data about a person. The first is the questionnaire. In effect, it asks the patient, "What do you think is your personality?" A set of questions, previously standardized and statistically treated in the manner of intelligence and achievement tests, leads the testee to expose his self-expressed attitudes, fear, wishes, etc. This type of personality test has come under sharp criticism, for it is fraught with shortcomings. Aside from the fact that psychological research reveals that a person seldom rates himself as others rate him, the testee can frequently see through the examiner's attempt to mask the import of the questions and is likely to answer in a way designed to put himself in a favorable light.[5]

The Minnesota Multiphasic Personality Inventory has taken precedence over other questionnaire personality tests. Many psychologists use this test to supplement other diagnostic instruments. Besides its individual administration in the clinic, the MMPI has been prepared for group administration on an adult and older-adolescent age level.

A second instrument for the investigation of personality is the rating scale. Persons familiar with the client are asked to rate him on certain qualities that they have observed in him. From these ratings, the psychologist can arrive at some estimate of those traits in his client which have social significance. It is clear that such ratings are merely an index to the response that the rated person stimulates in his associates. At best, the rating scale gives few, if any, clues to the inner dynamics of personality.

If a personality test [6] could be given to all school children to find those who might profit by psychiatric or psychological service, many mental disorders might be averted and many behavior difficulties might be cleared up before delinquency occurs. Unfortunately, no group personality test is adequate for screening all children on the elementary school level. Moreover, in the hands of an unskilled and untrained person, the interpretation of personality tests may be dangerous, leading to harmful labeling of children. The psychologist, perhaps more than anyone else, is aware of the danger of labels, having seen in some quarters the effect of the injudicious use of the I.Q. Frequently, an alert and experienced teacher is sufficiently well equipped to detect mental disorders and behavior patterns that call for the special attention of professional diagnosticians and therapists. If adjustments are made early enough, little or no permanent harm to the personality may ensue; but if pressures are permitted to build up, deep-seated neurotic conditions may develop. Moreover, psychological studies carried out early in life may give the psychiatrist precious information in later years if a personality disorder should develop. It is unfortunate that many parents who do not hesitate to visit a physician for the aches, pains, slight fevers, and other physical ills of their children refuse to permit those children to be referred to a psychiatrist, who, in turn, may refer the child to a clinical psychologist. Perhaps, the explanation is that these parents erroneously think that there is some stigma attached to clinical examination. Another reason is undoubtedly the number of quacks in this field. It is quite possible, too, that some may feel that they would be admitting themselves to be failures as parents if they were to seek advice on the serious behavior problems of their children.

The projective techniques constitute a third type of personality test—a type that finds wide acceptance among psychiatrists and psychologists. Such techniques aim to discover both the information that the patient cannot or will not give about himself because it is hidden or unacceptable and also the information that others cannot give about him because it is socially enigmatical. To bring information out of the *terra incognita* of personality, the individual is asked to give meaning and organization to ambiguous stimuli, such as inkblots, pictures, and finger paintings. Or, he may be asked to arrange objects, to fill conversation balloons in cartoons, or to fit facial expressions to cutouts in various social situations.[7] There are no "right" or "wrong" answers for these stimuli, as there are for the items of a standardized intelligence test. The testee is free to project his own personality into the meaning and organization of the stimulus. By an interpretation of this projection, the psychologist gains some knowledge about the individual's personality.

Of the various projective techniques used to investigate personality, the Rorschach Inkblot Test and the Thematic Apperception Test are most commonly used to aid in the diagnosis of mentally disordered patients. They have also proved to be valuable instruments in research on both normal and abnormal personalities. It is interesting to note that both these techniques were originated by psychiatrists.

The Rorschach Test consists of ten inkblots originally selected by Hermann Rorschach, a Swiss psychiatrist.[8] As each blot is presented, the subject is asked to say what the blot looks like to him. His responses are recorded. Later, he tells what part of the blot suggested his percept and the particular aspect of the blot that determined his response. In scoring the Rorschach Test, the psychologist takes into consideration not only what the subject sees but also what features of the blot (form, color, shading, etc.) remind the subject of the things he sees. From an interpretation of the whole configuration of the responses, the psychologist attempts to evaluate the psychological dimensions of the subject's personality and the interrelations of these dimensions.[9]

This test is designed to outline the structure of the individual personality. It helps to answer such questions as the following: How does the patient use his energies to meet the demands of his environment? What defenses has he set up? How firm are these defenses? Does he plan, or just coast, through life? Is he inclined to compulsivity? In general, the Rorschach Test is supposed to reveal a person's kind of thinking, his intellectual efficiency, motivation, control of emotions, ability to adjust within himself and in his environment. The proper use of the Rorschach Test requires intensive and extensive training. The more knowledge of psychodynamics, neurology, and abnormal psychology the psychologist brings to the interpretation of a Rorschach protocol, the more information the test reveals.

Like all psychological instruments, the Rorschach Inkblot Test is not intended to be used alone. Most clinical psychologists supplement its findings with a Thematic Apperception Test, commonly called a TAT. As the Rorschach Test reveals personality structure, the TAT indicates the content of personality, the specific problems, conflicts, anxieties, etc., that are disturbing the patient. One limitation of the TAT, however, is that sometimes a psychologically sophisticated person may realize that he is revealing more of himself than he desires. He can then obscure the record.

Pictures, ranging from clear magazine illustrations to vague abstractions, are presented one at a time to the subject taking the TAT. He is instructed to tell a story about each picture. These stories, recorded verbatim, are later analyzed by the psychologist. There is no set system for this analysis. Henry A. Murray,[10] the author of the test, interprets the stories according to "needs" that arise within the individual and "pressures" that impinge upon him from the environment. This system is cumbersome and not widely accepted by psychologists. Psychologists with psychoanalytic orientation rely on Freudian principles for their interpretation of the stories, but most TAT workers prefer a "common-sense" approach which evaluates the stories somewhat eclectically. They study recurring themes in the stories, presume identification with "heroes," and look for such factors as emotions, motives, attitudes, and feelings that are attributed to the characters. Certain formal elements of the stories play a part in this analysis; *e.g.*, the length of the productions, originality or stereotypy of ideas, logical development, and verisimilitude. The endings of the stories are important. Are they realistic or unrealistic? Predominantly happy, unhappy, or neutral? Consistent with the emotional tone of the whole story? A comprehensive analysis of these and similar elements gathered from ten to twenty stories often yield information that gives the psychiatrist objective data that he cannot acquire by routine observation.

Another form of projective technique, used extensively in England and gaining popularity in the United States, is the Mosaic Test, which was devised by Margaret Lowenfeld, an English psychiatrist, about 1929. The test may be considered as a nonverbal substitute for the Rorschach Test. The mosaics are small chips of plastic in various colors and of various shapes. The subject is asked to make a design with these chips. The result is, within the limits of the material, a *Gestalt* in varying degrees of organization. These configurations are then analyzed according to more or less established criteria. The test is supposed to illustrate, in the words of Lowenfeld herself, "what the individual can *do* with his intelligence and imagination; and whether his power of drive and his emotional facilitation or inhibition enable him to use such cognitive abilities as he possesses." [11] In that way the Mosaic Test reveals, according to its author, the basic personality structure of the subject. Using the usual statistical procedures, it is found that studies in validity and reliability have not given very satisfactory results, but blind interpretation by highly trained individuals has given extremely good results.

Finally, a word about the Szondi Test, devised by the Hungarian psychiatrist Lipot Szondi.[12] The test material consists of 48 photographs, each representing the face of a mental patient. The pictures are divided into six sets, each containing eight photographs. Each set contains the picture of a homosexual, a sadist, an epileptic, a hysteric, a catatonic schizophrenic, a paranoid schizophrenic, a manic-depressive in the depressive state, and a manic-depressive in the manic state. The subject is to choose from each series the two pictures he likes most and the two he dislikes most. The choice reactions of the subject are then analyzed according to certain criteria and are presumed to depict his basic personality structure. The value of this test is still under discussion.

This brief picture of the standardized psychodiagnostic techniques that the clinical psychologist has at his disposal shows that he is well equipped to meet the demands of an objective diagnosis. Whether he is better equipped than the psychiatrist, as some clinical psychologists themselves believe, is an open question.

In the neuropsychiatric team all the complex material gathered from test data, clinical observation, medical reports, interviews, and social histories, is pooled or, rather, interpreted. Because of his knowledge of psychodynamics, the clinical psychologist is able to outline a composite picture of the patient's personality.

With the completion of a carefully worked out diagnosis, the team is prepared to proceed to its second task, the selection of a method of treatment.

Therapeutic Task. In the neuropsychiatric team, the therapeutic role of the social worker creates, as a rule, no great difficulty. The social worker is responsible for such therapeutic procedures as the attempt to change the patient's environment or to change the attitude of his home and immediate family in case these environmental factors are the partial source of the individual's mental state. Therapeutic efforts with a child, for instance, can be successful only in proportion to the cooperation of the parents and other adults involved in the child's world.

As has been said repeatedly, the psychiatrist is the authority to handle cases that require medical care. But the division of labor between the psychiatrist and the clinical psychologist in the field of treatment is often enough a source of friction, for the latter's attempts to practice psychotherapy have met, and are still meeting, with the lukewarm or hostile attitude of some members of the psychiatric profession. Although recognizing the clinician's value, some psychiatrists would limit his role chiefly to testing.[13] The clinical psychologist takes a different attitude. Since 1896, when Lightner Witmer opened the first psychological clinic for children, psychologists have carried out therapy in schools and child guidance clinics —and with success, they claim. This success, they believe, is sufficient to warrant their continuance in the effort of alleviating some of the emotional disturbances and consequent behavior disorders of children. During its subsequent development in the armed forces, clinical psychology has been in continuous contact with abnormal personality cases among adults. Concentrating on the study of these years when pressures of environment and the development of physical, intellectual, and emotional capacities exert strong influences upon the formation of character and personality pattern, the clinical psychologist has learned about human nature much that adds to his effectiveness in dealing with adults. In other words, the clinical psychologist assumed some of the duties of a psychotherapist, even though he has no degree in medicine. The clinicians do not mean to say, of course, that the role of the psychiatrist should be confined to medical, somatic therapy and that the psychologist may monopolize psychotherapy, but they maintain that, in view of the ever-increasing number of mentally disordered patients and the qualifications of a competent clinical psychologist in the understanding of the psychodynamics and basic processes of human personality, a division of labor is in accord with professional economy. The psychologist can relieve the psychiatrist of some of the time-consuming burden of psychotherapy.

In discussing the relationship between the psychiatrist and the psychologist in administering therapy, one might ask what kind of mental disorders the clinical psychologist can successfully treat. The answer depends greatly, of course, upon the patient who needs treatment, upon the conditions under which the therapy is undertaken, and upon the clinician's training and competence. If the psychologist is able, for any reason, to reach a better relationship with the patient than the psychiatrist is, the psychologist might be assigned major responsibility for that case.

Generally speaking, the clinical psychologist treats persons of all ages who manifest behavior disorders or emotional disturbances. He offers psychotherapy to some neurotics, generally the milder cases, and to some psychopaths. Ordinarily, he does not undertake the treatment of psychotics, especially those so far out of contact with reality that rapport, upon which all psychotherapy depends, cannot be established.

One serious argument against the participation of the psychologist in therapy comes from the psychologists themselves. They fear that time spent in treatment is time taken away from research. There are clinicians who would reserve the title "clinical psychologist" for those who engage in research. Whatever opinion one may have on this narrowing of a title, there will probably always be psychologists primarily interested in helping the psychiatrist in diagnosis and in the immediate alleviation of mental disorders through psychotherapy; nevertheless, a vast and almost uncharted field lies before those psychologists who throw their energies into research.[14]

In reviewing the preceding discussion, it may be concluded that the clinical psychologist does practice certain forms of psychotherapy, and that he, because of his theoretical and practical training, thinks himself qualified to do so, at least in cooperation with the psychiatrist. As a matter of fact, most clinicians work under the supervision of a psychiatrist, especially when treating grave emotional disorders.

But a different tendency is exerting itself. There are at present two trends of thought concerning the position or the most appropriate role of the clinical psychologist. Some believe that his place is in the neuropsychiatric team, as it has been developed in the military service and as is still strongly advocated by the Veterans Administration. Those who take this stand point out that, so far as psychotherapy is concerned, psychology is not, as yet, prepared to cope with the responsibilities involved.[15] On the other hand, there is a rather strong movement against the team approach, for many believe that membership on the staff of a neuropsychiatric team is not the most desirable position for the clinical psychologist. As a matter of fact, many child-guidance clinics have abandoned the team approach.

The main reason for this attitude concerns the welfare of the patient. Although the team approach may be useful for diagnosis, it is deemed less beneficial for therapy because it does not seem advisable to have people of three different professions attack the problems of one client.[16] However, another very serious reason, underlying the whole dispute, is one which has been mentioned several times—*i.e.*, the friction that may occur, and often does occur, in the team between the psychiatrist and the clinical psychologist. Despite the well-meaning advice given by many authors with regard to a division of labor, it is hard to assign each one his own task in matters of psychotherapy. True, the Veterans Administration, which strongly advocates team work, has announced that the clinical psychologist should be considered a full-fledged member of the team, with a status comparable in every way to that of the psychiatrist. But many clinicians have their doubts about the sincerity of that statement, because the Veterans Administration, in continuing the description of the duties of the clinical psychologist, adds the provision that he should carry out "individual or group therapy under the direction of the responsible neuropsychiatrist." Many clinical psychologists resent this dominating role of the psychiatrist. Besides, they point out, there is little reason for this supremacy, inasmuch as they are better equipped than the physician in some respects: they have better diagnostic tools; they are more thoroughly trained for research; and they believe themselves to be better equipped also to handle competently the therapy of certain clinical problems that frequently arise in the schools—such problems as needs for vocational counseling, behavior problems in children, functional speech defects, defects in reading, etc.

For these reasons, some clinical psychologists set themselves up as private practitioners, independent of the medical framework. Here, of course, serious dangers may arise and, as a matter of fact, have already arisen. Because of the lack of sufficient supervision, many offices of clinical psychology—sometimes more fancy names are used—are set up by men and women who have only the most rudimentary notions of psychology or psychiatry. The number of such quacks in the United States is estimated to run into the thousands.[17] It is evident that only rigorous state legislation will be able to combat this evil successfully.

A final reason why some clinical psychologists work outside the usual team is of a simple, practical nature: shortage of trained personnel as well as the inadequacy of budget allowances rule out the team concept in many instances. The use of clinical psychology is no longer limited to government service agencies, hospitals, mental-hygiene agencies, and psychiatric clinics, for many other institutions and groups recognize its usefulness and its contributions to psychotherapeutics. Both industrial and social agencies use the clinical psychologist for the handling of human relationships; custodial and correctional institutions make a large use of psychotherapeutic principles and methods; pastoral counseling now recognizes the value of clinical psychology; and vocational-guidance counselors, who had formerly considered psychotherapy of no use to their procedures, now make use of it to help the client to realize the emotional conflicts standing in the way of his making a good vocational adjustment.

Since education aims not only at the accumulation of knowledge but also, and chiefly, at the development of the personality, it is natural that therapeutic principles and methods find ready application in the school.[18] Some of these institutions and agencies may well be in a position to afford a psychotherapeutic team, but it would obviously be out of the question, both because of shortage of manpower and because of financial reasons, to hope for an establishment of such teams in all of them. However, several such institutions could perhaps afford a clinical psychologist, and this holds true especially for schools and educational institutions.

Farsighted educators in elementary schools have recognized the importance of specialized training in psychology in coping with the "problem child." In many cities, the bureau of education has established psychiatric and psychological service for the children of the public schools. Despite the growing need for teachers in the classroom, several congregations of Sisters have trained some of their members in psychology to attend to the needs of children in their care. Likewise, a few Catholic universities, diocesan school boards, and charities organizations, as well as some other Catholic groups, have set up psychiatric and psychological centers for children and adults in various cities. There is a growing recognition that the psychiatrist and psychologist, working together with children either in the school or in the clinic, are doing a preventive work whose far-reaching benefits will be realized only in the future when, other factors being equal, one can reasonably hope that there will be a perceptible reduction in the number of neurotics and psychotics in our adult population.

Once clinical psychologists have set themselves up as independent therapists on a fee basis, it is understandable that they do not stop at symptomatic therapy. Many of these independent clinical psychologists, even though lacking in medical training, have gone further and practice depth psychology. The condition *sine qua non* of starting on such a therapeutic career is evident: that they be fully trained in depth psychotherapy. Here one meets the same problem that was pointed out in the beginning of this chapter; *i.e.*, whether the practice of depth therapy should be reserved to the medical profession alone. Those who believe that it should not be so limited point out the same reasons mentioned previously—the shortage of psychiatrists and the unwillingness or inability of many patients to see a depth therapist. In addition, they return to the observation referred to at the beginning of this discussion—*i.e.*, that depth therapy does not seem to include many medical elements properly speaking.

This picture may be concluded—as it began—by saying that the authors deem it unnecessary here to take sides in these controversies. They would like to add, however, that even those psychiatrists who are not unfavorably disposed toward the clinical psychologist consider his therapeutic training as yet insufficient. For instance, Kubie requires the clinical psychologist who is to become a psychotherapist to continue the study of anatomy, physiology, and pathology for two years longer than he would otherwise do.

THE SOCIAL WORKER

The problems that confront the social worker are as varied as the circumstances surrounding each individual or family that comes for help.[19] The main situations presented in which the child plays a major role are requests for child placement, requests for temporary shelter for children, behavior problems of children, difficulties in the parent-child relationship, vocational guidance of adolescents, mental deficiency or disease, parental neglect, and unmarried motherhood. In regard to the aged, there are problems in placement, health, family relationship, and economic maintenance. In addition, general family problems are presented in situations involving unemployment, desertion, inadequate housing, alcoholism, mental or physical handicaps in one of the parents, marital discord, and insufficient income and its allied household-management difficulties. Although not all these problems are directly of a psychological or psychiatric nature, the solution of them all requires on the part of the social worker, an insight and understanding of human nature, a knowledge of interpersonal relations, and a great skill in counseling techniques. When psychiatric elements are involved in a certain case, the social worker must have sufficient knowledge of the principles of mental hygiene to draw the case to the attention of the competent authorities. He must realize the weight and influence that early emotional experiences with their resultant attitudes have upon later disturbances and conflicts of the personality. Hence, it is obvious that the competent social case worker should be familiar with certain psychiatric concepts and the principles of mental health, particularly the counseling procedures.

Perhaps one of the best descriptions of case work was given a few years ago when the late Alfred E. Smith said that it is "the art of assisting our neighbor to help himself out of his own troubles, whatever they might be, and to assist him in such a way that he, as a human being, can keep his head up, maintain his independence and preserve his dignity." These troubles may be physical, emotional, or social in nature—and the Catholic case worker adds that often enough they are of a spiritual character. Hence, the task of the social worker is to help people who are beset by physical, emotional, social, and spiritual problems to help themselves within the compass of their own powers and choices.

When a problem arises within the family setting, the very foundation of happy and healthy family life can sometimes be seriously damaged unless outside help is available. One of the mediums through which this help is offered is social case work. This is not to imply that every problem that arises in the family needs case-work service. Problems are an essential part of life, if for no other reason than that mankind shares a nature wounded by original sin. Case-work service is focused on those families and individuals who need and want help in activating within themselves or their own family unit the necessary strength to meet and successfully combat the problems that confront them.

This art and skill of helping people to help themselves is carried out, first of all, through interviewing and talking with people beset by serious problems, *i.e.*, through an application of the techniques of good counseling. The case worker attempts, further, to bring about an adjustment to the environmental factors that have occasioned discord and unhappiness in families or individuals, or a readjustment of the environment itself. It is also his task to point out to his client the resources in his own community that will be of effective help to him; *e.g.*, he may bring an alcoholic in contact with the A.A., or a boy in contact with a good boys' club. Wherever psychiatric elements are involved, the social worker's contribution in diagnostics consists in exploring the environmental and family background of the individual; his therapeutic contribution is to carry out in practice the suggestions of the psychiatrist and to support them by his own personal counseling techniques. In his diagnostic as well as in his therapeutic work, he may operate within the framework of a neuropsychiatric team, but even if he does not, he will always keep in contact with competent psychiatric authorities. The social worker's task appears thus as largely practical, but, if he has time and talent, he may engage in research.

To become more specific, the social worker needs to understand what it really means emotionally for a child to be removed from his own home and placed in another. The foster-home placement or adoption of Johnny Smith is more than simply finding for him a house with four walls, a bed, a roof overhead, and an open door. The social worker must understand Johnny and what he needs. He must be sure that the adoption or foster home is able to give Johnny what he needs. Perhaps Johnny was conceived out of wedlock. His parents married in order to avoid scandal and to give the child a name. They were never meant for each other, had no genuine affection or love. Johnny became to both parents the object upon which they unloaded the burden of their personal unhappiness. He was never loved but regretted. He had no security, no sense of being wanted. His father eventually turned to drink and deserted the family. The mother feels that her life has become a blind alley, tied down as she is to a child with whom she associates only her own personal misery. She decides to surrender him for adoption or foster-home placement. Under such circumstances the social worker attempts to keep the family together whenever it is possible and constructive; he tries to have Johnny stay with his mother by helping her gain some realization of her own behavior and motivation, some awareness of what Johnny needs by the mere fact that he is flesh of her flesh. If this fails, another home must be provided. Perhaps Johnny most needs a congregate group experience with others of his own age in an institutional environment. Or perhaps adoption is indicated. Neither Johnny nor any child should be placed with a couple who request a child to adopt as a last futile gesture toward preserving their own unsteady marriage, for Johnny needs adoptive parents who will give him genuine love; he needs security, a sense of belonging. And so the process goes on. The social worker, through his awareness and use of mental hygiene and psychiatric concepts, is enabled to give the service to the situation that the circumstances require.

A young mother, bewildered and ashamed, comes asking for help in entering her seven-year-old girl in a special school. She says that the child is slow and has not been getting along well in several schools where she was entered. She cannot seem to grasp school exercises as well as other children of her age. The social worker patiently listens to the story, encouraging the mother to express the heartache that has been, and is, hers in realizing that her child is not as smart or as quick as other children in the neighborhood. Perhaps there is even expressed the fear that there may be something wrong with the child. The worker makes the necessary arrangements and has the little girl given psychological tests. It is found that the child is definitely a mental defective. She has been associating in school with children of her own actual age, but three or four years her senior in mental ability. Gently the social worker interprets the situation to the parents. Gradually they are brought to the realization that placement of their child in an institution for the mentally deficient is best for all concerned. Every human instinct may rebel against such a consideration; yet, with the skillful assistance of the social worker, with his deep awareness of the emotional factors involved, they themselves make the decision of placement. Again, it is precisely in such a situation that the psychiatric and mental hygiene concepts that are part of the social worker's equipment enable him to be of special help to the parents in facing and solving such a problem. The social worker helps the parents to realize what mental deficiency is and how it affects the child in her relationships to them and to other children both in and outside the home. He helps the parents to work through the feelings of heavy guilt, rejection, or overprotection—the feelings often characteristic of parents when they realize that God has given them such a child. The worker by his genuine understanding, compassion, and acceptance is the means whereby the experience is made endurable for this couple. Too often, such incidents can occasion a lifetime spent in unfounded self-accusation and fruitless protection of such a child, or a married life marked by mutual hostility and fear.

Catholic Social Work. Organized Catholic social work is carried on in the United States through the offices of Catholic Charities or Catholic social-welfare bureaus. These offices are generally under the direct supervision of the local ordinary. Trained men and women, who have secured a graduate degree in social service after completing their college courses, staff them. Priest directors, likewise equipped with a similar graduate degree, are directly responsible for the various programs of Catholic welfare activity. While it is true that many diocesan offices of Catholic Charities do not have a completely trained priest or lay staff, the trend is definitely in that direction. Most diocesan welfare organizations now expect and encourage prospective employees to secure a graduate degree in social service. The National Catholic School of Social Service of the Catholic University at Washington, D.C., is but one of several Catholic graduate schools from which both religious and lay graduates annually come to social work.

Many purposes characterize the functioning of diocesan welfare organizations. Primarily they coordinate and supervise the program of diocesan institutions and agencies such as those for dependent and delinquent children, hospitals, day nurseries, settlement houses, homes for the aged and chronically ill, business residences for young women, centers for the blind and handicapped, shelters for unmarried mothers, etc. More pertinent to the purpose of this chapter, however, is the fact that diocesan welfare organizations provide case work or counseling service to adults, youth, and children.

This counseling service is offered in various settings. There are medical case-work programs in Catholic hospitals and clinics. There are family and child case-work agencies. In addition, there are psychiatric case-work programs conducted in conjunction with child and adult psychiatric clinics. Moreover, an integral part of many Catholic camps, neighborhood houses, settlement, and recreational centers is the group-work service provided by trained personnel and essentially similar in its purpose and nature to case work.

Contrary to a widespread and deep-rooted misconception, private case-work welfare agencies such as Catholic Charities do not have as their primary purpose the dispensing of financial assistance to those in need. The inception of the Federal Social Security Program in 1935 and the prior existence of public-assistance programs made it unnecessary—and sometimes imprudent—for private welfare agencies to expend financial grants to meet basic necessities of life. Giving relief for subsistence has not altogether ceased to be a function of private welfare agencies, but today it is definitely subordinated to case-work programs. In 1929, approximately 98 per cent of all funds given in relief to the poor in the United States was secured through private contributions and distributed through private agencies. Today, the position is completely reversed, and it is estimated that, in 1949, about 98 per cent of such relief came from public agencies. In the year 1948, an average of 25 million dollars of public funds was expended monthly in the five boroughs of Greater New York through Aid to Dependent Children, Old Age Assistance, Aid to the Blind, Home Relief, Veteran Relief, and Unemployment Insurance benefits. It is evident, therefore, that the state has assumed the function of granting financial relief to the poor. This trend is entirely in accord with the encyclicals of Pope Leo XIII and Pope Pius XI, which maintain that agencies supported by public taxes should assume and discharge as their responsibility the task of providing the basic necessities of life to those in need. This does not mean, of course, that it is the intention of the popes to eliminate all personal charity.

The purpose, therefore, of private organizations such as Catholic Charities has a focus differing substantially from that of similar agencies a generation ago. The basic function is always that of dispensing the charity of Christ. But, whereas financial assistance was a major activity 20 years ago, case-work service or counseling programs are in the foreground today. The Catholic social worker has to acquaint himself not only with the basic concepts of psychiatry and mental hygiene, counseling procedure, and interpersonal relations but also with the concepts of theology. Certainly, the better he understands the workings of human nature and the influence of environment, heredity, emotions, and will power in personality development and behavior, the more he can be of real help to the confused, bewildered, and despairing people who come to him with problems that, to them, are overwhelming and unbearable. But, aside from this scientific preparation, the Catholic social worker must be equipped with a sound knowledge of theology, for he aims not simply at achieving the social adjustment of the families and individuals he serves, but rather at achieving their social adjustment as a means to an end—that of bringing men closer to God or back to Him. He understands human personality as a divine creation marred by the fall of Adam but redeemed by the saving sacrifice of Christ. His psychological knowledge is permeated by his conviction of the wounding and weakening effects of original sin, and this enables him to deepen his understanding and acceptance of those who ask his help. And in trying to help them, he will tell them that they can help themselves by asking God for His assistance and grace.

NOTES AND REFERENCES

1. A brief discussion of the question may be found in the editorial of the *American Journal of Psychotherapy,* Vol. 3 (1949), pp. 207–212.
2. This section was written in collaboration with the Rev. Louis B. Snider, S.J., Child Guidance Center, Loyola University, Chicago.
3. Concerning the status and development of clinical psychology, the training required for the clinical psychologist, and the diagnostic procedures that he uses, see the following:

Graduate Internship Training in Psychology, *Journal of Consulting Psychology,* Vol. 9 (1945), pp. 243–266.

KELLY, E. L., "Clinical Psychology," in DENNIS, W., *et al.*, "Current Trends in Psychology" (Pittsburgh: University of Pittsburgh Press, 1947), pp. 84 ff.; *id.*, "Training in Clinical Psychology" (New York: Prentice-Hall, Inc., 1950).

MCNEILL, HARRY V., Contemporary Developments in Clinical Psychology, *Proceedings of the American Catholic Philosophical Association,* 1950.

PENNINGTON, L. A., I. A. BERG, *et al.*, "An Introduction to Clinical Psychology" (New York: The Ronald Press Company, 1948).

Proposed Program of Professional Training in Clinical Psychology, Report of the Committee on Professional Training, *Journal of Consulting Psychology,* Vol. 7 (1943), pp. 23–26.

RAIMY, VICTOR C. (ed.), "Training in Clinical Psychology" (New York: Prentice-Hall, Inc., 1950).

ROSENZWEIG, S., Clinical Psychology as a Psychodiagnostic Art, *Journal of Personality,* Vol. 15 (1946), pp. 99 ff.

A *Journal of Clinical Psychology* is published in Brandon, Vermont.

4. For a summary of some representative tests, see ROSENZWEIG, S., An Elementary Syllabus of Psychological Tests, *Journal of Psychology,* Vol. 18 (1944), pp. 9–40; *id.*, "Psychodiagnosis" (New York: Grune and Stratton, 1949).
5. In an excellent summary of research on the validity of personality questionnaires, Ellis has listed 26 points that have been raised against paper and pencil personality tests. See ELLIS, ALBERT, The Validity of Personality Questionnaires, *Psychological Bulletin,* Vol. 43 (1946), pp. 385–440.
6. Concerning the tests referred to in this chapter, we wish to comment that Catholic moralists consider some of them objectionable and, in case they are, refuse the school authorities the right to apply them to the children without permission of the parents.
7. For a comprehensive review of the variety of these techniques, see ABT, LAWRENCE, and LEOPOLD BELLAK, "Projective Psychology" (New York: Alfred A. Knopf, Inc., 1950); BELL, JOHN E., "Projective Techniques" (New York: Longmans, Green & Co., Inc., 1948); FRANK, L., Projective Methods for the Study of Personality, *Journal of Psychiatry,* Vol. 8 (1939), pp. 389–413.
8. RORSCHACH, HERMANN, "Psychodiagnostics," translated by P. Lemkau and B. Kronenberg (New York: Grune and Stratton, 1942).
9. For a fuller treatment of this technique, see BECK, S. J., "Rorschach's Tests" (2 vols.; New York: Grune and Stratton, 1944–1945); KLOPFER, BRUNO, and DOUGLAS KELLER, "The Rorschach Technique" (Yonkers, N.Y.: World Book Company, 1942); VERNON, P. E., The Significance of the Rorschach Test, *British Journal of Medical Psychology,* Vol. 13 (1933), pp. 179–271.
10. MURRAY, HENRY A., "Explorations in Personality" (New York: Oxford University Press, 1938).
11. LOWENFELD, M., The Mosaic Test, *American Journal of Orthopsychiatry,*

Vol. 19 (1949). See also Lowenfeld, M., and A. Maberly, A Discussion on the Value of the Play Therapy in Child Psychiatry, *Proceedings of the Royal Society of Medicine,* Vol. 39 (1946), pp. 439–443; Diamond, B. L., and H. T. Schmale, The Mosaic Test: an Evaluation of Its Clinical Application, *American Journal of Orthopsychiatry,* Vol. 14 (1944), pp. 237–250; Reiman, M. G., The Mosaic Test: Its Applicability and Validity, *ibid.,* Vol. 20 (1950).

12. See Deri, Susan, "Introduction to the Szondi Test" (New York: Grune and Stratton, 1949).
13. For a report on some of the interprofessional problems that arise from the collaboration of psychiatry and clinical psychology, see "The Relation of Clinical Psychology to Psychiatry," Report No. 10, July, 1949, of the Group for the Advancement of Psychiatry. Topeka, Kansas.
14. In the study of personality, the psychologist has much to recommend him for research. His training has entered into the construction and administration of tests and other diagnostic devices. It continues to be valuable for the refinement of these instruments. Experiments throw light on the nature and concomitants of emotions. Experiments in learning and perception add to our knowledge of attitude formation, frustration, reaction times, psychological deficit, reflex activity, and levels of aspiration. Some experimental work has been done on induced neuroses to study psychodynamics under controlled conditions. All in all, there is a vast amount of experimental data which has never been adequately evaluated and incorporated into the practice of clinical psychology and psychiatry. A complete synthesis of these data is one of the outstanding needs of psychological research.
15. Clark, R. A., Psychologist and Psychiatrist, *Journal of Personality,* Vol. 15 (1946), pp. 101–104.
16. See Rogers, C. R., "Psychotherapy," in Dennis *et al., op. cit.,* p. 130.
17. Steiner, Lee, "Where Do People Take Their Troubles?" (Boston: Houghton Mifflin Company, 1945).
18. Cantor, N., "The Dynamics of Learning" (Buffalo: Foster and Steward, 1946).
19. The section on social work was written in collaboration with the Rev. Robert A. Ford, Associate Director of the Family Division of Catholic Charities, New York City.

Chapter 14

PSYCHOSES

The most striking mental diseases are the psychoses, whose victims the general public usually regards as insane or "crazy." Before entering upon a discussion of these diseases, it seems expedient to differentiate briefly between psychotic, psychoneurotic, and psychopathic patients.

The psychotic mind is separated from reality; consequently psychotics are unable to make a living or to conform to the rules of society. Such patients live in worlds of fantasy wherein every wish is satisfied: the one who wants power becomes Napoleon or the Pope or God; the woman who wants a child "gets a child daily"; the man who wants money is suddenly a multimillionaire. On the other hand, psychoneurotics are only partially disabled. Since they maintain contact with reality, they are able to make a living, to care for their families and sometimes to perform very valuable work. Whereas many psychotics, having lost the "hurt instinct," suffer little from their condition, psychoneurotics suffer intensely and continuously. Psychopathy presents a mixture of psychoneurotic and psychotic traits. The psychopath, although very close to psychosis, never experiences the full-blown psychotic attack. While psychopathic personalities sometimes do suffer as the psychoneurotics, yet most of the time they do not suffer, because they live a life of unreality similar to that of psychotics.

Some writers divide the psychoses into two major groups: the endogenous and the exogenous forms. Endogenous psychoses are, by definition, those disorders which arise from within the organism and are due to the patient's constitutional abnormalities. This endogenous group is further divided into the psychogenic and the organogenic psychoses. The general consensus of the modern psychiatric world posits schizophrenic and manic-depressive illnesses as psychogenic. It is true that little or nothing is known about organic factors as a cause of these two disorders; therefore, they might be the result of purely psychic causes. However, the possibility that there is some organic factor productive of these diseases still exists. Some European as well as American neuropathologists hesitate in endorsing the opinion that schizophrenia and manic-depressive psychoses are fully psychogenic, for they remember that general paresis was regarded as psychogenic until the discovery of the causative organism of syphilis, the *Treponema pallidum.*

The following two sections will deal with those psychoses which, according to the *Standard Nomenclature,* used in psychiatry and previously mentioned, are "disorders of psychogenic origin or without clearly defined tangible causes or structural change": schizophrenia and manic-depressive psychoses.

SCHIZOPHRENIA

Until some fifty years ago, the literature on schizophrenia was rather meager. Almost all those who wrote on the subject neglected to consider it as a clinical entity until, around 1900, Kraepelin completely modified the concept of this disease.

Kraepelin considered a gradual deterioration as the most significant symptom of schizophrenic patients. He also found a series of other clinical symptoms, such as hallucinations, delusions, odd and distorted emotional expressions, disorders of attention, negativism, stereotyped motions and attitudes, lessened capacity for work, disorders of judgment and impairment of thought processes associated with relatively intact perception and memory. Now Kraepelin was able to show that all these disorders were not symptoms of as many mental diseases but tended to run together in a well-defined syndrome. He therefore conceived of schizophrenia as a clinical entity. However, he did not use the term "schizophrenia," but termed the disease dementia praecox, because he established as fact that, whereas manic-depressives do not deteriorate until late in life, the deterioration of schizophrenics sets in at an early age.

Eugene Bleuler, like Kraepelin, felt that he was dealing with a clearly defined disease. To Bleuler, however, it was not essentially a condition of deterioration, for he demonstrated that some schizophrenics do not deteriorate, but rather show a splitting of personality. He therefore introduced the term "schizophrenia," which received a warm welcome in psychiatric circles. To substantiate his view that the patient's bizarre, unintelligible ways of thinking and acting are due to a split personality, Bleuler stressed in his symptomatology the presence of ambivalence, *i.e.,* the simultaneous existence of contradictory or contrasting thoughts in the minds of schizophrenic patients.

Adolf Meyer, in accordance with his psychobiological view, correlated the patient's schizophrenic mental state with his organic condition and found that the patient often reveals a long history of somatic diseases. In order to denote the odd and incongruous disturbances of the patient's behavior, Meyer made an attempt to introduce the term "parergastic reaction pattern"—a designation enjoying limited popularity. Meyer and his pupils, like Kanner, also pointed out that the behavior of the schizophrenics is reminiscent of the reactions in the primitive, archaic stages of human evolution. In this point they are in agreement with several spokesmen of the analytic schools. They, too, regard schizophrenia as a form of regression to the primitive tendencies observable in the early stages of development of the individual and among primitive peoples. According to this theory the schizophrenic's inability to differentiate between fantasy and reality is comparable to the state of early infancy. The shameless wetting and self-soiling of some schizophrenics may be seen as a confirmation of the regressive theory.

In brief, it is generally accepted today that schizophrenia represents a particular type of personality disorder, characterized by a splitting of the mind, a greater or lesser withdrawal from reality, and occasional unsuccessful struggles with both internal and external problems. The incidence of schizophrenia is high. One-fifth of the patients annually admitted to mental hospitals are classified as schizophrenics; about one-half of the permanent population in mental institutions are schizophrenic patients. The occurrence of schizophrenia is relatively rare before puberty and after the fiftieth year of life. Men slightly outnumber women in this disease, and its incidence is higher in urban areas than in rural environments—indeed, twice as high.

Classification. The four different types of schizophrenia described by Kraepelin form the basis for the classification used at present.

First, *simple schizophrenia* is characterized by a marked reduction of affective life, of ideas, and of the patient's interest in himself and his environment. These patients are quiet and listless. This type of the disease often endures throughout the patient's lifetime, and no treatment is known. A case may serve to illustrate some of the above points.

§ The patient was twenty-two years old when committed to the institution. He had an excellent school record and was about to complete his work for the bachelor's degree. At college, he had a perfect record during the first two academic years. Although he did have friends, he found it difficult to mix in larger groups and showed signs of oversensitivity. Two years previous to his commitment, he became careless in his personal appearance, went home to his parents, and refused to continue with his college studies. He thought that it would be unnecessary to work for a living as long as his father and mother were still alive. Contrary to his former habits, he slept until noontime. He would go out evenings and return about midnight without telling his family where he was or what he had done. After a lapse of six months, he returned, at the urging of his parents, to work on his college degree. However, shortly after his return, friends noted that he was not attending classes, that he avoided conversation, and that he acted in a silly manner. Continuing to neglect his physical and hygienic habits he would stay in bed the whole twenty-four hours of a day. When his parents visited him, he refused to talk with them, and a physician advised his parents to have him institutionalized. His emotional responses were shallow and inadequate. He showed no concern about his condition, and often indulged in silly laughter and strange mannerisms. In the hospital, his behavior was characterized by apathy, inattention, and preoccupation. He refused to leave his room and to take part in recreation with the other patients. He denied having hallucinations or illusions, although he was seen walking alone in the recreation rooms of the hospital, talking and laughing to himself.

Second, the *hebephrenic* type is marked by a complete withdrawal from reality, by development of delusions and hallucinations, by an inappropriateness of affect and thinking, and by silly behavior combined with autoeroticism.

§ Miss S. was nineteen years of age and had reached the senior year in high school. She originally came to seek psychiatric help, because she experienced difficulties in associating with the boys and girls of her school. Among the first things she mentioned was that she sometimes became confused about her "boy friend," who lived about five hundred miles away from her home. She wrote him regularly and he answered her letters. Notwithstanding this, she thought she saw him daily on the street, on the trolley car, or playing an instrument in the school band. A year and a half earlier she would have thought she was mistaken, but now she was sure that she saw him because he "winked at her" and gave her other signs of recognition. She related all these things in a monotone and with a blank, slyly smiling face.

About her life she related that she had been breast-fed, and that the picture of her mother's breast had been, from childhood on, almost constantly on her mind. She liked to be alone, and recalled among her most pleasant memories her solitary walks in the forest near her home. Once, when she was playing "post office," a boy kissed her; she cried and broke down. She said she intended to become a writer, but at the same time she disclosed that she hated school, which she never finished. She had always been a poor student, given to day dreaming and living in a world of fantasy. When she left school, her behavior became more and more apathetic, childish, and coquettish. When the doorbell rang, she thought that it was her "boy friend" calling; she also believed that friends of her brother came disguised as him. Eventually, she had to be committed to an institution.

Catatonia, the third form of schizophrenia, is manifested by such behavior types as negativism, stupor or excitement, and stereotyped mannerisms; it may be initiated in either an acute or subacute phase marked either by stupor or by excitement. The stupor is always connected with negativism. The patient is mute and hypersuggestible; his behavior is marked by command automatism, by catalepsy (*i.e.,* waxy flexibility—a state in which the arms, hands, or feet retain the position in which they may be placed by the attendant), echolalia (repetition of words or speech the patient happens to hear), and echobraxia (repetition of the actions of others). This stuporous phase may rapidly give way to the stage of excitement with a profusion of postures and gestures of an assaultive character. Some patients experience only the stupor, others only the excitement, but the vast majority show both stages. Violent suicidal attempts occur not infrequently. Quite commonly there is sexual excitement and erotic behavior with genital exposure and open masturbation. The duration of the states of catatonic excitement vary greatly, lasting from a few days or weeks to several months.

§ One catatonic patient was a single woman thirty-seven years old, the eldest of seven children. Her father was described as rigid and stubborn, and the mother as extremely nervous and excitable. The mother had experienced several convulsions of a hysterical nature. As a child the patient had been a behavior problem, being shy, timid, and frequently given to daydreaming. She was described as being stubborn and resistive. Content to play with her own dolls in her own room, she played very little with other children. During girlhood, she was the victim of an attempted rape. After her graduation from high school, she helped in taking care of the other children and with the household work. She was extremely religious and told of having had several visions, *e.g.*, she heard voices telling her never to marry because her life was to be sacrificed for a special purpose. She had the impression that people looked at her and made disparaging remarks concerning her virginity. At times, she had attacks of laughing and shouting without any apparent reason. As time passed, she withdrew more and more from society and became unmanageable, with the result that her brothers and sisters found it necessary to commit her to an institution.

In the hospital, the patient was described as small of stature and poorly nourished, with dilated pupils and hyperactive reflexes. At first, she was unmanageable; she struck the attendants, refused to eat or to speak, and showed many odd mannerisms. Her face was often expressionless and rigid, she paid no attention to questions, and there was no response to pin pricks or other painful stimuli. Artificial feeding became necessary until, four days later, she started to eat, though poorly. The patient's hallucinations occupied her attention. Sometimes she would say, "I am a saint. Everyone knows this." At other times, she became greatly excited and related that the devil was tempting her. It was often apparent that she heard voices of a frightening nature, for at such times, she would run out of the ward in a state of frantic anxiety, often without proper clothing. When asked why she was in the institution, she would reply, "You know as well as I do that the world is against me." She mentioned "rays" that were constantly directed at her in order to disturb her faith, and referred to them as atomic rays produced by a certain type of machinery to destroy her mind. The patient complained that she was sexually attacked all the time, and added that a certain man, who was actually far away, was constantly misusing her. She wished to talk to her mother, who had been long dead, but she did not recognize her brothers and sister when they visited her. Later, she became excited and said that she would save the world, that through the Pope she had invested large sums of money which would be used to destroy the bad world, and that only ten people would survive in it. Still later she mentioned that she was married to the King of England and claimed that all the honors that are normally bestowed upon the Queen should be given to her. These stories were related with no emotion and with an expressionless face. As time went on, she became quiet, walking along slowly and aimlessly without mingling with other patients.

The onset of *paranoia,* the fourth type of schizophrenia, usually takes place in the late thirties. The paranoid patient is characterized by the development of ambitions and suspicions which, through a process of rationalization and retrospective falsification, become excessive. He develops an uncompromising personality, which bends the facts rather than bend itself to the facts, thus engendering a complete and closely knit system of delusions. The delusions are usually of a grandiose nature, of being a king, a queen, a millionaire, or the Pope. They very often manifest compensatory gratifications for strong feelings of inferiority or inadequacy. Patients with intense guilt reactions see insulting faces, horrible animals, and threatening tortures. Patients with a religious bent see God the Father, or God the Son, or the Blessed Virgin, or the devil. The initial symptom is usually suspiciousness: the radio, the newspapers, and the speech of the passers-by, all make disparaging references to the patient. Thinking that strangers influence their souls and bodies, they misinterpret the actions of other people. In chronic cases, the ultimate stages closely resemble the other forms of schizophrenia.

The following example may serve to clarify the picture of paranoid schizophrenia:

§ Bill was described as a normal, average person, showing no unusual signs in his early life. As a boy he was active, healthy, and sociable, a great follower of, and participant in, athletics, especially baseball. The eldest of seven children, he went to work with his father in the coal mines as soon as he completed the seventh grade. No traces of mental disease were found in his ancestry or among his siblings. Bill's father was an alcoholic, but his mother succeeded in getting the father to work regularly. She managed the income in a competent way, with the result that the family had some property and owned a car. At twenty-nine, Bill married a girl whom he had been courting for eight years. They had four children, who, at the time Bill's mental disorder began, ranged in age from thirteen to three years.

After his marriage Bill was still considered an unusually pleasant, willing, and cooperative worker with an extrovert personality. He worked hard to fulfill his ambition of building his own home and providing a good environment for his children. He therefore bought and dismantled an old feed store, to provide lumber for the new house, since it was then impossible to secure lumber without priorities. Neglecting recreation and sleep, he worked a full day's shift in the mine and then spent the evening until midnight building his new home. At this time, he began to accuse his wife of infidelity, questioned his daughter about her mother's behavior, and threatened to kill his wife if he caught her with another man. At length, he refused to drink coffee prepared by his wife, for fear that she had put poison in it.

Finally, after being committed to a state institution, he became evasive and would neither admit nor deny his delusions concerning his wife's faithlessness. He showed no insight into his mental disturbance and claimed that he should not be in the institution. Although his delusions were fixed and unchangeable, he became in time more cooperative, social, and friendly. After he had received six electroshock treatments, his physical condition and behavior improved considerably; but his delusions remained. However, he was a willing worker and did every job assigned to him. The hospital staff felt that more electroshock treatments were indicated, but they were unable to predict whether or not he would recover to the extent of being able to return to his family.

One day he walked away from the hospital and went to another state. At last report, he had been working there for three years but would not let his family know his whereabouts, since he was afraid his wife would recommit him to the state institution. He said that he no longer loved his wife but that he did miss his children. His new friends and neighbors knew nothing of his background and thought him perfectly normal, for he never talked about his delusions. When last seen, all his delusions of persecution were well constructed, systematized, and rationalized. To support his assertion that his wife took drugs, he reasoned that his family had no savings, that his wife did not buy herself any clothes, and that therefore she must be spending all the money on drugs. He believed that, as a means of providing drugs for herself, his wife not only was unfaithful but drugged his coffee to kill his taste for cigarettes and so acquire his cigarette money for her narcotics. He further believed there was a narcotic ring, consisting of prominent people such as the parish priest and the local doctor, and concluded that he was placed in a mental institution in order to prevent him from telling this secret to the police.

This case will serve to illustrate that it is possible to live in close connection with a paranoid patient without being aware of his condition, for such people are pleasant, friendly, and logical as long as their delusional system remains untouched in any way.

Religious paranoia deserves special consideration. Such a case can be best illustrated by letting a patient speak for herself in a letter written to her therapist.

"Dear Doctor:

"I wonder what they done to me, a serious damage to my nervous system when last July at the clinic they put me to sleep in order to take my tonsils out, because I woke up, and from then on waves of frantic and fear went periodically over me, just like to snuff out my life, as if some one was pulling at my heart, making me gasp as if my breath was taken away.

"I believe they done serious damage unnecessarily to my nervous system (and I would never have another operation again), our nervous system being like a radio set, the finer the machinery, the better the reception. Before my operation, I lived in such a beautiful, spiritual world like a poet or artist, to cite a comparison, I loved this spiritual world and enjoyed it immensely. It gave me security, stability. Now it's all shut out. My reception is so coarse, so colorless, meaningless, it isn't funny. The radio set of my brain with its conducting nerve wires is on the blink. Where are my spirit and my mind? The creative part full of initiative, idealism, love? Love is creative and the best substance-sustainer of the mind. I mean actual true love which is the full possession of God. Does God's communication of his life to us thus depend on a nervous system? Of course they say 'a sound mind resides in a sound body.'

"Doctor, is rape not a fundamental, permanent injury to the nervous system because by force? And can't the same injury be done to a girl criminally while under anesthetic? I don't mean by ordinary means, but artificial ones. I had been injured and I think it is a horrible crime. It always reminds me of the passage in the Bible where the holy writer asserts: 'And the virgins know a song no one else knows.' Ever since that time I have in my mind and spirit been so dry, empty, not a bit elastic and reaching higher up in the fine spheres of the uncreative life. But Doctor why should I have to suffer for something some one done to my body, my nerves like that in my soul? They must know body and soul function together therefore it is such a crime to permanently disarrange vital parts, the finest, highest and noblest of the nervous system. It's a dirty, foul, hellish trick. And Doctor it showed in my face immediately. It had become so much more blank, the beauty of rightful innocence forcibly taken away like the freshness of flowers, a certain freshness that has nothing to do with years and keeps one younger looking on account of willfully preserved innocence. If I in my waking hours, with God's divine providence, have guarded my innocence, why should I be criminally robbed of it? My girlishness was gone, so from God I had a perfect right of its enjoyment, since according to his counsel I never wished to enjoy anything else."

Dynamics. The dynamics of schizophrenia are exemplified in the following account of the case of a veteran:

§ When the patient, the third youngest son of a family of eleven, was twelve, treatment of a hip condition necessitated his hospitalization in an orthopedic institute for two and one-half years. Although he had repressed this period of his life, he remembered his revolt at this institutionalization; although he had cried and begged his parents to take him home every Christmas, Easter, and birthday, the physician had always said that it would be harmful for him to go. He remembered, too, that he had been lonely. In the beginning, all his friends had visited him, but after a year, he had been practically deserted. Even his mother and his father, a well-known political and social figure, could not always find time for the regular visiting days. After his discharge, he returned to school, where he succeeded in his scholastic work, but as he had to wear an iron brace, he was unable to participate in such games as football and baseball. The result was that he found himself alone again.

When the war broke out, motivated by patriotism and loyalty to his country, he enlisted in the army. During this time, he made friends easily, but because he was continually transferred from one place to another, he was always losing these newly made friends. In the Asiatic theater of war, he followed the regulations of army life rigidly, and was thus deprived of much of the fun of his less disciplined companions. He avoided excesses in alcohol. When the war ended, he thought that he had satisfied his obligations of patriotism, and looked forward to being shipped home soon. At this time, he became tense and homesick for his family and was overjoyed when orders came to return stateside. He began packing up belongings. Two days later, he received word from his mother that one of his brothers had been killed in action. On the day after that, the order to return was rescinded, and he, with his companions, was ordered to Japan.

The almost simultaneous occurrence of these two events caused a furor of excitement in the young man, and reinduced the same feeling of constraint he had experienced in the hospital as a child. He lost, as he said, "consciousness," and attacked the commanding officer. Delusions of being persecuted and illusions of seeing his mother and his favorite sister manifested themselves. It was necessary to institutionalize him and send him back to the United States.

Three months after his return, his condition cleared up, leaving him, however, with a feeling of insecurity and a curiosity about the events that had occurred during his unconscious state. After the attack he was under observation for five years; during this time no schizophrenic reactions recurred. When last seen, he was a successful businessman, albeit somewhat sensitive to the stigma of having been in an institution.

The foregoing is a typical case, in which painful and unavoidable childhood events repeated themselves under war conditions. First in his youth and again in the war the patient was separated from his mother and relatives. The inability to escape these perplexing situations brought about the schizophrenic attack, which *au fond* was a flight reaction and an attempt to escape from reality.

Treatment. In recent years schizophrenia has been successfully treated. Metrazol, insulin, and electroshock treatment have proved helpful in many cases, but the use of some drugs such as Sodium Amytal and ephedrine sulfate has proved to be of only temporary assistance. In schizophrenic disorders, psychotherapy finds a very limited field because of the great difficulty in establishing any kind of rapport with the patients. Some analysts, *viz.*, Fromm, Reichmann, Brill, and Klein, report successful treatment, although in these cases most of the patients were admittedly only schizoid.

The best remedy is the prophylactic treatment of children whose behavior may suggest schizophrenia. The literature on this point presents many fine mental-hygiene measures aimed primarily at adapting the child to his environment in order to help him meet his problems directly rather than avoid and escape them. The question of how many people may be saved from a psychotic attack if given the proper mental treatment as children is hypothetical. However, it can be expected that children who are severely restricted and kept from ordinary contact with reality or who live in a fantasy world altogether remote from their school environment, unless given appropriate treatment, may easily become schizoid personalities and may later develop schizophrenic psychoses.

The prognosis in all cases of schizophrenia is questionable. However, with the development of modern medicine, it is hoped that in the future more effective treatment may be evolved.[1]

MANIC-DEPRESSIVE PSYCHOSES

Manic-depressive psychoses are characterized by attacks of depression, elation, or both. In earlier times, it was thought that the presence of the affective states, elation and depression, meant two different disease entities. But today, there is no doubt but that the two states represent one entity, a manic-depressive psychosis. There are cycloid conditions wherein one state, elation or depression, is the regular state and the other the exception. It also happens that people in the manic state are seemingly normal, but this regular condition is interrupted by a severe depression, *e.g.*, every three or four years.

In the *depressive phase,* the patient's psychophysiological processes are slowed up. A retardation in speech and a difficulty in thinking accompany the depressed mood, while physiologically, there occur loss of weight, constipation, anorexia (lack of appetite), sleep disturbance, general neglect of hygienic habits, and a decline in the sexual drive. For example, take the following case:

> § A man fifty-eight years old was a good worker, extremely industrious, and in every way a model father and husband. He was a good citizen with an excellent standing in his community. However, about every three to five years he started to complain about his job, that he had too much work to do, that he wanted to change his employer. He related over and over again many depressing stories. Although he was normally accustomed to getting up at five o'clock in the morning, during these periods he was unable to leave his bed before ten or eleven. He became irritable, grew hostile toward his wife and children, and did not want to see any of his neighbors or friends. While normal, he dressed to perfection, but during these periods of depression he was very negligent in his dress. He complained excessively about politicians, both local and national, and became easily unmanageable. After the lapse of about three months, he was able to return to his work and carry on in a normal way.

In the *manic phase,* the patients are extremely excited; they are plunged into a bewildering welter of thought, speech, and activity. People in this condition speak constantly and continuously—always, however, on a superficial level. They are absorbed by the environment and the outside world; there is a wealth of verbalized material about the environment, but nothing of their own inner life or personality. In normal people, this state is represented by the "holyday" or "Sunday" neurosis. These are the people who are always uneasy if they do not have work to do; they are always busy, always doing things. They are not daydreamers but doers and energetic thinkers. These are the people who work all the week, and then for recreation on Saturday and Sunday play at least thirty-six holes of golf. As an example, we may quote the following case:

§ A thirty-five-year-old patient was a quiet, reliable man living in a small community, belonging to the volunteer fire department and to various church and civic clubs. Suddenly, this patient became talkative, expansive, and was unable to sit at home or spend an evening with his wife. His condition seems to have started when he asked the landlord to renovate his apartment. The conversation concerning this matter was quiet and businesslike, the landlord mentioning the fact that it was difficult to obtain labor. However, the patient awoke at 5:00 the next morning, went to the landlord and spent a full hour in telling him "just what he thought of him." When the patient came home, he reported to his wife that he had seen the landlord to add a few things that he had forgotten the evening before, and that the landlord's reaction had been far from friendly. Among other things, the landlord had told him that he was crazy. From that day on, he went around telling everyone that he had a nervous breakdown. He began to play baseball all day with a group of high school boys. He expressed the desire to learn ping-pong and lawn tennis and was always on the go. He gave no thought at all to the support of his wife. He was extremely active in church work, mentioning over and over again that "if we do not live like Christ we never shall be saved." In the office, he talked incessantly and indiscriminately, accusing many people of misdemeanors. When it was mentioned that this behavior was incongruous with the teachings of Christian life, he became excited and very aggressive. He refused to sleep in a bed but chose the floor, saying that it was cooler. His ambition was to reform the whole world, and all with whom he came in contact became objects of his zeal. Three weeks later, he became quiet and slightly depressed. A month after this, he returned to work and seemed, to all appearances, normal. When the psychiatrist saw him, he said that he had experienced these episodes of excitement three times.

These two examples do not illustrate the classic manic-depressive psychoses that are commonly seen in mental institutions. They are, rather, the type of case handled in the psychiatric office, since they are receptive to treatment.

The incidence of manic-depressive psychosis is about 15 per cent of the first admissions to the mental hospitals. The onset, in either acute or subacute form, occurs twice as frequently among females as among males.

Types of Manic-Depressive Psychoses. There are different substates of elation, which are distinguished as follows: first, the *hypomania,* which is a slight elation and nearest to the normal condition; second, the *acute mania;* third, the *delirious mania;* and fourth, the *chronic mania.* The last three conditions should be treated in a mental hospital.

Depression, also, admits of several substates: the *simple retardation,* which is closely related to the normal and can be managed in the doctor's office; the *acute depression;* and the *depressive stupor.* The latter two should be treated in a mental institution. In depression, the gravest danger is the loss of life through suicide. It is often said that a person who threatens suicide does not commit it. This statement is not correct. As an example we may cite the following case:

§ The patient, a conductor, threatened his parents that he would commit suicide. Although unable to swim, he walked into the lake fully clothed and, when the water reached his neck, he cried for help. His parents regarded this behavior as a sham, but his psychiatrist refused to be responsible for him any longer and advised institutional care, to which the parents hesitantly agreed. In the institution, the patient was kept under steady observation which he tried to escape, *e.g.*, by asking the nurses to leave the room as he wanted to masturbate. He cloaked his suicidal drive with unreal and startling buffoonery, *e.g.*, he tried to cut his throat with a bone knife. At another time he obtained permission to walk outside the institution in the company of two attendants. When he was about three hundred feet from a bus, he lay down in the street so that the bus would run over him. The bus stopped at least a hundred feet before him, and the attendants brought him safely home.

With this last experience, the patience of the parents ended, and against the advice of the institution, he was discharged. When he arrived home, he went to his room, took a gun, filled the barrel with water, put a cork on top of it, shot it in his mouth, and killed himself.

Treatment. The treatment of manic-depressives consists mostly in institutional care. Hospitalization is definitely indicated in cases ranging from moderate to severe depression, because every patient suffering from such a condition is a potentially grave suicide risk.[2] It is not only necessary to preserve the life of the depressed individual, but it is also of paramount importance to keep him in good physical condition; for that reason, proper nourishment is essential. In all cases of depression the therapist should aim at restoring the patient to the feeling of security in himself and in his environment, and in reviving his trust in a better future. If it can be done, it would be of invaluable help to bring the patient to an understanding of the cause of his depression. Such an insight would enable him to avoid any future involvement through similar conditions. In the manic phase, it is necessary to use hydrotherapy and sedatives to give the patient the necessary rest.[3]

Involutional Melancholia. This term refers to an attack of depression that occurs during the period of "change of life" without any history of previous mental illness. Most people who do experience this disease are psychoneurotics, hysterics, and obsessive compulsives. Among women, the disease occurs most frequently between the ages of forty and fifty. It occurs less often among men, among whom it usually appears in a milder form and between the fiftieth and the seventieth year. The symptoms are some vague somatic complaints of general nervousness, restlessness, anxiety, and insomnia. In severe cases, typical attacks of anxiety and fully developed psychoses with hallucinations and delusions may be seen. The delusions are mostly of a nihilistic type, concerning death, poverty, and guilt feelings. Sometimes these people are extremely excited, agitated, and scrupulous.

§ Mrs. Q. was always regarded as a nervous personality; she was, at forty-five, unable to perform her household duties with her former customary ease. She became very sensitive, cried easily, and had an excessive fear of soon dying. One day, while strolling with her son near a playground, she was accidentally struck in the right temple with a soft rubber ball. Though there was no apparent damage, she complained of severe pains and was committed to a hospital, where no signs of injury could be found. After one year her condition improved so that she was able to return to her household work. However, she could not forget that she had been struck by a ball and regarded it as an attack on her life. She lives a retired life and shows no emotional joy in the development of her children or in the activities of her husband.

§ A man of sixty-two years experienced an unsuccessful coitus attempt with his wife. After this, he became very excited and accused his wife of having made his life miserable. In the following week, some people whom he met on the street remarked that he looked run down; again, while he was standing on a ladder, working on the ceiling of his garage, someone warned him that "that was no work for an old man to do." These incidents depressed him severely, and he began to complain of getting old. The physician's advice to have him institutionalized was disregarded. One-half year later the man committed suicide.

The cause of involutional melancholia is not known. However, the rapid physical change in the involutional period, which is comparable to the state in puberty, involves also mental changes. Many people in that period adopt a different outlook on life, the past, and the future. With some of them these thoughts take a morbid turn. They are afraid of death; they are tortured by the recollection of the sins of their past life and are frightened by the thought of retaliation; they feel that they have not made sufficient provision for their families; they consider themselves personally responsible for unhappiness in their families and sometimes even for the tragedy in the world. Such a condition not infrequently leads to an attempted suicide.

The milder cases may become difficult problems for priests, who often have been acquainted with these people for many years and are baffled by the change in their reactions. For example, they may wish to visit the church in the middle of the night, they become irritable in the confessional and continually ask for special privileges, they interfere in their neighbors' lives, and they continually gossip, often having no foundation for their stories.

Such psychoses may last from three to eight years, but their duration is often considerably shortened by electroshock treatments. The purer the psychosis, the shorter, generally, is the time needed for recovery. However, when the disorder is complicated by paranoidal persecution ideas, the prognosis is poor. Very often, involutional melancholia ends in a form of arteriosclerosis with defect of reasoning, memory, and judgment. The condition then becomes incurable. The diagnosis of involutional melancholia is not difficult to make if we keep in mind the fact that the climacterium may begin in women as early as the age of thirty-eight and in men at about forty-five. However, ordinarily, the time of onset is later.

It is rare for a woman with six to ten children to suffer from involutional melancholia, and the disturbance is certainly more frequent with women who have no children, or only one or two. Some writers explain the greater incidence in the latter case on the ground that the biological needs of these women are not sufficiently satisfied. Nor is it possible for them to sublimate the biological function by professional work, study, or cultural pursuits. In the time of the climacterium the woman especially feels the full weight of unfulfilled biological function because now it begins to become nonexistent.

PASTORAL PROBLEMS

All the conditions mentioned in this chapter have in common the fact that the thought processes of the patients are to a lesser or greater degree impaired. Since the full possession of one's intellectual processes is a necessary prerequisite for the exercise of one's free will, it follows that acts that the patient commits under the influence of delusion are imputable to him only in proportion to the degree in which his intelligence is unimpaired. It is, of course, impossible to draw the border line between complete and less serious disturbance of the thought processes. Hence, in many cases the confessor may give the penitent the benefit of the doubt. For these reasons suicide committed by persons in any of those mental conditions is presumed not to be a grave sin. This consideration is important in treating the question of burial in consecrated ground. Most psychiatrists go further and are of the opinion that suicide is always an act of insanity. From that opinion it would follow that any Catholic who commits suicide should be allowed an ecclesiastical burial. However, the Church is of a different opinion, for she lays down the rule (Codex Juris Canonici, Canon 1240, § 1, 3°) that ecclesiastical burial should be refused to persons who commit suicide with malice aforethought (*"deliberato consilio"*).

It happens that during the course of mental disease lucid intervals occur. From the pastoral standpoint it is useful to see how the ecclesiastical authority, the Rota, defines such periods. On the one hand, they are not to be confused with full and definite recovery; on the other hand, the periods of relative quiet as occur in maniacs or the mere absences of external symptoms of insanity are not lucid intervals [4] and the Rota warns that such intervals should not lightly be presumed. The same ecclesiastical tribunal declares, against the opinion of some physicians, that the mentally sick, during these intervals, recover the use of reason and are therefore capable of eliciting human acts. For that reason the Rota rules that such persons are capable of contracting a marriage.[5] Besides, the Codex Juris Canonici —after declaring that insane persons cannot be baptized unless they were insane from birth or became so before the age of reason—decrees that non-Catholics who during a lucid interval express the wish to become Catholic can be baptized.[6] And non-Catholics who expressed the wish to be baptized before the onset of the disease, and by implication also those who expressed that same wish during a lucid interval but relapsed before their wish could be fulfilled, should be baptized in imminent danger of death.[7] It is obvious that those who enjoy a lucid interval are bound to observe not only the natural law but also the positive laws, both divine and ecclesiastical.

If any rapport between patient and priest is possible—which may be the case with manic-depressives—the priest's greatest contribution to the patient's recovery will consist in reinforcing both his confidence in the physician who is treating him and also his trust in God.

Since manic-depressives in the periods of serious depression are not open to religious influences, the priest should refrain from speaking of religious motives, from exhorting them to pray or go to church or receive the sacraments. Only when they are recuperating may religious means influence them for the better.

In cases of serious delusions the priest can do next to nothing. If the patients talk to him about their delusional systems, he should try not to go into the subject. This negative attitude will require a great deal of patience and tact. Religious paranoiacs especially may single out the priest as the recipient of their stories; they will tell him that they are the greatest sinners on earth, that they are damned forever, etc. Any attempt to reason with them would not only be useless, but often harmful. For the characteristic of delusion is precisely that the victims are not receptive to reason or correction. The only avenue open for the listener is to use some sort of distraction method, leading the conversation in another direction.

NOTES AND REFERENCES

1. The reader may find further information in all books dealing with general psychiatry. Two may be mentioned here, as treating specifically the topic of schizophrenia: Hamilton, S. W., "The Treatment of Schizophrenia" (New

York: Paul B. Hoeber, Inc., 1928); CARP, E. A. D. E., "Bijdragen tot de Psychologie der schizophrene Psychosen" (Leiden: S. C. van Doesburgh, 1930).

2. On the topic of suicide, see JAMIESON, G. E., Suicide and Mental Disease: a Clinical Analysis of One Hundred Cases, *Archives of Neurology and Psychiatry,* Vol. 36 (1936).
3. Additional information may be found in HINSIE, L. E., and G. E. KATZ, Treatment of Manic-Depressive Psychosis: a Survey of the Literature, *American Journal of Psychiatry,* Vol. 11 (1931).
4. "*Lucida intervalla non sunt confundenda cum 'conspectu umbratae quietis,' sicut Glossa dicit, in quo saepe furiosi sunt constituti, aut cum mera absentia externarum manifestationum amentiae, neque cum plena et definitiva sanatione infirmi*" (Decisiones Rotales, 1930, p. 133).
5. "*Infirmi in lucidis intervallis actus humanos elicere et etiam matrimonium inire possunt. A qua sententia non est recedendum, etsi sint medici hodierni, qui dicant in omnibus lucidis intervallis adhuc semper haberi amentiam in statu latenti; nam hoc statu latenti, si revera existat, non obstante, infirmi de novo fiunt sui compotes et rationaliter agere valent, sicut experientia communis nos docet*" (Decisiones Rotales, 1930, p. 134).
6. "*Amentes et furiosi ne baptizentur, nisi tales a nativitate vel ante adeptum rationis usum fuerint; et tunc baptizandi sunt ut infantes.*" (Codex Juris Canonici, Canon 754, § 1). "*Si autem dilucida habeant intervalla, dum mentis compotes sunt, baptizentur, si velint*" (Canon 754, § 2).
7. "*Baptizentur quoque, imminente periculo mortis, si ante quam insanirent, suscipiendi baptismi desiderium ostenderint*" (Codex Juris Canonici, Canon 754, § 3).

Chapter 15

EPILEPTIC PSYCHOSES AND OTHER PSYCHOSES WITH ORGANIC BASIS

A great number of physical diseases may directly or indirectly affect the nervous system and thus cause psychotic conditions. Since these psychoses can be attributed to an organic cause, they are sometimes called organogenic. One such physical disease is epilepsy.

EPILEPSY

Epilepsy results from a diseased condition of the brain, which not infrequently gives rise to psychotic states involving a more or less pronounced estrangement from reality. In other words, an epileptic is by no means always a psychotic, but his condition may give rise to psychotic traits.

References to epilepsy date far back into history. The Greeks called it the "sacred disease," but Hippocrates, although retaining the name, found nothing sacred about it and simply identified it as a brain disease. History records many famous epileptics: Julius Caesar, Mohammed, Russia's Peter the Great and his daughter Elisabeth Petrovna, Napoleon, and Dostoevski.

It is estimated that in the United States there are some six hundred thousand epileptics, of whom forty thousand are cared for in mental institutions; of these latter, about ten thousand are confined to special epileptic colonies. About 10 per cent of all inmates of institutions for mental and nervous disorders are epileptic. It may be interesting to note that the cost to the American public for the care of institutionalized epileptics is $12,000,000 a year.

Epilepsy, the most serious of the convulsive disorders, is characterized by convulsions in which the subject usually loses consciousness. Epileptic convulsions should not be confused with fainting attacks resulting from a sudden fall in blood pressure or with unconsciousness due to shock or to organic disease. Nor should epileptic convulsions be mistaken for hysteric seizures; the former may occur anywhere, with nobody present; the latter happen only after emotional excitement and ordinarily take place in the presence of other people, for although the hysteric seems to be unconscious, he is, in reality, well aware of the reactions of his surroundings.

From the pathogenetic standpoint, two types of epilepsy are usually distinguished, the "essential" (idiopathic) and the "symptomatic" types. Symptomatic epilepsy is acquired during one's lifetime. It may be caused directly by some injury or tumor affecting the brain tissue, or it may be occasioned indirectly by some bodily disease or injury affecting the nerve cells in other parts of the body and thus, eventually, the brain. Among these causes are general paresis, arteriosclerosis, and toxic conditions brought about by certain drugs or uremia.

Essential epilepsy is a diseased condition of the brain that is present before the sufferer has manifested any seizures. Although neurologists hope eventually to find a specific cause for the condition, they have not yet succeeded; consequently, this kind of epilepsy is regarded as constitutional or hereditary. Typical of the less plausible hypotheses formerly advanced to explain the hereditary character of essential epilepsy was the alcohol theory. This theory supposed on the part of an alcoholic parent the proclivity of producing an epileptic child; some writers went so far as to suggest that the alcoholic excesses often in vogue at the wedding celebration plus the subsequent initiation into sex experience might result in an epileptic first-born. But psychiatrists for the most part abandoned these theories when experience proved their falsity. It is more likely that, instead of any one single factor being responsible for the condition, many factors together affecting the germ plasm form the cause of essential epilepsy. Among the factors that have been proposed as hypothetical causes are toxic conditions of the mother, birth trauma resulting from deformation of the pelvis, partial asphyxia of the fetus, etc. Essential epilepsy covers a large portion of convulsive disorders. It reveals itself usually in adolescence, rarely in advanced age, and it is of such a nature that the patient deteriorates rapidly.

Essential, as well as symptomatic, epilepsy consists in local changes in the brain tissue. These lesions, particularly in the case of essential epilepsy, are not always visible under the microscope, but they may be detected by means of the electro-encephalogram (EEG). Electro-encephalography is based on the fact that, during such mental processes as sensory perception, thinking, and feeling, the nerve cells of the cortex produce a small electrical current. With the use of an amplifying apparatus similar to that of a radio set, these currents can be picked up and recorded graphically on paper. The procedure is painless and consists in placing against the patient's head a pair of electrodes connected to the amplifying and recording apparatus. Since the normal pattern of brain waves is known, certain abnormal patterns can be easily detected. Of great help to the neurologist and psychiatrist, the method is of special importance for the child psychiatrist, enabling him to explain many behavior disorders of children on the basis of a pathological brain condition. Of the children with behavior problems tested in 1937 in the Child Guidance Institute of New York by means of the EEG, 7 to 8 per cent were found to present abnormal brain-wave patterns.

The following case will illustrate the typical development of an essential epilepsy:

§ The patient, a boy of fifteen years of age, small of stature, pale, and undernourished, required assistance in walking. His bodily movements were slow, his gait unsteady. His case history recorded that from the age of three onward he was reared in a foster home, after he had been deserted by his parents. His early development was normal until the age of fourteen when he began to manifest twitching in the face and arms. About a month after the commencement of the first twitchings, he suffered a typical major attack, followed by another the next day. Both occurred during sleep, and, upon awakening, the youth had no recollection of either attack.

He was hospitalized for half a year. During this time, his hands were almost continually cold and limp, and he looked seriously ill. Although he was able to feed himself, he usually spilled most of his food. Before these attacks occurred, he had been friendly, cheerful, cooperative, and polite; but afterward his attitude became hostile, quarrelsome, and uncooperative, and he began to masturbate without shame. Despite careful and specific treatment, his condition gradually grew worse for several months. After this period some improvement occurred, the attacks decreasing to about one a month, the optimum stage thus far in the course of his disease.

This is typical of the average development of an essential epilepsy with mental and behavioral deterioration. The prognosis for such a case is not hopeful.

Sometimes epileptic attacks take place without warning. More frequently, perhaps, the subject has an "aura" or a preceding period, lasting for hours or days, in which there is a feeling of impending disaster or danger. This aura is detectable by electro-encephalography.

There are four recognized types of epileptic attacks. The *grand mal* or *major attacks,* are the most spectacular. The subject loses consciousness, falls, and shows typical rhythmic movements of clonic or tonic muscular patterns. He may bite his tongue, may wet himself, and may sometimes even lose control of his bowels. These attacks may last from a few minutes to about twenty minutes (in contrast to hysteric seizures, lasting for hours). After such a seizure the subject may either be exhausted or appear perfectly normal.

In the *petit mal* or *minor attacks,* the subject shows some minor convulsive motions, but at times they are so slight as to go unnoticed by the uninitiated. In such an event the sufferer appears absent-minded, confused, and in a quandary for a few seconds; but immediately afterward he regains his composure and is able to go on with his work. Such lapses may occur hundreds of times a day.

The *psychomotor attacks,* on the other hand, do not result in a convulsion, but rather in a sudden change of temperament. The person suddenly flares up, is most unreasonable, and sometimes goes into severe temper tantrums. These attacks often are precipitated by external circumstances. During these periods, the subject may wander aimlessly around and perform senseless acts, showing usually at the same time some of the symptoms of either the grand mal or the petit mal attacks.

The so-called *Jacksonian attacks* may occur with or without loss of consciousness. One side of the body is agitated by an uncontrollable jerking or twisting, starting in the face and going down one side, down one arm, one leg, and to the toes, or vice versa.

Finally, there are various *epileptic equivalents.* In these states, the subject is free from convulsions but passes through periods of confusion, epileptic fugues, in which he may lose consciousness of his identity. In such a state, he may travel for great distances. He may commit serious crimes, such as stealing or murder, without any recollection of his actions. Perhaps a number of unsolved crimes could be explained by this type of epileptic equivalent.

Granting exceptions, many epileptics are inclined to live their own introverted life, paying little attention to their environment. Often irritable, jealous, irascible, oversensitive, egocentric, and stubborn, they are prone to emotional outbursts. A generation ago, the terms "epileptic personality" and "epileptic character," used to designate these traits, had wide acceptance. But the use of these terms was based on the theory that the character and temperament traits were the causes of the epileptic seizures. This theory has been disproved, for the EEG has shown that epileptic seizures are rooted in brain disorders. With the abandonment of the theory, the terms "epileptic personality" and "epileptic character" have disappeared from general usage. However, the fact remains that epileptics often present the personality traits just mentioned, and these traits at times may assume excessive proportions.

Sudden, drastic changes in the temperament of the epileptic may result in mean, perverse, and obstinate behavior. Catholics among this group are apt to avoid attendance at church and may attack the Church and its regulations bitterly and incessantly. The disease can in certain instances account for the behavior of some priests who, forgetful of their vocation, desert the Church and their priestly duties. When epileptic personality traits have been developed to the extreme, the patient falls victim to a psychosis characterized by progressive deterioration of intelligence and behavior.

The treatment of epileptics, primarily the concern of the neurologist and the neuropsychiatrist, has as its aim the prevention of convulsive seizures or a reduction in the frequency of the attacks. These effects are achieved by medicinal and dietary measures. In recent times many new drugs have been found which have successfully decreased the frequency of the attacks. Of these specifics, phenytoin has proved effective in grand mal attacks and in psychomotor seizures. It is not a hypnotic, and therefore not prone to aggravate the mental dullness to which epileptics are so susceptible. In the status epilepticus (a rapid succession of grand mal attacks), paraldehyde and Luminal injections are administered intravenously. For petit mal attacks, Mebaral has been used with success. The drowsiness caused by this latter drug is compensated by the use of Benzedrine sulfate. Moderation in eating and drinking, in study and work, and regular hours of sleeping are highly recommended. Since most attacks occur when mind and body are idle, the patient should take sufficient exercise, especially in the open air. Some psychiatrists, contrary to the opinion of most of their confreres, even permit epileptics to go swimming under the supervision of an experienced swimmer. Epileptic children should be kept in school, and adults at some light work; but hazardous employment, such as the driving of automobiles, should be avoided.

The proper treatment of the epileptic's personality characteristics is of great importance. To combat his irritability and emotional outbursts, sedatives like bromides and phenobarbital may be administered. But psychotherapeutic procedures should also be applied in order to teach the epileptic self-control, forbearance, and tolerance. In this respect, his environment can make a substantial contribution to his improvement. Although association with an epileptic is not always easy to bear, he should not be regarded as an outcast, but must be treated with sympathy and friendliness. It is important to remove from him every stigma of being unusual; his morale must be kept at a high level. This can be done most effectively by giving him occupations that not only keep him busy but are also suitable to his condition.[1]

Epileptics, especially those who suffer from essential epilepsy, should be discouraged from contracting marriage because of the danger of procreating epileptic offspring. Obviously this danger is more serious in case both parties are subject to seizures, but it cannot be ignored even when one of the parties is free from the disease.

With reference to the reception of Holy Orders, the Codex Juris Canonici (Canon 984, 3°) declares that those who are, or have been, epileptic must be considered *irregulares; i.e.,* unless dispensed by the Holy See, they cannot lawfully receive Holy Orders, even though they are completely cured. Further, to those who develop epilepsy after their reception of Holy Orders the same canon prohibits the exercise of their orders but permits the ordinary to grant an epileptic the resumption of his ecclesiastical duties upon his recovery. In the event that a priest suffers attacks at infrequent intervals, *i.e.,* a month or more apart, several authors hold that he may be allowed to celebrate Holy Mass privately in the presence of another priest who is still observing the eucharistic fast and who therefore is able to complete the sacrifice, if need be.[2] The aforesaid canon is also to be applied to *amentes; i.e.,* those who are, or have been, subject to psychotic conditions.

Epileptics, of course, are not responsible for their actions during acute seizures. Because their consciousness is heavily clouded during twilight states and epileptic fugues, they are certainly not fully responsible for the acts that they commit in such conditions; hence, there can be no question of grave moral guilt. Reduced moral responsibility for their emotional outbursts must also be admitted, because these reactions are indicative of a diseased condition of the brain. However, the reduction in responsibility is not necessarily to the exclusion of mortal sin, for the patient is not always unable to prevent or to control the violence of his temperament.

OTHER ORGANOGENIC PSYCHOSES

In addition to personality disorders due to epilepsy, there are a number of other psychotic conditions with an organic basis. These psychoses, called organic or organogenic, have in common that they are due to a disturbance of the brain, which in turn is caused by some physical condition or disease. Most organic psychoses can be treated by the neuropsychiatrist and the general practitioner. For the purpose of this book, it suffices to present only a brief survey of some of these conditions.

First of all, there are certain psychoses resulting from infectious diseases and characterized by delirium. Patients thus afflicted usually manifest impairment of consciousness and are more or less disoriented; *e.g.*, they may be confused and fail to recognize people. These disturbances often follow infectious diseases such as meningitis, syphilis, tuberculosis, influenza, pneumonia, typhoid fever, scarlet fever, and acute articular rheumatism.

Some personality disorders are directly due to diseases of the central nervous system. Multiple sclerosis, for example, sometimes results in mental deterioration, impairment of memory, and emotional indifference; hallucinations and "ideas of reference" are also present.

Paralysis agitans, or Parkinson's disease, is characterized by chronic muscular rigidity, and by a stony facial expression. The victims are very often irritable, peevish, and hostile.

Some psychoses are due to circulatory disturbances following cerebral hemorrhage or embolism. Cerebral arteriosclerosis, which deprives the brain of sufficient blood circulation and hence of oxygen nutrition, may cause psychotic conditions.

Other psychoses may be caused by disturbances of metabolism, of growth, of nutrition, or of endocrine function. Here are to be included also certain senile psychoses, characterized by self-centering of interests, reminiscence, and difficulty in the assimilation of new experiences. Patients suffering from these psychoses are childish, easily irritated, and sometimes without shame in sexual matters. The cause may be some bilateral cortical atrophy. In this group also belong the involutional psychoses, due to glandular disorder, and also those psychoses due to cancer and other intracranial neoplasms.

Toxic psychoses are conditioned by infections of the system through poisons such as lead, arsenic, mercury, and other metals, and also by alcoholic intoxication and drugs. Since the subject of alcoholism is treated in Chapter 20, it will suffice to give but a few words about drug addiction here.

Opium and its derivatives cause mental deterioration and paranoid states. In this country, morphine and heroin are used more frequently than is opium. To chronic morphine addicts no obstacle is great enough to stop them in their drive to obtain the drug. Since it can be acquired only surreptitiously and illegally, it is relatively expensive; hence none but the more wealthy of the addicts can continue to purchase it without neglecting the necessities of life. This general neglect, together with the cumulative toxic effect of the drug, gradually causes mental and moral deterioration. Eventually, the addict becomes a real delinquent; moral restraints disappear, and he may lie, steal, or commit any type of crime.

It should be mentioned in passing that drugs like phenobarbital, bromides, and others of this same type may be habit-forming. Over a prolonged period these may cause the same disorders as opium and marijuana, save that the symptoms are of a less serious nature.

While the layman, including the priest, may have no difficulty in accepting other types of psychotics as such, they may find it hard to regard drug addicts in the same light. In their case it is not always easy to distinguish between sin and sickness. Yet, in their present degraded state, these unfortunates must be regarded as mentally ill, and one of the most serious consequences of their psychic condition is abulia, *i.e.*, weakness of the will. All, or almost all, of the inhibitions that restrain normal people from doing evil have ceased to operate. With regard to the question of how far drug addicts can be held responsible for arriving at their present state, one should not overlook the fact that, in many cases, the very urge for some means of intoxication points to a preexisting morbid condition.

NOTES AND REFERENCES

1. For further information on the topic of epilepsy, the reader is referred to books on general psychiatry. A good manual for the patients themselves and for their families and friends, instructing the latter how to deal with them, is PUTNAM, TRACY J., "Convulsive Seizures" (Philadelphia: J. B. Lippincott Company, 1945).
2. See AERTNYS, J., and C. A. DAMEN, "Theologia moralis" (Turin: Marietti, 1944), Vol. II, n. 599; VERMEERSCH, A., "Theologia moralis" (Bruges: Beyaert, 1927), Vol. III, n. 700.

Chapter 16

PSYCHONEUROSES

Psychoneurotic disorders reveal themselves in a great variety of reaction forms. Psychoneurotics may suffer from maladjustments, anxieties, shyness, sensitivity, phobias, compulsions, and obsessions. In turn, these psychic reactions may bring in their train such functional disorders as disturbances of vision or speech, skin and respiratory ailments, stomach and colon disorders, and even convulsions. It would be a mistake, however, to suppose that any of these symptoms are readily noticeable to the average observer. Very often the psychoneurotic is tormented internally by psychic pains, although his anguish escapes the attention of everyone with the possible exception of a physician, a priest, or a very close friend acquainted with the symptoms of emotional disturbance.

CAUSE OF PSYCHONEUROSIS

As explained in the chapter on depth therapy, a number of theories have been presented as bases for understanding of neurotic behavior. Freud's main theory presupposes that a neurosis originates from an internal conflict between the libido and the superego. According to the psychoanalytic view, a person becomes neurotic when his sexual instincts are inhibited or his sexual life is fixated on an infantile level. The Freudian psychoanalyst looks upon the neurotic reactions as a substitutive satisfaction of the libido or as a compromise between the opposing forces, libido and superego. According to Adler, neurosis is due to a conflict between the will-to-power and reality; hence the neurotic is one who is frustrated in his urge to dominate. Jung holds that neurotic behavior is the result of a lack of balance and synthesis between the development of certain potentialities of the collective psyche at the expense of other potentialities. Rank ascribes neurotic reactions to the inability to overcome birth trauma. Horney considers neurosis an infantile form of helpless insecurity which grows out of the individual's inability to adapt himself satisfactorily to his social or cultural environment. All these theories have one point in common: they regard conflict as the origin of neurosis. But there is no reason why the idea should be limited, as some of these views limit it, to one or another particular type of conflict. There is no question but that sex plays an important part in the causation in various psychoneurotic disturbances. Often, patients suffering from these conditions have their moral life disturbed by ambivalence and conflicts; if they unsuccessfully suppress or repress their sexual life, they show typical neurotic symptoms, particularly in the form of phobias. It is also true that a frustrated will-to-power may lead to neurotic behavior. However, the problems and conflicts that the individual meets during his lifetime embrace much more than those which are created by the demands of the sex or power instincts, or of any other particular type of instinct.

The essential characteristic of all neurotic reactions is the inability to solve life's problems in a manner satisfactory to the particular personality. When confronted with the conflicts and the harsh demands of life, the neurotic is unable to face reality as it is. He solves his problem by unconsciously adopting a neurotic attitude, *e.g.*, by "choosing" defense mechanisms, flight into sickness, or regression to the infantile stage. This mental attitude, however, is not entirely satisfactory to him; at best it is but a feigned solution of his problem.

The personality organization of the psychoneurotic is disrupted, estranged from reality. It is this which distinguishes his personality from the normal one with its sensible appreciation of the difficulties, problems, and conflicts of life, and a practical sense of reality. It is quite true that well-balanced, normal people sometimes solve their conflicts in a manner that is less sensible, unrealistic, or even panicky. In this sense some degree of "neurotic" behavior is quite common, but transitory reactions are hardly sufficient to justify classifying those people as psychoneurotics. The psychoneurotic exhibits a more or less permanent state of mind, which is partially estranged from reality. He is, as it were, constantly struggling to live with reality, and in this struggle he feels that he is unsuccessful. He may state that he feels as if he were losing his mind and that he fears committing acts that are not socially acceptable; he may have a morbid fear of death; or he may fear that some silly behavior or minor misdemeanor of his past may be exposed to public censure or ridicule.

On the other hand, the personality organization of the psychoneurotic is only partially disrupted, and his estrangement from reality is far from complete. In that respect he is distinguished from the psychotic. Whereas psychosis is a very seriously defective ability or a complete inability to solve satisfactorily life's problems, the psychoneurotic's appreciation of, and contact with, his environment are at least partially maintained; and, therefore, the psychoneurotic is usually able to adjust himself acceptably to the outside world. Besides, a neurotic ordinarily has a better understanding of his condition, and because of that understanding he suffers more from his disorder than the psychotic does. The clinical distinction between psychotics and psychoneurotics is, of course, sometimes a difficult one, inasmuch as there are different degrees of severity between psychoneurosis and psychosis. Psychoneurotics are mental borderline cases between the sane and the insane. In the psychosis, the ego is overpowered; in the psychoneurosis, the ego is somewhat like a helpless spectator.

In the not too distant past, as was seen in Chapter 3, psychiatrists stressed the constitutional or organic nature of psychosis and what was then termed neurosis, for both were believed to be a dysfunction of the sensorimotor system. But a review of the present-day theories explaining the origin of psychoneurosis makes it clear that the great majority of authors consider exogenic influences to be the main factors in producing psychoneurotic behavior as largely determined by the events, the pressure, the stress and strains, occurring in an individual's life from infancy to death. These factors conditioning psychoneurotic reactions may be of a social and economic nature, or of a personal nature.

Social life today is so complex and exhausting that there is no question but that these conditions produce an atmosphere of strain and tension—an atmosphere that is very threatening to the average personality. It is well known that at times of economic depression the rate of suicide increases enormously. An interesting phenomenon observable in the depression era was that many people were unable to recover psychologically from the loss of their money in the stock-market crashes, although they had apparently experienced little difficulty in adjusting themselves to the loss of a father or son in the previous war.

On a personal level, differences in marriage may assume the character of a serious incompatibility; in mixed marriages these differences may concern the religious education of the children. When such personal difficulties are not adjusted in due time, they may initiate a psychoneurosis and finally cause a disruption of the marriage.

Lack of proper sex education may also play an important role in the development of psychoneurosis. Not long ago, treatment became necessary for a thirteen-year-old girl as a result of lack of proper instruction. While performing as a drum majorette at a football game, she experienced the onset of her first menstrual period. The shock of suddenly seeing blood coursing down her legs in public was too much for her. She fainted, and had to be hospitalized for four weeks; a year's treatment was needed to overcome her psychic trauma, a shock that could easily have been avoided through proper instruction.

Of particular importance are those events which occur during the individual's childhood. Time and again, it has been found that the real cause of psychoneurotic disturbances occurs in the patient's early life, and in this connection one must consider not only his sex experiences but also his other childhood experiences if one is to discover the contributing cause of his neurotic behavior in later life. For example, a too rigorous education may readily lead to the formation of an inferiority complex. Again, the overprotection of a pampered child may cause an attitude of fright and fear—an attitude that paves the way for development of anxiety conditions and phobias.

Such examples give evidence that the conditioning determinants of psychoneurotic behavior are to be found in the events that befall an individual during his life—or, rather, in the manner in which an individual experiences those events according to his own personality structure. Now, one's personality structure depends upon his physical and psychic constitution. Therefore a certain constitutional disposition must be assumed to make the exogenous factors operative in such a way as to cause neurosis. The postulation of such an endogenous constitutional predisposition in neurotic individuals is all the more compelling because it is necessary to explain the fact that they break down under the strain and stress of life's conflicts; whereas other people, although confronted with the same, or even more serious, problems, remain at peace with themselves and with the world. This predisposition to neurotic disturbances is probably present to some degree in every individual, since—as has been observed—every person is liable at times to neurotic reactions, but it is apparently more highly developed in the psychoneurotic. The normal person is possessed of a physical and psychic make-up capable of accepting and solving his life problems with relative tranquillity, but even for him there exists a breaking point. In certain personalities, this breaking point is rather low; when faced with problems and conflicts, they break down speedily and often permanently unless they learn how to face reality.

An illustration of how the constitutional and exogenous factors compensate and reactivate one another may be found in the puberal and involutional life periods of an individual. The changes that occur during these periods are, in the first place, of an organic nature, but they also have psychic, particularly emotional, repercussions. During the pubescent period the individual's outlook on life is confused, while for individuals of either sex the involutional time is marked by a feeling of insecurity and depression. The realization that one is definitely and rapidly aging has a discouraging mental effect. Both factors, the organic and psychic, deeply influence the personality structure of the individual. Here is present a disposition that may pave the way to neurotic disturbances. However, whether or not neurotic disorders will appear depends to a great extent on the person's life history; *e.g.*, a woman whose marital life has been quite normal and who has reared a number of children generally will pass through the involutional period with perhaps some temporary but little permanent harm.

Another reason compels the acceptance of a constitutional basis for the origin of neurotic reactions, *viz.*, it is necessary to explain why a neurotic person "chooses" to solve his life problems in such or such a manner. Sometimes, to be sure, the explanation is to be found in some life event; *e.g.*, a youth bitten by a dog may, in later life, develop a phobia for dogs, though he may have completely forgotten the incident. But it also happens that an individual's life history may offer no particular explanation of why he became, say, hysterical instead of neurasthenic. In fact, under apparently the same circumstances, some people adopt a hysterical attitude, others a neurasthenic attitude, and still others a compulsive attitude. Hence, the ultimate reason for the "choice" of a neurosis seems to hinge on the individual's constitution. In this respect, Carp [1] makes an interesting suggestion. Presupposing that the "choice" of the type of neurosis is largely determined by the individual's constitutional make-up, Carp suggests that a strongly developed emotional life might play an important role in the causation of hysterical reactions; the predominance of the intellectual functions, in the effecting of compulsive reactions; and the predominance of the striving functions, in the development of neurasthenic reactions.

What is this constitutional predisposition to neurotic behavior? According to a number of writers, it is to be found in the condition that is usually characterized as general nervousness. This condition is, of course, basically organic, but it has its repercussions in the individual's mental make-up. People affected by general nervousness are usually emotionally unstable and have vasomotor irregularities such as abnormal blushing and blanching. They may live comfortably in a dependent situation, *e.g.*, as a clerk or as an assistant, but they suffer under any of the ordinary strains of life.

Often they complain of organic symptoms like headaches and disturbances in cardiac activity. The following illustrations may clarify the picture:

§ An office clerk who suffered from time to time from rheumatic disorders was promoted to a vice-presidency. The burden of the new responsibility was so great that, on the day when his new job was to begin, he became violently ill and was unable to go to work. Only insight into the basis of his trouble—fear of responsibility—and encouragement to rely on his capacities for an executive position helped him to overcome his condition.

§ Another man, complaining of a pain in the back and the left side, presented himself for treatment. He stated that he had seen many physicians in the United States and in South America. Some of them had recommended surgery, but the patient had refused this advice. He explained briefly that he did not consider himself nervous and that he lived an upright and moral life. He further explained that he had been initially an office worker, but had shown so much skill in the mechanical handling of construction work that he had been offered a job as a foreman, with both a transfer and a material improvement in position and salary. It was at this time that the pain started. When he was at home in Mexico, living with his wife and doing office work, he was free of pain. The treatment enabled him to see that the responsibility for the greater administrative work as foreman overtaxed his capacity, and made him tense and upset. This man got rid of his symptoms after he returned to his former position as an office worker and gave up any thought of a more advanced position. If he had continued in his new job, he might have developed a full-fledged psychoneurosis.

In all types of neurosis the general therapy recommended as of prime importance is the discovery of the cause. But this discovery in itself is not enough. It must be supplemented by the psychagogic method, for the patient must be induced to adopt a different attitude toward life. Neurotic patients continually repeat that they cannot go on living as they do; hence, they themselves feel that a change is required. Only those become neurotic who awaken to the realization that being as they are or acting as they do is not satisfactory. It is precisely this dissatisfaction that presents them with the eternal problem of "to be or not to be." The neurotic tries to evade the problem, but no evasion is possible. His only solution is to adopt a new plan of life, and more often than not it will appear that such a new plan must imply moral and religious norms.

CLASSES OF PSYCHONEUROSES

Various writers have attempted to classify the neurotic reaction forms. Five groups are presented here, although the authors are well aware of the fact that, in actual practice, these conditions are very seldom found in a pure form but, rather, are mixed.

First Group: States of Tension, Irritability, and Weakness. In earlier times, people with such symptoms were classified as neurasthenics, suffering from nervous exhaustion. These individuals complain of chronic fatigue, sleeplessness, irritability, gastric disturbances, menstrual irregularities, and skin disorders; their habits are poorly organized. Under this general heading can be grouped the habitual masturbators, some of the married people who engage in abnormal sexual intercourse, and some sex perverts.

§ Mrs. Z., an only daughter who lived comfortably in the home of her widowed mother, had been engaged to a young man since her high school days. After a long courtship, when the war broke out, they decided to marry but continue to live with her mother. After the war was ended, the husband suggested that they set up their own home since there were some difficulties in living with the mother-in-law. He bought a small house, which was described as "adequate" although it did not have all the modern equipment of a fashionable home. Despite his sacrifices, the wife refused to move with him, and when the husband persisted, she showed all the classical signs of anxiety, fear, and tension. When it was finally agreed that they should continue to live with her mother, all her signs of anxiety disappeared.

§ Another patient who belongs in this group is a man who was one of a family of five children. They were all gourmets—stout people who enjoyed good food and drink. At the insistence of his parents, he began to think seriously of marriage. During the course of every attempted courtship he developed symptoms of anxiety, nervousness, loss of appetite and weight, and typical signs of depression. At last report, he was about thirty-five years of age; yet, in his most recently attempted courtship, he had developed, in addition to the other symptoms, a diabetic condition, which became latent when the engagement was broken.

The essential characteristic of these neurotics is a state of weakness and exhaustion, not only physical but especially psychic. It is not lack of will that makes them give up the struggle for life, but a feeling of inadequacy to meet its problems. Therefore, the main approach to helping them consists in the strengthening of their self-respect, confidence, courage, and of a reasonable sense of independence. The pastoral adviser, too, can help the patient to develop these qualities, particularly by deepening the patient's religion. Serious religious convictions are of the utmost importance in making them realize the real meaning of life and its difficulties. The state of psychic weakness of the neurasthenic also causes inhibitions with regard to their freedom of will—a fact that must be given serious consideration when the question of moral responsibility arises.

Second Group: Anxiety States and Disorders of Anticipation. These conditions are often called "anxiety neuroses." Although anxiety is treated here as one of the groups of neuroses, it occupies a very special place among all of the other groups, for neurotic anxiety is the most important and fundamental form of the neurotic reactions.[2] Anxiety phenomena, in a smaller or larger measure, are present in neurasthenic, hysterical, compulsive, and hypochondriac conditions. No wonder, therefore, that the study of the anxiety state occupies the center of interest among analysts and present-day psychiatrists. Their studies have supplied a better insight into the nature of neurotic disturbances in general.

The reactions of patients suffering from such neuroses are very changeable and are often the forerunners of a full-blown psychosis. A few of the numerous symptoms that mark anxiety states are attacks of difficulty in breathing, palpitation, perspiration, vertigo, feelings of weakness, and various complaints referable especially to the gastrointestinal tract. If one pays attention exclusively to the somatic symptoms, one may easily be led astray; thus it happens that the general practitioner sometimes treats such conditions as cases of indigestion, ulcers, functional heart disease, or suspected tuberculosis.

§ One patient, who had been cared for by general practitioners for about ten years, had received every kind of medical treatment, such as injections, various forms of physical therapy, and medication, without success. He was then referred to a surgeon and underwent two operations, an appendectomy and a cholecystotomy. Both these were unsuccessful; the attacks of abdominal pain continued in their usual form. This history is not intended to cast reflections on the ability or perspicacity of the attending physicians. In fact, the psychiatrist, who in the course of treatment later witnessed one of the attacks, stated that he, too, would have referred this patient to a medical man or to a surgeon, had he not known the man's history. The psychiatrist found in the patient's history a distressing childhood experience in which the patient's mother had been shot and seriously wounded in his presence. The patient then had developed a number of guilt feelings, which centered around the fact that he had caused his mother a great deal of trouble and had not defended her when she was attacked. She had been ill for three years, and during her sickness he had preferred playing games outside to staying with his mother; he remembered that once, when she asked him for a glass of water, he just laughed and ran outside. After the patient was made fully cognizant of these facts and given an understanding of the part these past experiences played in his attacks, he was cured within a year.

The somatic symptoms—only a few of them have been mentioned—that mark the anxiety neurosis are conversion phenomena. The cause of them is the patient's mental condition. Anxiety is a form of fear, but a fear emanating from within. Normal fear is inspired by some dangerous object or situation, and the individual who experiences such fear is thoroughly conscious of the reason of his fear. In the case of neurotic anxiety, the patient keeps on worrying about an anticipated evil, without precisely knowing the nature of the evil and without knowing the real cause of his anxiety. He may project his anxieties to certain events, either in the past or in the future, but they are actually not important. He may go out of his way to find motives for his fear (rationalization), but these motives are insignificant. The best proof that the reasons that harry the anxious worrier are not true motives, is the fact that once the so-called cause of worry is removed, another cause is placed in its stead, and so worry becomes continuous. Hence, it is apparent that the real source of the worry is something in the individual of which he is unconscious. Obviously, such a state of mind tends to make him tense, restless, ill at ease, and apprehensive.

The case that will now be presented at length illustrates rather completely the genesis and development of an anxiety attack. This is a typical case of an anxiety attack where the alleged cause is only the precipitating occasion, whereas in reality the whole life history, from early childhood on, contained the causative factors.

§ Mrs. B. came for treatment because she had experienced some kind of "heart attack" six months before. The "attack" occurred shortly after a friend, a married woman, died suddenly; Mrs. B. said that it was then that she became conscious of the possibility of dying without repentance. Following the "attack," she suffered a terrible fright and then chills. She was taken to the hospital, where ECG and x-ray examinations were given. All examinations showed a negative result. Since that time, she has had an attack of some sort about every two months, usually at night but sometimes at the movies. Even with the psychiatrist, she maintained her illusion of a weak heart.

Describing her home life as successful, she remarked, "I'm a great success with my husband. He thinks me both a wonderful mother and a wonderful woman. However, I feel miserable a great deal of the time." She said that her husband was faithful; she, however, carried on extramarital affairs. She spoke of herself in these terms: "I am not satisfied with my present condition. I am cruel, and I consciously hurt people."

Concerning her life history, she narrated that she was born in an apartment in a big city, and that her parents had a summer home near the ocean. Her family was wealthy, her parents were always on the go, and the pattern of family life changed rapidly. She remembered endless "boring" walks with her brother and a nurse.

Her continuous conflict with her brother stood out in her memory. "He was twenty months older than I, and I remember with disgust that I had to take an afternoon nap when he was excused because of his superior years." Her brother was "a perfect boy," and did everything better than she. "His bowels functioned as soon as he sat down, and I was always given to understand that I was to do likewise." Her brother always enjoyed his food, but she used to sit at the nursery table and look at "that revolting oatmeal, and the nasty little soft-boiled egg," and feel that she could not swallow a mouthful. All this she resented bitterly. She mentioned that she must have liked some food at this time, but she remembered only the foods she disliked—and there were many.

About the time of the poliomyelitis epidemic in 1916, when she was five years old, they left the city and lived somewhere near the ocean. At this time her father became seriously sick, "and Mother explained to us how ill he was; we thought he had the smallpox. I found out later that he really died of chronic alcoholism." She was about eight when her father died.

She remembered that after her father's death her mother had many affairs. The relationship with a physician, younger by several years than the mother, particularly impressed itself upon the patient's memory. "We all knew that he had a wife and three children. Our mother explained to us that this woman was a very unsuitable wife, that she made the doctor unhappy. She told us that she would like to marry him, but his wife refused to release him." The patient recalled that her mother, smiling and singing, would call her friend the physician on the phone and then complain of unendurable pain, forcing him to visit her at once. "It was plain to us children that she was not at all ill; that this was just a subterfuge to justify the doctor visiting her at home. I still remember resenting the disagreeable remarks made by my relatives concerning Mother and this doctor."

The patient admitted frankly that she and her brother hated their mother, that they called her "stinky old Mother who typewrites all day." She now thought that her mother had believed in the modern liberal concept of allowing her children to express their hostility, since no one was expected to love even his mother all the time. The patient thought that at present she loved her mother, and harbored no resentment or hostility toward her. Of her father, owing to his illness and early death, she had little more than a shadowy recollection of a figure in the background of her childhood. She thought of him with a kindly feeling.

When she went away to school she began to meet boys. She enjoyed kissing and embracing the young man of the moment, and it often seemed to her that perhaps the latest one was going to be the Prince Charming of her dreams. But she was more often bored with the boys' continuous petting, and submitted only because she had a great desire to be liked and wanted. However, she was not without passion, and as she grew older and began to have lovers, she found one who, while never able to stimulate her, showed her the vigorous love which appealed to her emotionally, at least for a time. Only in daydreams did she experience what she felt she should really receive from reality. Sometimes she imagined she was being kissed, and in the emotion of the moment she would have been glad to die.

She thought she had desired the man who is now her husband, and with him she had at one time achieved satisfactory sex relations. However, occasionally she would become restless and then would take another lover who was agreeable to her for a time. As the years of her marriage went on, and her husband's demands became seemingly more insistent and more frequent, she fell into the habit of calling up her old sex fantasies during intercourse with him. This difference between dream and reality worried her greatly, and she began to avoid intercourse with him whenever possible. Her whole sex life became, then, a bitter disappointment to her.

In her relationship with her children, she was unable to reconcile reality with her world of fantasy. She did not achieve fulfillment of her expectations of herself as a mother, because with her son she never was conscious of having the strength of feeling that she felt she should have. Only by repressing her preconceived notion of a mother's love did she find herself able to enjoy her child's affection. When her first daughter, a tiny premature infant, was born, she fell madly in love with her to the entire exclusion of all other interests and emotions.

Her social life was agreeable. The people in the community were warm and friendly toward her. She became active in community and church work. In the meantime, the financial position of her husband improved and made life easier for her. One of her main troubles was religion. At times deeply religious, she also had periods during which she was worried by her own disbelief. She had strong leanings toward the Catholic Church. She listened avidly to Monsignor Fulton Sheen's sermons, read his books, and envied her Catholic friends. Catholicism seemed to her such a real thing, so safe, so secure, so definitely delineated. It used to annoy her that some of her Catholic acquaintances seemed to think that Catholicism was a torment or a burden. She thought that they did not know how lucky they were, yet she remained in her own church—partly, perhaps, through dislike of change, but more because she felt that in the end, not having been born to Catholicism, she would not be able to accept the more controversial tenets of the Catholic faith. She remembered that in her childhood she sometimes slipped into the maid's room to prowl about and to see the pictures and statues depicting bleeding hearts and highly colored religious figures. She said that still, somewhere in her "snobbish little soul," as she described it, there remained a conviction, though she wished to get rid of it, that Catholicism was only for servants.

The "heart attacks" the patient suffered after the death of her friend were the manifestation of a deep-seated emotional condition built up over the years. The death of her friend was, so to say, the spark that set afire the inflammable material, made up of frustrations, resentment, hostility, anxiety, and guilt feelings. During treatment she expressed guilt feelings not only for her own life, but also for her mother's life. Before her anxiety attacks she repressed all moral considerations and compunctions, entertaining the hope of achieving "peace" at the price of complete capitulation and surrender to egotism. But this apparent peace was always being disturbed by guilt breaking forth from the unconscious, like an internal abscess working its way to the external surface, and it finally manifested itself in her anxiety attacks. The treatment relieved her of her "heart attacks," but increased her uneasiness and unrest because of a growing conscientiousness about her duties as a mother and a wife. When last seen, she was searching for a satisfactory adjustment, but seemed unable to make a real change of life. She looked to religion for support, but could not make up her mind; she entertained the illusion of being a faithful wife, but still carried on extramarital relations.

The cure of anxiety states lies in discovering and removing the real source of the anxiety, and not merely the cause to which the patient ascribes his condition. The theories that have been propounded to explain the origin of anxiety neuroses fall into the same groups as the theories about psychoneuroses in general. Some theories ascribe anxiety states to the frustration of one or another instinctive drive, such as sexual instinct or the drive to dominate. Somewhat connected with these theories is the view that anxiety is a reaction of the "conscience." Other theories explain anxiety as a remnant of childhood insecurity.

The Freudian explanation exemplifies the first viewpoint. According to Freud, anxiety is due to a disturbance of the demands of the sexual libido. When various circumstances prevent the sexual urge for shorter or longer periods from achieving adequate satisfaction, anxiety conditions may develop. This theory has met with considerable opposition from different quarters. Nevertheless many psychiatrists, even though not Freudians, believe, on the basis of their own experience with patients, that the theory should not lightly be tossed aside, on condition that one puts the accent on *psychic* satisfaction.[3] A great difference exists between the physiological, somatic aspects of sexual gratification and its psychological aspects, for there are many instances of somatic relief of the sexual instinct without any adequate psychic satisfaction. Such is the case with perversions, masturbation, coitus interruptus. On the purely psychological level, such practices may give rise to feelings of inferiority, dissatisfaction, and frustration and may eventually lead to anxiety attacks. Moreover, the practices just mentioned involve for many people a moral problem, a fact that holds true not only for inadequate forms of sexual gratification but also for adequate but illicit forms, like extramarital relations, and in fact for all activities that are sinful. The conflicts of conscience that frequently arise out of such activities are the responsible causes of a relatively large number of neurotic anxieties. Of course, the theory so extended takes on an entirely different aspect.

If it is found that neurotic anxiety is due to frustration of sexual urges, it is peremptory that such a cause be made plain to the patient, because he ought to know his enemy, if he is to do something about it. But what is he going to do about it? Two ways are open to the patient in order to solve the conflict. The first way consists in stilling the voice of conscience and giving free rein to the sexual passions; it cannot be denied that there are still psychiatrists who would give their patients this kind of advice.[4] But serious psychiatrists condemn such irresponsible advice, because, apart from its immorality, it would not serve any purpose. Not only does unrestrained sexual satisfaction fail to cure the patient, but not infrequently it worsens his condition, for it fails to give him psychic satisfaction and will increase in many individuals the pangs of conscience.

The other and only rational solution open to the patient is to give up his bad habit. He may feel powerless to do so, but here the help of the therapist and the pastoral counselor may turn the scales and lead him to summon up enough will power to fight his primitive passions. The pastor should urge him to pray so as to obtain God's assistance, and the therapist may help him to sublimate his lower impulses to higher and constructive strivings toward cultural, social, or ethical values. Experience quite often shows that even the average person is able to achieve some form of sublimation, if he is properly assisted and trained. Which method the therapist uses in promoting higher aspirations depends upon the circumstances and especially upon the personality of the patient. No single method is suitable to use with all individuals, for methods are made to fit personalities and not vice versa.

At this juncture, a remark is in order concerning abstinence or sexual restraint. Sexual abstinence may be a cause of neurotic behavior, particularly when it is practiced for motives of fear, such as fear of the consequences, fear of marriage or children, or scrupulosity. This fact does not in the least imply that all sexual restraint is conducive to anxiety conditions. In spite of the fact that, in one of his earlier works, Freud wrote, "So far as I know, the connection between sexual restraint and conditions of anxiety is no longer questioned," [5] he later changed his mind. Indeed, there is no evidence whatsoever that sexual restraint conditions neurotic disturbances if it is inspired by sound ethical motives and the person possesses a normal, healthy conscience.

As we said previously, neurotic anxiety is, in many instances, fear inspired by the individual's conscience; frequently, it is caused by feelings of guilt. Once more it is important to emphasize the distinction, which was made in Chapter 11, between guilt as a rational judgment or estimation of guilt, on the one hand, and guilt feelings, on the other. Guilt is an objective fact or condition and is the result of a voluntary transgression of a moral obligation—*casu quo,* of a legal or social one. Both the intellectual appreciation and the feelings of guilt are subjective phenomena. Normally—*i.e.,* when one's conscience is properly formed—his rational appreciation is in proportion with the gravity of his guilt, and this realization may be colored by feelings. A normal person, after having sinned and after realizing his guilt, usually experiences feelings of compunction, remorse, and shame, feelings of fear of retribution and punishment, and feelings of insecurity in anticipation of the future, particularly in the hereafter. With normal people, such guilt feelings are ordinarily in direct proportion to the intellectual estimation and the objective extent of their guilt. But in abnormal cases, feelings of guilt do not always run parallel with intellectual insight, because the quality and the intensity of men's emotions is determined not only by intellectual insight but also by temperament, physical constitution, and previous experience. The cynic and the criminal psychopath may have a perfect insight into their guilt, and yet remain emotionally untouched. On the other hand, there are cases in which a person experiences guilt feelings out of all proportion to his real guilt, or at least out of proportion to what the common run of people experience. This is the case with a number of anxiety patients. A normal Catholic, after confessing his sins, is convinced that his sins are forgiven and that therefore guilt as such no longer exists. He may still be sorry for having offended God, he may know that he has to atone for the temporal punishments attached to the transgression of God's law so as to avert future atonement in purgatory, but emotionally he feels reasonably secure. Not so the neurotic. Even after confession, he continues to bring up again and again to his mind his guilt in a self-perpetuating effort and ends up by feeling even more insecure. As a consequence, he may go to great length in an effort of self-punishment and expiation.[6]

The dynamic effect of guilt feelings as expressed by the "voice of conscience" may be exemplified by the following case cited by Nolan Lewis:

§ A thirty-year-old woman was the product of a mixed marriage. She was raised a Catholic until she was fifteen years old, when her Catholic mother died. After this, the girl never went to the sacraments or even to church. She was married twice, and had a history of several abortions, when she suddenly experienced an anxiety attack.

Dr. Lewis explained the attack succinctly by the comment: "Once a Catholic, always a Catholic."

Thus far, this discussion has dealt with guilt feelings that are the result of sin and with guilt of which the subject is perfectly conscious. However, it also happens that abnormal feelings of guilt develop on the unconscious level without any reasonable ground, and on the basis of such guilt feelings anxiety states may also arise. Some neurotics feel extremely guilty without being able to give any reasons for their fear, because the reasons they may indicate are quite inadequate to explain their fears. It would be altogether exaggerated to ascribe all neurotic conditions to unconscious guilt feelings, but the latter do play a role in the origin of certain neuroses. In this connection, some writers also speak of fear or anxiety of "conscience," but, obviously, in such cases we have no longer to do with "conscious conscience." The analysts attribute these conditions to that function of conscience which they say operates on the unconscious level and which they call the ego-ideal, and they think that the existence of such an unconscious function is an acceptable hypothesis precisely because it provides a basis for an explanation of the actual occurrence of unconscious guilt feelings.

Whatever the value of this theory, the fact remains that neurotic anxiety not infrequently originates as a reaction to unconscious feelings of guilt. The fact is, too, that patients in such a condition often exhibit an abnormal tendency to expiation, self-punishment, mortification, and certain masochistic practices. The exaggerated procedures of washing and purifying themselves that we observe in compulsive neurotics are an example of this morbid tendency.

Another group of theories concerning the cause of anxiety, as advanced by Horney and others, holds that anxiety is primarily a condition of insecurity. Since everyone is born a helpless individual, he must learn to find his way in the world and adjust to its demands through trial and error and with the help of adults. While most people get over their helplessness and secure a certain degree of independency, others stick to their childlike attitude of insecurity, and, when confronted with the harsh demands of life, ensuing either from their environment or from within themselves, they prove unable to meet their difficulties and conflicts and, as a result, furnish good soil for the development of anxieties. Since they try to cling to their mothers' apron strings, they go into a panic when their mothers are no longer there to protect them. Obviously, this viewpoint encompasses practically all life's difficulties, both from within and from without.

In the final analysis, neurotic anxiety—like any normal fear—is based on the instinct of self-preservation. In this respect, anxiety—again, like normal fear—has a teleological meaning: it warns the person of imminent danger. But, while normal fear is a useful, healthy reaction, anxiety oversteps the boundaries of usefulness and becomes positively harmful to the personality, for the individual does not know the exact nature of the danger, and therefore his fear is out of all proportion to the extent of the danger.

As for treatment, it is of course essential for the insecure, anxious person to learn to have a healthy form of independence. We stress the word "healthy" because excessive independence is just as harmful to the personality as excessive dependence. Some writers, particularly of the analytic schools, concentrate all their efforts upon creating in the insecure, anxious patient a high degree of independence, self-sufficiency, and creativity. But, as has been seen previously, a reaction has set in against the exaggeration of that tendency, because it is felt that supreme self-sufficiency also has its drawbacks and opens the path to many distortions of personality. Anyone who feels and acts in an almost completely independent way, the arrogant individual who asserts himself as a demigod, easily becomes a paranoiac, a fanatic, and an obsessive person, "and the last mistake will be worse than the first" (Matthew 27:64). The idea of healthy independency includes at the same time that of healthy dependency. The insecure person must be taught to depend in a sensible manner on his family, on the group in which he lives, on society, and, above all, on God, and it is in this connection that religion and pastoral treatment come into the picture.[7]

These discussions evince the fact that any *treatment* of anxiety cases must start with discovering the real cause. Sometimes the analytical method will be in order, but often the cathartic procedure, either with or without some hypnosis, will be sufficient. It is a remarkable fact that, even though the patient is not fully aware of the source of his anxiety, in many instances the cause is not so deeply hidden as it is in the case of hysterical or compulsive reactions.[8] Frequently, the cause is subconscious rather than unconscious, and the patient just plays hide-and-seek with himself. The cathartic method will gradually bring to light half-forgotten conflicts and memories or experiences that the patient wished to forget.

In so far as anxiety states often involve problems of conscience, they also fall within the province of the priest. The pastoral counselor should above all encourage the sufferers and try to instill in them a sense of security. It sometimes happens that people who come in contact with those tormented by anxiety are inclined to treat them roughly or even to ridicule them. Such treatment is unfair and harmful, and the pastoral counselor should be the first to show benevolence and understanding. Anxiety patients may find a rich source of security and peace of soul in religion. The idea should be planted in their minds that God is a father to be loved and not a tyrant to be feared, according to St. Paul's exhortations: "You have not received a spirit of bondage so as to be again in fear, but you have received a spirit of adoption as yours, by virtue of which we cry, 'Abba! Father!' " (Romans 8:15). Anxiety strongly influences the reason and will of the patient. Therefore, the *moral responsibility* for actions committed in an anxiety state is often so reduced that mortal sin is excluded, and in some cases there is no question of sin at all.

Third Group: Hysterical Reactions. To the layman hysterical conditions are the most puzzling of phenomena. He is often inclined to brand hysterical persons with the stigma of simulation, affectation, and histrionics. Yet, in spite of the fact that hysteria is basically a false and insincere attitude toward life, it is a genuine mental disorder. The dissembler simulates sickness, but the hysteric really gets sick because his psychic condition forces him to do so, even though he may give the impression that he voluntarily produces his hysterical reactions. At least, the hysteric does not consciously aim at simulating physical or psychic disorders. Until Sydenham's time, the opinion prevailed that hysterical reactions were the special prerogative of women. This was found to be incorrect, although it is true that women outnumber men in this respect.

The following two case histories illustrate hysterical conditions:

§ Mrs. P. was a very good-looking woman who dressed extremely well, somewhat in disproportion to the income of her husband. She complained of fainting and crying spells, of headaches, and of being unable sometimes to leave her bed for days on end. She was treated as an invalid child by her husband, her every wish being fulfilled. During the interviews with her therapist, it was revealed that as a little girl, when she did not know her lessons and was threatened with punishment, she promptly reacted with a fainting spell. She said that when her husband did not comply with her wishes, she reacted in the same way then. During these fainting spells, she was aware of everything in her environment and of the attention given her. Once, when she fainted in the physician's office, her husband, alarmed and concerned, remarked that this would last for an hour. Although he was reluctant to leave his wife, he was induced to go out of the office with the physician and leave the woman lying on the floor. When they returned five minutes later, she was seated in a chair and smilingly smoking a cigarette. She made most unreasonable requests, such as to be taken for a ride at three in the morning, or to have prepared for her at midnight special foods and delicacies, often requiring the husband to leave the house to obtain them; these dishes she would invariably refuse after they were prepared. Like all hysterics, she complained of muscular sensations and "paralysis" of the legs and arms.

§ The second case is that of a youngster who suddenly found herself unable to walk. After the diagnosis of poliomyelitis had been eliminated through careful physical examination, a psychiatrist was consulted. When he saw the child in her bedroom, he picked her up and tried to get her to stand, but she crumpled up on the floor, apparently with no muscular control at all. He discovered that the child had an intense dislike for school and a deep antipathy toward her teacher. Inquiring into her home habits, he was told among other things that she would never leave the house unless perfectly dressed. Toward the end of his first and only interview, he carried the girl, dressed only in her pajamas, downstairs and out of doors, where he stood her on her feet on the sidewalk. She promptly ran into the house!

Hysterical conditions reveal themselves in a great variety of reactions. On the mental side, we find amnesias, narrowing of the span of consciousness, dreamlike states, amnestic fugues (*i.e.*, impulsive, dreamlike wandering), extreme suggestibility, emotional instability with a tendency toward sudden outbursts, unpredictable moods suddenly changing from one extreme to another, and sometimes a dissociation of personality which may cause the strange phenomena of dual or multiple personalities.

The physical reactions consist of fainting spells, violent fits of weeping or of laughing, loss of voice or vision, anesthesia, hyperesthesia, paralysis, inability to walk or stand, such "motor neuroses" as occupational cramps, tics and spasms, hysterical convulsions and contractions such as strange bodily postures which seem impossible to endure for any length of time (*arc du cercle*). The peculiar feature of these performances is that the patient is usually well aware of his surroundings. The hysteric possesses in great measure the capacity to convert his emotional conditions into physical phenomena. An example in point is the wife who met her husband on the street with some other woman and could no longer, after that, leave her bed, as she seemed to be paralyzed and unable to carry about her own weight. Such conversion phenomena are, after all, only an exaggerated form of common emotional reactions. A sudden fright causes, even in the average person, shudders and, at times, momentary paralysis. These reactions are particularly strong with children and in primitive peoples, and they appear in an abnormal form in hysterics.

A survey of these hysterical reactions indicates that the diagnosis of hysterics is not always an easy matter, because persons who are not hysterical at all may show some of the same symptoms. The hysteric's convulsions may remind one of the epileptic; his moodiness, of a depressive patient. Hysterics sometimes seem to act like compulsives, and their morbid concentration upon their health may make the impression of hypochondriasis. Most hysterics are liars, bluffing, unreliable, dishonest, but so are the psychopaths. In fact, they may imitate and reproduce not only the symptoms of other mental disorders, but also those of various physical diseases. Hysterical women have been found to imitate the symptoms of pregnancy. A good test, which may be of some help to the layman who may be in doubt whether he is dealing with an hysterical or compulsive individual, is to treat him harshly. While the compulsive will accept the treatment as if he deserves it, the hysteric will show signs of resentment; the mere mention that one suspects one is dealing with a hysteric will make him protest vigorously.[9]

Since the symptoms mentioned may be observed also in other mental disorders, there is no set group of symptoms that would be characteristically proper to hysteria. If, therefore, hysteria is perhaps not a well-defined entity in the clinical sense, pathogenetically speaking one seems to be dealing with a single entity because the reactions are hysterical precisely in so far as they are the expression of an underlying cause, the so-called hysterical character.

What is the "hysterical character"? In other words, what is the *cause* of hysterical reactions? There are almost as many theories and suggestions about the nature of hysteria as there are writers who have made a study of it. Some say that hysteria is basically a splitting of personality (Janet), some that it is a phenomenon of autosuggestibility (Babinski), some that hysterical reactions are defense mechanisms against happenings and activities involving the prestige of one's personality (Claparède), some that hysteria is a regression phenomenon (Breuer, Freud), etc. An evaluation of the respective merits of these opinions is not pertinent to the character of the present book; therefore, it will suffice to say that the idea that hysteria is a condition of regression to a childish attitude toward life has met with wide acceptance, because it seems to explain many of the hysterical reactions and to form the basis from which several of the other views can be understood. According to this explanation, hysterical reactions are to be considered as the remnants of an infantile mind. Hysterics act in many respects like troublesome, whining children who by direct or devious means try to obtain what they want, and who, if they do not carry their point or if they want to avert punishment, use all kinds of intrigues, fainting spells, convulsive crying, flights into sickness, etc. Like frightened children, they try to escape the difficulties of life. Moody like children, they are unpredictable in their friendship and hostility. They show a great need for tenderness, they want to be pampered and coddled, and they crave signs of interest and sympathy. In brief, they are egocentric and strive to assert themselves *coûte que coûte*. This self-assertion, one of their main characteristics, is a result of overcompensation for their inferiority feelings. Like children, they are prone to boasting and bluffing and lying; hysterics sometimes do not know themselves what is true and what is false. They may play with one friend for a while, then lose interest and cast him aside. In doing so, they again show that they belong to that age level which is, as the French say, *sans pitié*. Obviously, these primitive, childish characteristics do not fit into the personality structure of an adult. The harmony and integration is lost, and thus one may sometimes witness cases of dissociation of personality.

How does the hysterical character originate? It is probably due to some hereditary disposition. In fact, it is often said that hysterical traits are present in every individual, but in a latent state. But this disposition needs activation to become patent. Improper education and too much coddling and spoiling may perpetuate the immature childhood traits so that some people never grow up mentally. Regression in the strict sense of the word may occur under the influence of life experiences—*i.e.*, psychic conflicts, as in love affairs and marriage trouble and emotional crises. Examples of cases in which emotions play the principal role in causing hysterical reactions are the traumatic neuroses due to accidents, war neuroses, and "shell shock."

Since hysterical reactions are probably a continuation of, or a regression to, the childhood attitude, any treatment is essentially a process of education or reeducation. The psychotherapeutic treatment, usually some form of analysis, consists in the first place in opening the patient's eyes. The hysteric must be brought to an insight of the origin and meaning of his reactions; *i.e.*, he must learn to see that he consciously or unconsciously uses his hysterical technique to escape the responsibilities, problems, and realities of adult life. Because most hysterics will accept this verdict only gradually and reluctantly, the treatment is usually a long-drawn-out affair. As long as the patient prefers his flight into sickness to being cured, no treatment will succeed. For that reason, there are some who maintain that it is not so much outside help as rather the stark realities of life that will eventually teach the hysteric his lesson of becoming more mature. In spite of all this, the prognosis of hysterical disorders is, according to most psychiatrists, comparatively favorable.

The patient's surroundings, his family and friends, may greatly contribute to his reeducation if they adopt the proper attitude, but if they do not, they will aggravate his condition. The proper attitude consists of a quiet and decidedly determined procedure; during emotional outbursts, fainting spells, and hysterical contractions, one should show little or no interest, let alone pity. The best way is to take no action, nor even notice such performances.

One individual may learn hysterical reactions from another; in that sense, hysteria may be said to be contagious. For instance, a hysterical mother easily initiates her children into the secrets and mechanisms of the hysterical technique, especially when the children have a weak psychic disposition. In such cases, prevention should be in order, but it is hard to see how it can be effected.

Prevention is of the greatest importance when hysterical reactions are due to sudden emotional shocks, *e.g.*, in the case of "shell shock." The immediate effect of the emotional shock (*i.e.*, tremors, paralysis, aphonia) usually disappear with time. Nevertheless, the individual may for some time feel a tendency to renew and develop the same reactions without any actual cause. If he is properly taught to inhibit at once these tendencies, which, in the final analysis, are based on the self-preservation instinct, he will overcome them with relative ease. But if he gives into such tendencies, he will gradually develop what Kretschmer calls a "bad habit" and acquire the hysterical character.

This discussion of hysteria will terminate with a few pastoral observations. Although it is true that the number of acute hysterical cases has been decreasing in recent years, priests know by experience that the number of less severe cases is far from negligible, for the emotional instability of the hysteric also shows itself in religious matters. At one time, hysterical people seem saintly, full of zeal, very devout, and tending toward mysticism; *e.g.*, they will say that during Mass they lose all contact with the environment, enjoy direct union with God, and receive private revelations. At some other time, these same people blaspheme and hate God as the supposed cause of their distress and misery.

In their urge for sympathy they always try to bind others to themselves, and often enough they single out for special attention the priests, particularly the young, inexperienced ones. In order to ingratiate themselves with the priest, they may send presents; or they may try to arouse his pity by playing the role of poor, misunderstood creatures. The old opinion which associated hysteria with abnormal sexual life is not altogether correct. True, their obvious desire to sit in the parlor as close as possible to the priest and their hints about sexual matters, uttered in a confidential, whispering tone, easily give the impression that they are out for something different from pastoral advice. Nevertheless, it is questionable whether the average hysteric is out for sexual relations. Usually, he just delights in playing and toying with these matters. Hysterics want to conquer and dominate, but they do not want to give themselves. But here another danger appears. When they do not succeed in binding the priest to themselves, they easily resort to slander in sexual matters, often expressed in anonymous letters to the superior. If these letters are addressed to the priest involved, the prudent thing for him to do is to keep them, after showing them to his superior or an older priest. It may be added here that hysterics sometimes write anonymous letters to themselves about other people.

All this emphasizes the truth of the age-old saying that hysterics are a *crux pastorum* (a cross for the priests). Yet, despite all the handicaps attached to the care of hysterics, the priest cannot leave them to their own devices. His task will be largely limited to moral and religious matters, but if he succeeds in giving the patients a better plan of life and restoring their peace of soul, he will greatly supplement the psychiatrist's work. In doing so, he should proceed with the utmost caution, reserve, and prudence, and in all circumstances preserve his independence and authority. The main obstacle will always be that the hysteric will take the lead also in spiritual and religious matters. Every attempt of the hysteric to assert himself should be turned down in a quiet but resolute manner. When he realizes that he cannot carry his point, he usually turns to another priest who does not yet know him. A good suggestion, given by several authors on pastoral psychiatry,[10] is to let the patient know that one sees through his plan. The priest might say to the patient: "Experience has taught me that persons in your condition will leave as soon as they have been told how the land lies with them and they feel that I see through them. You are perfectly free to go elsewhere; however, you will very probably meet with the same treatment. But if you want to stay and to listen to me, I may be able to help you."

In dealing with hysterics, the priest should never accept gifts from them, never become confidential with them, and always observe the necessary and proper reserve. He should, as a rule, refrain from answering their letters and drastically curtail the number and the time of their interviews. Furthermore, he should never allow them to do any extravagant or sensational things. They may suggest that they have a vocation for the religious life, but they are completely unfit for the convent, where they will be unhappy themselves, a nuisance for the superior, and a scandal for the members of the community. Moreover, because of their self-assertion, suspiciousness, and jealousy, hysterical women are also often a cross for their husbands; hence, in case they are single, the priest should be very careful in advising or allowing them to marry, for, contrary to a once more or less common opinion, it has been found that marriage is by no means always a cure for hysteria.

In the confessional, hysterics usually attempt to expatiate at great length upon their personal experiences. They dwell upon sexual matters in minute detail and delight in telling stories about other people. Sometimes, they assume a theatrical attitude by giving only hints or by abruptly stopping their narrative so as to draw closer attention or to bring about further questioning. In reply, the priest should insist upon matter-of-fact brevity.

All writers on pastoral psychiatry agree that the moral responsibility of hysterics' actions and omissions must be questioned. Müncker simply states that it is reduced; de Sinéty, Schulte, and Bless are of the opinion that reduced responsibility holds for less severe cases, whereas in severe cases the hysteric is not responsible at all.[11] In deciding the question of responsibility, one should take into consideration the fact that the violent emotions of the hysteric drive him frequently to actions which, because of their impulsive nature, are not fully voluntary. Of course, in concrete cases, it will often enough be difficult to determine whether the impulsive character of the patient's reactions impairs his freedom of will completely or only partially. With regard to actions committed in dreamlike or twilight states, the decisive factor is the narrowing of consciousness. In such conditions, the hysteric commits many acts without any forethought and without taking thought of consequences. The priest should also contemplate the possibility of *voluntarium in causa,* since there are cases in which hysterical persons consciously and willfully bring into motion the hysterical mechanisms in order to achieve their morally inadmissible ends.

Fourth Group: Obsessive-Compulsive States. Janet gives this group the name "psychoasthenia," and Freud calls it compulsion neurosis. Three types may be distinguished, although they often appear in combination with each other.

An *obsession* is an imperative, unmotivated, uncontrollable, and recurrent idea which an individual, enjoying unimpaired intelligence, recognizes as illogical and not in keeping with his own personality. When he tries to get rid of the idea, he suffers strong feelings of fear and unrest. In this group belong the people who have insistent doubts, who complain of losing their minds, who are afraid of committing acts that are socially frowned upon, such as exhibitionistic acts of childish behavior, *e.g.*, thumb-sucking; people who have impure thoughts in church and at the time of receiving Holy Communion, at the sight of the crucifix or the Host. Some are obsessed by the idea that they themselves committed a crime of which they heard or read in the newspapers. In short, obsessives are people who are forced to think what they do not want to think. Their mind is a battleground between reason and compulsive ideas. The insistent doubts that obsessive patients may suffer easily lead to endlessly repeated acts of verification. The average person, too, often is driven to acts prompted by such questions as: "Did I really turn out the light? Did I put enough stamps on the letter?" But such doubts become typically obsessive when they drive a person to repeat verification acts again and again.

Compulsions are closely related to obsessions. Whereas an obsession is a compulsive idea, compulsion is an imperative urge to perform some act that is unreasonable, unnatural, and unmotivated. The compulsive person knows that these acts are illogical or foolish; he hates and detests them; but he must carry them out even against his will, in order to feel at ease. Cases of compulsion are exemplified by the people who have impulses to throw themselves from trains, bridges, or towers although they hate the very idea of suicide, and by the people who have impulses to kill someone or to hurt their mother, their father, or other members of their family. Compulsives, even though very religious, feel the urge to disturb religious ceremonies by making noise. A compulsive may be irresistibly driven to touch his genitals, although he suffers terribly at the moment of satisfaction. Sometimes, these people seem to be forced to bite the Host when they receive Holy Communion. In such cases the mind is the battlefield between reason and compulsive urges.

Compulsive inhibitions consist in this, that the compulsive idea of being unable to do a certain thing inhibits in reality the execution of that act. They are known under the name of phobias. The idea of an act or an object is accompanied by such agonizing emotions of fear that they have a paralyzing effect on the person. Even though he recognizes his fear as unreasonable, he likes to suggest to himself that there is a basis for it. When a person who suffers from fear of open places tries, for instance, to pass over a square, he is seized by such violent fear that he begins to tremble and to perspire; eventually, he even becomes paralyzed. Some people suffer from fear of closed spaces, like the church or the theater; some are frightened by high places; others, by being alone; and still others, by being in company. Some cannot look at sharp objects or instruments without becoming frightened. Some suffer from fear of diseases or germs. Others are tormented by the fear of inability to fulfill their professional duties, *e.g.*, some priests who have a hard time getting through with absolution, consecration, baptism, or the reading of the breviary. In such cases, the mind is the battleground between reason and a compulsive emotion. When compulsive thoughts and fears pertain to the religious or moral domain, we call them scruples. The scrupulous person is always afraid of having transgressed God's law, and this thought keeps on recurring to him over and over again. Conditions of scrupulosity will be discussed in Chapter 19.

Compulsive ideas and phobias are often accompanied, or followed, by so-called protective acts. The individual who suffers from agoraphobia will take wide circuitous routes so as to avoid the open square. "Wash and brush" compulsions are another example in point; those who are afraid of germs wash their hands frequently—sometimes 200 times a day—and take a bath after every urination or defecation in order not to contaminate themselves or others. Hoping thereby to ward off temptations, scrupulous persons often use defensive movements with the head or the hands or feet.

Compulsive patients resort also to what are called compensation reactions in order to find relief from their fears and consequent guilt feelings. When performing some act that he fears is bad, the patient feels compelled to neutralize that action by attaching some sort of compensation or penance to it. Such was the man who, because he was vexed by impure thoughts, refused to shake hands with a woman unless he could also shake hands with a man. His compensation tendency went so far that when he had to go to a church dedicated to a female saint, he went right afterward to visit a church with a male patron.

The compensation urge takes sometimes the form of "vow compulsion." The patients make promises and straightway consider them as vows. Thus one who wanted to obtain freedom from sin promised himself, "If I succeed in not giving in to sin on this or that occasion, I'll walk up and down the whole Seventh Avenue 10 times." Another one, who wanted to avert evil by following superstitious deliberations, thought: "If I do not make the sign of the cross 25 times without interruption, surely a member of my family will fall ill." [12]

Contrary to the thought of earlier psychiatrists, a theory rather common among recent writers is to ascribe the cause of obsessive-compulsive states to a morbid fear. This fear is most evident in the case of phobias, but it is also thought to be the underlying factor of the other conditions. Although the fear underlying compulsive neuroses and the anxiety attack have much in common basically, there are certain differences. Common to both conditions is the patient's unawareness of the real cause of his fear. In the case of phobias the individual knows what he is afraid of, while in anxiety states his fears have a more vague and general character. In the latter state, when he projects his fear to a definite object, he does so in a make-believe manner, because his fears shift easily from one object to another.

According to the fear theory, fear throws the mind of the patient into a panic, and this emotional condition has a weakening, and sometimes paralyzing, effect on his will; consequently, ideas, impulses, and inhibitions impose themselves upon him against his will. The greater the fear of a thing, the greater the compulsion; hence, the intensity of the obsessive-compulsive states depends not so much upon the strength of the compulsive ideas, impulses, or inhibitions as upon the strength of the fear that causes them.

What causes this fear? At present, the common opinion is that the anxiety reaction either is due to some inner, mostly unconscious, conflict, or is to be considered as a caution signal for a threatening break-through of primitive instincts.

The theory is probably acceptable in the case of many obsessive ideas and inhibitions, but it does not seem to be sufficient to explain all the features of compulsive reactions. Why does fear or anxiety, whatever may be the cause, compel an individual to perform precisely the actions that he most ardently detests and to desire to do things that are, more or less, in opposition to his personality? The great variety of answers given to this question, such as a morbid disposition, or hereditary reaction type, the organization of infantile instincts, premature development of conscience, rigorous education, lowered degree of consciousness, exhaustion, weakened psychic energy, etc., serves only to reveal our ignorance in the matter.

The therapy of obsessive-compulsive states consists, of course, in removing the root of the evil, *i.e.*, the morbid fear. To that end the therapist must discover the cause of the fear, in so far as that is possible.

Obsessive and compulsive patients with religious and moral problems—such as those who are plagued by blasphemous thoughts and who feel the urge to destroy or smash the crucifix, and also, of course, those who are scrupulous—are among those who regularly call on the priest, in the parlor or in the confessional. The pastoral adviser can do a great deal to help them, for if he cannot remove the cause of the condition, he can, at least, considerably improve the patient's attitude by putting his conscience at rest. When the priest tells him that he did not commit any sin, he will greatly relieve the tension under which the patient lives. In some instances, once the compulsive character of the client's ideas, tendencies, or actions has been ascertained, the priest is justified in informing a compulsive person that he is not even able to sin because there can be no question of responsibility or sin. The very nature of psychic compulsions is contrary to freedom of will. Compulsion not only may reduce the exercise of will power but may completely paralyze it. The same holds true for phobias, where anxiety and fear can so confuse the individual's mind that moral responsibility is either reduced or totally abolished.

A final remark concerns the "freedom from fear" movement that is noticeable among modern psychiatrists, particularly the analysts. They sometimes seem to suggest that all fear is of the devil. This is an exaggeration. It is true that fear may be the beginning of much mental misery, but there is also fear that is the beginning of wisdom, *i.e.*, the fear of the Lord, as the Holy Scripture repeats several times (see Psalm 110:10, Ecclestiasticus 1:16, Proverbs 9:10). Fear of sin and of the punishment attached to the transgression of God's commandments will do no harm to anybody as long as this fear is in proportion to its cause. Reasonable fear is a valuable means to protect a person against dangers, including moral danger. Besides, one's actions should not be inspired by fear alone, for fear is only the beginning of wisdom, and perfect wisdom is achieved by love of and trust in God. St. John says: "In this is love perfected with us, that we may have confidence in the day of judgment. . . . There is no fear in love, but perfect love casts out fear." (I John 4:17–18) [13]

Fifth Group: Hypochondriac States. According to Meyer, hypochondriasis is characterized by the patient's being insistently and protractedly preoccupied with physical complaints. Such preoccupation is found in the "chronic complainers," who complain incessantly of almost any organ or organ-system of the body. These are the people who buy all the latest patent medicines and who study all the health books, imagining that they have contracted the weirdest diseases.

A typical hypochondriac is illustrated by the following case:

§ Mr. K., a successful architect, suddenly began to complain about bad eyesight, pain in his ribs, and weakness in his legs. He developed an unusual sensitivity to cold weather and declared that he could live comfortably only in a warm temperature of 80 to 90 degrees. He also stated that he had had a heart attack. Negative ECG and x-ray examinations could not convince him that his heart was not damaged. He even argued with a heart specialist that no one could really tell whether or not the heart was damaged, since one physician had unfortunately told him that even though, according to our present exploratory techniques, a damaged heart was ruled out in his case, there was still the possibility of undetectable heart disease. He had a constant feeling that he was losing weight; the scales revealed no changes, but this fact did not convince him. At last report, he was under the care of four physicians, receiving injections and other types of physiotherapy, but he declared that no treatment gave him more than temporary relief.

He repeatedly emphasized that he wished to recover in order to continue with his work. He had only a dawning cognizance that the psychological factor, the desire to parade his symptoms over and over again, was the real basis of his illness.

Because the hypochondriac may suffer from real physical disorders, it is sometimes difficult to determine what is imaginary and what is real in certain cases. Obviously, the physician is the only authority capable of differentiating between hypochondriasis and real sickness.

Hypochondriasis is frequently the forerunner of depression and schizophrenic and paranoid conditions, and it may also be associated with neurasthenia, hysteria, and other neuroses. There is, however, a difference between hypochondriasis and hysteria in that the hysteric seeks sickness as a means of safety, whereas the hypochondriac is basically afraid of it.

Since hypochondriac ideas are delusions, it is useless to try to convince the patient of the erroneous character of his complaints. Any such effort would only serve to worsen his morbid attitude. A hypochondriac, bent on recounting his ailments, presents the physician or pastor with a dilemma, for they should neither contradict him nor agree with him. In such a situation a change of topic would afford an escape from the dilemma, but a ruse of this sort often fails.

The therapist's task is to discover, if possible, the psychic cause of the patient's condition and, by the use of suggestive and occupational methods, to encourage him in the development of an indifferent attitude toward his complaints, thereby making him tolerably fit for his work. However, the indifference that the patient may gradually develop concerning his imaginary ailments is not always a sign of improvement but may be a manifestation of mental deterioration.

Hypochondriasis, like any other delusional system, forms a direct disturbance of the individual's thought processes, and for that reason, objectively inadmissible and illicit actions that are committed under the influence of hypochondriac ideas are often free from guilt of grievous sin.

NOTES AND REFERENCES

1. Carp, E. A. D. E., "De Neurosen" (Amsterdam: Scheltema & Holkema, 1947), pp. 11, 12.
2. For particular aspects of anxiety states, see the following:
   Benjamin, E., The Oedipus Complex in Childhood, *Nervous Child,* 1942–1943.

BERGMAN, P., Neurotic Anxieties in Children and Their Prevention, *Nervous Child,* 1946.

CAMERON, J. E., Autonomy in Anxiety, *Psychiatric Quarterly,* 1944.

COWLES, EDWARD S., "Don't Be Afraid!" (Chicago: Wilcox & Follett Co., 1948).

DESPERT, J. L., Anxiety, Phobias, and Fears in Young Children, *Nervous Child,* 1946.

HORNEY, KAREN, "The Neurotic Personality of Our Time" (New York: W. W. Norton & Company, Inc., 1937).

KLEIN, M., The Oedipus Complex in the Light of Early Anxieties, *International Journal of Psychoanalysis,* 1945.

MACKINNON, D. W., A Topological Analysis of Anxiety, *Character and Personality,* 1943–1944.

MOWRER, O. H., A Stimulus-Response Analysis of Anxiety and Its Role as a Reinforcing Agent, *Psychological Review,* 1939.

WILLIN, J. E. WALLACE, "Minor Mental Maladjustments in Normal People" (Durham, N.C.: Duke University Press, 1939).

3. See CARP, *op. cit.*, p. 260.
4. *Ibid.*, p. 261; MOORE, THOMAS V., "The Nature and Treatment of Mental Disorders" (New York: Grune & Stratton, Inc., 1944), p. 166. Moore quotes William A. White's condemnation of the practice of some psychiatrists to weaken the patient's religion and moral principles.
5. FREUD, S., "A General Introduction to Psychoanalysis" (Garden City, N.Y.: Garden City Publishing Company, Inc., 1943), p. 347.
6. One may make the remark that at times the saints, too, show extraordinary feelings of guilt, even with regard to venial sins and minor defects, and that their practices of expiation and mortification seem, sometimes, to go to extremes. However, there are important differences between their behavior and that of neurotics. In the first place, the gift of tears may be due to supernatural grace. But even though the issue be considered from the natural standpoint, one finds that the emotional expressions of the saints are in proportion with their rational appreciation of the evil they have committed. Possessing a tender conscience and an ardent love for God, they are more aware than other people that even a slight offense against God's majesty is an abomination, and they express their feelings of abhorrence accordingly. But usually they do not exhibit any of the signs of morbid fear which we notice in the neurotic, although they would not be human, if they did not at times show certain transitory neurotic phenomena. For an answer to the intriguing question whether the saints have at times shown neurotic characteristics, see BLESS, H., "Pastoraal Psychiatrie" (Roermond: Romen, 1945), pp. 200–202; ALLERS, R., "The Psychology of Character," translated by E. B. Strauss (New York: Sheed & Ward, Inc., 1943), pp. 346, 347; SINÉTY, R. DE, "Psychopathologie et direction" (Paris: Beauchesne, 1934), p. 5. The last author summarizes the answer when, with a fine touch of *esprit gaulois,* he says: "*L'Église ne met pas des fous sur ses autels, mais comme le dit quelque part joliment M. l'Abbé Brémond, il est bien permis aux Saints*

d'avoir leur nerfs. On peut ajouter que ces nerfs leur ont parfois joué de vilains tours en favorisant quelques illusions."

7. The reader may find a very good exposition of the mechanisms of flight, dependency, and independency in Sapirstein, M. R., "Emotional Security" (New York: Crown Publishers, 1948), pp. 1–92.
8. See Carp, *op. cit.*, p. 280.
9. See Schulte, C., "Nervous Mental Diseases," translated by C. Tschippert (London: Coldwell, 1938), p. 252; Müncker, Thomas, "Die psychologischen Grundlagen der Katholischen Sittenlehre" (Düsseldorf: Patmos-Verlag, 1948), p. 234.
10. Bless, *op. cit.*, p. 149; Schulte, C., Die pastorale Behandlung der Psychopathica, in Bergmann, W., "Religion und Seelenleiden" (Düsseldorf: Schwann, 1926), Vol. I, p. 114.
11. Sinéty de, *op. cit.*, p. 132; Bless, *op. cit.*, p. 147; Schulte, C., "Nervous Mental Diseases," p. 260.
12. Müncker, *op. cit.*, p. 220.
13. See Bless, *op. cit.*, pp. 105–106.

Chapter 17

PSYCHOPATHIC PERSONALITIES

Of all persons with mental disorders, the most enigmatic and paradoxical are those called psychopathic personalities, or constitutional psychopaths. For better understanding, the discussion will be prefaced with a general picture of such individuals.

Although the psychopath may never exhibit a really psychotic condition, his behavior at times resembles the behavior of insane patients. Impulsive and irresponsible, he lacks emotional control and is both inadequate and unstable in his educational, marital, occupational, and social adjustments. His inadequacy and instability may be evidenced by a quarrelsome aggressiveness toward his daily associates, by pathological lying, or by rebellion against the authority of society. He may forge checks, indulge in sexual perversions, or use alcohol to great excess; yet he cannot give a satisfactory explanation of his erratic behavior, for psychopaths do not understand themselves. Without realizing it they struggle against their environment, much as an animal struggles against the trap in his efforts to escape.

While psychopaths often turn up among the frequenters of Skid Row—the derelicts, the tramps, the alcoholics, the drug addicts, the prostitutes, the revolutionaries, the fantasts, and the quacks—they are also found among scholars, artists, and idealists such as conscientious objectors and leaders of religious sects. No matter where they are found, they always exhibit some form of asocial or antisocial reaction; for this reason, the layman often sums up his impression of one of them with, "That fellow ought to be in jail." However, considering the many evidences of psychic deviation that psychopaths reveal, even the layman will realize, on second thought, that jail is not the proper place for them.

The description of two cases may serve to illustrate a few psychopathic traits.

§ When he first met his wife, Mr. H. seemed to be a pleasant, friendly man, endowed with an overaverage intelligence, a persuasive manner, and some slight eccentricities. He was artistically inclined, had no definite job, but always seemed to have money. Mrs. H., in company with her family, was favorably impressed when she met him at a summer resort. He was well liked and seemed to be a devout Catholic. At the time of their engagement, he gave his bride-to-be a check for a diamond ring; however, the check proved to be no good. He explained that he had forgotten to make a bank deposit, an explanation that she accepted in good faith. Just before the wedding, he gave her $50 to buy a few things in New York. Shortly afterward, he called by phone and requested that she send back $20, as his landlady threatened to put him out, if he did not furnish that amount. Thinking that all would be different when they were married, the girl sent him the money.

The H.'s were married in the Catholic Church. On the wedding day Mr. H. drank so heavily that it was necessary to call the family physician, who found him in a semicomatose condition. The physician was unwilling to attend him, since he never paid his medical bills. Four days after the marriage, the groom asked for money to go to an important convention, where again he got drunk and passed a few worthless checks that his wife was forced to redeem out of her own money. He owed money to everybody, but promised to pay all his bills; however, he became furious if his wife reminded him of this fact. When his wife's money gave out, she returned to her parents, who were unwilling to support them any longer.

After half a year he called her on the phone and told her that he had taken a cure for alcoholism and that he was sorry for his past behavior. He promptly won back both her love and the opportunity to borrow money from her again. At this time, he was working in a publishing company, a position that he had secured through his family's influence. The president of this company mentioned some time later that he admired Mr. H. for cleverly defrauding his company of $1,800; Mr. H. had collected this amount in commissions for spurious orders. His family covered him and paid his debts. He promised to reform, to stop his drinking, and to work steadily. At this time, Mrs. H. became pregnant and had to stop work; from this moment on, Mr. H. relinquished all responsibility and disappeared. She had to go alone to a maternity hospital, and during her confinement she was never visited by her husband. He refused to defray the hospital expenses and manifested no interest in his child. After her release from the hospital, he never visited his wife, who had again gone to live at the home of her parents.

Although he entered the armed services in the Second World War, he made no arrangements for the support of his wife or child; she had to apply for the allotment before she received it. It was then that he wrote for the first time, told several hard-luck stories, and asked that some of his money be given back. In the army, he went A.W.O.L. several times, and the military police searched for him in his in-laws' home, where he had not appeared. The wife was told that he had been drinking heavily, had acted peculiar, and had had fits of anger.

What Mrs. H. did not know, in addition to the above-mentioned facts, was that Mr. H. had approached men for homosexual purposes and had, as a result, been known to the police. Mr. H. had mistakenly thought that Mrs. H. was wealthy, and he publicly explained that he had married her only in order to have sufficient money. People who knew Mr. H. described him as "no good," "never amounting to anything"; they said that he "spent too much money" and that he was "always a heavy drinker"; and his personality was characterized as "irresponsible" and as "having nothing favorable about it." One physician described him as unstable and unreliable, and suspected that he evidenced some symptoms of a neuropsychiatric nature. Another described him as lazy, queer, and manifesting definite signs of homosexuality.

This couple was eventually separated.

This case describes a marriage involving a psychopathic personality. Anticipating the problem of responsibility, it might be asked: Did such a psychopathic person understand the meaning of the marriage vow? Did this drunkard, this homosexual with a police record, really intend to marry? Did this man understand the obligations of a husband and father? These are the questions that naturally arise in one's mind. However, if such a marriage case were presented to a Catholic matrimonial court for annulment, it would be difficult to prove that this man was incapable of marriage, for the Church presumes sufficient understanding and free will unless the opposite is proved with certainty.

§ A nineteen-year-old high school senior was apprehended twice for the theft of an automobile, and came to a psychiatrist in hopes of being exonerated for his misdemeanors. He was antagonistic, morose, and embittered, but far above the average in intelligence. His school record, however, was poor, for he did not attend classes regularly. He complained that, although there were others involved in the theft, he was the only one who was caught and punished. When first caught, he was abandoning the fifth car that he had stolen and used until the gasoline ran out. Furiously, he stated that he would have killed the policeman who arrested him, if he had had a gun and nobody had been around. He exclaimed, "Don't tell me that kid stuff about 'crime does not pay,'" and said, "Don't forget that 65 per cent of murder cases are never solved." He continued, "Why, a friend of mine stole a car two years ago; he had it registered, and nobody found it out." He maintained that no one in this world is good or honest, and he criticized everybody; every judge could be bribed, he said, and the probation officer was just a bluff—knowing nothing and merely holding a political job. Of Catholicism he said that the Church had plenty of money and the Pope was a millionaire. His only ambition was to obtain money and to take revenge upon the persons who he thought had mistreated him.

His father and alcoholic mother were divorced. He remembered that when he was a small child his mother had once told him to lie down in the bathtub with his sister; evidently wanting to drown both children, the mother then let water run into the tub. At another time, he and his sister were sitting in the empty bathtub when the mother, drunk, came in and turned on the hot water, scalding both of them. At still another time, when they came home dirty, the mother put them into a tub of water while they were fully clothed; nor were they allowed to change their wet clothes that day.

Often, they had to roam from bar to bar, searching for their mother; invariably, they would find her drunk or engaged in promiscuous petting with some male patron of the bar. At one time, the mother came home with a drunken stranger and had intercourse with him in the presence of the children. The boy claims that he was often beaten unmercifully.

"My father," the boy said, "made a martyr of himself, and made you feel cheap. It was his fault that my mother drank and left him." The father frequently got into fights in restaurants. "He often went out with all kinds of girls. I never got any spending money, even for a show. Only when he was expecting one of his 'babes' did I get any money, and then I was thrown out of the house."

It is understandable that such an atmosphere and upbringing from early childhood onward must have a destructive effect on personality. The boy remembered his mother only as a drunkard, and his father only as a tyrant.

DEFINITION

It is not an easy matter to formulate an adequate definition of the psychopathic personality, *i.e.*, a definition that would include a clear-cut distinction from other mental disorders. A common way of defining the psychopathic person consists in stressing his lack of social adjustment, for the psychopath's behavior is maladjusted to the culture in which he lives, to society, his environment, his family, and his own self. This definition, based on the social viewpoint, even though correct, is not adequate because on the one hand psychotics and neurotics also show social maladjustment, and on the other even normal individuals occasionally show environmental maladjustment.

From this fact, some psychiatrists, *e.g.*, Eugene Kahn, draw the conclusion that no sharp distinction can be made between the normal and the psychopathic personality.[1] The psychopath gets into social difficulty much more readily than does the average person; hence, so Kahn claims, the difference between the two is only quantitative. However, why should the social definition be the only one to be used in defining psychopathy? After all, that definition describes the psychopath only from without. Kahn himself concedes that the psychopath's unsuccessful social adjustment is due to something from within, *i.e.*, to a deficiency or disproportion in his personality organization. Most authors lay great stress on this point. But all types of mental disturbance show personality disorders. What is the nature of this striking discordance in the psychopathic personality?

Psychometric tests show that psychopaths generally are average or better than average intellectually. In verbal testings, they do not show the typical sign of the psychotics; they are rational, free from delusions, and exhibit every indication of competency. However, in the practical tests of everyday living they reveal their deficiency—a lack of sound practical judgment, particularly in moral matters.

At first acquaintance with a psychopath one has no reason to suspect that he is dealing with an abnormal personality. He finds the person somewhat extrovert but pleasing and correct, well-mannered, intelligent, and gentlemanly—even suave and attractive. It may be possible to enjoy the friendship for some time before uneasiness arises about his smug actions and his presumptuous questions. He may ask for favors and material help, but he seems to be unable to return favors or to comply with his obligations. His moral viewpoint, his unreliability, and his complete lack of shame make one wonder whether the acquaintanceship should be continued.

Psychopaths are always interested in people who are newcomers in the neighborhood. They pay a visit to the new neighborhood physician, complaining of some small ailment or other, or patronize a new merchant to buy a small article, and then pay for it with a large check—which will, of course, turn out to be worthless. In one neighborhood a newcomer was greeted by such a person, who volunteered to help in sewing some curtains, and then afterward sent a bill for over fifty dollars.

Psychopaths seem to lack what is usually called "honor" or "moral principles." There is a conspicuous absence of emotions, and for that reason the psychopath is free from anxiety feelings or insecurity. Because his feelings are superficial, there is a lack of shame or delicacy. Egoistic, narcissistic, selfish, and given to excesses, the psychopath seems, according to Menninger, to have the "intention to exploit and distress others, to dissemble and flatter, and to have no constant loyalties." [2] He has no feeling of responsibility, and since he objects to any kind of authority, regular regime, or regular working hours, he is apt to seek his livelihood in the less restricted jobs. The sex life of psychopaths may be that of the homosexual, or the exhibitionist, or the bigamist. Although they seldom commit serious crimes like murders or grave felonies, they defraud, steal, and cheat, mostly in a minor degree, and, during the war many psychopaths were among the A.W.O.L.'s.[3] Several authors in describing psychopaths stress particularly this deficiency of moral responsibility. The English psychiatrist Prichard called attention to this characteristic as early as 1835, and therefore labeled as "moral insanity" the condition that today is called psychopathic.

Strecker and Ebaugh emphasize the same characteristic and, at the same time, show the difference between a psychopath and a mental defective.[4] They define the constitutional psychopathic person as one whose mental make-up reveals a defective rather than a pathological condition. Unlike the defect of mental deficiency, however, which involves the intellectual assets of the individual, they feel that the "missing something" is apparently a constitutional lack of responsiveness to the social demands of honesty or truthfulness or decency or consideration of others, as well as an inability to profit by experience. Even though the psychopath may repeatedly bring trouble upon himself, he never seems to learn his lesson.

A review of the analytical description that has been presented shows that the clinical symptoms that come to the fore in every psychopathic reaction form belong to the sphere of temperament and character. Although not every form of lack of self-control is an indication of psychopathy, every psychopath shows lack of self-control; he is unable to master his biological urge because of the imbalance inherent in his temperament. As a matter of fact he has not built up an equilibrious character. For the moment, the ethical question whether he might have been able to do so may be left unanswered. He habitually lacks what the theologians call *conscientia antecedens,* the conscience that warns and stimulates a person before he acts. Besides this defect, the psychopath shows very little sign of a *conscientia consequens,* the voice of conscience that rebukes an individual after he has committed a morally wrong act. True, the psychopath often seems to be sorry and promises better behavior, but *au fond* he is not affected by his deeds or actions, and he is insensitive to punishment. In this fact lies the significant difference between the neurotic and the psychopath: while the psychoneurotic personality suffers intensely, the psychopath suffers only occasionally and lets his family, or society, suffer for him. The feeling of guilt is much less intense in most psychopaths than it is in the neurotic, precisely because the psychopath's conscience—or, if we wish to adopt the psychoanalytical terminology, his ego-ideal—usually shows only a rudimentary stage. Consequently, the psychopath manifests few symptoms of either suppression or repression.

It is true that the picture of some of the mentally ill discloses an almost inextricable mixture of neuroticism and psychopathy. For example, most forms of sexual perversion reveal a mixture of psychopathic characteristics (due to characterological factors) and psychoneurotic characteristics (due to the psychic mechanisms of repression). Two patients may present exactly the same clinical characteristics, although in one case the reaction may be due to neurotic behavior, whereas in another case it may be symptomatic of a psychopathic personality. Moreover, it happens not infrequently that a neurosis develops upon a psychopathic basis, *e.g.,* a neurosis of hysteria may be due to the patient's constitutional character. For these reasons, some psychiatrists are rather inclined either to reduce psychopathy and neurosis to one and the same disease or, at least, to blur the dividing line.

Yet, such reasons are never sufficient to justify forgoing distinctions as a matter of principle, for mixtures and combinations never prove the identity of the things that are mixed. Every dog fancier knows that the majority of dogs are mongrels, but he recognizes mongrels precisely because he knows the specific differences between the purebreds. Furthermore, the fundamental distinction between neurosis and psychopathy should be maintained for very practical reasons. First of all, such a distinction is important for prognosis and treatment, because neurotic disorders are decidedly more responsive to treatment than are psychopathic disturbances. A second reason of practical importance lies in the evaluation of crimes. Knowing whether a crime is committed as a symptomatic act of a neurotic, or whether it must be considered the result of a psychopathic personality, certainly makes a great deal of difference, because the psychopath never learns from his experience while the neurotic does.

The above discussion implies that a distinction between neurosis and psychopathy based exclusively on clinical observation is often difficult to make. Therefore, several writers, in search of other criteria, believe they have found them in the etiological and pathogenetic factors of the two disorders. Koch, in 1891, advanced the opinion that what he termed "psychopathic inferiority" is determined by heredity.[5] Henderson and Gillespie [6] describe constitutional psychopathic personalities as those people who, from childhood on, present a habitually abnormal emotional reaction in general behavior. Carp [7] says that pure psychopathic disorders are preponderantly of an endogenous nature; their basis, although still unknown, seems to be a biological and hereditary disposition of the personality. According to this opinion, the pathogenetic difference between neurosis and psychopathy is one of accent; neuroses in an unadulterated form are predominantly of an exogenous nature, as they are due to influences that act upon the individual during his life span, whereas the great majority of psychopathic disorders spring from a special constitutional predisposition.

The biological basis of this disposition remains unknown. Some writers speak of endocrine or metabolic disturbances, and to them it must be conceded that the psychopathic constitution may reveal itself in the external physical appearance. George Henry [8] describes as follows the physical defects that are sometimes exhibited by psychopathic individuals. The brain may be large or small, or defective either in part or in whole. The abnormalities may be due to defective development, injury, tumor, infection, or vascular accidents such as cerebral hemorrhage, or they could possibly be attributed to interference with the circulation of the cerebrospinal fluid. The spinal cord may likewise be affected, with resulting weakness or paralysis. There may be gross physical defects, sometimes in the development of the eyes, ears, nose, mouth, hands, arms, legs, feet, rectum, and external urogenital organs. All such physical symptoms of degeneration may exist, but a great many psychopaths, criminal or no, fail to show them. What is meant by psychopathic constitution is a psychic disposition that in some way—not yet known—is founded in the biological constitution.

The defenders of constitutional psychopathy base their theory upon observations on children showing symptoms of psychopathic personality structure. Their thesis is as follows: although our knowledge of such children is still inadequate, it is a fact that, at a very early age, certain children reveal psychopathic characteristics, and it is equally a fact of experience that such children seem almost predestined to turn into full-fledged psychopaths, even though they grow up under the most favorable environmental conditions. However, this is not to be taken to mean that every form of psychopathy is always innate; exogenous factors, like encephalitis epidemica, may also cause psychopathic reaction forms. It means still less that psychopathy is due to inborn factors exclusively. The great importance of environmental occasioners should be fully recognized. To mention only a few instances of the factors that may activate the general constitutional disposition to psychopathic reaction forms, some psychopaths give a history of premature birth, or of great disability of the mother preceding birth. Other cases owe their existence to malnutrition in early infancy, and a few indicate diminished action of the thyroid gland. Still other factors are bad example, seduction, and, particularly, neglect during childhood: the majority of psychopaths have undergone an unfortunate childhood environment and tell a history of grave defects in childhood training. If neglect of perfectly normal children promotes juvenile delinquency, a fortiori is it true that neglect of children with a psychopathic predisposition fosters it. A great many psychopaths are the result of rejection or of broken homes. Rejected, unhappy children, deprived of affection during their youth, readily develop into restless, changeable individuals in later life. So too, do children, rich or poor, who are raised in institutions or foster homes as a result of their parents' separation and divorce. Foster homes often breed psychopaths if the foster parents are poorly chosen. This can be illustrated by citing the following case:

§ A boy at the age of ten was placed in the care of a wealthy couple with two other children. Previous to this, the lady of the house had suffered a depression, the result of the delivery of a stillborn child. Shortly afterward, this boy was adopted and taken to the wealthy home as "treatment" for her depression. He was told every night to pray for his parents, whom he did not know and who—so he was informed—would not accept the responsibility of raising him.

Such a "home" atmosphere can help to develop a psychopathic personality. When brought up in such a manner the child, granted a certain constitutional make-up, lives in a dream world and, when abruptly brought back to reality, suffers mental trauma from which he is practically never able to recover.

Clearly, environmental factors should not be minimized in the etiology of psychopathic disorders. But, on the other hand, these observations do not lessen the importance of a constitutional predisposition. It still remains true, as Carp [9] says, that the great majority of psychopathic cases, even of those cases which take on a more or less definite form only at a later age, should be attributed to a special constitutional make-up.

How far this constitutional make-up is hereditary is a difficult, but intriguing, question. The history of notorious psychopathic families seems to furnish support to the thesis that heredity plays a role in the production of a degenerative disposition. This is not true, however, in all cases. It may be true that psychopathic children are sometimes born from psychopathic, neurotic, syphilitic, or alcoholic parents; but the theory that this is always so is incorrect and has been scientifically disproved. Moreover, even the disorders of those children who are the offspring of abnormal parents are not always to be attributed to true heredity, for at times they are attributable to an unwholesome family milieu.

CLASSIFICATION

Kraepelin, the indefatigable classifier of mental diseases, divided the psychopathic personalities into the following groups: (*a*) the excitable; (*b*) the unstable; (*c*) the impulsive; (*d*) the egocentric; (*e*) the liars and swindlers; (*f*) the antisocial; and (*g*) the quarrelsome.[10] Although this classification is still used today, many contemporary authors find it faulty. And indeed this division, based as it is exclusively on clinical observations, is little more than a list of types which could be extended almost indefinitely. Hence, modern writers prefer a more systematic division based on the pathogenetic viewpoint. However, the usefulness of the present book would scarcely be advanced by a detailed discussion of this problem.

TREATMENT

The treatment of psychopathic disorders is anything but an inviting task. For the most part, all authors agree that the prognosis is well-nigh hopeless for complete recovery. This opinion is quite understandable if one keeps in view the assumption that psychopathic disorders are due to a diseased psychic constitution. Yet, despite the fact that complete recovery is almost excluded, some improvement—and even considerable improvement—can be achieved.

It would seem that the more purely psychopathic the case is, the less the chance of success, but—as has been seen—the greater part of the cases are of mixed pathogenesis. The treatment is a long process, consisting of intensive forms of psychotherapy. Although psychotherapy is difficult to initiate, there are practically always some emotional or mental traits upon which the therapist can establish some satisfactory relationship. Naturally, the attitude of the psychiatrist is important; he should never give the impression that he is dominating, nor, on the other hand, that he is being dominated. But psychotherapy alone will hardly be effective if it is not accompanied by an extensive reeducation program, for, as has been seen, a neglected or distorted education is one of the main contributory causes for the development of psychopathic personalities. In this respect, the social worker can help a great deal by finding for the patient a favorable milieu where the chances of lapsing are greatly reduced and where some sort of work therapy can be applied.

There are also those who believe that reeducation may be better served by rigorous discipline and who, therefore are not averse to the infliction of punishment on the patient for his every infraction. Experience has shown that many psychopaths are sensitive to disciplinary measures and that such measures are often the only method of making them behave, at least for some time. However, most psychiatrists take an unfavorable view of these practices.

From the social standpoint, the best treatment is prophylactic. Social workers and others should endeavor to discover children and youths with psychopathic symptoms and find the means to withdraw them from dangerous environment. Even granted the proper education, success is certainly not ensured in all cases, but neither is there reason for the fatalistic opinion that all preventive measures will inevitably fail. Chance for success rests on the fact that the youth's character is still in the process of development;

children show a great deal of plasticity and—to borrow a term from psychoanalysis—identification power.

PASTORAL OBSERVATIONS

Previously it was seen that the psychopath's instinctive life—in scholastic terms, his passions—is very strongly developed. But that in itself does not abolish his freedom of will or the responsibility for his actions. For the excessive or abnormal strength of an individual's passions does not inevitably involve an incapacity to resist these passions. True, many psychopaths show little practical judgment, and their inability to build up a harmonious character is an indication that their will power is weak. So there are certainly those whose power of resistance and self-control are decidedly weakened, with a consequent diminution of moral responsibility. It is those who seem almost predestined to fall from abyss to abyss in the underworld of crime. Yet, to say that all psychopaths should be exculpated of responsibility for their immoral or antisocial activities would be altogether false. However, with regard to responsibility, another very important point must be taken into consideration. It was pointed out that many psychopaths reveal only a rudimentary, or infantile, form of conscience; they suffer from psychic infantilism, as Kraepelin called it. Like children, they scarcely realize their guilt and show little feeling about the sinfulness of their actions. Often one wonders if they have real contrition, and one may wonder even more if they have any firm purpose of amendment, even though they make the most sacred promises under a flood of tears. Tears may be, according to some moral theologians, a sign of a perfect disposition of the penitent, but the tears of the psychopath often give the impression of crocodile tears. Like children, the psychopaths find ready reasons to excuse themselves, and, what is worse, they usually try to lay the blame on someone else. A properly formed conscience is lacking in all psychopaths, also in those whose intellectual endowment is quite normal but whose practical judgment is impaired. If those psychopaths who by good luck manage to stay clear of the judge lack a properly formed conscience, this is all the more true for criminal psychopaths in the strict sense. These are, for the most part, typical cynics who fail to see any difference between good and evil, decline any responsibility with a shrug of the shoulders, and consider all punishment as utterly unfair. They are the "morally insane" of whom Prichard was speaking. Since conscience is the subjective norm of morality, it follows that people possessing erroneous consciences of this type can hardly be held responsible for their deeds. Because of their elastic consciences most psychopaths may be considered the direct opposite of scrupulous people. While this clear-cut distinction generally is true, some psychopaths may evince a curious blend of laxness in their general behavior and scrupulosity in matters of minor importance. For instance, when one young man who revealed all the symptoms of a psychopathic personality returned home from one of his periodic escapades, in the course of which he had committed an impressive number of misdemeanors, his father ordered him to remain in his room. His serious misdemeanors appeared to bother his conscience only moderately, if even that much. The one thing that deeply disturbed his conscience was his act of momentarily leaving the room in disobedience of his father's orders. Here we have the perfect case of those "who strain out the gnat but swallow the camel" (Matthew 23:24). And it would be very difficult to decide whether such people are sincere or merely play-acting.

Since one of the most striking characteristics of psychopaths is their lack of social adjustment, it is clear that they are completely unsuited to religious community life. They are an intolerable burden for the superiors, for the other members of the community, and for themselves, and a source of continuous scandal. Oddly enough, some superiors are deceived by their inane promises to behave better in the future, a future which for them is continuously postponed.

Can religion aid the psychopathic personality? With the possible exception of the downright cynics, the psychopaths are not inaccessible to religious influences. If a sound and genuine religious life can be fostered in the psychopath—a task that will require a great deal of patience but is not impossible—he will find in the religious ideals the motives for the reformation of his character.

Basically the psychopath needs a more harmonious character formation. The human soul naturally tends to some form of harmony. Hence, if the psychopath efficaciously strives to support this natural tendency, he may at least reduce the disharmony of his character. Moreover, Catholics believe that the formation of character is due, not only to natural factors, but also to the supernatural factor of grace. But God gives His grace only to those who work and pray for it. Hence, if we succeed in inducing the psychopath to pray and to receive the sacraments despite his frequent lapses, there is a solid reason for hope that God will do His share in the reform of the individual.[11]

NOTES AND REFERENCES

1. KAHN, E., "Psychopathic Personalities," translated by F. Dunbar (New Haven: Yale University Press, 1931).
2. MENNINGER, K. A., Recognizing and Renaming Psychopathic Personalities, *Bulletin of the Menninger Clinic,* 1941.
3. See CALDWELL, G. M., Constitutional Psychopathic Studies of Soldiers in the U.S. Army, *Journal of Criminal Psychopathology,* 1941.
4. STRECKER, E. A., and F. G. EBAUGH, "Practical Clinical Psychiatry" (Philadelphia: The Blakiston Company, 1940).
5. In the term "psychopathic inferiority" Koch included psychoneurosis, hence making it, too, a hereditary disease—an opinion that will hardly find followers at present.
6. HENDERSON, D. K., and R. D. GILLESPIE, "A Textbook of Psychiatry" (New York: Oxford University Press, 1948).
7. CARP, E. A. D. E., "De Psychopathieën" (Amsterdam: Scheltema & Holkema, 1941), p. 10.
8. HENRY, G. W., "Essentials of Psychiatry" (Baltimore: The Williams & Wilkins Company, 1938), p. 232.
9. CARP, *op. cit.,* p. 9.
10. KRAEPELIN, E., "Psychiatrie" (Leipzig: A. J. Barth, 1915), Vol. IV, Part 3.
11. For further information about psychopathic disorders, the reader is referred to the following works:

    ALEXANDER, FRANZ, The Neurotic Character, *International Journal of Psychoanalysis,* 1930.

    ARIEFF, ALEX J., and DAVID B. ROTMAN, Psychopathic Personality, *Journal of Criminal Law and Criminology,* Vol. 39, July and August, 1948.

    CASON, HULSEY, The Character of the Psychopath, *American Journal of Psychiatry,* Vol. 105 (1948–49).

    CLECKLEY, H., "The Psychopath Viewed Practically," in SELIGER, R. V., E. J. LUKAS, and R. M. LINDER, "Contemporary Criminal Hygiene" (Baltimore: Oakridge Press, 1946).

    HENDERSON, DAVID K., "Psychopathic States" (New York: W. W. Norton & Company, 1939).

    KARPMAN, BENJAMIN, The Myth of Psychopathic Personality, *American Journal of Psychiatry,* Vol. 105 (1948–49).

    LINDNER, ROBERT M., Formulation of the Psychopathic Personality, *Psychiatry,* Vol. 7 (1944).

    PREU, W. P., "The Concept of Psychopathic Personality" in HUNT, J. MCV., "Personality and Behavior Disorders" (New York: The Ronald Press Company, 1944), Vol. II; *id.,* Psychopathic Personalities, in "Encyclopedia of Medicine, Surgery and Specialities" (Philadelphia: F. A. Davis Company, 1940).

    SPRAGUE, G. S., The Psychopathology of Psychopathic Personalities, *Bulletin of the New York Academy of Medicine,* 1941.

Chapter 18

MENTAL DEFICIENCY

Mental deficiency is, primarily, an impairment of the intellectual functions. The person with normal intelligence is able to use his memory, his power of concentration, and his ability to judge and to reason in an orderly, socially acceptable way, without undue emotion or bizarre operations of the mind. The feeble-minded person lacks these abilities to a lesser or greater degree.

Two types of mental defectives may be distinguished: the mentally incapacitated, *i.e.,* those who have lost a certain amount of mental ability that they previously possessed (a loss that may be due to brain damage occurring in later life or, in dementia senilis, to old age); and the mentally undeveloped, or mental defectives proper, *i.e.,* those who began life without even a fair stock of mental ability. Normal people, as they grow physically, also grow mentally, showing a gradual maturation of the mind; mental defectives also develop physically, but their mental growth is arrested. It may be noted in passing that some of the feeble-minded show not only arrested mental development, but also symptoms of psychosis and other disorders.[1]

Stressing the arrest of mental growth as the special feature of mental deficiency, Tredgold in 1908 defined what then was called amentia as a state of restricted potentiality for, and arrest of, "cerebral development, in consequence of which the person affected was incapable at maturity of so adapting himself to his environment or to the requirements of the community as to maintain existence independently of external support."[2] This definition brings out at the same time the existence of the defective's intellectual immaturity and the consequences of his mental deficiency—*i.e.,* inadequacy in adapting himself to his environment. Later writers concentrate particularly on this social characteristic and suggest that, because of it, the term "intellectual inadequacy" be used in place of "feeble-mindedness" or "mental deficiency." Furthermore, these writers point out that mental deficiency, considered from the social standpoint, is a rather relative concept. For instance, Goodenough says that, practically speaking, a person may be feeble-minded in one kind of social setting and normal in another; according to this writer, "it does not imply a universal condition . . . rather it necessitates the question, inadequate for what?" [3]

These writers hold that the principal shortcoming of the feeble-minded is an inability to comply with the intelligence requirement of their society; their deficiency is an ethnologically determined phenomenon relative to local standards, and, even within those standards, relative to educational demands, vocational ambitions, and family expectations. This relativistic viewpoint may possibly have something to commend in it as far as it goes. In a less complex society, a moron might perhaps have less trouble in making a living; he might, for example, make a successful hunter or fisherman. But whether the mentally better equipped members would take him for a full man is an open question, while it is certainly very problematic whether the idiots and most imbeciles would be considered normal people in any group, even in the most primitive one that the evolutionist could picture. A man who would starve with food lying beside him is inadequate as a member of any society.

Whatever the value of these disquisitions may be, they tell little about the etiology of mental deficiency. Mental defectives are inadequate in adapting themselves to their surroundings because their mental development is arrested. But why is their mental growth arrested?

PATHOGENESIS OF MENTAL DEFICIENCY

The differentiation between the two forms of mental deficiency, mentioned above, is based on pathogenetic criteria. The first group comprises the types of deficiency that the individual acquires during his lifetime: *i.e.*, the cases in which the mental abilities develop normally until some accident or incident causes damage to the brain, when mental development is arrested or regression takes place, as in senile dementia. Since almost all the forms of acquired deficiency are caused by outside factors, they are sometimes called exogenous. The second group comprises the inborn, or congenital, deficiencies; *i.e.*, the cases in which the mental capacities present little or no development after infancy. Since, in these forms of deficiency, the defect originates from within, they are sometimes called endogenous. Of the two groups of deficiencies, the congenital forms are the more numerous.

Because of the constitutional character of a great many forms of mental deficiency, some writers [4] relate them to psychopathic reaction forms;

they consider feeble-mindedness as a subgroup of psychopathy. They hold that, pathogenetically speaking, in both conditions the accent is on constitutional factors. The important difference is that in psychopathy impairment involves, primarily, the individual's capacities for development of character, while in feeble-mindedness, impairment involves, primarily, his capacities for intellectual development.

If this theory is correct, it would fit in with the distinction made by some philosophers between theoretical and practical intelligence. Psychopaths, more often than not, have plenty of theoretical intelligence but show a deplorable deficiency of practical intelligence; on the other hand, the feeble-minded have a deficit of theoretical intelligence, and because they have little or nothing to start with, one cannot except too much from them in such practical matters as adaptation to society or to their own instinctual life.

The cause of exogenous mental deficiency is obviously to be found in any disease or accident that affects the brain; *e.g.*, any inflammatory process in the brain, like meningitis or lues, may cause mental deficiency. But little is known about the etiology of the congenital types of mental deficiency except for a few cases in which the organic basis is apparent. It is known that hydrocephalitis (a condition marked by an enlarged head) is due to a blocking of the ventricular system, which causes degeneration of the brain substance. Several endocrine diseases, *e.g.*, myxedema, gigantism, and similar disturbances of the pituitary gland, may also cause endogenous mental deficiency. Some writers are of the opinion that birth injuries may cause trauma of the brain in the same way as a serious accident or disease does.

The fact that many forms of mental deficiency are congenital, leads again to the problem of heredity. Here, too, as in the case of psychopathy, the pedigrees of the Markus, Jukes, Kallikak, and Zero families are cited to lend support to the thesis that congenital deficiency is hereditary. In 1920, Hollingworth claimed that in 90 per cent of the cases feeble-mindedness was inherited,[5] but in later years, the trend of opinion has tended to minimize hereditary factors. In 1934, Penrose claimed heredity to be involved in only 29 per cent of the cases,[6] and several writers like Kanner[7] seemed inclined to accept this figure as the more accurate statement. However, most writers remain firmly convinced that in certain types of feeble-mindedness there is a hereditary, familial transference originating in injury to the germ plasm. Although heredity cannot be dismissed, it is not the only cause, for there are the other etiological factors, some of which have been mentioned. Besides this, even in the cases in which a role is played by heredity, its effect is greatly enhanced by environmental factors, which will be discussed in the section on the social aspects of feeblemindedness.

DIAGNOSIS AND CLINICAL CLASSIFICATION

The recognition of mentally deficient children is relatively easy in a classroom or catechetical situation. The life history will usually tell enough about the behavior of such a deficient child; *e.g.*, it will be apparent that the child had a peculiar cry, was slow in its responses, and was late in showing any improvement or development, or that he always liked to play with children half his age. It will perhaps be learned that he started to laugh at about eight months, that he developed his first tooth at the age of a year and a half, and that he was slow in sitting up. It may be found that he has been subject to many diseases. Perhaps it was not until he was in his third year that he uttered some unintelligible baby talk; but his tardiness in beginning to talk has, possibly, been mistaken for a speech defect, and the child may be described as nervous and high strung. Moreover, it may be observed that he constantly craves affection and is friendly with every adult, liking the attention of strangers quite as much as that of his mother and father; the result is that he often accepts suggestions that bring him to mischief. Such is the average picture, with some slight variations, of a deficient child. Many of the points mentioned will also help in the recognition of the adult defective, but a more correct diagnosis requires more specific criteria, which will, at the same time, enable one to arrive at a clinical classification.

The first step in classifying mentally deficient individuals by clinical means consists in the use of such psychometric media as the Binet, the Terman-Merrill, and the Wechsler-Bellevue intelligence tests. In these and in other like tests, mental capacities are evaluated in terms of the individual's mental age and intelligence quotient. The mental age represents his successes on the test scale; *e.g.*, although he may be fourteen years old, he may pass only enough tests to give him a mental age of ten years—a mental retardation of four years. The I.Q. is determined by dividing the mental age by the chronological age and multiplying by 100—a procedure that gives us the I.Q. on a scale where 100 represents approximate normality. If one says, for example, that a person has an I.Q. of 50, one means that his mental age is half his chronological age; or, vice versa, if a twenty-four-year-old man has a mental age of twelve, his I.Q. is 50.

It is on the basis of their I.Q.'s that the mentally deficient are classified into the three groups: idiots, imbeciles, and morons.

The evaluation of mental defectives obtained through the psychometric tests is definitely of great help in recognizing them. However, psychological testing alone is not sufficient to formulate a diagnosis. This fact may be made clear by referring again to the example of the twenty-four-year-old man. Even though his mental age is twelve, he should not be considered as the equivalent of a normal twelve-year-old. The man is not normal even with regard to his own mental age level.[8] He has acquired much more experience than a normal twelve-year-old; while his intellectual development was arrested, his other mental powers as well as his biological powers continued to develop further. It is precisely this inequality of development that created the disharmony of his personality. This implies that the I.Q. is meaningless, unless it is related to the total personality structure of the individual and to his life history. It should always be remembered that the "mind" of a man comprises much more than what is tested by the intelligence tests. In addition to the intellectual functions, there are also present the volitive, conative, and emotional functions, together with a great many forms of experience gathered during his lifetime.

Therefore, in order to diagnose mental deficiency properly, the total personality should be studied. Besides knowing the patient's mental age and I.Q., the psychiatrist should know as much as possible about his patient's origin, development, childhood history, sickness, experiences, patterns of behavior and action, speed and type of responsiveness, alertness, etc. In general, the psychiatrist, in order to arrive at an over-all picture of the patient, must orient himself on six sets of determinants: the genetic, the mental, the physical, the environmental, the educational, and the emotional.

On the basis of this information, a brief general description of the three main classes of the feeble-minded may be formulated. A few lines of interest to pastors are included.

The *idiot* has a mental age up to two or three years, and an I.Q. up to 25. He is often physically deformed, paralyzed, or subject to convulsions. Deprived of judgment and unable to foresee or measure the consequences of his actions, he does not recognize physical danger and is unfit to help himself. In many instances idiots lead a purely vegetative existence. Usually they either die at an early age or must be cared for in mental institutions. Idiots must, of course, be baptized, and they can and should be confirmed. They are unable to commit any sin, hence they do not need the Sacrament of Penance. Inasmuch as they lack the necessary disposition and understanding, they cannot receive the Holy Eucharist. Since some parents find it difficult to accept the verdict that their child is an idiot, they sometimes insist that he make his First Communion. It has even happened that they express the hope for a miraculous cure as the result of it. Pointing out to such parents that miracles may happen also without the danger of irreverence to the Sacrament, the priest is obliged to refuse the request.[9]

The second group are the *imbeciles.* With a mental age of three to seven years and an I.Q. of 25 to 50, they are often able to take care of themselves. These individuals are very often emotionally unstable and have been known to commit murder for such petty offenses as being deprived of candy. Unable to judge the consequences of their behavior, they easily fly into a rage and are frequently given to sexual perversities. Only some of the higher grade imbeciles may be permitted to go to confession and to receive Holy Communion.

The third group, the *morons,* vary in mental age from six to twelve years, and have I.Q.'s ranging from 50 to 70. Under supervision, they are able to do routine work. Quite open to suggestion, they can be easily led, either into good or into bad ways. Lack of common sense, of good judgment, and of discriminatory ability is often apparent in them. This group provides society with many of its petty thieves, drunkards, prostitutes, homosexuals, exhibitionists, liars, and other minor criminals. These people can usually receive the Sacraments of Penance and Holy Communion, but not indiscriminately. They should be screened carefully, for it may happen that they are able to memorize the necessary facts of religion without, however, understanding their real meaning.

As an example of the limitations inherent in morons, the following cases may be cited:

§ A moronic girl frequently allowed herself to be sexually misused by a group of men. These men would promise her a quarter of a dollar, which she never received but always hoped to get.

§ A moronic married woman, Mrs. K., had an I.Q. of 65. When Mrs. K. became pregnant, she regularly visited the prenatal clinic. Toward the end of the pregnancy, she was told that when labor began she was to call on the public health nurse, who would take her to a hospital where she could be delivered of her baby. However, one day at the prenatal clinic, she appeared to be no longer pregnant. When inquiries were made, she explained that she had had two violent bowel movements the night before. When she was questioned further, it was found that she had used a commode. Upon investigation, it was discovered that the baby and the afterbirth were still in the commode. Naturally, the infant had drowned.

The Subnormal Groups. Psychometric tests have tended to cause the discarding of the old notion that humanity is precisely divided into two groups, the normal and the deficient, because these tests have shown conclusively that there is a continuity bridging the two categories. Accepting an I.Q. between 90 and 110 as the index of normality, the gap between normal members of society and high grade morons is bridged by the subnormal group. This subnormal group is subdivided further into the borderline group, with an I.Q. of 70 to 80, and the dull normal group, having an I.Q. between 80 and 90.

The differentiation between the normal and subnormal groups in terms of I.Q. is an easy matter, but differentiation on the basis of other clinical symptoms may create more difficulty. Generally speaking, the subnormal group has trouble with any kind of memory work that requires special effort; furthermore, capacity to think in terms of the abstract or to use arithmetical symbols effectively is lacking. The members of this group seem normal, and often appear to fulfill the expectations of their family, community, and school until about the last year in grammar school or the first year of high school. Only then is it noticeable that these children are subnormal and are unable to manifest any higher intellectual capacity.

An example of this late recognition of existent subnormality is to be found in the following case:

§ A forty-year-old woman, a Catholic, had eloped from home at the age of seventeen to get married before a justice of the peace. Although she had five children, she was never able to cope with the duties of a housewife: she slept until noon and neglected her children and her husband. Absolutely egocentric and possessing limited reasoning power, she squandered money recklessly, with the result that she would arrive home from a shopping trip burdened with clothes she did not need because she could not resist the suggestions of saleswomen. Only the financial resourcefulness of her husband kept the house and children

> from complete destitution. In her case history she stated that she had procured for herself several abortions, but she explained to her therapist that, when she went to confession, she told the priest that she had never committed a serious sin. She fell in love with another man and was seen publicly with him everywhere, although she shamelessly explained that this man only wanted her money. In addition to all this, she was a drug addict.

Such a case as this would be classified as ranking between high-grade moron and subnormal.

Many subnormal people succeed in creating the impression that they are considerably more intelligent than they are in reality. The general public may regard them as normal or even above normal. In this category belong certain people with phenomenal memories, or the man who is a "lion," and nothing else, in society. Often, such persons are borderline mental cases or individuals who are, practically speaking, unable to deal effectively with the ordinary problems of life.

In this group, too, belong many of the people, mostly women, who claim to have had visions or who come to the pastor to tell him, for instance, that in a few days the church will collapse or burn. Here, too, belong many of those who are overly zealous in mixing in parish affairs and still more in the affairs of the parish household. They are always underfoot, have always questions to ask of the pastor or want to have medals and other articles of piety blessed. One such girl claimed that every wish for which she prayed was fulfilled. She also modestly related how once, when she went over an ice-covered bridge in the winter, she saw roses blooming on the bridge.

THERAPY

Up to the present time, there have been very few medical means of treating the feeble-minded.[10] One of the classic examples of these means is the treatment of myxedema with thyroid preparation. Recently, a new drug, glutamic acid, is being freely used, although as yet not enough is known about it to predict with certainty its effectiveness in the field of mental deficiency. Glutamic acid is an amino-acid product found in cow's milk. It occurs in such small quantity that it is estimated that, if patients were to obtain it by drinking the milk, it would be necessary for them to drink about twenty quarts daily to get the required amount of acid. Reports of studies performed in the laboratory of the Neurological Institute of New

York indicate the use of the acid to be beneficial, and it is claimed that regular doses raise the subnormal child's I.Q. from 10 to 20 points. Although the reports from other clinics are not quite so favorable, they, too, acknowledge for the most part a positive effect of glutamic acid on mentally retarded children. Definitive evaluation of the drug must await the completion of further research.

PSEUDO FEEBLEMINDEDNESS

In addition to true mental deficiency, there exist conditions that simulate it. Genuine mental deficiency cannot be corrected beyond the pattern of the limited brain ability, but pseudo feeblemindedness can, in several instances, be cured. In the category of the pseudo-feebleminded are found (*a*) those with special disabilities, such as spastic paralysis, which have been confused with poor general ability; (*b*) those whose speech was delayed far beyond the normal limits, but whose nonverbal ability was developed; (*c*) those subjected to some severe early illness that delayed, but did not prevent, mental development; (*d*) victims of a brain injury (occurring either at birth or, later, in an accident) that interfered with some kinds of intellectual activity but not with others; (*e*) those with such physical handicaps as impaired vision and hearing, which may interfere with academic learning and influence the accuracy of intelligence measurements; and (*f*) victims of emotional maladjustments resulting from such factors as adverse home conditions.[11]

Since the conditions that simulate mental deficiency can be alleviated and often cured, one of the most important tasks of the teacher lies in distinguishing pseudo feeblemindedness from real mental deficiency. For this purpose, he may secure the help of the clinical psychologist, who, by testing, is often able to recognize the pseudo-feebleminded.[12] Although the teacher and the psychologist are in a position to recognize the condition, the therapy is usually to be entrusted to the psychiatrist, for each type of pseudo feeblemindedness must have its own special therapy, according to the rule that "the surest road to the patient leads not through the broad highway of diagnostic classification, but through the narrow trail of individual personal study."[13] Nevertheless, the teacher may also have a share, at times, in the rehabilitation of some of the pseudo-feebleminded, for a frequent source of mental retardation is found in the fact that children for one reason or other failed to learn how to read properly—a defect that can be corrected by remedial reading.[14]

SOCIAL PROBLEM

The number of mentally deficient persons in the United States has been variously estimated at figures ranging from 600,000 to 6,000,000. The enormous difference between these two figures can be explained, perhaps, by the narrower or wider limits that different writers assign to the concept of mental deficiency. Perhaps, too, the explanation is to be sought in the writer's lesser or greater propensity for guesswork. At any rate, it is certain that at the end of 1948 the population of the institutions for mental defectives in the United States was 121,426.[15] This large number of mentally deficient individuals creates a social problem because these persons easily fall prey to delinquency and antisocial behavior. The most common forms of such behavior are crimes and delicts against the property of others, vagabondage, sexual misdemeanors, fighting, and alcoholism.[16]

Environmental factors that promote delinquency include broken homes, premature loss of one or both parents, poverty, poor accommodations, alcohol abuse, temptation, seduction, amoral education, examples of delinquency at home and in the near milieu, and neglect. It is obvious that if these factors foster delinquency in normal persons, they are all the more liable to bring the feeble-minded to ruin.

The removal of such conditions and the prevention of neglect is, therefore, a duty of society. Proper education can prevent delinquency among the young defectives, but experience teaches that reeducation may achieve good results even with adult defective delinquents.

PASTORAL PROBLEMS

The moral responsibility of idiots creates no problem; that of imbeciles, hardly any greater problem; but in connection with the moral responsibility of morons and subnormals, problems do arise.[17]

Theologians used to consider a seven-year-old normal child as having arrived at the age of reason. But a feeble-minded person is not normal. As we saw, a twenty-four-year-old person with a mental age of seven is in no way on a par with a seven-year-old normal child. Biologically, he is an adult with the full physical strength needed, for instance, to commit certain crimes. Furthermore, he has the emotions of a grown-up man, and the instincts proper to adults—greed, hostility, vengefulness, and sexual tendencies—demand satisfaction when the occasions arise. It can hardly be expected that the feeble-minded individual, with his poor mental equipment, will be in a position to master his instincts and to inhibit his impulses.

A feeble-minded person's most characteristic failing is that he lacks thoughtfulness or advertence (*advertentia*) to an even greater extent than does the child. He cannot reflect; he fails to see the implications of his actions and their consequences, unless they have been drilled into him—a matter that will be discussed presently. For the feeble-minded, the present is everything and the future is almost meaningless. He shows his "inadvertence" not only with regard to the dangers of the external world, but also with regard to the moral dangers of his internal world, his instincts and passions. Everybody, even the most normal person, may go through moments of "inadvertence," but the whole life of the feeble-minded consists of such moments.

Now one of the conditions necessary to make any act a mortal sin is full advertence to the grave malice of that act. The description just given of the feeble-minded makes it clear that this condition is often lacking in the defective; thus, it may easily happen that there is no advertence at all, the presence of which is the necessary condition for any sin, mortal or venial.

Does the moron have a conscience? It is not at all impossible to form the consciences of higher grade morons; indeed, it has been noticed that some develop a rather tender one. But many of the feeble-minded exhibit a kind that can scarcely be called a moral conscience, *i.e.*, a conscience that tells them what is morally good or bad. Often the conscience of the mentally deficient person is nothing but the result of drilling: the feeble-minded can be drilled not to do evil things, much the same as animals can be drilled to be housebroken. But then their "conscience" makes them do the right thing, only because they do not dare to do the wrong thing for fear of punishment. In the eyes of the feeble-minded, maltreating animals is not permissible because they bite, and striking a big dog is a greater "sin" than striking a small dog because the big dog bites harder.

This picture of the mental defective's attitude in moral matters holds good for imbeciles and low-grade morons. It can be expected that there is more chance of "advertence" and a moral conscience in high-grade morons and subnormals; however, we should not expect a mathematical proportion. Theoretically speaking, it may be true that moral responsibility increases with a higher I.Q., but our practical evaluation of the responsibility of the feeble-minded should not be decided by the I.Q. alone, because it gives only one facet of the defective's personality.

Lack of responsibility in the feeble-minded raises the question of marriage. It has been observed that two feeble-minded persons often feel instinctively attracted to one another. Since heredity, as we have seen, plays a role in the causation of mental deficiency, it is to be feared that the marriage of two mental defectives is apt to produce like offspring. This need not always come true, but even if it does not, the danger that the defective parents will neglect the proper education of their children is always present.

Extending the limits of this problem to include also the marriages of psychopaths and of others where similar defective offspring may be produced, it may be asked: What is the Church's attitude toward such marriages? The Church, by the mouth of her highest authorities, has answered this question by setting forth the principles of the natural law. Pope Pius XI in his encyclical "On Christian Marriage" ("Casti connubii") does not disapprove of eugenics in so far as it "gives salutary counsel for more certainly procuring the strength and health of the future child—which, indeed, is not contrary to right reason," but he condemns those "who, oversolicitous for the cause of eugenics . . . , wish to prevent from marrying all those who, in their opinion and according to the norms and conjectures of their investigations, would, through hereditary transmission, bring forth defective offspring, even though these persons are naturally fit for marriage." True, the Pope suggests that "often these individuals are to be dissuaded from entering into marriage." However, they cannot be forbidden to do so, if they are mentally capable of contracting matrimony. "Certainly it is wrong to brand men with the stigma of crime, because they contract marriage, on the ground that, despite the fact that *they are in every respect capable of matrimony,* they will give birth only to defective children, even though they use all care and diligence." It will be noticed that the Pope speaks explicitly of those abnormal persons who are capable of matrimony, *i.e.*, those whose mental condition does not prevent them from having a sufficient notion of the nature of marriage or from giving proper consent. In that case the public authorities have no right to promulgate laws prohibiting marriages between abnormals. The reason is that such laws infringe "upon the natural right of man to enter matrimony." In answer to the objection that the procreation of abnormals might endanger the mental health of the community, the encyclical replies that "the family is more sacred than the state and that men are begotten not for the earth and for time, but for heaven and eternity." [18] Of course, mental defectives and other abnormals will often be found to be incapable of marriage precisely for the reasons stated above. Furthermore, if abnormals are unbaptized, the state has the right to outlaw their marriage, because the marriages of unbaptized persons are subject to the authority of the state.

The Pope also condemns the artificial practices that are intended to incapacitate persons for the procreation of children—*i.e.*, sterilization by such procedures as salpingectomy, vasectomy, ovariotomy, surgical castration, and x-ray castration—for no one, not even the public authority, is allowed to destroy or mutilate the body or a part of the body without a very serious reason. According to some theologians, punishment for committed crimes may be a sufficient reason; but in the case of abnormal persons who have done no harm to society, there is no justification for such a punishment. Another legitimate reason for artificial sterilization is to cure the individual of an existing disease. The emphasis is here on "existing," because the use of artificial sterilization not for the purpose of curing a patient of an existent disease but for the purpose of preventing future procreation is condemned.[19]

If sterilization may be used, when necessary, as a means of curing organic diseases, the question has been raised, whether sterilization may also be employed as a possible cure of disorders that include a mental component, as in the case of sexual psychopathy or abnormal sexuality. Vermeersch[20] is of the opinion that in such cases sterilization is permissible, if the method is really effective and no other means are available.

NOTES AND REFERENCES

1. Cassell, R. H., Mental Deficiency and Psychosis, *Journal of Clinical Psychology,* Vol. 5 (1949).
2. Tredgold, A., "A Textbook of Mental Deficiency" (Baltimore: William Wood & Company, 6th ed., 1937), Chap. 12.
3. Goodenough, F. L., "Developmental Psychology" (New York: Appleton-Century-Crofts, Inc., 1945), p. 631.
4. For instance, Carp, E. A. D. E., "De Psychopathieën" (Amsterdam: Scheltema & Holkema, 1941), pp. 112, 415.
5. Hollingworth, H. L., "Psychology of Functional Neuroses" (New York: Appleton-Century-Crofts, Inc., 1920).
6. Penrose, L. S., "Mental Defectives" (New York: Rinehart & Company, Inc., 1934).
7. Kanner, L., Feeblemindedness: Absolute, Relative and Apparent, *Nervous Child,* Vol. 7 (1948); *id.,* Feeblemindedness, *Digest of Neurology and Psychiatry, Institute of Living,* May, 1949.
8. The misconception alluded to in the text is due to a mistaken notion concerning the meaning of M.A., C.A., and I.Q. Mental age (M.A.) is a *score* made

on a particular test. It is expressed in terms of years and months. It is presumed to represent the level of mental development. Chronological age (C.A.), likewise expressed in terms of years and months, might also be looked upon as a *score* that represents the expected average performance of children of that age. The intelligence quotient (I.Q.) is the ratio between these two scores, an index of intelligence. It indicates the *rate* of mental growth.

It must not be thought, however, that a ten-year-old child with an I.Q. of 80 is on a par with a child of eight who has normal intelligence. Actually, their mental development (M.A.) may be approximately on the same level; but the older child with the I.Q. of 80 will soon be surpassed in achievement by the younger child whose rate of mental growth is normal. Likewise, the younger child with an I.Q. of 120 is not equal to an older normal child, but superior. A common misconception in this matter comes from considering a child as *normal* on his M.A. level, *i.e.*, to regard a child of ten with an I.Q. of 80 as equivalent to a normal eight-year-old.

9. For the problems concerning the relationship with the patient's parents, see the following:

Sampson, A. H., Developing and Maintaining Good Relations with Parents of Mentally Deficient Children, *American Journal of Mental Deficiency,* Vol. 52 (1948).

Walker, G. H., Some Considerations of Parental Reactions to Institutionalization of Mentally Defective Children, *ibid.,* Vol. 54 (1949).

Wardell, W., Case Work with Parents of Mentally Deficient Children, *ibid.,* Vol. 52 (1948).

10. See Doll, Edgar A., Is Mental Deficiency Curable? *ibid.,* Vol. 51 (1946–1947).

11. For the problem of pseudo feeblemindedness, see the following:

Debra, S., and E. Harans, Social and Educational Impairment Wrongly Diagnosed as Feeblemindedness, *Nervous Child,* Vol. 7 (1948).

Hearsey, M. E., Problems of the Handicapped Child, *Family,* May, 1937.

Rautman, A. L., Society's First Responsibility to the Mentally Retarded, *American Journal of Mental Deficiency,* Vol. 54 (1949).

Stone, M., Parental Reactions to Retardation, *ibid.,* Vol. 53 (1948).

12. See the following:

Altable, J. P., Role of Psychometry in the Differential Diagnosis of Some Forms of Pseudo-feeblemindedness, *Nervous Child,* Vol. 4 (1948).

Blanchard, Phyllis, Interpretation of Psychological Tests in Clinical Work with Children, *Mental Hygiene,* Vol. 15 (1940).

Waskowitz, Charlotte, Psychologist's Contribution to Recognition of Pseudo-feeblemindedness, *Nervous Child,* Vol. 7 (1948).

13. Kanner, L., Feeblemindedness, *Nervous Child,* Vol. 7 (1948), p. 376.

14. For the treatment of reading difficulties in elementary school children, see the following:

Durrell, Donald D., "Improvement of Basic Reading Abilities" (Yonkers, N.Y.: World Book Company, 1940).

Kirk, S., "Teaching Reading to Slow Learning Children" (Boston: Houghton Mifflin Company, 1940).

Russell, David H., "Children Learn to Read" (Boston: Ginn & Company, 1949).

For the treatment of the same problems on the high school and college level, see McCullough, C., R. Strang, and A. E. Traxler, "Problems in the Improvement of Reading" (New York: McGraw-Hill Book Company, Inc., 1946).

For the treatment of speech defects, see the following:

Abney, Louise, and Dorothy Miniac, "This Way to Better Speech" (Yonkers, N.Y.: World Book Company, 1940).

Schoolfield, Lucille D., "Better Speech and Better Reading" (Boston: Expression Co., 1937).

15. Deutsch, A., "The Mentally Ill in America" (New York: Columbia University Press, 1946). Concerning the problems of institutionalized mental deficients, see "An Outline of Practices and Aims for Children's Institutions" (New York: Committee on Institutions for Children of Welfare Council of New York City, 1935); Bender, Lauretta, There Is No Substitute for Family Life, *Child Study,* Spring, 1946.

16. For further information, see the following:

Carp, *op. cit.,* pp. 415–428.

Davies, St. P., "Social Control of the Mentally Deficient" (New York: The Thomas Y. Crowell Company, 1930).

Hartogs, R., The Pseudo-feebleminded Child and Adolescent in Court, *Nervous Child,* Vol. 4 (1948).

Healy, W., A. Bronner, *et al.,* "Reconstructing Behavior in Youth" (New York: Alfred A. Knopf, Inc., 1931).

Johnstone, E. L., What Shall We Do with the Mentally Deficient? *Mental Hygiene,* Vol. 30 (1946).

"The Needs of Mental Defectives," pamphlet published by the New York City Committee of Mental Hygiene, 1939.

Schumacher, H. C., Contribution of the Child Guidance Clinic to the Problem of Mental Deficiency, *American Journal of Mental Deficiency,* October, 1947.

17. The reader may find information in Cammack, J. S., "Moral Problems of Mental Defectives" (New York: Benziger Bros., 1939).

18. Encyclical "Casti connubii." *Acta apostolicae sedis,* Vol. 22 (1930), pp. 539–592. The excerpts used in the text are taken from the English translation published by the National Catholic Welfare Conference. A very good summary of these and connected problems may be found in Bless, H., "Pastoraal Psychiatrie" (Roermond: J. J. Romen, 1945), pp. 36–42.

19. Concerning the problem of sterilization, the encyclical says that there are some who "wish to legislate to deprive these [who would perhaps bring forth defective offspring] of that natural faculty by medical action despite their unwillingness; and this they do not propose as an infliction of grave punishment under the authority of the state for a crime committed, nor to

prevent future crimes by guilty persons, but against every right and good, they wish the civil authority to arrogate to itself a power over a faculty which it never had and can never legitimately possess. . . . Public magistrates have no direct power over the bodies of their subjects; therefore where no crime has taken place and there is no cause present for grave punishment, they can never directly harm, or tamper with the integrity of the body, either for reasons of eugenics or for any other reason. . . . Furthermore, Christian doctrine establishes, and the light of human reason makes it most clear, that private individuals have no other power over the members of their bodies than that which pertains to their natural ends; and they are not free to destroy or mutilate their members, or in any other way render themselves unfit for their natural functions, except when no other provision can be made for the good of the whole body." The Holy Office, too, has declared direct sterilization illicit; see *Acta apostolicae sedis,* Vol. 32 (1940), p. 73.

20. See Vermeersch, A., "Theologia moralis" (Bruges: Beyaert, 1927), Vol. II, n. 323; Bless, *op. cit.,* pp. 40–41.

Chapter 19

SCRUPULOSITY

Scrupulosity can be understood only by those who believe in the reality of the supernatural, of sin, and of moral conscience. Etymologically, the term "scruple" derives from the Latin. *Scrupulus* means, literally, a small, sharp pebble which in a shoe causes discomfort in walking, and its neutral form *scrupulum* was a Roman weight unit, a little more than our present gram (1.137 gram). Applying these two meanings in a metaphorical sense, one may identify a scrupulous person as one who allows minute, insignificant moral considerations to hamper his progress on the road to spiritual perfection.

This word picture comes fairly close to the real definition of scrupulosity. Although definitions of scrupulosity have been formulated in various ways, they all have in common the notion that scrupulosity consists in those dispositions of fear and insecurity which tend to make an individual see evil where there is no evil, mortal sin where there is no mortal sin, and obligations where there are no obligations.[1] These delusions are based on futile, groundless, or unreasonable motives.

Scrupulosity is a special type of anxiety, closely related to neurotic ruminations, obsessions, and compulsions, but the anxiety of the scrupulous person presents this peculiar feature: it focuses attention on the commandments and their infractions. The scrupulous individual dreads sin, but in contrast to the normal person, this fear of sin becomes an obsession with the scrupulous man in such a way that his state of mind makes him see sin where as a matter of fact there is none, or certainly not to the extent that it exists in his anxious mind. This unwarranted fear of sin puts him out of contact with reality; he lives in a world of his own imagination, in which he continually worries and frets and wears himself out about the past and the future, instead of living confidently in the present.

A scrupulous conscience is—as was seen in Chapter 2—altogether different from a tender or strict conscience. A person of tender conscience correctly distinguishes between imaginary sin and real sin, and between sin and imperfection, and precisely because of his exact estimation of sin, he tries to avoid all sins, however small they may appear. He is careful even in smaller matters, in a quiet way, without worry or anxiety.

A scrupulous conscience differs from other forms of erroneous consciences in so far as the judgment of a simply erroneous conscience is rooted in ignorance, whereas the judgment of the scrupulous conscience is due, not so much to lack of knowledge, as to the emotional condition of anxiety. In point of fact it happens quite frequently that a scrupulous person is deeply disturbed by an imagined guilt, even though his reason assures him that he is free of guilt; but, as a result of his fear, he refuses to trust his judgment.

This peculiar antinomy between reason and emotion is confirmed by the following fact. If the scrupulous person were really convinced of the enormity of his imagined sins, he should feel, as normal repentant sinners do, the obligation to expiate his sins by appropriate acts of penance. However, that rarely happens. If a confessor mistakenly places credence in the scrupulous penitent's tale and imposes a severe penance, the penitent meticulously fulfills the penance, but in his innermost heart he is convinced that he has not deserved such rough treatment.

In certain instances, however, anxious people may resort to symbolic acts of penance; *e.g.*, persons who have been guilty of sexual sins in the past may become obsessed by the notion of filth and attempt to cleanse themselves to excess.

§ A woman patient had compulsive acts of cleansing which sprang from an unconscious drive to wipe out her very conscious sins. The therapist discovered that during five of the seven years of her married life the patient had consistently been indulging in extramarital relations. Her husband complained that living with his wife was almost intolerable, for she imperiously demanded cleanliness at any cost. Her insistence extended not only to her own personal hygiene, but also to her house, her clothes, and her children. An immaculately groomed woman, she had a withering contempt for anyone who did not approximate her self-imposed standard of cleanliness. Yet, she stoutly maintained that in this she did nothing more than conform with the social manners of the average American.

During the treatment she disclosed that she had been rigidly educated and had always been told that sex in thought or deed was unbecoming for a girl of her social stratum, and that only "dirty" people talked about the subject. By that way sex became in her mind strongly associated with physical dirt. As a result of this mental association of sex and filth, when the patient became involved in sexual misbehavior in high school, she developed a compulsive urge for cleanliness, an urge that was constantly fomented during marriage by her promiscuous behavior.

Scrupulosity is a fairly common condition. There is probably no priest who, in his confessional work, does not come in contact with scrupulous persons. Opinion about the incidence of scrupulosity varies; by way of example we quote the inquiry made by Joseph J. Mullen who found the following figures for his group: "Of 400 students in a girls' private high school where the student body represents American-born students of very varied national descent, 26.25% admitted that they feel themselves habitually scrupulous." [2] Nearly 50 per cent of the 400 students said that they suffered from passing attacks of scrupulosity.

ETIOLOGY

What causes the emotional disposition of fear and insecurity so characteristic of scrupulous people? The theories proposed in the etiology of scrupulosity are substantially the same as those which attempt to explain anxiety neuroses. In general, one group of them stresses constitutional, another environmental factors.

Environmental factors are the individual's experiences during his lifetime, with particular emphasis on those of childhood. An overprotective education, naturally enough, inculcates in a child a feeling of insecurity, the very basic trait of scrupulosity. Youth's conflicts, if not solved successfully, provide another ready source for future scrupulosity. Such cases of repression are especially frequent at the time of puberty. A too rigorous education also is conducive to scrupulous ideas, especially when coupled with either an exaggerated, or a false, moral instruction. Here should be mentioned the lurid tales of terror with which some parents, priests, ministers, and teachers attempt to frighten people into being good. The origin of many a scrupulous conscience can be traced to some fire-and-brimstone sermon about hell. It is far from the intention of this book to discredit the efficacy of sermons about hell, but it is, in many cases, advisable to keep scrupulous persons away from these so-called thunderous sermons. However, this is not always necessary, for the authors know of several cases in which very scrupulous people attended all the sermons of a mission, even the so-called powerful ones, without being frightened in the least. At one time in their youth, such sermons may have frightened them and may have been the concomitant cause of their present scrupulosity, but now they listen to them as if these thunderclaps are meant not for themselves, but for others. This fact is worth mentioning because it shows again that many a scrupulous adult is *au fond* not convinced of his guilt.

After reviewing the more common sources of scrupulosity, there remains, as in all similar problems, the question of how it is that these experiential factors cause anxiety and scrupulosity in some individuals, while they do not affect others who have been exposed to the same experiences. Terrifying experiences or stories which for some children prove real sources of scruples are for others merely thrilling affairs, leaving them perfectly unscathed.

Could it be, therefore, that environmental influences affect predominantly those who are inherently timorous or neurotic? Indeed, some psychiatrists hold that experiential factors build upon a certain constitutional predisposition, both psychic and physiological. This interpretation harkens back to P. Janet's theory of psychasthenia, according to which certain individuals may possess a lowered psychic tension. The lack of psychic tension creates a feeling of insufficiency and insecurity with consequent repercussions on the conscience. In the opinion of J. Mayer, scrupulosity consists, in most cases, of an infantilism of conscience. The conscience of the scrupulous adult has remained on the level of a child. A child, incapable as yet of forming sound judgments, seeks and relies on those of his elders; his questions are prompted by ignorance. The intellect of the scrupulous person can, and does, possess theoretical knowledge; but in practice his intellect is prevented from arriving at the formation of a practical judgment, because this normal activity is suspended by his insecurity and fear of error.[3]

Some writers feeling that the diminution of psychic tension and the consequent sense of insecurity call for further explanation, think it can be found in the physiological constitution of the individual. Scrupulosity, so they reason, is due to a lack of balance in the person's emotional life. Now, it has been found that emotional experiences, like fear and sadness, may be brought about not only through intellectual insight into a situation that inspires fear or sadness, but also directly through the stimulation of the emotional centers in the brain; *e.g.*, too much adrenaline in the blood stream is likely to irritate these centers and cause not only the organic expression of emotion, like the acceleration of the heartbeat, but also a psychic experience of anxiety. If that is so, it may be assumed that the physiological condition of certain subjects throws the emotional centers off balance and causes a native disposition to fear and anxiety, which may be called an anxious temperament. Such a temperament may, in turn, be the organic source of scrupulosity.[4]

There are, indeed, certain facts that seem to confirm the organic explanation. As mentioned before, the onset of scrupulosity is common to puberty, an age characterized by strong physiological changes. Also, temporary scrupulous conditions quite frequently occur during periods of exhaustion following illness. Moreover the temporary relief from scrupulosity or anxiety afforded by the injection of adrenal cortical extract seems to furnish an indirect proof that these conditions have some physiological causation.

Combining the environmental and the constitutional interpretations of scrupulosity, one might say that in a number of cases the physiological and psychic constitution determines whether or not a person will become scrupulous, whereas the experiential factors will determine the direction his fears will take and to what class of objects they will attach themselves.

This explanation seems to embrace a majority of cases, but not all. Certain cases involving the presence of a defense mechanism demand another explanation. Instances of this type of case are found in candidates for the priesthood or for membership in a religious order who develop a very severe state of anxiety and scrupulosity prior to their ordination or their pronouncement of vows. The fact that such conditions sometimes disappear as soon as the person makes up his mind not to take the intended step is probably the best indication that a defense reaction is operative, *i.e.*, a mechanism which develops because the person is confronted by a situation from which he secretly would like to escape, but which for other reasons he feels himself constrained to accept. From his own experience, Thomas V. Moore [5] cites instances of persons who used anxiety as a defense against the religious vocation to which they were attracted, but for which they had no real calling. When they left the religious life, the scrupulous condition suddenly disappeared. The cases mentioned here were the more severe ones. Milder cases of scrupulosity occur quite frequently under the same circumstances, but they usually clear up when the person determines to take the step.

Another group of sufferers apparently evince the desire to rid themselves of their scruples, but actually they cling to them because of a certain satisfaction afforded them by the attention, and perhaps sympathy, of their spiritual directors. In these cases scrupulosity seems to be so closely akin to hysterical reactions that some psychiatrists and spiritual advisers incline to the view that this craving for attention is at the root of practically all scrupulosity. As a consequence, this type of scrupulous person is recognizable by three outstanding characteristics: incessant demands on the services of his directors and spiritual advisers, obstinate adherence to his own erroneous judgments, and a childish sensitivity in the sphere of his scruples. These symptoms have led some writers to advance the theory that the basic source of most cases of scrupulosity is pride, selfishness, egocentricity, and self-assertion. It cannot be denied that pride—mostly unformulated—is the major factor in some cases of scrupulosity. However, it is questionable if this theory does justice to the greater majority of scrupulous people. With the possible exception of those cases which appear to be on the border line between scrupulosity and hysteria, most scrupulous individuals present a picture of utter dejection and pitiful insufficiency. Their constant calling upon their confessor is attributable to their helpless insecurity rather than to the craving for attention, and their obstinacy in clinging to their little scrupulous sphere is due to their tormenting fears, rather than to pride. In this respect, the present authors cannot agree with R. Allers' remark that there are no genuinely scrupulous persons worrying about the commandment of love of one's neighbor.[6]

Scrupulosity may be occasioned also by past sins. One who has spent a period of his life in sin and has mended his ways may develop a tender conscience; but although he avoids even the shadow of his former sins, he cannot completely break with the past. To all appearances he is completely normal, in good physical health, and possessed of a wholesome personality, but actually he suffers from rumination, *i.e.*, a tendency to go over and over past experiences in an obsessive way.

Such suffering is well illustrated by the following case:

§ The patient was a middle-age woman—polite, friendly, charitable, and healthy. She seemed well adjusted, with no compulsive traits. She complained to the psychiatrist that she had sinned often against the commandment "Honor thy father and thy mother." What tortured her were the circumstances surrounding her mother's death twenty years before. Several months before her death the mother had written to the patient to the effect that she was ill and in dire need of money; but the patient thought that her mother was merely scheming to make her return home. Although having an adequate income, she failed to send her mother the money. She suffered a severe shock when the news reached her that her mother had died in the hospital as a charity patient. Again and again she had confessed this sin of negligence, but was unable to rid herself of a terrifying feeling of guilt. Objectively speaking there was probably no serious sin on her part; but the patient's feeling of having neglected her mother and her desire to include this negligence in her confessions were understandable. However, the anxiety fostered by this guilt feeling evidenced scrupulosity.

Lastly, there are cases that apparently are attributable to preternatural or supernatural causes. Catholic theology holds that scrupulosity is, at times, a trial which God sends in order to teach the soul self-detachment. Some writers on asceticism, spiritual directors, and religious superiors seem too often to foster the mistaken notion that scrupulosity is a disciplinary measure employed by God as a means to the justification and sanctification of souls. It is true that it may contribute to spiritual progress, but it is entirely false to believe that scrupulosity in itself is a means of perfection.[7] Scrupulosity as such is a hindrance on the way to perfection; St. Alphonsus, speaking perhaps from personal experience, says that there is nothing more damaging to the soul that longs for God or is devoted to Him than scrupulosity. It is for that reason that Catholic theologians hold that some forms of scrupulosity may be due to the intervention of the devil working for his own purposes. Spiritual progress is not advanced by scrupulosity in itself, but only by the manner in which an individual manages to overcome his condition. At any rate, a word of caution seems appropriate here: one should not be too generous in ascribing scrupulous conditions to supernatural or preternatural causes, for the great majority of scruples have a natural origin.

In summing up, it would seem that scrupulous conditions are occasioned by a variety of causes and that most theories about the origin of scruples have some commendable features.

DEGREES OF SCRUPULOSITY

The criterion for distinguishing various types of scrupulosity is the lack of balance between reason and emotions. It seems appropriate here to enumerate a few of these types in an ascending order of gravity. The first form might be called pseudo scrupulosity, inasmuch as it is basically due not to serious emotional disturbance, but rather to lack of knowledge. People afflicted with this kind of scrupulosity are those with a tender conscience. They have perhaps the makings of scrupulosity in themselves, but given the proper instruction, they may never develop it. If from ignorance they do develop a scruple, they easily overcome it, when given assurance and the necessary guidance. The following is a case of this type:

§ A twenty-six-year-old girl had been engaged for two years to a professional man; she was a quiet, polite, well-educated young woman. She frequented the sacraments regularly, receiving Holy Communion at least once a week and confessing biweekly. She was extremely sensitive, was conscientious, and possessed high moral principles. Once when she asked her confessor what intimacies were permitted to an engaged couple, she was told that she should not allow herself to be aroused by passion. Since the girl had only a very vague notion of the term "passion," uncertainty began to prey upon her mind. She often found herself wondering if a harmless kiss or embrace had not aroused her, and at times she shied away from her fiancé because she thought that closeness to him might be wrong. After the difference between affection and passion had been explained to her in plain, simple terms, her scrupulous behavior ceased.

Emotional disturbances become more apparent with another type of people who, even though properly instructed, never are sure of themselves in moral matters. They are the doubters who feel as if they might be in sin. Such persons may go to confession on Saturday night, but the next morning they wonder if they can receive Holy Communion, because they are doubtful whether a person can live twelve hours without sinning. Typical of this case is the girl who, after holding hands with her fiancé and kissing him in a harmless way, feels her conscience stirred by uncertainty whether or not she has committed a mortal sin.

Still more serious is the condition of those in whom doubt begins to give way to misgivings and suspicion that they have actually committed a sin, *e.g.*, the married man who feels guilty of adultery because in an innocent way he looked at a woman.

The most serious kind of scrupulosity is found in the individuals whose reason in moral matters is almost completely overpowered by emotions and who therefore live in a constant state of anxiety. Such are the poor creatures who are afraid of the past, because they feel guilty about practically everything they did in their lives, and who now try to atone for their "many sins" symbolically in some absurd way. These persons are frightened by the future, because they presume that they simply cannot avoid sin. Such is, for instance, the man who avoids marriage because he regards sex and everything connected with it as sinful.

The following case may help to clarify some of the details of this condition:

§ An eighteen-year-old girl attended a party at which the young people present played "post office." During the game, one of the boys kissed her; and, being in total ignorance about sexual relations, she feared that she had become pregnant. Menstruation ceased immediately and a doctor was consulted. Recognizing her nervous condition, he prescribed sedatives, and, shortly after, menstruation recommenced. The girl then went to confession and told the priest that she had had "sexual relations," that menstruation had not occurred, and only through medication of a physician did it again start. The priest, apparently not understanding the girl's confused confession, refused to give her absolution. Upon learning this, she became inconsolable and she informed her mother of these complications. Fortunately, the girl's mother understood the situation and had the prudence to explain it tactfully to the girl's confessor. Later on, the girl became engaged and remained so for 12 years. She resisted her fiancé's amorous advances, permitting him neither to touch nor to kiss her. She practiced cleanliness to excess and was in the habit of washing her body for two hours after every visit to the bathroom. She cleaned carefully every opening of her body, including the rectal passage, until she fell into a state of exhaustion. At times she remained in the bathtub for five hours before going to bed. Diagnosis of the patient's condition indicated the use of intensive psychotherapy. This treatment, coupled with a complete course of moral instruction by a priest, proved successful, and enabled the girl to overcome her aversion toward marriage.

In this case the starting point of the girl's scrupulous behavior was to be found in ignorance regarding sex matters, but the lack of knowledge was no more than an occasion, the real reason being a profound emotional disorder.

THERAPY

A person who suffers from scrupulosity will, because of its very nature, usually reveal it to his confessor or spiritual adviser. When the penitent discloses his scrupulosity in the confessional, it may in some instances be advisable for the priest to ask the penitent to consult him outside the confessional, because such conferences afford both parties a better opportunity and more time to discuss the problem. Many scrupulous individuals will bring their troubles to the parlor of their own accord anyway, because in their helpless insecurity they are searching for guidance and eager to accept any that is offered. However, this eagerness for assistance is, at the same time, seriously handicapped by a lack of trust stemming from their state of fear. Invariably, when the pastoral counselor presents concrete advice as to what such a person is to do, the latter will immediately reveal his attitude of fear and doubt by asking himself whether the counselor understood him fully, whether he expressed himself correctly, whether he took sufficient time to examine his conscience to give a proper account. Hence, the priest who is faced with a scrupulous penitent should continually bear in mind that he has before him one who in his torment is grasping for any aid, but who, on the other hand, is reluctant to accept the judgment of another person.

During the first interviews the experienced counselor wisely permits his patients to "talk themselves out," as long and as repetitiously as they wish. He should avoid interrupting them, and his primary purpose should be to make them believe by his attention, gestures, and an occasional encouraging word that he understands their problem thoroughly. Before long, the patient will bring up the inevitable question of his responsibility, because this problem is uppermost in his mind. But in those first interviews a direct answer to the patient's question would be premature; any decision at this time, however sound it may be, tends to shake the patient's confidence in the ability of his adviser. The counselor might say, for instance, that he needs some time to study all the complications and ramifications of the case, but he must leave the patient with the hope of a complete answer, when the solution is arrived at.

The counselor's immediate concern is to make the patient realize that he is a sick person. Usually, it will not be too hard to convince a scrupulous individual of this truth, because in the depths of his heart he is well aware of it. To be sure, his emotional condition will make him protest, but if the counselor succeeds in bringing about a better frame of mind in spite of the patient's emotional disturbance and can at least make him believe that his troubles are pathogenetic in origin, an important step has been made in the right direction.

In any event, the pastoral adviser soon faces a crucial problem, *i.e.*, he must decide whether he is capable of handling the case alone or whether he needs the help of a psychiatrist. Certainly, not all cases of scrupulosity require the latter's assistance, and age-old experience has shown that prudent, tactful, and patient pastoral counseling often leads to a satisfactory solution. On the other hand, numerous cases call for psychiatric treatment. The physical condition of the patient may be a complicating factor, and the cause of the trouble may be of such a nature that the prudent pastor does not feel qualified to deal with it. Hence, the pastor's decision—whether or not to send the scrupulous person to a psychiatrist—should be governed by considerations of the person's physical health and the seriousness of the motives of his anxiety. The decision is a crucial one and demands detailed knowledge of the nature and pathogenesis of scrupulosity. Naturally, in a great number of cases the question will remain somewhat academic, for many persons simply cannot afford to incur the expenses of psychiatric treatment. Under those circumstances there is no choice left to the pastor but to treat the case as best he can, unless other priests trained in psychology are available to lend professional aid.

Suppose the case is of the milder type with no apparent physical complications, so that the priest feels reasonably competent to cope with it. He then must realize that there is no known treatment applicable to all cases, because no two scrupulous persons present the same problems. But there are certain general directives that may guide him in his efforts. One of the main rules is that the adviser should concentrate upon the appeal to the patient's will and emotions, rather than to his reasoning power. It would be completely useless to descend to argumentation, because the patient, with his secret aprioristic conviction that after all nobody really understands him, will always find a loophole in even the most perfect syllogism.

From the very beginning the confessor or spiritual adviser must assume a dominant role. With most Catholics this should not prove too difficult, since the priest has unquestioned authority in moral matters by the very nature of his sacerdotal profession. And he could add to his prestige, if he would make his patient aware that he also is versed in psychology. Naturally, such authority should be blended with kindness and sympathy.

Undisputed authority on the part of the counselor will strengthen the counselee's confidence and will reinforce the counselor's reassurance technique. Because of his sense of insufficiency, the scrupulous person needs constant reassurance that his troubles stem from a morbid emotional condition.

Authority demands obedience on the part of the penitent. Traditionally, moral theologians recommend the rule that the confessor should exact blind obedience. This, of course, is not always possible; besides, the rule is at times misinterpreted. It would, for instance, be hardly advisable for the confessor to extract a direct promise of obedience, at least in the beginning; but by the assertion of his authority he should bring about a certain confidence and a wholehearted willingness to obey. Furthermore, at the start of the treatment certain orders should be avoided. Some confessors tell the penitent not to dwell upon his past sins, because, they add, everything is forgiven: "I take upon myself all the responsibility." Such instructions, however well intentioned, are useless, and even harmful in the beginning of the treatment. The penitents cannot obey them, and if they attempt it, they usually do so under the pressure of extreme anxiety, thus throwing their emotional state still further out of balance. Hence, this precept of obedience should be applied with great discretion.

But when the counselor feels that sufficient progress in acceptance of his commands has been made, his orders should be short, direct, and categorical. He should seldom rescind an order or change it, because in so doing he "loses face" in the eyes of his charge, whose attention is extremely alert in detecting uncertainty in the adviser. If, in later interviews, the counselor learns that the patient has not put his advice into practice, he should inform him in a restrained, but firm tone that his disobedience is the best way to prolong his miserable condition. In other words, he must constantly appeal to the patient's will to health.

As in all similar relations, there exists a danger both for the pastor in his role of an authoritative counselor and for the patient in his role of a more or less obedient receptor of advice. The very tendency of the patient to trust his counselor implicitly, despite lapses of rebellion and hostility, brings with it the danger that he may begin to lean too heavily upon his counselor and to relinquish to the latter his own share of the work. Confidence in the adviser is necessary in the first stage of the treatment, but gradually the bond upon which it rests should be dissolved. In other words, confidence in the counselor should be changed gradually into self-confidence.

The scrupulous person should not accept guidance merely in a passive manner, but he must learn to take the initiative. It is not sufficient that such a one avoid reading ascetical books or communicating with people who suffer from the same condition, nor that he be convinced that he commits no sin in those actions which formerly he regarded as sins. One who can bring him that far certainly may speak of progress. Yet even this progress may prove ephemeral, for the patient may shift his fears and doubts to other objects and events so long as his sense of insecurity is not altered. The ultimate goal of the treatment is to make the patient the equal of other responsible persons, *i.e.*, capable of forming a correct judgment concerning the culpability or nonculpability of his acts.

In many cases, this goal can scarcely be achieved without the intensive psychotherapy reserved to the psychiatrist. But in many other cases the spiritual adviser is well enough equipped to aid the patient positively by effecting changes in his character formation. He should bring his patient to an understanding of his childish personality, change his introspective attitude, make him avoid the interminable self-examinations, make him pay less attention to his feelings, and help him to develop gradually into a more mature person who can make his own decisions in moral matters without suffering interminable nagging doubts. In other words, the counselor must reeducate the patient by helping him to develop new principles, habits, and attitudes toward life.

During the entire course of treatment the priest should try constantly to correct or change the patient's concept of God. Rather than regard Him as a revengeful, rigid, unbending Master, he must learn to appreciate His kindness, mercy, and goodness. Of course, all scrupulous persons admit theoretically that God is goodness, but, in practice, most of them concentrate on His frightening justice, exclusively. When, at the inception of treatment, the priest places before him the picture of God's infinite goodness, the patient will believe him, but these words make no real impression. Eventually, however, this picture must become the woof and warp of the patient's mental attitude toward God, if any lasting success is to be achieved.

As has been said before, the scope of this book permits only an outline of the general directives of the treatment, and not a discussion of more specific points, such as the cathartic value of general confessions, the choice of a confessor, the treatment of specific types of scrupulous people, the value of occupational therapy, distraction, hobbies, hygienic living conditions, the influence of the proper environment, etc.

Thus far, this discussion has dealt with what the priest can accomplish in cases of scrupulosity. But every priest will meet with cases the treatment of which he feels incapable of assuming. These are, for instance, the cases in which the anxiety extends to every action of a person's life, or those in which scrupulosity is only one of the symptoms of a severe psychoneurosis or psychosis, or those in which obsessional and compulsive actions interfere with the proper performance of the individual's regular duties. In such instances, pastoral help alone is not sufficient, and the prudent pastor should refer such persons to the psychiatrist, provided the patient's financial position permits him to seek psychiatric help.

Obviously, some scrupulous patients directly contact a psychiatrist on their own initiative; for they are reluctant, even though they are Catholics, to consult the priest. The following case gives one such instance:

§ A married woman with five children had had scruples about the observance of the commandment "Thou shalt not commit adultery" since her school days. Marriage did not improve her condition, as marital adjustment was almost impossible. Her history revealed a fervent religious background. Four of her brothers were priests. She regularly attended Sunday Mass, and she had her children enrolled in the parochial school, but when she presented herself for treatment to the psychiatrist, she admitted that it had been nine years since her last confession. The reason was that in three consecutive confessions she had received harsh treatment from the confessors in the matter of her scruples. She now rationalized her avoidance of the sacraments by the statement that confession was the cause of her scrupulosity. Several attempts were made to induce her to see a priest but without success. She was distrustful of priests not only because of the stern attitude they had taken toward her in the confessional, but also because she had been told that a certain kindhearted pastor regarded her as a "saint." This remark angered her, and she referred to the good pastor as a person who "does not understand his business." She complained bitterly against being treated by a Catholic psychiatrist, saying, "In back of your mind exists only the thought that I should go to confession and Holy Communion."

As long as a patient remains in such a state of mind, it is utterly useless to bring him into contact with a priest.

When a scrupulous person accepts the advice of his spiritual adviser to see a psychiatrist, he implicitly accepts the fact that he is a sick man—a state of mind that will immediately facilitate his treatment. The nature of the treatment naturally will be dictated by the psychiatrist's concept concerning the nature of scrupulosity. For instance, the Freudian analyst who envisions every form of scrupulosity as the result of sexual repression will, of necessity, deal with it in a manner different from a follower of Janet, or an existential analyst. As a general rule, a Catholic psychiatrist is best qualified to treat Catholics suffering from scrupulosity, since both he and his patient have identical beliefs in the existence of God, sin, guilt, and conscience. However, other psychiatrists have been known to treat understandingly cases involving a delicate religious and moral nature.

When the psychiatrist concludes that the patient's state of psychic insufficiency is due to physiological causes, he will probably apply some physical means, *e.g.*, injections, to raise the lowered psychic tension. But most of the treatment will be of a psychotherapeutic nature.[8] The primary goal is the discovery of the cause of the scruples and any possible complexes. The patient's life history, his past experience, and his interpersonal relationships form, as always, the sources of information. The attitude of the patient's father and mother toward religion, his own religious and moral formation, and the methods used by others in this formation—all these are factors of fundamental importance. Of special interest also are any failures in the patient's life that may be contributory to his feeling of insecurity. In many instances, a thorough review of the person's psychosexual development may yield important clues as to the cause of his condition.

Obviously, there is in these procedures little that an experienced pastoral counselor could not handle, provided of course that emphasis be placed on the word "experienced." But since intensive treatment requires a great expenditure of time, most priests, burdened as they are with their ministerial duties, will find themselves unable to assume such treatment. Moreover, in some cases of scrupulosity the unearthing of the cause may require analytical treatment, and this should be left to experts.

In the discussion of pastoral treatment, it was pointed out that a large part of the therapy consists in the patient's reeducation to a more mature attitude toward moral problems; this holds equally true for psychiatric treatment. In fact, here is a field in which psychiatrist and pastor can collaborate effectively. Though certain psychoanalysts regard the collaboration with confessors and spiritual advisers as an invasion of their own jealously guarded domain, the majority of psychiatrists welcome such cooperation for its beneficial effects to the patient. The patient himself feels the need of such help, and ordinarily he is more than willing to grant the permission required for an extrasacramental discussion of his case. Due safeguards for preserving the integrity of the seal must be observed. The cooperation of priest and doctor aids in the achievement of their common goal, the psychic and moral well-being of the individual. This can be gleaned from the following case, in which the patient initially was opposed to combined treatment:

§ A conscientious and intelligent Catholic was referred for treatment of a sexual perversion (transvestism) which he had attempted in vain to overcome. His psychic state was complicated by the presence of two paradoxical factors: a scrupulosity that the sins arising from his perversion were unforgivable, and a deep-seated fear and suspicion of priests and the confessional. The first factor forced him to seek relief, according to his own estimate, from one hundred different confessors, despite the fact that he had been advised and warned to limit himself to the ministrations of one confessor. His reluctance to follow this advice was inspired by the second factor—a suspicion and distrust of priests, engendered in his early youth by a traumatic experience with a priest. In order to resolve the antithetical dynamics of the patient's personality, the psychiatrist deemed it advisable to include in the course of treatment a series of interviews between the patient and a priest versed in psychology, a stipulation to which the patient agreed. The treatment, lasting for a year and a half, was successful.

The psychiatrist may approach the matter from the psychiatric standpoint, and the priest from the moral and spiritual standpoint, but in cases of scrupulosity considerable overlapping can be expected. Both the priest and the doctor are faced with the problem of moral responsibility and duty. The patient is tortured continuously by doubts and by a million questions such as "Were my former confessions really good?" "Is this or that act a sin?" "Did I give into bad thoughts last night?" and "Am I not bound to restitution?"

If there is any collaboration between psychiatrist and confessor, the two should reach an agreement regarding answers to such questions, for any contradiction between the two will retard the progress of the patient. In general, this policy is always the best: questions concerning moral responsibility are the sole concern of the spiritual director. If the psychiatrist observes this agreement to the letter and shows in his treatment that he approves of it, he can contribute greatly to the patient's recovery.

In the matter of deciding the moral responsibility of a scrupulous individual, a few general remarks suffice.[9] A number of moralists lay down the guiding principle that a scrupulous person is unable to commit a grievous sin. Their opinion is based upon the fact that the patient is the victim of a compulsion neurosis. However, in practice they admit that this rule holds true only with the verification of one condition—that the case be one of serious and pure compulsion. By pure cases they imply those in which the individual's scrupulous fear of sin is not complicated by a moral laxity and a spiritual tepidity that might cause him, when tempted, to give in to real sin. In other words, the condition is that the confessor be reasonably sure that the penitent is a person of high moral standards, who will not take advantage of the liberty which the rule gives him; *e.g.*, it is reasonable to believe that a soul habitually pure and religious will continue to behave in that manner.

The mixed case presents a very different picture. A married man may accuse himself of adultery because he looked at a woman, although he did so without any bad intentions, but he may feel justified in masturbating at a time when his wife is too sick to allow normal sexual intercourse. Clearly, such a person, being both scrupulous and lax toward the one moral precept, cannot be given the advice that he is unable to commit a mortal sin. In fact it is practically impossible to set down any definite rules in this type of case.

A final remark concerns the prophylaxis of scrupulous conditions. Since prevention is much easier than cure, and since scrupulosity generally arises in the pubescent period, parents, teachers, and priests bear a great deal of responsibility for the mental hygiene of our youth.[10] Those in authority should exercise constant vigilance, lest by word or deed they frighten the young, even though their intention be good. They must appeal to the higher nature, to the idealism, and to the hero worship of youth in helping them to form noble characters.

NOTES AND REFERENCES

1. St. Alphonsus ("Theologia moralis," I, I, II) defines a scrupulous conscience as follows: *"Conscientia scrupulosa est ea quae ob levia motiva absque rationabili fundamento (scrupulus est enim inanis apprehensio) saepe formidat de peccato ubi revera non est."*
2. Mullen, Joseph J., "Psychological Factors in the Pastoral Treatment of Scruples" in "Studies in Psychology and Psychiatry" (Washington, D.C., The Catholic University of America Press, 1927), Vol. I, pp. 29–30.
3. Mayer, J., "Religiöse Fehlentwicklungen, eine Entstehungsursache von Psychopathien," in Bergmann, W. (ed.), "Religion und Seelenleiden" (Düsseldorf: Schwann, 1928) Vol. III, pp. 170–172; 367–369.
4. Moore, Thomas V., "Personal Mental Hygiene" (New York: Grune and Stratton, 1945), pp. 16, 32–49.
5. *Ibid.*, pp. 42, 43.
6. Allers, R., "The Psychology of Character" (New York: Sheed & Ward, Inc., 1943), p. 357.
7. See Sinéty, R. de, "Psychopathologie et direction" (Paris: Beauchesne, 1934), p. 47: *"Il n'est pas rare que des directeurs, égarés par je ne sais pas quelles idées fausses, s'imaginent que ces états sont des épreuves spirituelles destinées à purifier et à sanctifier les âmes."* See also Bless, H., "Pastoraal Psychiatrie" (Roermond: J. J. Romen, 1945), pp. 211, 220.

8. Lasko, Ernest F., A Psychotherapy for Scruples, *Homiletic and Pastoral Review,* Vol. 49 (1949), pp. 617–623, 906–914, presents a psychotherapeutic method based on the principles of Vittoz, Roger, "Traitement des psychonévroses par la rééducation du controle cérébral" (Paris, 1947).
9. For the problem of the moral responsibility of scrupulous persons, see the following:

   Bless, *op. cit.*, pp. 228, 229.

   Doyle, W., "Scruples and Their Treatment" (Dublin, 1936).

   Eymieu, A., "L'Obsession et le scrupule" (Paris, 1913), pp. 248, 268.

   Gearon, P., "Scruples: Words of Consolation" (St. Louis, 1927), p. 66.

   Gemelli, A., "De scrupulis" (Florence, 1913), p. 311.

   Müncker, Thomas, "Die psychologischen Grundlagen der Katholischen Sittenlehre" (Düsseldorf: Patmos-Verlag, 1948), p. 231.

   Vermeersch, A., "Theologia moralis" (Rome, 1933), I, pp. 357 ff.

   Turco, Natale, "Ad uso degli ammalati, medici e confessori: il trattamento morale dello scrupulo e dell'ossessione morbosa" (2 vols.; Turin: Marietti, 1919–1920).
10. See Jersild, Arthur T., and Frances Baker Holmes, "Children's Fear" (New York: Teacher's College, Columbia University, 1915).

Chapter 20

ALCOHOLISM

The Bible cites, as the first recorded instance of drunkenness, the patriarch Noe, who we are told was unaware of the strength of sweet wine. (Genesis 9:21). Ever since that day man has used alcoholic beverages of one kind or another. The peoples of primitive races and those of some ancient civilizations often surrounded with quasi-religious ritual the use of intoxicating beverages. Poets sang paeans to the rubied cup, and a phase of Greek drama is said to have developed out of the worship of Dionysos, the wine god. Nevertheless, use has so often become abuse that religious teachers and leaders of all ages have repeatedly condemned the excessive use of alcohol.

Whatever the condition may have been in the past, in modern times the excessive use of alcohol is one of the major social problems. When the effects of alcohol on our economic system are considered, it is small wonder that alcoholism has become the subject of so much investigation.

E. M. Jellinek, Director of the Yale Summer School of Alcoholic Studies, estimates that, of 50 million Americans who drink alcohol in some form, the total number of excessive drinkers is 3 million, 750,000 of whom become chronic alcoholics. He further estimates that of the 3 million excessive drinkers, 2,600,000 are men.[1] In the course of one year each of these men lost an average of 22 working days; this absenteeism caused by excessive drinking is indicative of the problem that alcoholism presents in the field of economics alone.

Scientific research into the why and wherefore of alcoholism received impetus in 1937, with the establishment of the Research Council on Problems of Alcoholism. Since that time much research and experimentation have been attempted, notably by the Yale University Laboratory of Applied Science. Summarizing its research, the Yale Summer School of Alcoholic Studies makes the following general statements: (*a*) what used to be considered alcohol's three primary functions—food value, medicinal value, and religious-ecstasy value—can be practically disregarded; (*b*) the needs for integrative mechanisms adapted to the complexities of modern society have become increasingly evident; (*c*) the anxieties of the individual members of our complex society are increased; (*d*) social drinking has become a custom wedded to wealth, social position, etc.; (*e*) control of drinking has become more difficult; (*f*) the individual within such a society has a far more formidable task in establishing satisfactory interpersonal relationships, is faced with more choices, and belongs to looser, more specialized groups that provide fewer personally satisfying associations.

Prohibition, together with the years that followed the repeal of the Eighteenth Amendment, called attention to the fact that society's attitude toward alcohol conditions the manner of indulgence. For instance, drinking was taboo among women, for the most part, until prohibition made it fashionable. The recent increase of drinking among women of all strata of society is evident from the statistics of police courts, jails, and mental hospitals.[2] Society not only tolerates drinking of both men and women, but actually seems to encourage it. The result is that alcoholic beverages form not an inconsiderable item on the budget of the average society man or woman.

Between the social drinking and chronic alcoholism range various degrees of alcoholic addiction. Many persons indulge occasionally in excessive amounts of alcohol, but that does not necessarily make them chronic alcoholics. The term "chronic alcoholic" has been defined in various ways. Some definitions simply list the effects of alcohol and describe a chronic alcoholic as a person who, through the use of alcohol, endangers his job and his health, and fails to support his family. A causal definition would describe the chronic or habitual drinker as one who is driven to repeated excess in drinking by an almost irresistible craving for alcohol. Probably, the most typical characteristic of a chronic alcoholic is his inability to take one drink without having to become drunk, even though he may have stayed sober for many years.

Among chronic alcoholics there is a special group termed periodic alcoholics. The periodic alcoholic, or dipsomaniac in the strict sense, is a person who, after staying sober for three or four months or longer, is seized by a recurrent, compulsive attack of drunkenness. It is believed that this periodic drinking is a reaction to situations of stress.

EFFECTS OF ALCOHOL

The old-fashioned opinion that alcohol has nutritional value, or helps in treating such diseases as heart attacks, is quite commonly discarded,[3] although lately some claims have been made that a weak solution of alcohol in water given intravenously might be used as a mild anesthetic.

As yet, no evidence has been educed to support the contention that small amounts of alcohol are greatly harmful to the average person. Nevertheless, even small amounts, when assimilated into the blood stream, cause dilation of the peripheral blood vessels, which in turn lowers the skin temperature and thereby the resistance to cold.[4] It has also been demonstrated that even a very moderate amount of alcohol reduces the imbiber's discrimination and muscular control.

Large quantities of alcohol, however, seriously affect the drunkard in both body and mind, albeit the power of resistance varies in different individuals. In the first place an alcoholic easily falls prey to organic diseases, because his diet is frequently inadequate, to start with. Then too, alcohol produces physical changes in the stomach which prevent proper digestion, and in this way any dietary deficiency already present is further aggravated. The body of the alcoholic, weakened by nutritional inadequacy, is predisposed to several types of diseases, especially pneumonia and cardiac ailments, which complicate his case and lessen his chances of recovery. Moreover, poor nutrition often results in notable vitamin insufficiency, especially of vitamin B complex, which may result in lesions of the brain. Such a condition is degenerative in nature and soon renders the case definitely pathological.

Alcohol has furthermore a direct effect on the nervous system, including the brain. To cite but a few instances, the action of alcohol on the brain centers disturbs the metabolism of the body; it affects the control of vasodilation and vasoconstriction, resulting in headaches or faulty digestion. Practically every case of intoxication disturbs the balance between the activities of the sympathetic and parasympathetic system. Since this balance is necessary for the regular functions of the organs, its derangement results in the increased activity of such organs as the heart. Alcohol has a devastating effect on the higher brain centers controlling voluntary behavior.

Through its effects on the central nervous system and the brain, alcohol causes extensive mental and personality disturbances in the drinker; it impairs consciousness and reduces mental activities. Excessive use of alcohol impairs judgment, numbs the will, and so beclouds memory that the more complicated and recent experiences are the first forgotten.

During the drinking bout the raw material of the drunkard's personality comes to the fore; some become excited, some irritable, and some melancholy, according to their original temperament. Using Jung's "persona" concept, one might say that the drunkard casts off his conventional mask and shows his "true self." Character traits disappear to a great extent, because the alcoholic's will and judgment fail to function properly; moral inhibitions fall away, and during a heavy drinking period, only the animal is left.

Thus far the discussion has dealt with the effects of alcohol as they appear during the "lost week ends" of occasional drinkers. The effects of chronic alcohol intoxication, although far more disastrous and permanent, follow the same general pattern.

Chronic alcoholism may cause very serious physical disorders. Tremors, paresthesia, circulatory and gastrointestinal diseases, cirrhosis of the liver, nephritis, and generalized arteriosclerosis are not infrequently found. Doubtless, too, anemia is often present and so are vitamin deficiencies which, as we said, may produce degeneration of the brain. In addition to this type of brain degeneration, the brains of almost all chronic alcoholics are found to have shrunk, especially in the frontal lobes, with a corresponding increase of fluid in the subarachnoidal space. This shrinkage may result from degeneration of nerve fibers, simple dehydration, or both.

The intellectual and mental deterioration is no less appalling. Ethical degeneration, clouding of finer sentiments, impairment of judgment, inability to concentrate, loss of memory—all these are characteristic of the chronic alcoholic, even during periods of sobriety. Instability of the personality is the most marked feature and is often accompanied by paranoic tendencies. Whereas the occasional drinker regains his personality after he has slept off the effects of his debauch, with the habitual drinker the change of personality becomes more or less permanent. The alcoholic addict is very susceptible to emotional upsets which are due to the function of the endocrine system. Though the symptoms may have preceded the drinking spree, or, in the case of the chronic alcoholic, the onset of the addiction, they seem to manifest themselves to a greater degree during the so-called "hangover" period. The most common of these endocrine disturbances affect the gastric and arterio-circulatory systems. The emotional spells lead eventually to insomnia.

Alcoholic intoxication, particularly of the chronic type, may give rise to psychotic conditions. Among the best known alcoholic psychoses are delirium tremens and the Korsakoff syndrome. Delirium tremens is unmistakable even to the layman because of its violent symptoms. Occurring in some 4 per cent of heavy drinkers, it largely affects persons with a high tolerance for alcohol who have shown no apparent or marked abnormalities after even ten to fifteen years of habitual excessive indulgence. Contrary to popular opinion, its onset is not sudden but is preceded by such signs as anxiety, restlessness, fears, sleeplessness, nightmares, and terrifying dreams. The characteristic of the psychosis is the appearance of vivid and frightening visual hallucinations and sometimes of auditory hallucinations, but always accompanied by violent activity. Such attacks are sometimes fatal because of heart failure or because the patient's lowered resistance causes pneumonia or some infectious disease. The attack itself usually lasts from three to six days. Recovery begins when the excitement gives way to sleep. Unfortunately, one attack does not guarantee future immunity, and most patients, once recovered, return sooner or later to the hospital with another attack.

The Korsakoff syndrome is most frequently encountered in chronic alcoholism, but it occasionally appears in other conditions, such as cerebral arteriosclerosis, lead poisoning, or chronic infections. When occurring as a result of alcoholism, it is frequently preceded by an attack of delirium tremens and is accompanied by polyneuritis. Mentally, there is marked memory disturbance, disorientation in space and time, and the tendency to fill in memory gaps with haphazard snatches from immediate happenings. The course of the disorder is usually a long one; and although these cases often begin to show some improvement in six to eight weeks, many take a considerably longer time. However, the prognosis for complete recovery is poor, especially with regard to memory. Some residue of mental deterioration remains even after all physical symptoms have disappeared.

CAUSES OF ALCOHOLISM

The discussion of alcoholic psychoses shows that alcoholic intoxication may be the cause of mental disorders. On the other hand, alcoholism is often the effect of mental disturbances. In such cases alcoholism is rather a symptom of some form of insanity or an occasioning factor that precipitates the onset of the disorder and aggravates its character. Some statisticians hold that 20 per cent or more of alcoholics belong to this type.

As research in alcoholism has progressed it has become apparent that many people formerly considered as true alcoholics are actually suffering from schizophrenia, manic-depressive psychoses, general paresis, epilepsy, or some mental disease having no relation to alcohol other than that the use of alcohol affords the patient escape from the bewildering sensation he experiences, or provides him with the sensation of well-being he may otherwise lack. When alcohol is not the cause of the condition, but a symptom of it, the patient is classified as a symptomatic drinker.

Likewise it is now agreed that excessive drinking is, at times, the result of low intelligence rather than its cause, as was once considered to be the case, for mental defectives, as a group, are especially prone to indulge in alcohol on account of their lack of inhibitions and its self-aggrandizing effect. These are the habitual drinkers who seem to spend their lives shuffling in and out of jail.

Another group of alcoholics is made up of the psychopaths. These alcoholics are the social misfits, the drifters and derelicts, for whom alcohol is about the only pleasure in life. Some psychiatrists think the majority of alcoholics are psychopaths. Whatever value one may accord this opinion, the fact remains that many people are alcoholics because they are psychopaths, and not vice versa.

This fact—that many alcoholics are mentally ill—has shed an interesting light on the remaining types of alcoholics, on those who are not psychotics and who do not seem to be psychopaths. It is of especial interest in the case of a third type of alcoholic, the neurotics. Because alcohol affords a means of escape, or a personality crutch, neurotics often seek in it a temporary escape from insecurity and frustration. After a period of time they, too, become true addicts precisely because they are mentally unbalanced.

From this discussion of the psychotic, psychopathic, and neurotic drinker, it seems to follow that alcoholism—at least in a fairly large percentage of the cases—is a disease or, rather, the result of a pathological condition. These cases seem to refute Wexberg's opinion that there is no such thing as an alcoholic personality, prior to drinking, and that alcoholism is due to habit formation. Another reason militating against Wexberg's opinion is that the recovered alcoholic, after having cultivated the habit of sobriety for six, ten or more years, is sure to become inebriated once he takes the first drink.

That alcoholism is frequently a disease is a formula of the greatest importance. As this idea becomes more widely diffused and more generally accepted, the problem of alcoholism can be more effectively approached.

What are the dynamics that drive certain persons to alcoholic excesses? In treating of chronic alcoholism Alexander and French contend that the standard psychiatric textbooks describe the symptoms of the disorder but are not interested in the motivations of the chronic alcoholics.[5] However, numerous solutions have been presented to explain the behavior of the problem drinker.

Karl Menninger holds that alcoholism is a suicide drive, but he evidently confuses cause and effect, for the suicide drive may be the result of the mental grief and guilt feelings of the alcoholic, but it is not the cause of alcoholism.

The opinion of some psychiatrists that repressed homosexuality is the essential basis of alcoholism has never been substantiated; nevertheless it can be admitted that some persons may very well find in alcohol a temporary relief of sexual tension and guilt feelings.

Bergler believes that the alcoholic reverts to the stage of his earliest infancy by substituting the whisky bottle for the milk bottle—the mechanism of orality.

Another psychoanalytic interpretation of the alcoholic is offered by Simmel.[6] He holds that "the ego finds a way of denying reality by reestablishing infantile pleasure principles as a release from superego prohibitions through pharmaco-toxic elation." Simmel feels that alcohol spares the ego the mental expenditures involved in neurotic and psychotic defenses. He classifies drinkers as social, reactive, neurotic, and addicts. The social drinker uses alcohol to make his social relationships with people more comfortable and congenial, and it is the community ethos which imposes restrictions on social drinking. The reactive drinker places the restrictions on himself. Both these classes defend their ego from external forces. The neurotic alcoholic escapes from himself. Sometimes the neurotic ego disintegrates regressively, and as the ego goes back beyond the early stages of development, the person becomes an addict. Simmel finds the basis of neurotic alcoholism in a childhood where parents were indulgent to themselves but puritanical toward the child. Strecker, too, suggests that an undesirable parent-child relationship is often to blame for the children's alcoholism: "In about eighty percent of alcoholic cases I have studied, 'momism' in childhood was the basic underlying cause."[7]

Barbara tries to fit Horney's theory to the compulsive drinker.[8] To him alcoholism is a product of distorted childhood, inasmuch as a severe upbringing may result in the formation of a rigid personality with a harsh superego that strives unbendingly toward perfection. But in later life such a person realizes that his drive for perfection is continually thwarted and renders his interpersonal relationships excessively difficult. The result of this clash with reality is a state of frustration and anxiety. Once arrived at such a state, an individual may well try to alleviate it by reaching for the bottle. Continuous excessive drinking creates more conflicts and so the vicious circle is closed.

Apart from these rather theoretical considerations, a number of studies have been undertaken, based on psychological tests. A study of 50 alcoholics, by Karlan and Heller,[9] with psychiatric and Rorschach evaluations, showed that nine suffered mild anxiety states, eight showed hypochondriacal trends, but all drank to relieve suffering. The sexual urge was weak in most of them. The Rorschach Test indicated an excessive number of restricted responses; these responses, believed to be due to inadequate security, were generally similar to those of any group of psychoneurotics. Therefore, Karlan and Heller concluded that there was no essential difference between psychoneurotics and alcoholics; except for the one feature that the neurotic is usually dissatisfied with the way he tries to solve his problems and will seek help, while the alcoholic is frequently quite satisfied with his solution.

Omitting extravagant opinions which seem only to reflect their author's capacity for fanciful description or esoteric terminology, one finds one common factor in the majority of studies: alcoholics consciously or unconsciously employ alcohol as an escape mechanism. Often enough they hate alcohol and its consequences, but they cannot live without it. Unable to meet the conflicts of everyday life, they seek respite in alcoholic stupor. After the drinking bout, they are tortured by terrific guilt feelings and remorse, and, in turn, they drown these feelings in a new flood of alcohol.

This search for an escape mechanism is the sign and the result of emotional immaturity. Normal, well-balanced people who may have the same or greater problems face reality squarely and solve their problems in a rational way. But the alcoholic runs away from life's problems as a child who seeks protection in an all-powerful father or clings to the apron strings of a caressing mother.

But precisely why do certain people reach for the bottle while others employ such escape mechanisms as daydreaming, cynicism, or unreasoned optimism? Unless one has a perfect insight into an immature individual's personality traits, it is impossible to predict what means of escape he will take. Both kinds of factors that concur in the formation of a personality—*i.e.,* constitutional and environmental—probably play a role in determining the choice of escape mechanisms. The psychic factor—emotional immaturity—not only accounts for the fact *that* an individual looks for escape, but also partly for the *form* of that mechanism. But purely psychological factors do not seem to be sufficient to explain why a certain individual prefers alcohol to other forms of escape. Certain physical constitutional factors would seem to play a part too. All in all, it appears that the psychic disposition forces them to look for an escape mechanism while organic and environmental factors determine alcohol as this mechanism.

Alcoholism does not seem to be hereditary.[10] True, the children of alcoholic parents often become alcoholics themselves, but this may be due to the parents' example, or to neglected education, or to a psychopathic disposition, or to a combination of these factors.

Thus far, this discussion has reviewed the alcoholic types that are clearly unbalanced. But there is another group of alcoholics that creates more difficulties in the explanation of their behavior. They are those who, prior to their alcoholism, were normal. They had their everyday problems, but who has not? Why is it that with hardly any more problems than the average person, they turn to alcohol? Probably, environmental factors are very important motivating factors, but these factors seem to presuppose a certain predisposition. As a matter of fact, in the first stages, the motive is largely hedonistic; but that precisely indicates a physical disposition because to many other people alcohol is distasteful. Because of this inclination, the gratification of the desire becomes more frequent, and the person contracts a habit. Here, then, the alcoholic becomes an inebriate along the lines of simple habit formation. In the beginning there is no more sickness, physical or psychic, than there is in the case of those who contract a habit by repeatedly gratifying sexual desires.

MORAL RESPONSIBILITY

The review of the above categories of alcoholics paves the way to a judgment about their moral responsibility.

Once an individual has become an alcoholic, no matter from what cause, he is definitely a sick person, as may be seen from a consideration of the physical and psychic effects of alcoholism. His personality is changed; his will power is greatly weakened; and, therefore, one may seriously question his moral responsibility when again he turns to the bottle. But this statement does not exhaust the entire problem. How far is an alcoholic responsible for his condition?

The answer depends on the type of alcoholic. The feeble-minded, the psychotic, and the epileptic are on the whole not responsible for becoming alcoholics, as they can do little or nothing about it. One may also question the responsibility of the periodic drinker if his urge is really the result of an epileptoid constitution. The responsibility of the psychopathic drinker is as hard to judge as any other act of the psychopath.

The question is different with regard to the other types of alcoholics, particularly with regard to those apparently normal persons who turned alcoholic through sheer habit formation. They were no sicker than any other normal person who acquires a bad habit or vice. It should be repeated that not every sinner is a sick person. If the alcoholic of this type is sincere and honest with himself, he will admit that he could, and should, have stopped before he crossed the boundary line between normal and compulsive drinking. Because he did not, there is *voluntarium in causa* with regard to his becoming the alcoholic he now is. The fact that no one knows where that invisible line runs, does not alter his moral culpability in the least. He is also responsible for the sins he commits during his drinking bouts, except for those which were not foreseen when he contracted the habit.

The same holds true to a great extent for the neurotic drinker, although culpability is reduced according to the strength of his neurosis.

A third question concerning responsibility is whether, once the chronic alcoholic is reformed, he is responsible for relapse.[11] He knows that he will not stop if he takes one glass of alcohol, even after a period of sobriety for many years. No recovered alcoholic is able to resume social drinking. The first drink so affects his judgment and will power that he will inevitably continue drinking. For him it is either total abstinence or total collapse. In view of these facts, a recovered alcoholic should be considered, theoretically, fully responsible for his first drink. But, in practice, the alcoholics themselves tell, in all sincerity, a different story. It happens, they say, that even after staying sober for months or years, the idea of taking a drink builds up to such an extent that they take the drink automatically without realizing the consequences.

With regard to periodic drinkers, the solution of the present question is complicated by the probable relationship between dipsomania and epilepsy. If dipsomaniacs are basically epileptics, they cannot be regarded as responsible for their periodic relapses.

TREATMENT

The first step in the treatment of alcoholics is medical and consists in getting the patient over the effects of alcohol. The second step is psychological and consists in teaching him how to live without the need of alcohol.

In order to build up the patient's physical health and resistance, baths, exercise, and a special diet are often prescribed. Since the role of vitamin deficiency has been recognized, vitamin therapy is widely employed. The "conditioned reflex" treatment consists in giving the patient alcohol in association with certain drugs, such as apomorphine and emetine; the combination of alcohol and drug has an unpleasant aftereffect.[12] One of the latest drugs on sale is Antabuse (tetraethylthiuramdisulphide), a chemical compound to be taken in tablet form. A patient who takes alcohol after a dose of Antabuse suffers serious physical disturbances, such as nausea, vomiting, sweating, respiratory difficulties. Hence Antabuse acts as a deterrent. However, the drug should be used only under medical supervision, because if improperly used, it may cause illness and even death. When used upon the doctor's prescription, the drug may eliminate the necessity of the patient's institutionalization, but Antabuse by itself is no guarantee for curing the alcoholic of his drinking. In order to obtain favorable results, its use must be coupled with psychotherapy.

Because psychotherapy aims at readjusting the partially disorganized personality of the alcoholic, it is an extensive process and only certain types of persons can be expected to respond.

It is hardly necessary to state that symptomatic drinkers of the psychotic type cannot be reformed until the underlying personality disorder can be treated and cured. As for the mental defectives, the hope of any cure is, of course, out of the question; the only solution would be to segregate such people in an institution. Not much hope can be held out for the cure of a psychopathic drinker. A psychiatrist will usually accept a neurotic alcoholic for treatment, but he will seldom accept a psychopathic one, for these cases are, with a few exceptions, beyond treatment.

With regard to the remaining groups of chronic alcoholics, psychotherapy at the present time is successful in about 25 or 30 per cent of the cases. Neurotic victims with an anxiety complex respond well to psychotherapy, and it is the only method that affects them. It is interesting to note that young drinkers, under twenty years of age, are frequently more difficult to cure than older ones. Experience has shown that psychotherapy is effective only if it succeeds in changing an alcoholic into an abstainer. How is this change to be effected? Anyone—the psychiatrist, the counselor, the priest—who tries to help the alcoholic must refrain from adopting a patronizing, condescending, or superior attitude. He must be convinced that an alcoholic is a sick person, and he must blend infinite patience with tactful authority.

It is not enough to remind the alcoholic of his present degradation; he must be shown that his recovery is possible. Encouragement in this matter is of great help. The counselor or the priest must help the patient acquire an insight into his condition by showing him that the causative factors are not found in the present situation, but go back into the past, *e.g.*, into a maladjusted and unhealthy childhood or adolescence.

If the patient accepts this disclosure about the origin of his disorder, if he accepts the fact that he was an emotional failure even before he became an alcoholic, if he "surrenders," an important step has been made on the road to recovery. However, such an insight must be followed up by inducing the patient to adopt a reeducation program, which is often best achieved by group therapy in one of the existing organizations.

This lay therapy exercised by recovered alcoholics among themselves in organizations and societies like the Total Temperance League, the Salvation Army, the Sons of Matt Talbot, the Society of St. Jude, the Society of St. Dismas, and Alcoholics Anonymous, presents one of the most intriguing features in the treatment of alcoholics.[13] The A.A. especially should be singled out as the most effective organization for helping alcoholics.[14] The remarkable success of group therapy achieved by the A.A. at times puzzles even psychiatrists. This is what Harry M. Tiebout said at a meeting of the American Psychiatric Association: "After observing personally for years the interesting effects of the A.A. program upon my patients and having watched at close range numerous other examples of their work, I feel it highly imperative that we, presumably open-minded psychiatrists, view wisely and long the efforts of this group of former alcoholics who are now achieving so many remarkable recoveries in our field. At first I was amazed and chagrined when A.A. accomplished a change in a patient who was a failure under my therapy, now I am amazed and astonished when the patient fails under the A.A. program." [15]

What is the secret of the remarkable recoveries made in A.A.? In the first place, organizations such as A.A. fulfill the social demands of an individual living in a complex society, by recognizing his desire for close companionship—a companionship that society often enough refuses to give the alcoholic by ostracizing and avoiding him. Besides, A.A. is not just an organization but a fellowship and brotherhood, where the alcoholics can openly and freely discuss their problem. And it seems that they can talk to each other more easily than to an outsider, including the psychiatrist. As one ex-alcoholic put it: "Apparently God Almighty gave us a gift that is not given to non-alcoholics. He gave us the ability, each of us, to talk to one another. One alcoholic can always talk to another one, drunk or sober, either one or both of them."

It was said previously that one of the most difficult tasks of the therapist is not to adopt a superior or condescending manner toward the alcoholic. For one ex-alcoholic talking with another, no such danger exists. This frankness and free exchange of ideas contributes to reform. In addition there is present the will, or at least the desire, to reform because otherwise the patients would not join the organization. Each member is filled with compassion for his fellow member, and in order to help him stay sober, has himself to set the example. But the main source of A.A.'s success is to be found in its education program which emphatically stresses spiritual and religious values.

As was pointed out previously, the basic cause of alcoholism is a childish emotional immaturity that causes the patient to run away from the conflicts of everyday life and revert to an infantile state; instead of seeking protection from an omnipotent father or mother, he now finds escape in alcoholic intoxication. This sense of dependency, so characteristic of the alcoholic, may be used to good advantage by developing a sense of filial dependence upon the all-powerful and merciful God. Thus an unhealthy dependency is converted into a healthy one. As a matter of fact, A.A. and similar organizations emphasize the importance of religious motives in aiding the alcoholic.

Several psychiatrists, Catholics and non-Catholics alike, are also of the opinion that recovery of an alcoholic hardly is possible without the help of religion.[16] Hence, a psychologically trained priest who has an open mind for the problem of the alcoholic may often be as successful in the treatment of alcoholics as the psychiatrist. At least, the priest working with the physician may achieve considerable success. When the priest is dealing with alcoholics, it is of great importance to stress the value of basic religious motives, of our purpose in life, and of the necessity of trust in God—a trust springing from a realization of our dependence upon Him. The priest should point out that spiritual strength through confidence in God can be far more forceful than the strength of physical habits.

Every priest is capable of treating cases of slight alcoholism. He need not be a formally trained psychologist, but he should have an understanding and appreciation of personality which springs from priestly sympathy, zeal, and interest. He may try to induce an alcoholic to take the pledge, because experience shows that it works with some cases, but he should avoid insisting too strongly on pledges and vows, for the ambivalent trends of the alcoholic personality may lead the alcoholic who is unduly constrained toward abstinence to exactly the opposite, making "the last state of that man worse than the first."

Again it should be pointed out that in the severe cases the priest should work with the psychiatrist in helping the patient to understand the underlying causes of his excessive indulgence.

An example will illustrate the importance of sending the patient to a religiously orientated psychiatrist.

§ Mr. W. was thirty-two years old, a devout Catholic, and married. He had been an alcoholic for several years. His excessive drinking cost him several jobs, and finally resulted in his passing forged checks. The first psychiatrist whom he consulted advised him to have sexual relations with men, since his basic conflict, according to that psychiatrist, was of a homosexual nature. Naturally, the patient rejected such advice and objected to any kind of marital infidelity. The point is that the patient was first referred merely "to a psychiatrist." Later he was advised by a priest to see a Catholic psychiatrist, one with his own religious ideals. The advice proved to be correct, because the psychiatrist by stressing these ideals was able to treat the patient successfully.

The development of spiritual and moral values within the patient changes his negative attitude to a positive one. Such a change comprises loss of hostilities, disappearance of the perfectionistic drive, lessening of the egocentric power drive, a better response to work demands, greater capacity for objectivity, and a certain disposition to serenity.

Once an alcoholic has recovered, he is evidently no more free from temptations to relapse than any other person in any other field. He should be careful to avoid mental conflicts, emotional upsets, depressions, and overfatigue, because many an ex-alcoholic confesses that, if he does not avoid these conditions, he will automatically return to King Alcohol. And every day he must ask God for the strength to stay sober at least for that day.

The increase of alcoholism in the United States has created a serious social problem. The more the problem is studied, the more we discover that there is a great need for a wider understanding of alcoholism as a disease, and a greater need for preventive treatment. The main solution lies in prevention rather than cure. Today's mothers can help reduce the number of tomorrow's alcoholics by providing their children with a more secure environment with which to ward off the dangers of later life and by giving them religious motivations.

The present problem may eventually be solved if society awakens to the recognition that alcoholism is among the most serious of social problems and takes steps to cope with it.

NOTES AND REFERENCES

1. "Alcohol, Science and Society" (New Haven: Yale University Press, 1945), pp. 23 ff. This volume consists of 29 lectures which were given at the Yale Summer School of Alcoholic Studies and which were first printed in the *Quarterly Journal of Studies on Alcohol.* For further study on the problem of alcoholism, the following are recommended, besides those works referred to in the notes below:

   CARVER, A. E., Alcoholism from the Psychosomatic Point of View, *British Journal of Addiction,* Vol. 45 (1948), pp. 45 ff.

   HAGGARD, HOWARD, and E. M. JELLINEK, "Alcohol Explored" (New York: Doubleday & Company, Inc., 1942).

   JELLINEK, E. M., "Alcohol Problems Dissected" (New York: Federal Council of the Churches of Christ in America, 1945).

   SILLMAN, L. R., Chronic Alcoholism, *Journal of Nervous and Mental Disease,* Vol. 107 (1948), pp. 129 ff.

2. For studies on alcoholic women, see the following:

   CURRAN, FRANK J., Personality Studies in Alcoholic Women, *Journal of Nervous and Mental Disease,* Vol. 86 (1937), pp. 645–667.

   VAN ANBERG, ROBERT J., A Study of 50 Women Patients Hospitalized for Alcohol Addiction, *Diseases of the Nervous System,* Vol. 4 (1943), pp. 246–250.

   WALL, JAMES H., A Study of Alcoholism in Women, *American Journal of Psychiatry,* Vol. 93 (1937), pp. 943–955.

3. Concerning the effects of alcohol, see JELLINEK, E. M., and K. M. BOWMAN, "Alcohol Addiction and Chronic Alcoholism," Vol. I of "Effects of Alcohol on the Individual," edited by E. M. Jellinek on behalf of the Scientific Committee of the Research Council on Problems of Alcohol (New Haven: Yale University Press, 1942).

4. MAGGARD, N. W., The Physiology of Alcohol, *Yale Review,* Vol. 35 (1945), pp. 295 ff.

5. ALEXANDER, FRANZ, and T. M. FRENCH, "Studies in Psychosomatic Medicine" (New York: The Ronald Press Company, 1948), p. 23.

6. SIMMEL, E., Alcoholism and Addiction, *Psychoanalytic Quarterly,* Vol. 17 (1948), pp. 7 ff.

7. STRECKER, E. A., "Fundamentals of Psychiatry" (Philadelphia: J. B. Lippincott Company, 1947), pp. 144–154; See also STRECKER, E. A., and F. T. CHAMBERS, "Alcohol: One Man's Meat" (New York: The Macmillan Company, 1947).

8. BARBARA, D. A., The Neurotic Character Structure of the Alcoholic Personality, *Psychiatric Quarterly,* Vol. 19 (1945), pp. 503 ff. For further study on the personality structure of the alcoholic, see HARRIS, R. E., and V. M. IVES, A Study of the Personality of Alcoholics, *American Psychologist,* Vol. 2 (1947), pp. 405 ff.; LANDIS, C., "Theories of the Alcoholic Personality," in "Alcohol, Science and Society," *op. cit.*

9. KARLAN, S. C., and E. HELLER, Chronic Alcoholism: Psychiatric and Rorschach Evaluation, *Journal of Clinical Psychopathology,* Vol. 8 (1946), pp. 291 ff.
10. For a study concerning this problem, see JELLINEK, E. M., "Heredity of the Alcoholic," in "*Alcohol, Science and Society,*" *op. cit.*, pp. 109 ff.
11. See O'BRIEN, P., "Emotions and Morals" (New York: Grune and Stratton, 1950), pp. 118 ff.
12. See THIMANN, J., The Conditioned Reflex Treatment of Alcoholics, in GLUECK, B., "Current Theories of Personality Disorders," pp. 101–106.
13. See MCPECK, F. W., "The Role of Religious Bodies in the Treatment of Inebriety in the United States," in "Alcohol, Science and Society," *op. cit.;* FALLON, N. P., "The Social Recovery of Inebriates" (Washington, The Catholic University of America Press, 1948).
14. The basic work of A.A. is "Alcoholics Anonymous" (New York: Works Publishing Co., 1942). Among the large number of writers on the subject of A.A., the following may be mentioned: TIEBOUT, HARRY M., "Psychological Factors Operating in Alcoholics Anonymous," in GLUECK, *op. cit.,* pp. 154–165; *id.,* The Therapeutic Mechanism of Alcoholics Anonymous, *American Journal of Psychiatry,* January, 1944; SMITH, PERCY E., Alcoholics Anonymous, *Psychiatric Quarterly,* January, 1941.
15. The ninety-ninth annual meeting of the American Psychiatric Association, Detroit, Michigan, 1943, discussion on the paper "Basic Concepts of Alcoholics Anonymous," read by a contributor identified only as "X."
16. NIEDERMEYER, A., "Pastoral Psychiatrie" (Paderborn: Bonifacius Druckerei, 1936), p. 85.

Chapter 21

MASTURBATION, FRIGIDITY, AND IMPOTENCE

MASTURBATION

According to its probable etymological derivation, the term "masturbation" means sexual self-abuse caused by the manual manipulation of genital organs, but in this chapter the term will be used in a wider sense to designate any kind of self-stimulation of the genital organs tending toward the production of an orgasm. This self-stimulation may be produced by manual manipulation or any other form of physical excitation as well as by psychic stimulation, such as indulgence in sexual fantasies.

Masturbation is usually followed by erection of the sexual organ, *i.e.*, of the penis in the male or of the clitoris in the female. An erection, though often induced by manipulation of the organ, can follow from any number of causes such as pressure from the bladder, constipation, stimulation due to friction from the clothing, emotional disturbances which seem to have no direct connection with the genital organs, overeating, glandular disturbance, or simply as a sequel of normal sleep, *i.e.*, tumescence. It is clear, therefore, that the cause of an erection need be neither conscious nor voluntary; it may occur without the subject realizing that an erection is taking place. The statement that, whereas sexual intercourse often must be taught, masturbation needs no teacher is especially true, for an erection may easily follow from a cause in itself asexual.

Relative to the emotional life, three variations of masturbation can be distinguished, *viz.*, prostitution, homosexuality, and contraceptive intercourse. The principal difference between masturbation and prostitution is that masturbation is a solitary act. In neither masturbation nor prostitution is there love, mental compatibility, or mutual desire; both are mechanisms for the relief of physical tension. In homosexuality also a partner is used, and the same pattern is present, *viz.*, sexual stimulation or manipulation leading to an orgasm. It is true that in homosexuality some kind of mutual affection may be present, but it is a distorted caricature of love. Contraceptive intercourse has been described rather satirically by George Bernard Shaw as nothing but mutual masturbation. Whether or not this is a just description, contraceptive intercourse is regarded by some of its own proponents as both psychologically and physically unsatisfactory, if not harmful.

The Genetic Development of Masturbation. Even very young children may manipulate their genitals; as early as at the age of two months, the normal boy may have an erection, resulting from improper hygiene. Such an erection seems to be accompanied by some vague sort of autoerotic feeling, a "tingling" sensation, which is still far remote from the sexual satisfaction that follows manipulation and erection at a later age. In this sense it may be said that, although one is not conscious of ever having masturbated, still at some time, perhaps in early forgotten childhood, he has indulged in some form of self-stimulation.

When the child approaches the age of three years, self-stimulation is not an uncommon practice because his increasing interest in almost every visible organ of his body extends also to his genitals. When an erection follows manipulation it does not necessarily indicate that the child has any sex consciousness; in fact, it is extremely doubtful that a child at this early age has any specific sex awareness. It is obvious that a child who has not yet attained the use of reason, usually around the seventh year, can incur no moral guilt in an act of self-stimulation. Parents on noticing an erection in their young children sometimes become upset; but they should regard the phenomenon simply as an automatic response of the child's interest in his own body. Therefore, the parents should then educate the child in such a way as not to cause him fear or shame, because such fear and shame will only mar with a false attitude his first consciousness of sex. Rather they should discuss the matter frankly, in an unemotional and objective way suitable to the child's intellectual level, not giving him the impression of being a criminal caught in the act but persuading him to discontinue the practice. This period of his training is extremely important in the building of his character for later life.

The sensual feelings produced by manipulation of the genitals increases after the child, male or female, reaches the sixth or seventh year. Although there is as yet no question of orgasm, the feelings become more pronounced. Children of this age may become masturbation addicts through the example and seduction of older children or adults; this happens frequently when the child lives in an institution. When the child is removed from such an environment and is given sufficient instruction, these masturbation habits soon disappear. Sometimes, however, they remain despite environmental change and educational advice, especially in those children who reveal such abnormal personality traits as excessive mendacity and an aggressive, domineering disposition.

The following case is one of a normal child whose masturbatory habits were altered through a change in environment:

§ This seven-year-old boy engaged in frequent masturbation and coital attempts with his mother. The history revealed that he had had a normal development, that he had scarcely indulged in such childhood habits as thumb-sucking and infantile "masturbation," and that he had developed physically, socially, and educationally in a normal manner. Because the mother had to undergo an operation, he was sent to the paternal grandmother who suffered slightly from a dementia. The boy developed masturbatory habits during his stay with the grandmother. How he acquired the habit was never fully explained, but it was believed that his senile grandmother induced him to masturbation and coituslike behavior. It is understandable that the mother experienced a great amount of anxiety and guilt because she, knowing her mother-in-law's senility, had given the boy into her care. It did not seem necessary to give the lad psychotherapeutic treatment, but the mother was advised of the course of action to be followed. Investigations made a year and a half later showed that the boy had ceased to masturbate, had developed normally, and—as the mother said—had forgotten everything.

When the child reaches the age of puberty—roughly between thirteen and seventeen—masturbation causes orgasm, the height of sexual excitement. Experience and statistics show that most children practice masturbation at least occasionally, if not habitually, during the period of puberty. Although masturbation would seem to be less frequent among girls than among boys, yet it occurs among the former much more often than is generally believed. From the psychological standpoint, a rather sharp difference exists between extrovert and introvert personalities relative to masturbatory practices. It has often been found that the extrovert may practice masturbation without experiencing serious pangs of conscience and without creating internal conflicts, but things are different with those of a more introverted, sensitive, timorous nature. These, despite high ideals of purity, may find their ideals shattered time and again. They may experience trials so severe as to form inferiority and guilt complexes which will exercise a pernicious influence on their life for many years, for these individuals' sexual difficulties, if not solved adequately and in time, may well be the source of neurotic disturbances in later life.

The age of puberty, therefore, is the proper time for serious sex instruction. Curiosity and interest in the parts of the body, and particularly erection, is usually all that is needed for a boy to learn masturbatory practices. But it is also true that the boy's tendency toward such practices may be greatly increased through seduction and the example of other boys or adults.

For girls conditions are somewhat different; they may be induced to these practices by accidental physiological experiences. Moods of depression and frustration are notable among such factors leading to masturbation in girls. Since this is so, one can readily see the possibility of a vicious circle. Depression may drive a girl to masturbation, but at the same time she may be profoundly religious. The result will be deep remorse of conscience. But these pangs of conscience cause new feelings of depression, and depression is relieved through masturbation. So the trap is sprung, the circle closed. The masturbatory practices of girls—and the same holds for adult women—show certain features that differ from those of boys and men. The masturbatory practices of women, young and old, are characterized by extraordinary and intense passionateness. Once the woman's passion has been aroused, she may stimulate herself a great many times in succession on one and the same occasion. This frequent abuse is not necessarily a sign of abnormality, but can be explained by the woman's particular constitution, for a woman allows herself more easily to be carried away by her passion. Besides, masturbation does not afford a girl or woman the same complete satisfaction as it does a man. Another characteristic is that masturbatory habits in women are very stubborn and hard to eradicate. Despite good will and despite periods relatively free from such practices, a woman may easily relapse. This periodical recurrence of masturbation is probably due to biological factors, since it has been observed that some women give in to masturbatory practices more readily during the period of menstruation. For example, one young girl was able to overcome a periodical masturbatory habit with the exception of masturbating one day before the start of her period. Though her menstrual cycle was irregular, she always masturbated the day before beginning menstruation, for she was of the opinion that, if she did not masturbate, she could not menstruate.

Although the masturbation of pubescents is certainly not a symptom of abnormality, there are circumstances that indicate the presence of an abnormal psychic constitution. In the first place, the fantasies and dreams which precede, provoke, or accompany masturbation should be taken into consideration; if they are of a perverse nature, they may well indicate some form of abnormality. Moreover, masturbation, if practiced to an excessive degree, may point to a compulsion, similar to excessive addiction to alcohol or drugs. Such habitual, chronic masturbation should be differentiated from masturbation as a temporary relief. In the latter case masturbation is used as a temporary measure for the relief of sexual tension, and also as a means for overcoming insomnia or conditions of nervousness produced by work, strain, and fatigue. Symptomatically, temporary masturbation is less serious than chronic masturbation, but it is clear that the former easily leads to the latter because sexual tension, once released, builds up again and again demands release. In this way, masturbation is very similar in nature to alcoholism. Both are but temporary measures of escape from some kind of tension, but when used as a means of release from such tension they tend to create a conditioned reflex; *i.e.*, should tension arise again, there will seem to be but one means of release. In other words, temporary masturbation easily leads to the formation of a compulsive habit.

After the turmoil of puberty has subsided and the psychosexual development gradually settles upon the opposite sex, adolescents who have not learned to control themselves may still continue their masturbatory practices. Continued chronic masturbation at this age may result from a habit contracted during puberty; but it may also be the manifestation of a strongly developed sexual hyperesthesia. In both cases, there is question not of abnormal behavior but of unbridled passion. In certain cases, however, postpuberal chronic masturbation may indicate a psychosexual disturbance; it may be a symptom of a narcissistic, homoerotic disposition, of infantile fixation, of abnormal fear of the opposite sex, and of morbid depression. In order to judge the abnormal nature of the individual's disposition, one must consider, in the adolescent as in the pubescent, the compulsive character of his practices and the content of the fantasies and dreams accompanying or inducing the act. Other evidence of the abnormality of such an individual can be found after marriage: those who have been enslaved to masturbation often show impotence or frigidity in marriage. Masturbation is a narcissistic condition in which the object of satisfaction is exclusively the person's own body. Chronic masturbation may well arrest the normal sexual development, and when a person remains fixated at that stage, the result may be impotence.

Relative to the psychological aspects of masturbation as practiced by married adults, the distinction between temporary and habitual types should be repeated. Married people often resort to temporary masturbation in situations such as exist in war, when men are separated from their wives, or in institutions where many of only one sex are living together. On the other hand, there are also married adults who continue habitual masturbation despite every opportunity for marital intercourse. In this case, masturbation is a serious symptom, usually indicative of deep emotional problems, especially when the one who practices it seems to derive more satisfaction from masturbation than from marital intercourse. Although it is often thought that masturbation in married adults is nothing more than a habit carried over from adolescence, the authors maintain that such a practice is a sign of psychoneurotic disturbance and for that reason should usually be treated by a psychiatrist.

The Effects of Masturbation. Not so long ago, the notion that masturbation damaged physical health prevailed; it was supposed to weaken the nervous system and to cause tabes dorsalis and even tuberculosis. This same notion is still used occasionally in the pulpit or in the confessional as a kind of deterrent. However, scientific medical investigation seems to indicate that masturbation in itself will not produce physical illness.

Nevertheless, masturbatory practices may well induce emotional disturbances in certain personalities. Of course, the physical act of masturbation does not cause mental disorders, but masturbation has also a psychological context in that it takes place in a specific personality contrary to the attitudes and convictions of that personality. Given a certain personality, particularly the more introvert or conscientious type, the practice may have serious psychic repercussions. Since, considered from the psychosexual standpoint, masturbation is an inadequate form of sexual satisfaction, it may leave feelings of dissatisfaction, insufficiency, inferiority, and lack of self-confidence. Even though it may produce a somatic relief of tension, psychic satisfaction is lacking; after all, masturbation is, morally speaking, a sin against nature. It may also cause self-reproach, intrapsychic conflicts, and feelings of guilt, conscious or unconscious, which in turn may produce neurotic anxiety. The peculiar feature of these neurotic conditions is that they appear not infrequently when the individual, after indulging for a longer or shorter period, calls a halt to his unnatural practice. In interpreting this fact, some psychiatrists claim that the libido calls for satisfaction, but others see in it the result of the function of conscience and a need for self-punishment.

It would be straining the point to say that all individuals in whom masturbatory activities produce psychic conflicts because of their particular personality structure are abnormal. They may be introspective, introvert, idealistic, shy, or even timorous, but that is not sufficient to classify them all as abnormal. Yet it is true that some forms of masturbation are often a symptom of latent neurotic disorders. In such cases, masturbation, rather than being a cause, is a result of a psychic disturbance and a warning that a psychotic episode may possibly be in the offing. This is especially true of habitual chronic masturbation that continues during adult age; this type of practice is frequently found in psychopathic personalities.

Moral Responsibility and Treatment. Voluntary masturbation is a mortal sin for everyone possessing a normal, healthy mind and a free will. This is the general principle of moral theology. But in deciding the moral responsibility of an individual case, one must take into account the personality of the individual, the causes of the masturbatory practice, and the efforts that the individual makes to get rid of his practice. Each case deserves individual consideration, *i.e.,* one must consider the person's age, his life history, his individual constitution, and his environmental background. When a person's psychic balance or psychosexual development is disturbed, his moral responsibility is reduced. However, even abnormal personalities must evince an honest desire to regain self-possession and to control such inclinations, particularly by avoiding dangerous occasions.

Are masturbatory practices during the age of puberty and adolescence to be considered abnormal? Decidedly not, at least in the majority of cases. However, the masturbation practices of adolescents reflect their general maladjustment in their new form of life. The intellectual development during puberty does not always keep step with the physical and emotional changes that take place in that period. To be sure, the adolescent's reasoning powers are fairly well developed, but the moral principles that the adolescent fully understands and accepts theoretically are sometimes obscured by the turmoil of strong passion. This state of affairs makes for extenuating circumstances. It is perhaps interesting to note that there are psychiatrists who are less lenient in the matter of responsibility than some confessors, precisely because they realize that too much leniency weakens the patient's will to fight.

How can we *cure* masturbation? A certain group of psychiatrists will counter this question by claiming that one should do little or nothing to cure this practice in an individual but rather advise him to give free rein to his sexual passions, supposedly to avert neurotic disturbances. Whether the number of such psychiatrists is increasing or decreasing is of no importance, for it is not the number of advisers but the principle underlying the advice that counts, and the principle is false. This type of counsel, far from preventing or curing neurotic conditions, often causes or aggravates them. Besides, it happens not infrequently that those afflicted with this habit are themselves only too anxious to get rid of it.

Granted, therefore, that one should help to cure a masturbator, what can one do? The answer is somewhat disappointing, for the simple reason that there is no single remedy or panacea applicable to all masturbators. In theory, one should distinguish between the normal individuals who masturbate temporarily or habitually, and those whose masturbation is the result of an abnormal disposition. In practice, of course, the demarcation line between the two categories is not always easy to draw; in doubtful cases the decision should be made by a reliable psychiatrist.

With regard to the normal group, the treatment consists in healthy sex education and sound counseling. With young children the treatment will consist in prophylactic measures. There is no need for calling the physician or the priest, since the parents are the important therapists. The parents must increase the love and affection they are giving to the child, but make sure that they do not give the child morbid attitudes before there is any possibility of his realizing that he is doing wrong. Restrictive and punitive measures should not be used; warnings and threats that disease will arise, that the genital organs will be destroyed or cut off, should be completely avoided, as these form the basis for future morbidity.

With adolescent masturbators, a confessor or religious counselor is the first line of defense. Here, the axiom that "prevention is better than cure" is all-important. If the adolescent anticipates a danger of habit formation, he may have sense enough to consult an older person about it either on his own accord or on the persuasion of his parents. The priest or religious counselor will realize that it is the adolescent personality as a whole that must be considered. The adolescent does have special problems and special difficulties. While the authors cannot recommend a specific cure for masturbation in adolescence, they do highly recommend a common-sense program of life including sufficient exercise and sleep, fresh air, healthy companionship with members of both sexes, and absorbing occupations. At the same time, they also recommend that the parents of adolescents, and those who are in charge of them at school or otherwise, should try to give them all the sympathy and understanding possible. It is unnecessary to point out that our modern adolescents live in an atmosphere of liberality. Now, the sophisticated adolescent who indulges in "heavy necking or petting" can almost certainly be expected to be sexually tense a great part of the time, and may thus easily form the habit of masturbation. While the authors are not recommending an oppressive, restrictive regimen for youth, they do recommend a healthy, virile discipline, and training of the will. Self-discipline is the only means to prevent masturbatory habits. If the youth is taught self-discipline, if he is taught that he *must* restrain himself and that he *can* restrain himself, and if he seriously attempts to discipline himself in all the phases of his life, in food and drink as well as in sex, he will have the tools within himself whereby he can control the tendency toward masturbation.

Presupposing that the youngster shows an honest wish to get over his trouble, the counselor should advise him to fight against his practice with indirect methods, *i.e.*, the adolescent should learn to divert his attention from things sexual. Introverts, especially, are too much concerned with their own fantasies and inclinations. The religious counselor should not minimize the sinfulness of their acts, but should inspire in them such courage and confidence that they will gradually overcome their habit. In order to strengthen their courage, it will be a good thing to tell them that the current tales about the physical effects of masturbation hinge on ignorance. Such advice will remove fears which often cause depression. In view of the penitent's psychic condition, lectures on punishment and God's avenging hand, although theoretically justified, will sometimes have deleterious effects. The priest should not omit to recommend supernatural means, like prayer and the sacraments, because these means will secure the individual the divine grace he needs to overcome his habit; they have also a therapeutic value, in as far as a person who sincerely prays for his conversion will automatically strengthen his will to do his share toward effecting it. But when his habit is due to an abnormal disposition, supernatural means alone fall short of the mark; one would be asking for a miracle, if one neglected to use suitable therapeutic remedies.

Whenever there is a serious suspicion that masturbation is caused by an abnormal disposition, the patient should consult a psychiatrist, who then will try to discover the root of the trouble. He may find that the habit is due to compulsion, anxiety, or a psychotic condition. An illustrative case of each of these conditions is presented here.

§ One twenty-eight-year-old man, who started masturbating at the age of nine years, was introduced to the practice by his own sister, who was thirteen at the time. He explained that one day when everyone else was absent his sister called him into her room and showed him her breasts. The sister told him to watch what she did when she was playing with her breasts and her nipples and later with her vagina. Some time later, the girl showed him how to get "pleasure." This relationship endured for half a year until the sister repented and had a serious talk with the boy in which she denounced their behavior as sinful. But the boy was never able to overcome the habit he had contracted, despite pastoral counseling and psychiatric help. He was able to abstain from the practice of masturbation only for relatively short periods of one or two weeks. When last seen he was a pleasant, friendly young man, liked by girls but extremely shy. He preferred girls who behaved like boys, and shrank from any amorous inclinations. This seemed to be a case of compulsion so deeply rooted as to be incurable.

§ A twenty-two-year-old girl was extremely shy in the presence of men. Previously she had been troubled at certain sensations in her vagina. An old-fashioned doctor gave her a vaginal massage, after which she felt "exhausted, but better." In time she developed a compulsive urge to clean her vagina; every night she spent two full hours on that performance, using two cakes of soap. The girl did not consider this masturbation. But analysis disclosed that she suffered from a deep-lying fear of committing sins against sex, experiencing at the same time strong sexual desires. She resorted to the practice of cleaning her vagina as a compromise that would satisfy her desires without arousing her fear of committing sin. This case is a classic example of a severe psychoneurosis of anxiety combined with hypochondriac sex symptoms.

§ A senior high school girl of nineteen years complained of being unable to do her regular work. She was tense, anxious, and masturbated several times daily. During her masturbatory actions she had illusions that her "boy friend" was watching her. She knew that these thoughts were nonsense, but they continued to plague her. In the first half of her senior year, she found she was able to surmount the tension created by a test by masturbating immediately before the test. This practice helped her to relax, she said. However, when she was last seen, the desired release was achieved only by repeating the performance several times during a test. This was evidently an incipient psychotic condition.

During the course of psychiatric treatment, there may come a time when the drafting of a reeducation program necessitates collaboration with a priest on the solution of pertinent moral problems.

Is marriage desirable as a cure for masturbation? If no psychoneurotic symptoms are present, masturbatory practices may be only a habit acquired in adolescence. Should such be the case, then marriage, which will afford the masturbator a legitimate opportunity for sexual activity, may cure the habit. But marriage is not to be recommended when masturbation is due to a psychoneurotic disposition, for as has been seen, chronic masturbation in an adult is only too often a symptom of serious emotional disturbances. In such cases marriage would be harmful rather than helpful, because such persons often suffer from psychic impotence and, even though not impotent, usually remain victims of their perverse or narcissistic attitudes. In both instances they continue their masturbatory practices despite their marriage. Consequently, confessors should be cautious in advising marriage as a cure for masturbation, and in doubtful cases a priest should seek advice from a reputable psychiatrist.

§ Mrs. D. was brought up in a rigid home situation. During her college years, she lived at home with her mother, as her father had died when she was very young. A likable, socially adjusted girl, she had many dates. She strenuously objected to any petting and reported it to a personal pastoral adviser, yet she masturbated—at first infrequently, but indulging more and more in the practice, until at twenty-eight she was confirmed in the habit. Her mother, finding her moody and depressed, consulted her son, a priest, who suggested that she should marry. For two years she went with a young man of a steady income. On the advice of her brother and contrary to her mother's objections, she married. However, the objections of her mother, who went to live with the married couple, kept preying on her mind to such an extent that after every intercourse she felt guilty and expected maternal reproach. Finally she discontinued marital relations, preferring masturbation to the marital act, for she did not fear that her mother would object to this practice.

§ Another woman, whose case presented compulsive-obsessive features, masturbated regularly before her marriage. After she married, sexual intercourse never gave her full satisfaction. She complained that her husband was stupid, and inexperienced in sexual matters. Finding that her masturbatory practices satisfied her needs better than marital intercourse, she soon opposed sexual relations altogether and returned to her old habit.

§ Mrs. Y. applied to the psychiatrist for treatment of her depression, stating that she felt hostile toward everyone, including God and her husband. She explained that she had been married seventeen years and had a good husband who took excellent care of her, but that her marital relations were far from satisfactory to her. She related that her husband had intercourse with her on their wedding night and only once more in all seventeen years of their marriage. Further investigation disclosed that her husband had been a habitual masturbator prior to their marriage. He had married in the hope that regular intercourse would make him cease his masturbatory practice. But he soon found that he preferred masturbation to marital relations and so refused intercourse.

This last case shows that marital relations not only were not a cure for the husband, but also brought grief and severe depression to the wife.[1]

FRIGIDITY AND IMPOTENCE

Such sex disturbances in married life as frigidity in women and impotence in men are practically all emotional in origin. Physical abnormalities probably do not cause more than one-tenth of 1 per cent of these disorders.

By frigidity is understood the inability of an adult woman to achieve sexual satisfaction by experiencing an orgasm. It is estimated that among women more than 50 per cent never achieve an orgasm in sexual relations; others achieve it only at times or at intervals of years; besides, some women are only able to attain sexual satisfaction when on vacation or outside the usual home environment.

Impotence is the inability of a man to experience an erection in the normal performance of the sex act. With some men, erection may occur but only for a short time, too short to complete the action. To this group belongs the man who has premature ejaculations—ejaculations that take place before the sex act has really started. In one case, a man, although married for eighteen years, had had sexual intercourse with his wife only once after marriage; after that, he had never succeeded again. In another case, a married couple were able to have sexual relations no oftener than once a year.

Frigidity and impotence are symptoms of a basic psychoneurotic make-up; the causes of these disturbances are many. One is lack of sex education, abetted by the unreality and untruths with which many persons surround the whole field of sex. If children have been taught to regard legitimate sexual relations as a God-given means of enjoyment between two sexes participating in the propagation of the race, frigidity or impotence is not likely to develop in later life. But if children are punished for the natural sex curiosity and are kept ignorant of all matters pertinent to sex, the inhibitions thus created may make it difficult or even impossible for them to rid themselves of the feeling that sex is wrong and detestable. After they are married and attempt to indulge in legitimate sexual pleasure, they may fear they are doing wrong because of such an unconscious or unformulated feeling of guilt or shame induced by their parents' attitude toward sex.

Improper sex instruction may avenge itself in later life in another way. When the boy who indulges in masturbation is told by his parents or other people that this habit will influence his later sex life and perhaps render him impotent, this false advice may, indeed, prevent him from enjoying normal marital relations. The mother in particular may cause serious damage by repeatedly telling the boy that sex is a "dirty" business. In marital life, that same boy may be unable to have an erection because during the marital act he recalls, consciously or unconsciously, his mother's admonitions. It is known that some men have regained their potency upon the serious illness or death of the mother. Impotence can also develop in the man as the result of boyhood overdependency upon his mother. If such a boy marries a woman who has adopted a motherly attitude, he may unconsciously substitute, because of these motherly qualities, his wife for his mother, and develop the same impotence toward his wife as he would consciously maintain toward his mother. For the most part, the same could be said of the "spoiled son" who, when he marries, seeks in his wife the same type of glorified servant he always had found in his overprotective mother.

The therapy of such cases of impotence consists in reeducation. It should be impressed upon the husband that his wife is a personality in her own right, working with him on an equal basis and bearing responsibilities in the house that are equal to those of his work and earning power in the support of his family. Many a man fully realizes this fact only when he becomes a widower and must hire a housekeeper to care for his children and himself.

A too rigorous education, even apart from sex matters, can create unconscious hostility toward the opposite sex. For example, a boy treated harshly in his youth by an overly strict mother, foster mother, aunt, or teacher unconsciously relates cruelty, harshness, and injustice with women and acts accordingly; a daughter brought up by an unjust and rigid father acts in the same manner.

Another cause of frigidity and impotence is too frequent petting before marriage. When for years the boy or girl has been accustomed to receiving high satisfaction from tactile relationships without intercourse, sex feelings become so perverted that normal sex relations become impossible and undesired.

These are some of the causes of impotence and frigidity that are found in the youth and the premarital life of individuals. Other sources of trouble are found in marital life itself, and these sources are often nourished by the concepts of our modern society and culture about sex, marriage, and the family.

Women very often have a fear of being injured or lacerated in some way by the sex act. Consciously or unconsciously, they fear pregnancy, thinking that pregnancy may age them prematurely or ruin their good figures. In our modern era of the "emancipation of women," it often happens that the woman rejects the male sex as a whole with its seemingly preferred status of life, and projects her jealousy and hostility on the person of the one male she knows best, her husband.

Temporary frigidity or impotence may arise at such times of great sorrow as the death of a beloved member of the family, during times of unusual economic stress, or when the married couple must depart from their usual well-ordered regime and must, for instance, live with relatives.

Every inhibition in married life causes disturbances of some sort in marital relations. At present people seem to be more egocentric and more self-centered than ever before and do not want to bear the burden of a large family. The parents who might have had from six to ten children a generation ago believe today that they should not produce more than two or three. Although there may perhaps be reason sufficient to warrant the exercise of natural birth control (the rhythm method), this practice cannot be justified merely on the basis of satisfying the parents' desire to take care of only one, two, or three children. Frigidity and impotence may supervene when a person fears that his practice of birth control may fail, or when there is a fear of pregnancy with all its burdens.

A very important factor that should not be forgotten here is the wedding day, a day on which frigidity and impotence may begin. For everyone this day is one of tension, excitement, and unrest. Unfortunately, the importance of this day, combined with the turmoil of mixed feelings, is too often surrounded by excesses in alcoholic indulgence. This abnormal excitement may do permanent harm to the sex relations that are legalized on this day. A drunken bridegroom or a drunken bride on the wedding day may be disgusting to the other partner, so disgusting as to establish at the beginning of the marriage an attitude that may never be eradicated. For many couples it should be a rule that this day and the following days should be used to rid themselves of the tension, excitement, and apprehensions of the wedding day. In that way they may avoid permanent trouble in their marital life. Actually, it is one of the purposes of the honeymoon to achieve a satisfactory initiation into married life in as relaxed a manner as is possible.

Very often, frigidity and impotence can be remedied only with the help of a physician or psychiatrist, and because of the moral problems involved the collaboration of a priest may be a definite asset. In the great majority of cases psychotherapy is indicated. Sometimes it is not very easy to make people understand that sexual adjustment is adjustment of the emotional life. Fears and false beliefs must be dispelled, and the basic meaning of sexual relations must be clarified and explained. If necessary, the question of natural birth control should be discussed between husband and wife, and evaluated in a relaxed, informal, and objective manner. The couple should be made to understand that married life has as its natural destiny the procreation of children; and women should realize that being a housewife and a mother is a full-time job much more important than a career in business.

The counseling of the maritally maladjusted calls for understanding and patience. Blaming either partner for an unsatisfactory sex situation should be avoided, for sexual incompatibility indicates that both partners are guilty of some misunderstanding. There is no question that, in truly peaceful and mutual love, sexual relations will attain the summit in efficiency and pleasure. Physical and psychological compatibility, mutual consideration and understanding, gentleness and patience are all aspects of that oneness and harmony of the ideal married life for which men and women should strive. Where one spouse is failing in his or her contribution, the other has to suffer; where there is continual quarreling, misunderstanding, and mistrust, the most normal and adaptable sex partners fail to achieve true marital relations.

Here again it must be emphasized that marriage is not a cure for psychoneurotic behavior. Alcoholism, compulsions, and phobias will not improve in marriage; on the contrary, the added burden of responsibility will increase them. Psychoneurotic personalities, the unstable and indecisive, often break down in marriage, for even such normal events as pregnancy increase tension, insecurity, depression, and aggression. Too well known are the many "postpartum psychoses." In mixed marriages, the problems involved in the religious education of the children usually cause disturbance and turmoil.

The marriage relationship embraces not only physical compatibility and satisfaction, but also psychological and intellectual compatibility, social understanding, and mutual emotional satisfaction. It would be foolish for one spouse to seek his own satisfaction, neglecting his partner, and still expect a happy marriage. It is impossible to lay down definite rules as to the time and frequency of the marital act, since this depends upon individual personalities with individual needs and differences. However, there should occasionally be a thoughtful investigation of the feelings of the partner, so that the maximum of enjoyment and satisfaction in sexual life take place for *both.* As a rule, it may be said that those who seek primarily to satisfy their partner will be richly rewarded and experience a high degree of satisfaction in married life. Preparation for the marital act should not be postponed until just before retiring but should be present in the thoughtful consideration and affection shown throughout the day.

The authors wish to emphasize that legitimate sexual relation in marriage is a perfectly natural, God-given function, with no stigma attached to it. We who live in the middle of the twentieth century, are still inclined—unconsciously, perhaps—to place certain taboos on sex habits; but sex can be spoken of in the right circles, under the right circumstances, freely and without shame. Marriage is a vocation, just as is the religious life. Grace comes from God to persons in the married state, just as it does to those in the religious state. Both have the right to perfect satisfaction and contentment, and both should be helped to achieve the maximum benefit from their respective vocations.[2]

NOTES AND REFERENCES

1. Practically all works of general psychiatry, psychotherapy, sex education, sexual adjustment, and sexual behavior contain sections treating of masturbation. The Catholic reader, however, is advised that the opinions expressed in most of these works is unacceptable from the standpoint of Catholic ethics.
2. For further information on frigidity and impotence the reader is referred to the following publications: HAMBLEN, E. C., "Facts for Childless Couples" (Springfield, Illinois: Charles C Thomas, Publisher, 1950); HITSCHMANN, E., and E. BERGLER, "Frigidity in Women" (New York: Nervous and Mental Disease Monographs, 1936); HOTCHKISS, R. S., "Etiology and Diagnosis in the Treatment of Infertility in Men" (Springfield, Illinois: Charles C Thomas, Publisher, 1950); PORTNOY, L., and J. SALTMAN, "Fertility in Marriage" (New York: Farrar, Straus & Young, 1950).

Chapter 22

HOMOSEXUALITY

Homosexuality has been known all through history: the Bible mentions it, and in some nations of antiquity homosexuality was so rampant that it may be regarded as one of the first steps in their degeneration and fall.

An important distinction must be made between pseudo homosexuality and true, or genuine, homosexuality. Pseudo homosexuals are individuals who in normal conditions would be heterosexual, but who turn to persons of the same sex as a means of satisfying sexual tension produced by the stress of particular circumstances. Instances of this type occur among soldiers, sailors, prisoners, and inmates of some institutions who are unable to find a partner of the opposite sex. It was this variety of homosexuality at which Napoleon hinted during his campaign in Egypt: *mes hommes se suffisent*. And a number of the male prostitutes who practice homosexuality only out of pursuit of gain belong to the same category. The pseudo homosexual feels no psychic attraction to members of the same sex, and his homosexual activities are only a substitute for heterosexual life.

With the genuine homosexual, however, the attraction toward members of the same sex is of a psychic nature, in as far as they arouse in him more or less permanent erotic, affective feelings. Although the term "inversion" is often applied to both types of homosexuality, it is particularly apt to designate the genuine type, because in this case the psychic and physical roles are inverted, inasmuch as the psychosexual make-up of the genuine homosexual is in contradiction to the physical sexual body build. Some writers restrict the term "genuine" to those homosexuals who are supposed to be biologically determined, but since—as will presently be seen—the question whether there is inborn homosexuality is not completely solved to everyone's satisfaction, the term will be used here for all those who are "genuinely" attracted to the same sex, leaving it undecided whether such attraction is inborn or acquired.

Both men and women may be homosexuals. The active homosexual, either man or woman, plays the "male" part in the relationship with a member of the same sex, while the passive partner plays the "female" role. A third variety, the mixed homosexual, plays both roles, now one and now the other.

With regard to sexual appeal, some homosexuals feel attracted to adults; others, to adolescents; still others, to children below the age of twelve; and finally, there are some who prefer their homosexual relations with old people. Not all perform the sexual act (coitus) with their partner, but some find sexual satisfaction in exhibitionism, transvestism, voyeurism, mutual masturbation, fetishism, and other perversions. Although the homosexual proper is exclusively, or almost exclusively, attracted toward members of the same sex, some belong to the so-called bisexual type whose affections are drawn to both men and women. They are sometimes referred to as psychic hermaphrodites.

Magnus Hirschfeld estimated the number of homosexuals in Germany who are exclusively interested in members of the same sex at about 1.5 per cent of the total population. Taking into consideration those who are predominantly attracted by the same sex, the percentage rises to 2.3. Others give different figures, and several writers hold that none of the statistical data is reliable. In the United States, Kinsey estimates that 6.3 per cent of the total number of orgasms are derived from homosexual reactions.

When one becomes acquainted with a male homosexual, one notices a certain formality and reserve together with a somewhat labored refinement; with the development of more intimate acquaintance, the homosexual usually becomes ambiguous, makes suggestive remarks, and eventually reveals a fondness for obscene expressions and salacious stories.

Homosexuals seem to have a compulsive need for comradeship and friendship, not in the broad sense of needing a group of friends, but in the more restricted sense of needing a friend. It has been repeatedly observed that most homosexuals are highly sexed, with diffuse bodily distribution of sexual sensitivity; the breasts in particular are in many cases the more sensitive part.

Certain psychic characteristics are almost regularly present. Homosexuals are usually introverts, shy personalities, people who seem to be akin to the psychotics of the schizophrenic type. True, various personality types are found among them, but there is considerable evidence to show that a special relationship exists between schizoid or autistic personality and homosexuality. Homosexuals, as a rule, are unhappy and disturbed individuals characterized by basic anxiety abetted by loneliness, fears, and indecisiveness.

The disturbance is often due to repression, a factor that, under the influence of social conventions, is common enough with heterosexuals, but that is undoubtedly much more common and more damaging with homosexuals. In severe cases, psychotic disorders may develop, for the most part, in the form of paranoid states in which the delusional or hallucinatory trend is of a homosexual nature. On the other hand, the delusion of being homosexual is often the first symptom of a psychotic breakdown.

Probably as many degrees of intelligence are found among homosexuals as among heterosexuals, but one gains the impression that above-average intelligence is more common among them than average or below. It seems, also, that they have contributed more than their share to literature and the arts, owing possibly to their finding themselves more generally forced to find an outlet for psychosexual energies through channels of sublimation.

The choice of occupation may be determined by homosexuality. One factor affecting such choice is a preference of male homosexuals for feminine artistic activity. Thus, one finds them engaged in dressmaking, millinery, beauty-parlor work, and embroidery; others work at window trimming, drapery, pictures, and in art shops. Another factor is their desire for the opportunity of association with males, or for an environment affording a measure of freedom from conventional restraints. Thus, others are to be found among painters, sculptors, musicians, and actors; others, again, are in the army or navy, in the police force and among prison guards, among male nurses, masseurs, and public bath attendants. This is not to say, of course, that all men in the above professions and occupations, or even a large part of them, are homosexuals, but only that some homosexuals sometimes enter those occupations for the reasons listed above.

ETIOLOGY OF HOMOSEXUALITY

The problem concerning the causes of genuine homosexuality is of profound importance, for its solution will largely determine the nature of therapy that can be applied. It therefore deserves to be discussed in some detail. Although there are few, if any, writers who hold that all genuine homosexuality is biologically determined, a number of them believe that, in addition to an acquired form of homosexuality, there should also be recognized an inborn organically determined type. Among those expressing this view are Karl H. Ulrichs, R. von Krafft-Ebing, Magnus Hirschfeld, Iwan Bloch, Thomas Lang, and Arthur Weil. The biological theory holds that some homosexuality is organogenic, *i.e.*, that some homosexuals constitute a biological intersex variety of the human race. The upholders of this theory, when calling the homosexuals sex intergrades (Hirschfeld's

Zwischenstufen), mean by this term that male homosexuals—to limit ourselves to them—are, biologically speaking, women in disguise. Normal men are of the XY biological type, because they have an X chromosome from the mother and a Y chromosome from the father; women have an X chromosome from the mother and an X chromosome from the father, so that they belong to the XX type. Now homosexual men are, according to this theory, supposed to belong to the same XX type, because they are supposed biologically to be women camouflaged in the external disguise of men. Male homosexuals usually have well-developed male sex organs; people with imperfect development of the sex organs are rare exceptions and are by no means always homosexual. But despite the disguise of clearly developed sex organs, the individual's inclinations are toward the same sex. Because of their concept of organogenic homosexuality, many of the writers named above find in it not a pathological abnormality but a biological variation.

Many other writers, hesitant in accepting the evidence that is offered to show the existence of inborn homosexuality, consider it as a psychogenic rather than an organogenic disorder. This is the theory of analytical psychiatrists and of many other writers, including Freud, Stekel, Adler, Binet, Ferenczi, J. Sadger, A. Moll, A. A. Brill, K. Menninger, Thomas V. Moore, E. Carp, and E. Allen.

These writers hold that homosexuality is due exclusively or predominantly to early life experiences. Inasmuch as environment and upbringing may teach a child homosexual practices or make it averse to the opposite sex, they believe that homosexuality is psychogenic, at least to a great extent. Some of these writers, and particularly the psychoanalysts, admit a certain genetic predisposition to homosexuality, not only in homosexuals but also in heterosexuals. In their opinion, there is a latent heterosexual component in every homosexual and a homosexual component in every heterosexual individual; in other words, a homosexual disposition is normal for everybody. This concept of homosexuality is in line with the Freudian trend of thought, which assumes that all individuals are born bisexual. Hence, bisexuality is the normal constitutional condition of the child; but with the appearance of puberty either disposition may prevail, since environmental influences cause the child to repress either its homosexual or its heterosexual disposition. Homosexuality, therefore, develops under the influence of environmental factors, regardless of its constitutional disposition. Non-Freudian authors question the truth of this bisexual theory and are not sure whether it is based on clinical experience or the conclusion of a preconceived trend of thought, but they agree that homosexuality is at least mainly due to experiences that occur during the individual's life from early childhood on.

Although a thorough discussion of the pathogenesis of homosexuality would take this discussion too far afield, a brief survey of the pros and cons of both the organic and psychological theories seems necessary to clarify certain points.[1]

Some advocates of the constitutional character of genuine homosexuality stress the fact that the earliest sexual experiences that appear in the life of true homosexuals are of a homosexual nature. They conclude from this fact that the patient's condition is biologically determined. The fact itself is not well substantiated, since it rests on the testimony of homosexuals themselves, who may feel inclined to give a justification of their life or to convince the psychiatrists of the uselessness of any therapy. However, leaving aside this observation, the main objection is that the argument is fallacious, as Thomas V. Moore rightly points out: "One might perhaps say: If a patient's homosexuality rests on organic factors of development, his earliest sexual experience will be homo- rather than heterosexual. But one cannot invert the statement and conclude: This man's earliest experience was homosexual; therefore his homosexuality is organically determined." [2]

The problem of the pathogenesis of homosexuality has also been approached from the genetic standpoint. If it can be proved that the disorder is hereditary, there must be an organic basis for it. Now Hirschfeld and others observed that homosexuality sometimes is found in more than one member of the same family or even in father and son. And more recent studies made on pairs of identical twins, one of whom was homosexual, show that in a large percentage of cases the other twin was also. But the difficulty of such studies is the perennially recurring question whether the condition being examined is due to hereditary transmission or to the fact that identical twins are usually brought up in an identical or similar environment.

Other writers find proof of the biological theory in the difference between the anthropological measurements of the body build of homosexuals and heterosexuals.[3] The measurements show indeed that there are anatomical differences of the width of the hips, the length of legs, the development of arm muscles, distribution of hair and of fat, etc., between a normal and a homosexual group. According to other writers, however, these differences are too slight to substantiate the theory that homosexuality is an intersex state between man and woman, because the mean of measurements for the male homosexual lies much closer to the male norm than to the female norm. The mean refers, of course, to a group. With regard to individuals, the anatomical differences just mentioned are by no means a sure sign in detecting homosexuals, because these characteristics may not be found in individual homosexuals, while, on the other hand, they may be seen in heterosexuals.

There are, to be sure, other characteristics that may serve to indicate that an individual is homosexual, such as affected gestures, gait, posture, pronunciation and choice of words, style of dress, certain feminine "airs" in males, etc. The overt male homosexual often shows evidence of thoughtful discrimination, of careful choosing and harmonizing of colors, and considerable individuality, but he seldom, if ever, shows any unpleasant conspicuous eccentricity. Similar care is bestowed upon such things as the style of haircut, manicure, and the decoration of his living quarters. However, such characteristics are not necessarily due to a biological structure, for they may be acquired by imitation.

The hormonal theory of homosexuality presents another piece of evidence for the biological, innate character of the disorder. After it had been found that all people carry in their blood both androgen, the male hormone, and estrogen, the female hormone, investigators have examined these hormone values by measuring the ratio of androgen and estrogen in the urinary output of both normal and homosexual people. They found that male homosexuals as a group, have less androgen and more estrogen than normal men, as a group; in other words, the androgen-estrogen ratio is lowered. They therefore concluded that homosexual tendencies are due to the relative preponderance of the hormones of the opposite sex.[4]

It cannot be denied that these findings form a rather significant contribution to support the innate biological theory of homosexuality, but more data seem to be needed to make the evidence conclusive. For one thing, the findings concern homosexuals as a group, but do not hold for homosexuals taken individually, for it has been found that a low androgen-estrogen ratio can coexist with heterosexuality. If it is true that homosexuality is determined by the relative predominance of the hormones of the opposite sex, it might be expected that the homosexual would be cured of his disorder by the transplantation of the gonads of a normal individual into his tissues or by the administration of endocrine extract. Now, none of these biochemical treatments seem to score lasting success, as will be seen in the section on therapy.

After the evidence in favor of the biological explanation of homosexuality is reviewed, it may be concluded (*a*) that there is not sufficient reason to admit that homosexuals form an intersex group, and (*b*) that the evidence for the biochemical nature of the disorder has thus far not been entirely conclusive.

As a conclusion from a case study carried out on a hundred homosexuals in the medical center for prisoners at Springfield, Missouri, Roy A. Darke states, "The statistical analysis of findings gives little supportive evidence in favor of the genetic determination of homosexuality." [5]

How do the advocates of the environmental, psychological theory of homosexuality explain the origin of the disorder? The Freudians, as we saw, hold that man is genetically bisexual and that the child learns to repress either the homosexual or the heterosexual component in his personality. Why do some children repress the latter? Freud and the psychoanalysts lay much stress on the castration complex. When a male child is caught playing with his male organ, the angry parents sometimes scold him and even threaten him with cutting off the organ if he does not stop. The fear of mutilation may cause in the child a sense of overevaluation of the genital organ and, in turn, a kind of contempt for girls because they lack a penis. This frame of mind may eventually develop into an aversion for women (Stekel's *Angst vor dem Weibe*).

This attempt to explain homosexuality has not met with general approval outside the psychoanalytical school. The castration complex may play a role in rare instances, but it is too exceptional to be accepted as a general explanation. Besides, it would hold true only in the case of male homosexuality.

Another factor presented by Freud is the fixation on the mother. Some children may become so fixated on the mother that there is little room in their heart for other women. This view in which the overprotecting mother is to be blamed for fostering in the child an attitude of immaturity has been given prominence by many writers. For instance, Edward Strecker, in explaining the causes of homosexuality, states: "There are many instances in which it seems reasonable to impute an immaturity determined by Mom and her wiles." In a later paragraph he says: "Since it is universal that every male child, at least at first, is in love with his mother, it naturally follows that a very large portion of sex development and progress towards heterosexuality is determined by the attitude of the mother." [6] Strecker feels that homosexuals are made and not born, and that while innate factors often go into the making of homosexuality, environmental influences exerted by "Mom" and "Pop" are of primary importance. Homosexuality, according to this view, then develops when parents, especially mothers, refuse to assist their children in developing a healthy, independent outlook; when they refuse to untie the apron strings by which they hold and protect their boys; when they do not stimulate their boys to a mature outlook upon life, especially upon sex life; when they "love" their boys so much that they cannot bear to see them leave the family.

It cannot be denied that certain parents, because of their own immaturity and oversolicitude toward their children, may sow the seeds of homosexuality in their own families. They should be educated along these lines, for an understanding of the causes of homosexuality will prevent much suffering for themselves as well as for their children.

Several other factors have been pointed out as nourishing a homosexual attitude in children and adolescents. There are the parents who desire the expected baby to be a girl but get a boy or vice versa and, when their wish is not fulfilled, subject the child to the pattern of their wishful thinking by rearing and dressing it as if it were actually a member of its opposite sex. Sibling jealousy is also worthy of mention; the boy may see his sister preferred—or the other way around—and, feeling rejected in his own sex, may adopt the attitude and characteristics of the preferred sex in gait, gestures, and behavior in order to win favor. A lack of manliness and virility in the male members of a family may induce other members to imitate these manners and thus become a cause of inverted tendencies. Some adolescent boys have been known to turn to homosexual relations as a kind of protest action, after they have been unsuccessful in their interpersonal relations with one girl after the other. Adolescent girls may acquire homosexual habits from fear and disgust at the rudeness of men in sexual matters. Of course, both boys and girls may be drawn into bad society by the seduction of other homosexuals, who often group together in clubs and associations, especially in the larger cities.

These and other factors are presented in pertinent literature as possible causes of homosexuality. Some of these possibilities seem to be quite acceptable, but others give the impression of being farfetched. Moreover, when discussing these possible etiological factors of homosexual disorders, the writers do not always make it clear whether they have in mind genuine or pseudo homosexuality.

When one weighs the pros and the cons of both the constitutional and the environmental theories, after everything has been said concerning the etiology of homosexuality, one may well feel doubtful about the advisability of taking sides in favor of either the biochemical or the psychic nature of the disorder. It can be expected, therefore, that some writers will try to strike a compromise. This is what Rosanoff, for instance, does when he concludes: "The facts of clinical experience would seem to indicate that homosexuality, like other psychic constitutional anomalies, has in its etiology both inborn and environmental factors. Here, as elsewhere . . . , heredity determines what one can do and environment determines what one does." [7]

THERAPY

Hirschfeld, Rohleder, H. Blüher, and others who hold to the exclusively constitutional etiology of homosexuality considered the disorder as completely incurable—an attitude that has been dubbed therapeutic nihilism. All that these authors have to offer to homosexuals is the advice to indulge in their tendencies but in such a safe way as to stay out of the hands of the law and avoid social ostracism.

The majority of writers, however, have gradually become less pessimistic concerning the curability of the anomaly—an attitude that does not mean that they are overoptimistic. The treatment they choose depends largely on the stand they take in the matter of etiology.

Those who believe in the biological determination of homosexuality will preferably resort to physical treatment, because they reason that, if the disorder is due to a disturbance of the glandular functions, it should be possible to cure it by glandular treatment. Earlier writers, such as E. Steinach, R. Lichtenstein, and their school, attempted to transform male homosexuals into heterosexuals by implanting into their tissues the gonads of a normal man.[8] But these efforts, at first welcomed with enthusiasm, proved to be an illusion; the operation scored mild success only when it was preceded by castration. More recent investigators, on the basis of the biochemical theory, have tried sex-hormone medication by injecting intramuscularly testosterone propionate and other endocrine extracts. L. A. Lurie reported some success with this treatment, but only in cases of eunochoid homosexuals.[9] In the cases of other homosexuals, a number of American and European investigators have found that glandular treatment not only fails in most instances to reverse the direction of the libido, but sometimes causes an intensification of the homosexual drive.[10]

Again some success has been reported with the injection of Metrazol; after causing a number of Metrazol convulsions, Owensby observed a change from homosexuality to heterosexuality in six individuals.[11] On the other hand, electroshock treatment of homosexuals produced no success.[12]

Sometimes castration of homosexuals has been recommended as a very last resort. The moral aspects of this operation will be discussed later in this chapter.

In conclusion, it is clear that the results obtained with physiotherapy in the treatment of homosexuals are only moderate, and many writers find in this fact a confirmation of their opinion that homosexuality is due not so much to organic causes as to psychic ones.

Those who favor the psychogenic concept of homosexuality maintain that, before anything else, psychotherapy should be attempted in the treatment of patients; they intend to change not his organic constitution, but his mental attitude. The absolute prerequisite of any such treatment is the patient's willingness to get rid of his abnormal condition. But the lack of sincere desire to be cured is, in many cases, precisely the stumbling block. Yet, it has to be removed before any effective psychotherapy can be instituted.

Most homosexuals do not want to be cured; like other immature individuals, they only want to be accepted as they are. This is one of the main reasons why relatively few homosexuals come to see the psychiatrist. If they come at all, it is often because they are driven by fear of the police, scandal, or blackmail, or because they want to have their mind and conscience set at ease so they can continue their life more comfortably. But as long as the patient has no honest desire to be cured, all attempts on the part of the psychiatrist will almost invariably fail. The latter's first effort, therefore, should be to stimulate the "will to health" in the patient, and since the psychotherapist is supposed to believe in his own view of the psychogenic nature of homosexuality, he is mentally well equipped to make the patient realize that he is not determined by an hereditary constitution.

The next step is to trace the psychological factors that brought about the individual's perverse condition. Psychoanalysts, as well as other psychiatrists, maintain that they often find such factors in a patient's life history, particularly in his childhood. Analysis may also lay bare the patient's hidden disposition to heterosexuality which, according to the analysts, is sometimes latently present despite overt homosexual tendencies.

The difficulty in helping the patient to accept the idea of such an environmental factor and such a latent disposition lies, again, in his own mental attitude; he often refuses to admit any such factor, because he is convinced of the inborn character of his anomaly. Even if the therapist succeeds in giving the patient an insight into the acquired nature of his condition and into his own potentialities, there is still a long road for him to travel because insight alone will not be enough to make him discontinue his homosexual tendencies, which may be deeply ingrained through many years of habit formation.

The aim of any effectual treatment is, in the final analysis, to bring about a radical change in the patient's attitude. A. Moll and Bechterew have tried to achieve this goal through association therapy, which proceeds somewhat along the lines of the conditioned-reflex method; but results seem to be questionable.[13]

And what about the results of psychotherapy, with or without analysis? Although psychotherapeutic procedures have shown that homosexuality is not incurable, the results are rather modest. Some psychoanalysts—Stekel [14] is an example—seem to feel satisfied if they can bring the individual back to the bisexual stage which, according to their theory, is the original normal condition of man. But many other psychiatrists wonder if that is much of a solution of the problem—and so do those homosexuals who honestly wish to be cured. These other therapists, therefore, earnestly strive for a radical change and feel that their therapy is a failure unless they have changed the homosexual into a heterosexual. A number of them report from moderate to complete success. Among these may be mentioned Ferenczi (1914), J. Sadger (1921); J. Vinson and S. Nacht (1930), E. Frey (1932), E. Carp (1941), A. N. Foxe (1941), and Thomas V. Moore (1945).

E. Carp and others rightly insist on a reeducation process in which a strong appeal is made to the patient's will to take himself in hand. Thomas V. Moore, too, recommends this course as the only possible method for achieving permanent results. This author, furthermore, holds that the tedious, time-consuming procedures of psychoanalysis are not always necessary by any means. Moore starts from the self-evident premise that psychiatrists can only help the patient to help himself. Presupposing the patient's sincere willingness to free himself from his homosexuality, the therapist should try to stimulate his continued cooperation and a proper sense of his moral obligations.

The patient's first moral duty is, of course, to give up all homosexual contacts as well as all seemingly innocent attachments to members of the same sex, and to exchange these private relations for a normal social life. Moore believes that the treatment of homosexuals is, in many respects, similar to that of alcoholics, and that in both cases lasting results can be obtained only when the patients seek help from a Higher Power. However, the comparison with alcoholics should not be pushed to the extreme, for there is a significant difference: whereas alcoholics find strong mutual support by banding together in such societies as Alcoholics Anonymous, such attempts among reformed homosexuals would obviously be disastrous.

A favorable prognosis depends largely on the duration of the homosexual tendencies, the age of the patient, the sincerity of his desire to become a normal person, and his personality structure. There is more hope of a cure for the active than for the passive homosexual.

In many instances, the most that psychotherapy can achieve is to restore the patient's mental balance without producing in him a change from homosexual to heterosexual. But even this seemingly negative result is of great importance, because a person who regains his mental balance will be in a better position to control himself. If a homosexual cannot be changed into a heterosexual, it is his moral duty to resign himself to a nonsexual adjustment in life. This is not asking the impossible, for the countless numbers of heterosexuals who live a life without sexual outlet show that it is possible. Some homosexuals may object that theirs is an abnormal drive and that such drives are stronger than normal heterosexual inclinations. Granted that this is true, the numerous reformed alcoholics prove that an abnormal urge can be controlled. Persons who are afflicted with homosexual tendencies but who control themselves show a high degree of character and compel admiration and respect.[15]

PASTORAL AND SOCIAL ASPECTS OF HOMOSEXUALITY

It is probably safe to say that, as far as Catholic homosexuals are concerned, many more go to see the pastor, either in or outside the confessional, than to see a psychiatrist. The pastoral care of these people is indeed a difficult task, demanding patience and perseverance, and fraught with much disappointment. If psychiatry often fails in effecting a cure, the pastor cannot be expected to work miracles; yet, his assistance can be of the utmost importance. True, he only too often will have to resign himself to the fact that he cannot change a homosexual into a heterosexual —not even in collaboration with a psychiatrist—but any priest would act in an altogether irresponsible manner if he should try to pass off such cases with impatience or disgust because he thinks he can do nothing about them anyway. The pastoral counselor or confessor can do a great deal for the homosexual counselee or penitent; he can effectively help the individual to control himself and in that manner reduce to a minimum the grief that the homosexual brings upon himself and the harm that he may do to other people.

The necessary condition for any fruitful relationship in pastoral counseling consists, as always, in creating an atmosphere of charitable understanding and confidence. The homosexuals who turn to the pastor—and those who do so are by no means the worst—expect at least to be heard and treated in a spirit of Christian charity. There is no justification for regarding homosexuals as a class to be abhorred as depraved and degenerate. They, like all sick people, deserve to be understood and to be given the same sympathetic assistance that is willingly given to other types of people. Scorn, contempt, and undue severity will only increase the feeling of inferiority that predominates in many homosexuals despite an outward appearance of insouciance or defiance. Of course, kindness does not mean weakness on the part of the counselor, who should insist on the giving up of all homosexual practices and relations. As long as the counselee does not give definite signs of his intention to do so, the case is well-nigh hopeless; but even then the pastor should try to form in the penitent the right intention, particularly by educating him to the use of supernatural means. Where natural means fail, divine grace may still prevail.

Once an atmosphere of confidential understanding is established, the counselee will feel that he no longer has to fight alone. The pastoral counselor then may proceed to decrease the patient's inferiority feelings by making him realize that, despite his perverse passion, he possesses many good and desirable qualities, and that he should sublimate his sexual tendencies by employing his energy in the development of his desirable traits. This development the homosexual can effect by engaging wholeheartedly in intellectual, charitable, social, artistic, or other activities, according to his own preferences and capacities. The satisfaction which the patient will experience in his own work will take his mind off unhealthy sexual fantasies, decrease his feeling of inferiority, and increase his courage. The sincere practice of his religious duties will put his life on a higher level and thus become one of the best forms of sublimation.

However, despite all such efforts and despite the best of intentions, miracles should not be expected, relapses are to be feared, and continuous control on the part of the counselor is necessary. But the very fact that the patient submits to such a control is the best sign of his good intentions.

With regard to the homosexual's moral responsibility, the basic rule is that voluntary actions and desires of a homosexual nature are objectively a grievous sin against the natural law. Granted, for the sake of argument, that some forms of homosexuality have a biological organic cause, one cannot claim that the homosexual therefore has a right to give in to his urges. A heterosexual may be said to be biologically urged to normal sexual activities, but that does not give him the right to sexual satisfaction outside marriage. Neither can one claim that, again granted a biological disposition to homosexuality, the individual's will is necessarily determined in such a manner that he cannot act differently. However, there are cases in which homosexuality is like a compulsion that blindly drives the individual to give in to his passion, and even to seek the occasion to do so. In such cases, the action may be said to be willed, but it is no longer freely willed; hence, complete guilt may be questioned. But, as in all other similar conditions, reduced responsibility does not give the penitent a *carte blanche* to continue his practices; in other words, the most important question in deciding the subjective guilt of the homosexual is whether he sincerely strives to control himself. Now, it has been seen that the honesty of the willingness to do so may, sometimes, be seriously called into question. This is a point that the confessor should keep in mind. The homosexual may sincerely repent his past sins in the confessional, but the purpose of amendment is sometimes rather weak. The reason is, as we pointed out, his conviction that he cannot get rid of his habit anyway—a conviction that frequently is strengthened by the reading of propagandistic literature. In such a case, words of encouragement are needed to lift up the penitent's morale and to prepare the proper disposition for receiving absolution. We may add that the Church has laid down the canonical regulations and penal laws concerning homosexuals and other sexual delinquents in Canons 2357 to 2359 of the Codex Juris Canonici.

Is marriage indicated as a solution in cases of homosexuality? For pseudo homosexuals, as we have defined them, marriage or a return to regular marital life will often be the best and only solution. But it would be disastrous to advise marriage to a genuine homosexual as long as he has not been changed into a heterosexual by some method of therapy, regardless of whether his condition is supposed to be organogenic or psychogenic. Marriage does not cure the genuine homosexual from his perverse inclinations, and because he does not feel any real psychic attraction toward the other sex, his condition will cause his partner untold grief. Should a homosexual, before being cured, insist upon marriage, he is morally bound to reveal his condition to his partner.

At this point, the question arises whether castration is permissible as a possible cure of homosexuality (and other sexual perversities). Some Catholic moralists give an affirmative answer, presupposing, of course, that the necessary requirements are met. They argue that medical castration is an act with a double effect, one good and one bad, and that it may be permitted as a last resort after all other therapeutic means have failed, because they deem the conditions required for the permissibility of such an act to be then fulfilled. The good effect is supposed to consist in the individual's being cured of his abnormal sexual drive. The bad effect is that he remains permanently deprived of his function of reproduction; in addition, the operation may eventually result in dizziness, palpitation of the heart, and, on the psychological side, in feelings of inferiority and depression. Now it is argued that, if the good effect does not outweigh the bad effect, at least it balances the other.

The authors wish to express some reservations concerning the validity of this argument, particularly in view of the preceding discussions about the etiology of homosexuality. A first reservation concerns the good effect. Several serious investigations have proved, indeed, that castration may considerably and lastingly reduce the sexual urge in such a way that the victim more easily controls himself, but the operation does not present an absolute guarantee that such a reduction will be effected. However, this is not the main point. Our main concern regards the character of the operation itself. The first condition for the permissibility of an act with a double effect is that the act is in itself licit, because we are not allowed to effect good results by means of an act that is itself evil. In other surgical operations this condition is fulfilled; the act itself is good, inasmuch as it removes a sick organ which endangers the health of the entire organism. Now it is argued that similar conditions prevail in the operation under discussion; castration, it is said, is in this case not a mutilation, but the removal of a sick part of the body. However, is this statement true in the case of homosexuality? It seems to rest on the premise that homosexuality has an organic cause, presumably hormonal disturbance. But this premise is doubtful in individual cases. It is true, as we saw previously, that the androgen-estrogen ratio in male homosexuals as a group is lower than it is in heterosexuals as a group. But a surgeon does not operate on groups; rather, he operates on an individual. And, as Thomas V. Moore points out, "one would not prove an individual to be normal or homosexual by determining his androgen-estrogen ratio. . . . The male hormone may or may not be dominant in either normal or homosexual individuals. . . .

There is some evidence to show that the amount of androgen is associated with the intensity of the sex drive, but does not determine its character as homo- or heterosexual." [16]

Suppose an indubitably male homosexual has androgen values below normal and estrogen values above normal. One might argue that in such case the lowered androgen-estrogen ratio is apparently the cause of the individual's sexual disorder. But even then the causal connection between the two facts is not as clear as it seems, for, as has been seen, the administration of androgen does not generally change such an individual into a heterosexual.

Therefore, as long as the organic character of homosexuality in an individual case has not been undeniably proved, it seems doubtful whether such a drastic operation as castration can be called licit.

It must be emphasized that this discussion deals with only the *moral* aspects of castration considered as a possible therapeutic measure. It leaves undecided, as not relevant to the nature of this book, the legal question whether the state has the right to order castration of a delinquent homosexual as a punishment for his crimes and in consequence as a protective or preventive measure for the benefit of society.

For the most part, society has been unfair to the homosexual. The average man views him with suspicion, scorn, and hostility. Particularly the uneducated make him the butt of their equally uneducated humor in the poolroom, the bowling alley, and the beer parlor. It even happens that they single out a man as a homosexual solely because he is a refined person or because he shows his friendly love toward his fellow men, when he is not a homosexual by any stretch of the imagination.

The reaction of the homosexuals to this attitude of society is understandable. In constant threat of social ostracism, blackmail, economic ruin, and legal persecution, they clan together in cliques, clubs, and circles. There they have their parties or "drags" to which only homosexuals are admitted and at which some appear in the dress of the opposite sex.

The attitude of the man of the street is doubtlessly unfortunate; but on the other hand, society as a whole does have a right to protect itself against the spread of homosexuality. It is like a contagious disease, and the propaganda disseminated by homosexual societies contributes to its spread. The lawmaker has the right and the duty to protect at least the minors from becoming afflicted with the contagion. True, homosexuals counter by observing that they are not criminals but sick people because they are biologically determined, but certainly not all homosexuality is constitutional, and it is precisely the spread of the psychological contagion, due to environmental influence, that the laws try to prevent. Hence, there is no reason to repeal the laws against homosexuality, as Hirschfeld and others advocate. Nevertheless, as more and more writers believe, these laws should be modified, inasmuch as delinquent homosexuals should be considered as mental patients and, for that reason, should be sent to a mental hospital instead of to jail.

NOTES AND REFERENCES

1. For a critical discussion of the literature on the controversy concerning the etiology of homosexuality, see Moore, Thomas V., Pathogenesis and Treatment of Homosexual Disorders: a Digest of Some Pertinent Evidence, *Journal of Personality,* Vol. 14 (1945), pp. 47–83. We express our indebtedness to this excellent article.
2. *Ibid.,* p. 79.
3. An important anthropological study of homosexuals was made by Arthur Weil; see his article entitled: Sprechen anatomische Grundlagen für das Angeborensein der Homosexualität? *Archiv für Frauenkunde und Eugenik,* Vol. 9 (1923), pp. 23–51.
4. See Glass, S. J., H. J. Duel, and C. A. Wright, Sex Hormone Studies in Male Homosexuals, *Endocrinology,* Vol. 26 (1940), pp. 590–594; also Neustadt, R., and A. Myerson, Quantitative Sex Hormone Studies in Homosexuality, Childhood and Various Neuropsychiatric Disturbances, *American Journal of Psychiatry,* Vol. 97 (1940), pp. 524–551.
5. Darke, Roy A., Heredity as an Etiological Factor in Homosexuality, *Journal of Nervous and Mental Disease,* Vol. 107 (1948).
6. Strecker, Edward A., "Their Mothers' Sons" (Philadelphia: Lippincott, 1946), p. 129.
7. Rosanoff, A. J., "Manual of Psychiatry" (New York: John Wiley & Sons, Inc., 1927).
8. Steinach, E., and R. Lichtenstein, Umstimmung der Homosexualität durch Austausch der Pubertätsdrüsen, *Münchener medizinische Wochenschrift,* Vol. 65 (1918), I, pp. 145–148.
9. Lurie, L. A., The Endocrine Factor in Homosexuality, *American Journal of Medical Science,* Vol. 208 (1944), pp. 176–186.
10. Barahal, H. S., Testosterone in Psychotic Male Homosexuals, *Psychiatric Quarterly,* Vol. 14 (1940), pp. 319–330.

    Gallot, H. M., Homosexualité mâle et testosterone, *Annales médicopsychologiques,* Vol. 100 (1942), pp. 207–210.

    Myerson, A., and R. Neustadt, Bisexuality and Male Homosexuality, *Clinic,* Vol. 1 (1942), pp. 932–957.

    Rosenzweig, S., and R. Hopkins, A Note on the Ineffectualness of Sex-hormone Medication in a Case of Pronounced Homosexuality, *Psychosomatic Medicine,* Vol. 3 (1941), pp. 87–89.

11. Owensby, N. M., Homosexuality and Lesbianism Treated with Metrazol, *Journal of Nervous and Mental Disease,* Vol. 92 (1940), pp. 65–66.
12. Liebmann, S., Homosexuality, Transvestism and Psychosis, *Journal of Nervous and Mental Disease,* Vol. 99 (1944), pp. 945–958.
13. Moll, A., "Die Behandlung sexualer Perversionen mit besonderer Berücksichtigung der Assoziationstherapie" (Stuttgart, 1911); Bechterew, V., Die Perversitäten und Inversitäten vom Standpunkte der Reflexologie, *Archiv für Psychiatrie,* Vol. 68 (1923).
14. Stekel, W., "Störungen des Trieb- und Affektlebens" (Berlin: Urban und Schwarzenburg, 1923), Vol. II, p. 167.
15. For more complete information concerning sex anomalies, the reader is referred to Bergler, Edmund, "Neurotic Counterfeit Sex" (New York: Grune & Stratton, Inc., 1951); Cory, Donald Webster, "The Homosexual in America, A Subjective Approach" (New York: Greenberg: Publisher, Inc., 1951); Ellis, Havelock, "Study of Psychology of Sex" (New York: Random House, 1936); Henry, G. W., "Sex Variants: A Study of Homosexual Patterns" (New York: Paul B. Hoeber, Inc., 1948); Hirschfeld, M., "Sex Anomalies" (London, 1944); Kinsey, Alfred C., "Sexual Behavior in the Human Male" (Philadelphia: W. B. Saunders Company, 1948). With regard to Kinsey's report and similar works, it would be hard to find a more incisive and more logical criticism than the one expressed by M. R. Sapirstein in his "Emotional Security" (New York: Crown Publishers, 1948), pp. 99–100: "Almost every possible cultural variation has been described in our own culture by Kinsey, and the experimental biologists use this as evidence that man is basically an 'animal.' They use this evidence to encourage a greater permissiveness toward socially unacceptable practices in our own society by bringing forth evidence that 'perversions' are acceptable in other cultures and other species of animals. This type of reasoning which is rapidly becoming fashionable, further destroys conformity of sexual patterns as a means of finding security. The anthropologists and the biologists do not suggest that we adopt the religion, the family organization or economic practices of the many societies which they describe. Yet they seem to indicate that any variation of sexual practice, taken out of context, is 'normal' for our society."

    See also London, Louis S., and Frank S. Caprio, "Sexual Deviations" (Washington, D.C.: Linacre Press, 1950); Thompson, Clara, Changing Concepts of Homosexuality in Psychoanalysis, *Psychiatry: Journal of the Biology and Pathology of Interpersonal Relations,* Vol. XX (1947), p. 183.
16. Moore, *op. cit.,* pp. 65, 80.

Chapter 23

SEX EDUCATION

It is significant that sex education must be discussed as a problem. Children are educated in all the sciences of living. But sex—that is a part of man's nature that is obscured both by controversy and by misunderstanding. Parents are failing in their God-given right and duty to educate children in the true and wholesome knowledge of sex because they have come to consider it as something embarrassing and shameful. Yet, what is wrong with sex? Why should sex furnish us with more problems than any other realm of living? Possibly it is because on the one hand sex is quite *natural,* like the intake of food and other aspects of living, and yet on the other hand sex is *sacred,* and concerned with the basic mysteries of time and eternity.

The sex impulse is a normal phenomenon and causes in every growing child a curiosity that demands explanation. On turning, naturally, to his parents for this information, he finds—sometimes at an amazingly early age—that they are ill at ease or even horror-stricken at the very mention of the word. He concludes that something is wrong with the whole idea of sex and will probably no longer seek their advice in the matter. When his valid desire for knowledge is rebuffed he either retreats within himself, where the seeds of sexual maladjustment develop, or he turns to some source of information other than his parents—a source too often corrupt if not altogether vicious.

Sex instruction is a part of the educational mission that the parents hold directly from God. Why do most parents fail to include the very important subject of sex in the program of their children's education?

Traditionally, it has been a subject discussed only in medical, psychological, or theological circles and sometimes only in some esoteric medium, such as Latin. It was assumed formerly that knowledge of sex was dangerous knowledge, especially for the young. One should not be too eager to discard this more or less traditional reserve, for it is fundamentally based upon sound reasoning, *viz.,* upon the fact that, with the subject of sex, theory and reality cannot be well separated. Sex knowledge has a personal relation with its possessor that knowledge in other fields has not; and with sex, knowledge tends to be more operative and experimental. Recognizing this to be true, the authors still maintain that parents should, if possible, personally supervise the education of their children in this matter and should, themselves, give the guidance necessary for maturity and common sense in matters of sex.

Every child at times experiences some kind of sexual curiosity, and every parent, whether prepared or not, will be confronted with questions from children on sex. Evasions or manifest emotional upset over such questions will not go unnoticed by the child and will either inhibit or thwart the complete confidence that children should have in their parents.

If the parents refuse to give this information, or if they are emotionally unable to do so, what is to happen to the child who does not have his natural curiosity in sexual matters satisfied? To this question, in itself a problem of great importance, there is only one possible answer that will permit the growth of a well-adjusted child: he must be given sex instruction outside the home. This, we admit, is only a substitute, for education should come primarily from the parents; but the matter of sex is so vital to the child's well-being that some adequate substitute must be found and utilized.

What substitute form of sex education is adequate? This can be ascertained from an investigation of the essentials of sex education. Is the mere knowledge of sex sufficient for the child? Certainly not. It is true that many children who become involved in sexual difficulties will plead ignorance, but are they really ignorant? "The real reason for the general breakdown of personal morality is not that the boys and girls do not know enough about sex matters. They know too little about God," [1] says an authority on juveniles who has had much experience with the young. And God has no part in the street-corner course in sex. Knowledge itself is no virtue, although it is a necessary prerequisite to virtue. But it is especially by supernatural means that children obtain the self-control necessary for the practice of chastity. Prayer and the grace of the sacraments will do more to make a child pure than mere indoctrination on the facts of the sex life.

It is for this reason that sex education is best imparted in a religious atmosphere in which recognition is given to objective norms of morality and objective motivation toward observance of moral law. Sex education, divorced from religious motives and religious principles and imparted in a completely secular atmosphere cannot possibly teach the true nature of sex. Since a secularized milieu does not recognize sex as a function related to God, it cannot treat sex crimes as sinful; nevertheless all sex offenses, whatever else they may be, are objectively sins against God. Sex education should, therefore, be given in an atmosphere of religion.

No doubt our modern methods of communication, the popular press, radio, movies, and cheap literature, are tainted with sly innuendos and salacious nuances giving an improper turn to legitimate sex knowledge. Whether we will it or not, our youth are getting sex information, and much of it is incorrect and provocative. It stirs their curiosity and throws their parents, teachers, and religious ministers into doubt and confusion.

Urban H. Fleege [2] reports the following observations taken from actual responses of high school boys to a questionnaire on the subject of sex education:

"I think it would be an aid if a law were made making the schools teach something on this subject. I know that if I were instructed in the beginning I would have saved myself a lot of mental grief."

"I do believe that boys and girls should be told certain details, so that they would not be so curious and so anxious for the thrill of sex experience."

"Why do elders dislike discussing sex problems and explaining them, when they should know that it is a help and not a hindrance in our lives?"

"I feel that the school should give us a fuller explanation of sex and its intricacies, so as to better acquaint us with what we will have to face later on. I, for one, am puzzled about many sexual problems."

"I think a Catholic book on sex should be printed which would be clean and clear for boys of my age."

About 50 per cent of the boys whom Fleege interviewed did not think the school furnished the information on sex that they should have. More than 90 per cent of the high school freshmen interviewed claimed that grade school had never given them a simple clear interpretation of the commandment "Thou shalt not commit adultery." Not only the youth, but the pastors feel the same need. Fleege found that 349 pastors out of 369 thought it *necessary* that our youth should be instructed in sex matters.

Today, many marriages are shipwrecked. Broken homes and divorce are signs of our modern society. The headlines of the newspapers scream forth sex crimes and juvenile delinquency. One cannot help wondering how much of this condition is the result of faulty sex education, of a bizarre attitude on sex, of a moral penury bred of puritanism.

The question is no longer, "Shall we instruct our youth?" It is, rather, "*How* shall we tell them? *How much* shall we tell them? *Who* will tell them?"

Two extreme views are frequently presented on the subject. One group of educators believe that very thorough instructions should be given in sex matters even before children reach puberty. The other groups would give no sex instruction before puberty, or merely the barest minimum, and this only when asked in each individual case. It would seem that a *via media* or combination of the best features of both views would be the solution.[3]

A few basic considerations ought to underly the philosophy of our sex education. First, sex is not something isolated or superimposed upon man's personality; it is a part of an integrated whole. Second, man is not only a body but also a spirit, and sex has a spiritual and psychic, as well as physical and somatic, implication. Third, sex education should be integrated into the educational process in much the same way as instruction in other fields and should then be adapted to the intellectual and emotional level of the students.

The last consideration is not intended to imply that imparting sex education is the same as teaching catechism or mathematics. As has already been observed, sex knowledge has personal and intimate overtones not possessed by other subjects in our curricula. Nevertheless, the evidence shows that a serious attempt to integrate it into our educational system must be made.

In a matter that has such intensely personal implications it is difficult to lay down a generalized program that will be suitable for every individual child, but keeping in mind the above considerations and always allowing room for adaptation, it is possible to indicate a broad outline of sex education that seems both practical and suited to the mentality of our time.

What should be the purpose of sex education? The underlying purpose is to assign sex its proper place in the life of an individual. Now, the proper place in the life of the individual implies first the knowledge of the necessary facts of sex, and secondly the appropriate attitude toward the facts. The appropriate attitude will be largely taken care of if the necessary knowledge is wisely imparted.

On considering the youngsters who are to receive this proper knowledge and attitude, one finds that sex development is distinguished by several periods. Allowing for overlapping in retarded and advanced cases, these periods will correspond to the divisions outlined in the following paragraphs.

The first period covers the time from infancy to early childhood. There is little to say here, as it is doubtful whether the child has any sex consciousness. If he receives all the attention, love, and care that an infant needs, he will be well started on his way to normal adjustment to sex life.

The second period, extending from early childhood to late childhood, is marked by an awakening of sex consciousness. The child is apt to discover for the first time the male and female sex differences. The formation of proper attitudes toward sex are most important during these years because the child is so impressionable. It is during this period that sex education should begin. The parents, especially the mother, have an ideal opportunity—and obligation—to start the first steps. Unless the children are very precocious, the mother could arrange, for example, for the very young children, girls and boys, to take their baths together, in an atmosphere that is quite natural to children. This gives the mother a chance to furnish the necessary explanations. One father approached the problem with his four-year-old son by explaining how to use the bathroom. A child at this age accepts quite easily and without morbidity the difference in sex.

The third period includes late childhood to pubescence. It is rather in the latter part of the previous period or in the early part of this period that children can become acquainted with the correct answer to the perennial children's query: "Where do babies come from?" The fable of the stork may have its usefulness at times, but it decreases in plausibility in inverse proportion to the number of playmates a child has. According to the law of averages, there are usually one or two children in every neighborhood who use the "shock treatment" to assert superiority. Sometimes the shock is quite real, resulting in psychic trauma that lasts for years. The damage is effected not only by the shock that the child receives, but also by the distrust that the child learns to feel toward his parents, who did not tell the truth in this matter. The result is that a sensitive child may suffer all his life, never trusting again. However, the parents, and again especially the mother, can anticipate this difficulty. The occasion for giving instruction in this matter presents itself quite naturally when a younger brother or sister is on the way, or, if this opportunity fails to occur, the story of Christmas may furnish an opening. A Catholic mother can use the words of the "Hail Mary."

A mother may tell her children when they are quite young how they were carried and grew in her womb and how they were finally delivered through the laborious process of childbirth. The growth of the human embryo, the general process of pregnancy and childbirth, can be explained in a manner that is intelligible to children and that will give them respect and reverence for the obligation of parenthood. The children may love their mother much more after this story has been told, respect her, obey her, and behave much more thoughtfully than before.

Two observations about the explanation of conception and childbirth are worth making. First, explaining conception and pregnancy is not the same as explaining the details of marital intercourse. The former can be explained with but an allusion, if even that, to the latter. Second, when a child introduces the subject of babies, this need not necessarily imply sex curiosity. Questions about babies are very often only manifestations of a general interest in things and in changes—a sort of incipient, vague appreciation that all effects have a cause.

The fourth period takes the child from puberty to adolescence. The onset of puberty for both boys and girls carries with it many radical physical and mental changes. Very often, it is a time of great stress. Adjustment is difficult; personality is not well integrated. Mysterious, scarcely perceptible processes are going on, and the boy or girl runs a long gamut of question marks. It is highly desirable that girls should look upon the phenomenon of menstruation as a normal, physiological process, and not as an illness or sickness. The adolescent boy should be prepared for the perfectly normal event of nocturnal emissions. The actual beginning of puberty in individual cases can best be handled by fathers with their sons and by mothers with their daughters; if for any reason that is impossible, another reliable and trustworthy person should impart the necessary orientation. Explanations can be candidly and gently given about the powers of parenthood that are just beginning to develop. Just how much detail can be given at this time, whether or not marital intercourse can be referred to, how much the psychology of sexual attraction can be discussed—all this depends upon the maturity of the child, the skill and tact of the parent. In any case, the onset of puberty should be definitely met by the parents or guardians. In general, it is a good principle to follow the axiom, "Answer what is asked."

The period of adolescence is a critical time for youth, and quite often their problems are ignored or depreciated. Grown-ups, caught in the vortex of their own problems, are apt to forget the problems of youth—it has been too long since they had them! The normal adolescent boy or girl experiences new interests, new feelings and impulses. In spite of good will, they are often betrayed by weakness, surprise, or lack of maturity into undesirable patterns of behavior. They are often acutely conscious of their failings and, therefore, are susceptible to excessive remorse and inferiority feelings. The storms of adolescence come and go, and no one can exactly anticipate them, least of all the parents. However, the wise father and mother will find chances to have an occasional chat with the adolescent boy or girl. An evening stroll or drive, or movies together—these will furnish the sympathetic parents and the adolescent boy or girl with the opportunity to discuss such problems. It is on occasions like this that subjects such as the psychology of sex and temptations can be tactfully discussed.

The question arises whether the older adolescent boy or girl should be enlightened as to the details of marital intercourse and, if so, how and when. It is fairly safe to assume that most boys and girls nowadays, at least in their later teens, will know these details more or less clearly and will have gotten their knowledge explicitly or implicitly by reading, by hearing allusions in movies, in chance conversation, and in other ways. But the great danger is that unless the child himself definitely broaches the subject, the parent will not know whether he has the proper knowledge. This is perhaps the most delicate subject of sex education, and because of its significance for married life, it is probably the most important.

In brief, it may be said that young men and young women before they are twenty-one—and earlier, if there is an early marriage—should be given complete instructions and details of marital intercourse. The instructions should be given either by the parents or by a physician or nurse of good moral character, or by the pastor, if he feels qualified to do it and circumstances warrant it. Such instruction may be given perhaps even better through printed matter, provided it is sure that this printed matter is completely in accord with good ethics.

Proper sex instruction should avoid the danger of unilaterally overestimating the moral obligations concerning sex; *i.e.*, it should not give the youngsters the impression that the sixth and the ninth are the only commandments that count. For quite a few people, virtue and morality are simply synonymous with the observance of these commandments, but this is an inaccurate concept.

Another danger to be avoided is repression. The youngster certainly should learn to control himself and to fight temptations, but he should also be told how to do this. Emotional violence and tenseness in warding off temptations may not only have the opposite effect, but may also produce psychic trouble. Not our emotions, but our reason and resoluteness must counteract and lead the sexual impulses. The impetuous youth will find it hard to learn the quiet approach to sexual temptations, and that is another reason why the youngsters need an experienced counselor.

The parents will not always be sufficiently equipped to tackle these problems. They themselves might need some training in such matters. In some places, therefore, the parish or other Catholic agencies arrange courses in which the parents receive instruction as to how to handle their children, particularly the pubescent and adolescent, in matters of sex.

Thus far, sex instruction has been discussed as being in the first place the task and the obligation of the parents. The Catholic authorities have always insisted upon this parental duty. Pope Pius XII in an address to Catholic mothers gave these directives to parents whose children are approaching adolescence: "The day will come when the child's heart will feel new impulses stirring within it; new desires will disturb the serenity of those early years. . . . In that time of trial . . . you will have a task of the highest importance to fill. . . . With the discretion of a mother and teacher, and thanks to the open-hearted confidence with which you have been able to inspire your children, you will not fail to watch for and to discern the moment in which unspoken questions have occurred to their minds and are troubling their senses. It will then be your duty to your daughters, the father's duty to your sons, carefully and delicately to unveil the truth as far as it appears necessary, to give a prudent, true and Christian answer to those questions, and set their minds at ease." [4] And the cardinals, archbishops and bishops of the United States, in their statement "The Child: Citizen of Two Worlds," issued at the close of their annual meeting in Washington, in 1950, said, "Fathers and mothers have a natural competence to instruct their children with regard to sex. False modesty should not deter them from doing their duty in this regard. Sex is one of God's endowments. It should not be ignored or treated as something bad. If sex instruction is properly carried on in the home, a deep reverence will be developed in the child and he will be spared the shameful inferences which he often makes when he is left to himself to find out about sex."

At the present time, there is a rather widespread movement which advocates imparting sex instruction to children in public, particularly in school. But sex education indiscreetly handled in that manner will amount to little more than sex propaganda. Very often, this kind of instruction is concerned not with the virtue of chastity, but with the prevention of venereal diseases. In secularized education, sex abuses are evil, not because they are sins against the Creator, but because they tend to bring disorder in the community. Pope Pius XI in his encyclical "On the Christian Education of Youth," recalling that this kind of sex instruction is based on educational naturalism, says, "A very grave danger is that naturalism which nowadays invades the field of education in that most delicate matter of purity of morals. Far too common is the error of those who propagate a so-called sex education, falsely imagining that they can rearm youth against the dangers of sensuality by purely natural means, such as a foolhardy initiation and precautionary instruction for all indiscriminately, even in public. . . . Such persons grievously err, because they refuse to recognize the inborn weakness of human nature . . . and also because they ignore factual experience which clearly shows that, particularly in young people, immoral practices are not so much the result of ignorance of the intellect, as rather of weakness of a will exposed to dangerous occasions and unsupported by the means of grace." [5]

The bishops of the United States, in the statement just mentioned, reiterate the Pope's warning in the following words: "We protest in the strongest possible terms against the introduction of sex instruction into the schools. To be of benefit such instruction must be far broader than the imparting of information, and must be given with the sacredness and the uniqueness of the human personality. It can be fully and properly appreciated only within a religious and moral context. If treated otherwise, the child will see it apart from the controlling purpose of life, which is service to God."

Although the task of instructing their children in matters of sex falls in the first place on the parents, it cannot be denied that they only too often shy away from that task for one reason or other. Sometimes they are at least sensible enough, when the time comes, to refer the youngster to a priest, a doctor, a teacher, or some other qualified person. But sometimes they are altogether negligent and do not seem to care. In such cases, it may be the task of the priest or of the teacher to take the initiative in so important a matter. The teacher should so instruct the child as to give him a healthy, and at the same time reverent attitude toward sex. If the child is curious, he has a right to know the right answer. The answer should be complete enough to satisfy present curiosity without arousing morbid curiosity about something else. It should be given reverently and, at the same time, matter-of-factly, without any tension or anxiety on the part of the teacher.

In summary, it should be repeated that "sex" refers not merely to a somatic function, but also to a spiritual and psychological component. Adjustment to sexual life implies a blending of both the spiritual and the physical aspects of the sexual life. One cannot really love a body; one must love a person. Perfect love is consummated not by a physical union alone, but by a harmony and a oneness of the spirit. Sex education implies not only sex knowledge, but, in addition, a certain training, a certain discipline. If the knowledge is properly presented, there will be formed those attitudes toward sex which are most conducive to self-discipline. One can further encourage self-discipline, for maintaining self-discipline in other matters helps to make for self-discipline in regard to sex. Besides, sex education should not be isolated but should be integrated in the larger pattern of Christian education. The spirit of sacrifice, the art of which lies in giving up something of value for something of greater value, is essential to this pattern.

Sex in itself is beautiful, sublime, sacred. It can be kept so if this touchstone of all education in sex, is deeply imprinted in young minds: God, the Creator of all things, has, in His infinite wisdom, made His creatures of different sex for His own honor and glory.

NOTES AND REFERENCES

1. Editorial, *Extension Magazine,* August, 1948.
2. Fleege, Urban H., "Self-revelation of the Adolescent Boy" (Milwaukee: The Bruce Publishing Company, 1946).
3. A discussion of the various problems connected with sex education may be found in the following works:

   Allers, R. (translated by Rahmers), "Sex Psychology in Education" (St. Louis: B. Herder Book Company, 1937).

   Bergman, O., Neurotic Anxieties in Children and Their Prevention, *Nervous Child,* 1946.

   Bergmann, W. (ed.), "Religion und Seelenleiden" (Düsseldorf: L. Schwann, 1930), Vol. IV.

   Connell, Francis J., Sex Instruction in High School, *The Catholic Educational Review,* September, 1949, pp. 442–447.

   Fleege, *op. cit.; id.,* "Guiding the Adolescent" (Washington, D.C.: Superintendent of Documents, Government Printing Office, 1946).

   Kelly, Gerald, "Modern Youth and Chastity" (St. Louis: Queen's Work, 1943).

   Lord, Daniel, "Love, Sex, and the Teenager" (St. Louis: Queen's Work, 1947).

   McCarthy, Raphael C., "Training the Adolescent" (Milwaukee: The Bruce Publishing Company, 1946).

MOLL, ALBERT, "The Sexual Life of the Child" (New York: The Macmillan Company, 1913).

SCHUMACHER, HENRY, "The Adolescent: His Development and Major Problems" (Washington, D.C.: Catholic Conference on Family Life, 1945).

SEWARD, GEORGENE, "Sex and the Social Order" (New York: McGraw-Hill Book Company, Inc., 1946).

THOM, D. A., "Normal Youth and Its Everyday Problems" (New York: Appleton-Century-Crofts, Inc., 1932).

VAN WATERS, MIRIAM, "Youth in Conflict" (New York: Republic Publishing Co., 1925).

4. Address to Catholic Mothers by Pope Pius XII, October 26, 1941, *Acta apostolicae sedis,* Vol. 33 (1941), pp. 450–458.
5. Encyclical, "Rappresentanti in terra" ("On the Christian Education of Youth"), *Acta apostolicae sedis,* Vol. 21 (1929), pp. 723–762.

Chapter 24

PSYCHIATRIC AND PSYCHOLOGICAL ASPECTS OF MARRIAGE PROBLEMS

An analysis of the nature and purpose of marriage reveals that the fundamental, objective reason for marriage is the propagation of the human race. Marriage also affords an opportunity for close conjugal comradeship, for the expression of mutual love between man and woman. Marriage is not a mere remedy for concupiscence; marriage is a privilege, because by it two human beings cooperate with God in the conception of a child destined to share the eternal bliss of Heaven.

The family is the basic unit of society, because from it develop the community and the state. If, therefore, the institution of marriage is disintegrating, one must be prepared to find that society itself is also disintegrating. Everyone is aware of the alarming statistics of the divorce rate; in city areas in the United States, there is one divorce for every three or four marriages. One may well raise the question why, if marriage was instituted by God and if it was raised to the dignity of a sacrament by Jesus Christ, there are so many failures in marriage today.

A great many people come to see the psychiatrist, and probably even more see the pastoral counselor, because they feel that their marriage is a failure and wonder why that is so. Why is marriage failing? Or perhaps, we may better phrase the question: "Why are married people failing?"

If we compare the modern pagan concept of marriage to the Christian concept of a monogamous union, a number of the factors disruptive of Christian marriage become evident.[1]

Since marriage demands a state of adulthood, one of the most obvious sources of marital breakdown is immaturity. Many people never attain that full state of intellectual, volitional, and emotional maturity which is necessary for happy married life. The mature man may be described as one who has as much appreciation for his spouse as he has for himself, as one who can accept responsibility, as one who has an appreciation of home life and a respect for civil and ecclesiastical authority.

Deserving of special mention is sexual maturity, which implies that a person has an appreciation, reverence, and respect for his own sex life and that of his partner. We are well aware of the necessity of the child's developing in an atmosphere of healthy sex attitudes. An example of the development of wrong sex attitudes is presented by the following case:

> § A mother complained that her twenty-year-old daughter was unable to have dates with young men. The daughter shied away from any male companionship, even though she had a strong desire to get married and raise a family. During the psychiatric interview, the daughter became very disturbed emotionally and shouted at her mother, "When I was fourteen years old, you warned me that I should keep away from all men because they would only get me into trouble, would give me diseases, and would make me pregnant, and all for selfish motives of their own. At that time I obeyed you sincerely, and now after all these years I am not able to change."

Everyone is familiar with cases of boys and girls who, on arriving home from a date, are subjected to an exacting and inquisitive parental examination. Now, the parents have not only the right but the duty of supervising their children's conduct, as the bishops of the United States emphatically pointed out in their pastoral statement of 1950: "Parents should carefully regulate the company and the hours that their child keeps. They should not treat him as an adult. He needs to be warned against, even forbidden, certain associations. Particularly during adolescence, this is extremely important. A vigilant watch should be kept over the type of entertainment in which he indulges, the motion pictures he attends, the books he reads, the radio and television programs to which he is exposed in the home." [2] But, although keeping a vigilant watch over their children's behavior inside and outside the home, the parents should avoid implying in their interrogations an a priori suspicion that the youngster probably did something wrong. The wisest policy would be to induce the child to freely and honestly talk over his social activities and then, if necessary, help him to see what is wrong or dangerous.

The approach to sex instruction, as a remote preparation for marriage, should be positive and should always imply that sex is in itself something beautiful, a gift from God whereby man and woman cooperate with Him in the mystifying and beautiful work of creation. Woman is a shrine wherein man deposits the precious seed quickened by the touch of God into a new life, a new person. Marital union is a unity not only of bodies but also of spirits—a unity blessed in the eyes of God. The ultimate goal of sex is not the pleasure of physical union but the completion of that union in the generation and education of the child.

Today, about 50 per cent of all women are frigid, and approximately 20 per cent of all men are impotent; a large percentage of such cases is undoubtedly due to improper sex education. By improper sex education is meant the lack of a gradual, progressive integration of sex knowledge into the child's general educational system, as provided by the home, church, and school.

The basic fundamentals of a healthy sex life must be part of the intellectual equipment of those about to marry. The following case will serve to illustrate the point:

§ Mr. L., a college graduate, explained that after five years of marriage his wife had never conceived. Their case history revealed that neither of them had ever received adequate sex instruction. Their initial attempts at intercourse were painful to the wife, so both husband and wife agreed to refrain from intercourse. They found mutual embraces without intercourse very pleasant and thought that this was the purpose of sexual activity. As time went on, they were surprised and disappointed that no children were born. On pastoral advice, they sought the counsel of a physician; a simple instruction on the mechanics of marital intercourse was sufficient to resolve the problem.

Mixed marriages pose a special problem, for they menace the psychological and emotional unity of husband and wife. Although it may be agreed before marriage that each one shall practice his or her own religion, nevertheless, such basic differences are by their very nature apt to cause disturbance and anxiety in subsequent marital and family life. One must realize that no systems of knowledge or bodies of truths are so emotionally charged as religious ones. A mixed marriage involves two people with two entirely different attitudes on a very basic concept of life. Although they may love one another greatly, these very basic concepts are apt to influence their way of thinking and acting in even the very ordinary decisions and activities of everyday life. It is, for example, to be expected that a deeply religious person can become tense and extremely fearful for the salvation of the soul of the spouse. Children of mixed marriages often ask, "What will happen to Mother [or Dad] when she [or he] dies?" A very intelligent Catholic boy, studying his catechism with his non-Catholic mother, remarked to her, "You certainly wouldn't want anybody to teach me an untruth, would you?" He then continued, "Mother, I have never seen you go to Mass or to confession or to Holy Communion. Isn't that a mortal sin?" The mother, of course, was very much disturbed and could not frame a suitable answer to his question. Another young lad, a child of a mixed marriage, refused to go to the parochial school because, when there, he felt a fear and anxiety that his father, being of a different religion from his own, might be condemned to hell. There are other cases where the non-Catholic party fulfilled his obligation of sending the child to the parochial school, but at the same time, by continual criticism, influenced the child against the school and against the teaching Sisters. For the sake of peace many Catholic parents in mixed marriages will allow themselves to be drawn away from Catholic practices. Many Catholics need psychiatric treatment because their happiness has been shattered on the rocks of religious differences.

Another factor contributing to the breakdown of marriage is the so-called "emancipation of woman." In the Bible, it is written "Let women be subject to their husbands as to the Lord" (Ephesians 5:23). However, in modern times woman, refusing to be subject, has renounced her dependence on man. She has accepted, instead, the ideal of the equality of the sexes, and too often insists on financial independence to the detriment of marital harmony. The basic function of the married woman is pregnancy, and this is one function of the marriage state that cannot be replaced by the male partner. Modern inventions have shortened traveling distances and have accelerated traveling speeds, but they will never be able to replace or to accelerate the slow, natural process of pregnancy. Many of the basic difficulties of modern marriage can be found in the overrapid and overextensive emancipation of woman from many of the functions granted her by God.

A peculiar manifestation of this inordinate independence is seen in the modern woman's attitude toward breast feeding. Although a happy reaction has lately set in, breast feeding is in many circles still unfortunately out of fashion, and by the same unfortunate token, physicians who do not recommend ersatz baby food are out of fashion and unpopular. Such is our modern mentality that a perfectly natural function is considered outmoded. Another type of emancipated woman is the "very spiritual" woman who, after bearing several children, announces that she will now have only spiritual children, these in the form of Catholic Action.

On the other hand, men are not without blame either, for men have become immature and more emotionally dependent on woman than was the case formerly. The school system of today, in which women are the instructors of boys through grammar school and into high school, may be responsible for the submissive and immature attitudes of our males today.

Physiologically speaking, the two sexes are very different. Man is stronger in shoulder, broader of back and of chest, has narrower hips, and is usually taller than women. A woman, on the other hand, is shorter, frailer, and broader in the pelvis. The generative organs in man makes him the aggressor, whereas the female generative organs cause the woman to adopt a submissive role. Because of the unity of the person, the somatic differences induce the psychological differences between the two sexes. Man is the provider; he accepts the responsibility for the marriage and for supporting his wife and should therefore be competent and responsible. On the other hand, the woman is dependent, submissive, and the domestic custodian of the home. It *is* she who is to care for the children and to prepare the food. For these reasons she is the strongest psychological influence in the education and the formation of the younger, coming generation. The functions of man and woman overlap and are interchangeable in many respects. However, only a man can become a father and only a woman can become a mother. Each sex in itself is incomplete, and only man and woman together can form a unity of the sexes, something that is biologically and sexually complete.

Men and women must, as individuals, attain their end, the saving of their souls. However, in marriage husband and wife form a unit, sexually and biologically. The total surrender in intercourse of male and female is a surrender to unity, to harmony; as the Scriptures say, they become "two in one flesh." God created Adam first and from his side fashioned Eve, indicating the superiority of man in a juridical sense. Nevertheless, it was only from Adam and Eve, both cooperating with God, that the entire human race was to descend. To these two God gave equal responsibility for the propagation of the race. Man alone could not do it, nor could woman.

Woman, since she cooperates with God and her husband in conception, should feel honored and should have a position of dignity in society. However, the modern woman often rejects the dignity of her femininity. It is no longer unusual to see a woman refuse the courtesy of entering a room before a man or of having a man offer her his seat in a public conveyance. What she wants is equality of salary. Feminists are proud of the economic emancipation of woman; they are happy to be in an income bracket equal to, or superior to, that of the male competitor, and to be delivered from pots and pans—the symbols of their slavery. Pregnancy is often considered an illness instead of the crowning period of the woman's life. The "emancipated" mother rejects the child because the child takes her away from playing an active part in her business or social environment. A generation ago, the Catholic mother had an average of about six children; today, she has an average of two or three children. How different is this modern attitude from that of the Catholic mother who went to the doctor some time after the coming of her seventh child and complained that she was no longer conceiving! Yet, there do remain a few who know the joys of true womanhood; *e.g.*, one Italian woman has had 22 children, all living, and all of whom, to use her own words, "continually contribute to her happiness and her joy."

There is no doubt that life is more competitive than formerly. The average modern man coming home from work today does not care to play with his children or to enter actively into family affairs; he prefers to be soothed and pampered, to have his tired brow smoothed by caressing hands. The modern man wants to enjoy his baseball game, his game of golf, without having to participate in the internal activities of family life. In a way, he is spoiled. Too often he cares to see his wife only when she is well coifed, glamorized with lipstick and rouge, and dressed in her best. He does not care to be seen in public with a pregnant wife. He too easily repudiates the dignity of pregnancy, perhaps fearing that the coming baby will disturb the routine of his daily life and recreation.

Contraceptive practices disrupt marital unity much more than is suspected. In the marriage state, man and woman are to form a unity—man the father, woman the mother. In contraceptive intercourse there is no unity. "Planned parenthood" is an intended physical frustration of the natural sex functions, and a psychological frustration of the natural instinct to propagate. Although differing in physical and psychological structure, both men and women are intended to complement one another. Sexual intercourse for married people is as much a psychological as a physical matter. To have marital relations for merely physical reasons and with the use of contraceptives was once characterized by a patient as an "unsatisfactory and delusionary act." Such dissatisfaction leads to quarreling; and couples who are always quarreling will never have satisfactory sexual relations, since harmony of mind is just as important as unity of the body.

Contraception employs devices to keep the sperma of the man from meeting the ovum of the woman. There are mechanical and chemical ways of doing this, some of which are fairly successful. However, the psychological and natural feeling of unreality induces abnormality and artificiality in the relations of the husband and wife. The artificial means of avoiding procreation should always be regarded as abnormal conditions; obviously, a contraceptive instrument placed between the bodies of the man and the woman cannot be considered a normal condition.

It is wrong to have sexual relations freely without accepting the consequences; but the Church does not want childbearing to be a disaster. The only normal alternative, then, is not to have intercourse. However, this would be, for the average person, a strained and unnatural condition dangerous to the happiness of the marriage. There is, as a final recourse, a natural means of birth control. As time goes on science is gaining more and more knowledge about the so-called "safe periods" in which conception is highly improbable. Medical authorities generally agree that this method is not absolutely secure, since the physiological mechanism of the woman is not always uniform in its periods. This so-called rhythm theory has in recent times undergone a refinement in the method of computing maximal expectations of fertility from the highest of temperature variations during the menstrual cycle. Neither the rhythm method nor its refinement, computed on basal body temperature, can be dependably used to ensure either fertility or sterility without consultation with a competent physician.

In addition to the factors thus far considered—immaturity, mixed marriages, feminine overemancipation, and birth control—it is obvious that the general breakdown in private and public morality has had its influence on the Christian tradition of monogamous marriage.

Sterilization deprives individuals of their sexually creative functions, a privation that is unjust in the eyes of God and against the laws of nature. Is it any wonder that modern man should pay the price for so flagrantly disobeying the laws of God and of nature? What purpose can modern society have in ignoring the differences in sex, for trying to plan parenthood by contraception, for facilitating divorce proceedings to the extreme? Books like the Kinsey report indicate statistically widespread conditions of free love and sexual license. It is important to note, however, that the Kinsey report does not give the statistics on how many of those reporting to the interviewers believed in God or His law.

Economic factors are sometimes most important for the success of the marriage. Unquestionably, one of the results of the Second World War was that many who were forced to live with in-laws experienced unhappy marital relations. At the same time, the lack of a just family wage has in some instances forced the woman to share in the earning power of the family. The growing tendency of young men and women in college to marry without adequate means of support should be heartily discouraged.

Many couples nowadays marry after too short a courtship. A great deal of the unhappiness of married couples could be avoided if the couple contemplating marriage had to undergo a course of instruction lasting from three to six months, dealing with the purpose and functions of marriage and the psychological significance and implications of the marriage state. How many couples were married during the war on a mere emotional whim and on a purely frivolous basis! Yet in discussing marital problems with clients, parents were rarely found to have discouraged such precipitate marriages, or to have tried to make the couples realize that they were taking a very important step in being united in a holy and sacramental state. In the marriage of the average twenty-one-year-old boy and eighteen-year-old girl, one can hardly expect that maturity of consideration which is necessary for a holy and permanent state of life. No couple can be adequately prepared for marriage by merely one or two lectures given by the parish priest.

Another factor in marriage failure is marital infidelity. Cocktail and other drinking parties lay the groundwork for this failure in marriage. Unstable persons very easily fall prey to temptation. Everybody wants to please others and to be accepted by others. Men and women in middle age feel proud when they are courted or appreciated by the other sex. Without sufficient reasons, many happy marriages have been broken only because of vanity, only because of a man's wish to be regarded as a superman at fifty years, or a woman's to be wanted and desired at forty-five.

It is beyond the scope of this book to attempt to mention all of the factors that contribute to unhappy marriages, but as a final instance there may be mentioned the overprotective mothers who, either consciously or unconsciously, destroy the happiness of the marriages of their children by their insistent demands for personal attention and by their oversolicitous interference in the private affairs of the young married couples. In one family of 12 children, none was able to get married because the mother overstressed the children's obligation of caring for her. In another case an overprotective mother let her children marry but, through her interference and constant demands upon filial obligations, succeeded in getting them all separated.

This review clearly indicates that many marriage problems have a moral basis. The solution, therefore, is to be found in the straightening out of the moral problems and marriage counseling often should aim at an insight into the moral causes of marital difficulties. Many people go to the psychiatrist with their marriage problem, although in many cases the problem can be solved only by helping them to behave better. It is possible that, in cases in which immaturity is the reason for an unhappy marriage, some analytic procedure may do good; but even then the main point is to bring the counselee to a realization that he has to take himself in hand and correct whatever is amiss.

A real appreciation of the true meaning of sexual intercourse between husband and wife is essential to a happy marriage and should be rooted in devotion to the loved one. Whenever there is a lack of reverence for womanhood and for parenthood, there can be nothing but delusion for both husband and wife. In a full and proper marriage, both husband and wife need each other; there should be one mind and one heart. Sexual adjustment is indispensable for a happy marriage, but sickness and disability, which make an active sex life impossible, should not be allowed to interfere with the love that should exist in the marital state. Here again, it is important to stress the importance of psychological as well as physical unity. If two people truly love one another in the proper physical and psychological sense, both nature and God will reward them with true peace of soul.

Would it not be helpful if all pastors encouraged each couple coming to them to arrange for marriage to take a thorough and intensive course, offered under Catholic auspices, on the physiology and psychology of marriage, and on the full significance of all its duties and functions? Would it not be wise to urge that every couple wishing to be married should wait from three to six months? If during this waiting period the couples had the opportunity to receive such instructions and were given the proper appreciation of the full significance of the state they were about to assume, not a small number of couples would find that they were not yet properly equipped, and in this way many unhappy and broken marriages would be prevented.

NOTES AND REFERENCES

1. With regard to marriage and family problems and marriage counseling, see the following works:

   Brown, Fred, and Rudolph T. Kempton, "Sex Questions and Answers: A Guide to Happy Marriage" (New York: McGraw-Hill Book Company, Inc., 1950).

   Burgess, E. W., Emotional Factors in Marriage, *Collier's,* January 31, 1948.

   Foster, R. G., "Marriage and Family Relations" (New York: The Macmillan Company, 1944).

   Fromme, Allan, "The Psychologist Looks at Sex and Marriage" (New York: Prentice-Hall, Inc., 1950).

   Gerrard, Thomas, "Marriage and Parenthood, The Catholic Ideal" (New York: Joseph F. Wagner, Inc., 1948).

   Goldstein, Sydney E., "Marriage and Family Counseling" (New York: McGraw-Hill Book Company, Inc., 1945).

   Good, Frederick L., and Otis F. Kelly, "Marriage, Morals and Medical Ethics" (New York: P. J. Kenedy & Sons, 1951).

   Kothem, R., "Marriage the Great Mystery," translated by E. J. Ross (Westminster, Md.: Newman Press, 1942).

   LeClerq, J., "Marriage and the Family" (New York: Frederick Pustet, 1947).

   Messenger, E., "Two in One Flesh" (3 vols.; Westminster, Md.: Newman Press, 1948).

   Meyer, Fulgence, "Plain Talks on Marriage" (Cincinnati: St. Francis Book Shop, 1927).

   Mudd, Emily, "The Practice of Marriage Counseling" (New York: Association Press, 1951).

   Odenwald, Robert P., Psychiatric Factors in Marriage Counselling, p. 111, and Counselling Problem Parents with Problem Children, p. 130, in book by Clemens, Alphonse H., "Marriage Education and Counselling" (Washington, D.C.: The Catholic University of America Press, 1951); *id.,* Why is Marriage Failing? *The Family Digest,* Vol. 7, No. 1, October (1951), p. 22.

   Schmiedeler, Edgar, "An Introductory Study of the Family" (New York: Appleton-Century-Crofts, Inc., 1940).

   Thorman, George, "Broken Homes," Public Affairs Pamphlet, No. 135, 1947.

2. Statement on Catholic education issued by the cardinals, archbishops, and bishops of the United States at the close of their annual meeting in Washington, 1950.

A SURVEY

Statistics provide the following data on mental health in the United States. More than 170,000 patients are annually admitted to public mental hospitals, which have a resident population of half a million. The number of hospital beds reserved for mentally sick is larger than the number of all other hospital beds combined. Large appropriations of the public revenue—in some states, as much as one-eighth—are allocated for the care of the mentally diseased. These figures refer only to institutionalized patients. The number of mentally and emotionally unbalanced persons not institutionalized is probably much greater.

Among those who directly or indirectly come in contact with the mentally ill are the Catholic clergy. Since priests are not only moral theologians but moral psychologists, they ought to have an understanding of the various classes of mental diseases and the theories attempting to explain them. One objective of the present book is to impart that knowledge. In presenting a description of the main forms of mental disorder, the authors have tried to show what pastors and other nonpsychiatric counselors, when confronted with mental cases, can do and what they should avoid. For the same reason, the counseling procedure and symptomatic methods of psychotherapy have been discussed in some detail because these can —*suppositis supponendis*—more readily be applied by advisers who are not psychiatrically trained than other methods of treatment.

The second objective of this book is to point out the principles which, according to Catholic philosophy and theology, should govern the theoretical and practical approach to the problem of mental disease. The authors' rather extensive experience indicates that many psychiatrists, clinical psychologists, nurses, social workers, and educated lay people are interested in this objective.

It has sometimes seemed to the authors that modern psychiatry is paying homage to Kant's hypothesis, systematized by Hans Vaihinger in his *Philosophie des Als-ob*—the *as-if* philosophy. There are psychiatrists who, going back to La Mettrie's materialism, consider man theoretically as a machine or a robot, but, in practice, treat him *as if* he were a living being. Many psychiatrists proclaim that man is just another animal, but deal with him *as if* he had reason and will; they even appeal to the latter *as if* man had a free will and could decide for himself. Why such a gap between theory and practice? Catholics hold, theoretically and practically, that a human being is neither an automaton nor brute, but a person, composed of a body and a spiritual soul, endowed with intellect and will.

Conscientious psychiatrists treat their patients *as if* they should abide by certain moral norms. But they should also recognize that the observance of moral precepts will yield lasting results only if they are considered as having an objective basis. Much mental grief can be avoided and many patients can be restored to mental health, if they regulate their conduct according to the commandments of the natural law, laid down by the Supreme Lawgiver. And since a person's conscience, if rightly formed, reflects the norms of the natural law, the proper formation of conscience is of the greatest importance for the preservation and restoration of mental disorders. The Norwegian poet and dramatist Hendrik Ibsen, in his "Rosmersholm," makes the raffish Ulrik Brendel complain that an insecure conscience is our common inheritance and that mankind is uncurable because God has forgotten to give him wings, external and internal. But, when Brendel resignedly decides to continue his dissolute life, he is apparently not driven by an insecure conscience but rather by a wicked desire. In moral matters, he is incurable who refuses to be cured. But if one earnestly strives to recover, God gives him internal wings, His supernatural grace, which supplements man's natural powers. Since the human soul is spiritual, it is immortal. The hard and grueling experiences of this life on earth are real enough; but the Catholic knows that his real life lies beyond the grave, and that it will be dependent upon the way in which he lives this present life.

These are the main principles of Catholic psychology, both philosophical and theological. It is in the light of these principles that the various theories of psychotherapy have been reviewed in this book. Here once more the *as-if* philosophy is encountered. Many depth psychologists speak and write *as if* they were faithful Freudians, whereas in reality they deviate far from their Viennese master in many essential points. To mention only a few such departures from original psychoanalysis, the libido is no longer considered omnipotent, the death instinct and the Oedipus complex are relegated to the background, the importance of the patient's will to health is extolled. Some speak and write *as if* Freud had written the last and final work about the causation of neuroses, but there are few who would claim that neuroses are exclusively caused by libidinal conflicts. St. Paul (II Timothy 3:2–5) says: "Men will be lovers of self, covetous, haughty, proud, blasphemers, disobedient to parents, ungrateful, criminal, heartless, faithless, slanderers, incontinent, merciless, unkind, treacherous, stubborn, puffed up with pride, loving pleasure more than God, having a semblance of piety, but disowning his power." All these unwholesome drives may cause neurotic attitudes, and the Catholic psychologist refuses to consider these drives as misdirected sex-derivations.

In the event that indulgence in any of these drives has made an individual neurotic, the first aim of psychotherapy will be the disclosure of the cause of his condition, be it conscious or unconscious, but the release of the negative, destructive forces in the individual should be followed up by the release of his positive, constructive propensities. For Catholics believe not only in original sin, but also in original virtue. The final aim, therefore, of psychotherapy should be psychagogic—an aim in which Freud showed but scant interest. The psychiatrist should positively assist the patient in actualizing his constructive potentialities. The authors agree fully that the aim of therapy consists in making the patient a mature and responsible person. But they disagree with those psychiatrists who speak *as if* the ultimate goal of reeducating the patient is complete self-sufficiency and independence, although they know that such qualities also create neurotics. A reasonable sense of independence is consonant with dependence on human and divine authority. "Son, when thou comest to the service of God, stand in justice and in fear" (Ecclesiasticus 2:1). The service of God is religion. And it is decidedly a good omen that several psychiatrists, abandoning—although hesitantly—Freud's antireligious attitude, have begun to recognize the value of religion for mental health. But then again, why present a nontheistic system of vaguely defined moral rules, *as if* that were religion? Why speak of "the religion of nonreligion" *as if* such overt contradiction ever could make sense?

In this book it has been shown that Freud's futurism is a thing of the past. Many analysts reject some of the basic ideas of the original psychoanalytical system. Why then pose *as if* they are Freudian? It should be admitted that depth psychology has given a better appreciation of the unconscious elements in the conflict that often underlies the appearance of psychoneurotic symptoms. But much of what is presented as new in the description of that conflict has been known for ages, although under different terms. The conflict between the pleasure-seeking self and the self of moral greatness has been described in less technical but more glowing terms by St. Augustine in his "Confessions," by Goethe in his "Faust," by Strindberg in his "Inferno," by Oscar Wilde in his "Ballad of Reading Gaol," by Francis Thompson in "The Hound of Heaven." That eternal struggle has succinctly been expressed by Ovid when he says: "*Video meliora proboque, deteriora sequor*" and by St. Paul (Romans 7:23): "I see another law in my members, fighting against the law of my mind, and captivating me in the law of sin."

The authors also believe that to some theories of depth psychology can be applied St. Paul's word (II Timothy 4:3–5): "For there will come a time when . . . they turn away their hearing from the truth and turn aside rather to *fables*." Many psychiatrists make use of a jargon that is worse than the *abyssus potentionabilitudinalitatum* of which the "Centuriatores Magdeburgenses" accused the Scholastics, and they act *as if* their gibberish has real meaning.

The *raison d'être* of this book is the disproval of modern attempts to integrate man in an *as-if* environment. To these attempts, the authors oppose the Christian principle of integration, which is rooted in the natural law and in the belief of a personal God.

INDEX

N

O

P

R

T

U